Marxism and Freedom was first published in 1958 and was widely acclaimed as a serious, scholarly study of the development and vicissitudes of the Marxian theory of liberation. It has since been translated into Italian, Japanese and French.

Its scope is the modern machine age, from its foundations in the industrial revolution to the present day, tracing through the development of three strands of thought:

1 The evolution of English political economy, French revolutionary doctrines, and German idealist (Hegelian) philosophy, in relation to the actual social development of the period 1776 to 1831.

2 The development of Marxism in Marx's day and since, in relation to the actual class struggles in the epoch of the Civil War in the United States and the Paris Commune, as well as World War I and the Russian Revolution.

3 The methodology of Marxism to the problems that arise from the trend towards state capitalism, on the one hand, and a movement for total freedom, on the other.

Marx's theory, as the author argues, is 'the generalisation of the instinctive striving of the proletariat for a new social order, a truly human society' and this work is offered as a contribution towards the realisation of that goal.

Raya Dunayevskaya was secretary to Leon Trotsky during his exile in Mexico, but broke with him at the time of the Hitler-Stalin pact because he insisted that Russia had to be defended. She, on the contrary, asserted that the Russian Revolution had degenerated into a state capitalist tyranny. Since the 1940s she has been closely associated with American workers' struggles and has written on numerous aspects of the class struggle as well as lecturing widely on the subject in the United States, Western Europe and Africa. She is at present chairman of the National Editorial Board of the American publication *News and Letters*.

including a new chapter
Cultural Revolution or Maoist Reaction?

Preface by Harry McShane

PLUTO PRESS

MARX ISM AND FREEDOM

. . . from 1776 until Today

RAYA DUNAYEVSKAYA

First published in 1958 © Raya Dunayevskaya 1958
Second edition with a new chapter on Mao Tse-tung
and the Sino-Soviet rift © Raya Dunayevskaya 1964
Third edition published 1971 with a new chapter on
Cultural Revolution or Maoist Reaction?
© Pluto Press 1971

ISBN 0 902818 04 x (hardback)
ISBN 0 902818 05 8 (paperback)

PLUTO PRESS LTD
Cottons Gardens, London E2 8DN

Printed in Great Britain by Redwood Press Ltd, Trowbridge

ACKNOWLEDGEMENTS

I thank the following for permission to quote from their publications:

American Economic Association, Evanston, Ill., for quotations from my translation of *Pod Znamenem Marxizma* (*Under the Banner of Marxism*), commentary and rejoinder, "A New Revision of Marxian Economics," in the *American Economic Review*, September 1944 and September 1945;

Joseph Buttinger, *In the Twilight of Socialism*, published by Frederick A. Praeger, Inc., New York;

Harcourt, Brace and Company, Inc., New York, *The Letters of Lenin*, translated and edited by Elizabeth Hill and Doris Mudie;

Harvard University Press, Cambridge, *The Formation of the Soviet Union, Communism and Nationalism, 1917-1923*, by Richard Pipes, copyright by the President and Fellows of Harvard University;

Henry Holt and Company, New York, *Vorkuta* by Joseph Scholmer;

Humanities Press, New York, *Reason and Revolution*, by Herbert Marcuse;

International Publishers, New York; *The Civil War in the United States*, by K. Marx and F. Engels, *Selected Correspondence* of K. Marx and F. Engels, *Selected Works*, Volumes I and II, by K. Marx and F. Engels, *Selected Works*, Volumes I-IX, by V. I. Lenin, and *Essays in Literature, Philosophy and Music*, by Andrei A. Zhdanov;

Charles H. Kerr & Company, Chicago; *Capital*, Volumes I-III; *A Contribution to the Critique of Political Economy;* and *The Poverty of Philosophy;* all by Karl Marx;

The Macmillan Company, New York, and George Allen & Unwin, Ltd., London, *Phenomenology of Mind*, translated by J. B. Baillie; and *Science of Logic*, by Hegel, translated by W. H. Johnston and L. G. Struthers;

Oxford University Press, Inc., New York and London, *The Logic of Hegel*, and *Hegel's Philosophy of Mind*, translated by William Wallace;

Pioneer Publishers, New York, *The Stalin School of Falsification*, and *The Suppressed Testament of Lenin*, by Leon Trotsky;

Random House, Inc., New York, *The Poems, Prose and Plays of Alexander Pushkin*, edited by Avrahm Yarmolinsky;

St. Martin's Press, New York, and Macmillan & Company, Ltd., London, *The Second International*, Part I, by G. D. H. Cole;

Stanford University Press, Stanford, *The Bolsheviks and the World War: The Origins of the Third International* (Publication No. 15, The Hoover Library on War, Revolution, and Peace), by Olga Hess Gankin and H. H. Fisher, copyright by the Board of Trustees of Leland Stanford Junior University;

The University of Chicago Press, Chicago, *Early Theological Writings*, by Hegel, translated by T. M. Knox and edited by Richard Kroner; and *The Political Community*, by Sebastian de Grazia;

The George Wahr Publishing Company, Ann Arbor, *Materials for the Study of the Soviet System*, by J. H. Meizel and E. S. Kozera;

Yale University Press, New Haven, *Ferdinand Lassalle, Romantic Revolutionary*, by David Footman.

I also wish to thank the newspaper, *News & Letters*, Detroit, and its worker-editor, Charles Denby, for permission to quote his and other workers' articles on conditions in the shops and mines.

R. D.

"Freedom is so much the essence of man that even its opponents realize it . . . No man fights freedom; he fights at most the freedom of others. Every kind of freedom has therefore always existed, only at one time as a special privilege, another time as a universal right."

—Karl Marx

"When individuals and nations have once got in their heads the abstract concept of full-blown liberty, there is nothing like it in its uncontrollable strength, just because it is the very essence of mind, and that as its very actuality . . . If to be aware of the idea—to be aware, i.e., that men are aware of freedom as their essence, aim and object—is a matter of *speculation*, still this very idea itself is the actuality of men—not something which they *have*, as men, but which they *are*."

—G. W. F. Hegel

TABLE OF CONTENTS

PART III. MARXISM: THE UNITY OF THEORY AND PRACTICE

ORGANIZATIONAL INTERLUDE

PART IV. WORLD WAR I AND THE GREAT DIVIDE IN MARXISM

PART V. THE PROBLEM OF OUR AGE: STATE CAPITALISM VS. FREEDOM

PREFACE

It is a great honour to be asked to write a Preface to the British edition of this book. I have hesitated because of doubts as to whether I am qualified to introduce such a scholarly work to readers in this country.

The publication of *Marxism and Freedom* marks a departure from the dull and stereotyped material sent out by those who seek to be regarded as the *authorised* custodians of Marxist wisdom. Raya Dunayevskaya has produced a work that will be of great service to all who are ready to involve themselves in the struggle for a free and humane society.

Marxist theory never found a foothold in Britain. Mr Morgan Phillips was not entirely wrong when he rated the influence of Methodism on the British working-class movement higher than that of Marxism. The religious evangelism, financed by the ruling class after the fall of Chartism, did not prevent the rise of working-class militancy, but it did have a retarding effect. Most of the working-class leaders had a religious outlook which favoured a policy of restraint rather than one of struggle. In later years, the Labour movement took on a semi-religious character.

The readiness of the British workers to battle with their class enemies gave encouragement to the Marxists who, despite their heroic efforts, were unable to stop the spread of opportunism which is now a fully developed feature of British Labour politics. The Marxists were handicapped by the fact that the works of Marx, such as were available, did not receive the attention given to those of Hyndman, Bax and Kautsky. Ideologically, the British movement lagged behind most other countries.

The Russian Revolution stirred up a new interest in Marxist literature. Serious-minded workers grabbed at the works of Lenin and found that there was more to Marxist theory than that contained in the publications put out by the various Socialist organisations. The inspiration that came from Russia had a gratifying result when the British workers took a stand against their own government making war on Soviet Russia.

Unfortunately, internal forces in Russia destroyed what Britain and her allies were not allowed to destroy. The Russian workers became a subject class under the domination of the One-Party State. The British Communist Party, like its brother parties elsewhere, churns out literature which makes use of Marxist phraseology to justify the enslavement of the Russian workers. Having covered up every criminal act of Stalin, these so-called Marxists now try to bring the British workers to the support of the present Russian regime on the plea that the principles of the Russian Revolution have been adhered to. The change that has taken place in Russia is tragic in its consequences for the world.

A situation like this makes a re-statement of the fundamental principles of Marxism a necessity. That is what this book consists of. "Marxism," says the author, "is a theory of liberation or it is nothing." By a combination of deep thinking and research she proves that assertion to be correct.

The efforts of the supporters of the Russian regime to make that regime acceptable to British workers have been helped by the widespread belief that the state ownership of capital is the guarantee of freedom. Britain has made a big contribution to this misconception. It was boosted by the Fabians and accepted by many sections of the British working-class movement. It was significant that when the Webbs returned from a visit to Russia they said they had seen Fabianism in practice. As the author of this book points out this has nothing in common with Marxism.

The transfer of capital to the state places the workers in the same relation to capital as in Britain and America. The constant renewal and extension of capital by labour is as real in Russia as elsewhere. Because of the intensive production drive from above the portion of capital spent on means of production increases while that spent on labour power diminishes. Speed, and more speed, becomes the rule. As Marx pointed out, it cannot be otherwise "in a mode of production in which the labourer exists to satisfy the need of self-expansion of existing values instead of, on the contrary, material wealth existing to satisfy the need of development on the part of the labourer."

The chapters dealing with Marx's *Capital* are a pleasure to read. The wiseacres who turned away from *Capital* because it was "too dull" should be persuaded to read *Marxism and Freedom* to whet their appetites. Behind all the trouble Marx took to deal with commodities, the two-fold character of labour, the composition of capital, accumulation of capital and crisis, was his passionate desire to see destroyed the tyranny of capitalism.

His analysis does not become obsolete when capital is transferred to the state. The same laws continue to operate. The position of the workers is really worse because every act of resistance brings them into conflict with the state apparatus. Because of its control of the press the facts about any dispute are hidden from the outside world. The machinery of the law is there to ensure that the plans from above are fully carried out. This was condemned by Marx before it happened. Everything he wrote about capitalism applies to the system that now prevails in Russia, even as it does in Britain.

Nothing has happened since Marx was working on *Capital* that detracts in any way from the conclusions he arrived at as a result of his exhaustive study of the capitalist system of production. Those conclusions are confirmed by every move to deal with Britain's present crisis. The ruthless legislation directed against the militants on the factory floor reflects the determination of the ruling circles to curb the efforts of the workers to improve their conditions of labour. They demand more production from workers who, despite three agreed cuts in working hours since 1919, have been working longer hours than before the first world war. They want a greater proportion of production to go towards profits. The Chancellor of the Exchequer complained that "the share of company profits has fallen from $14\frac{1}{2}$ per cent in 1964 to about 10 per cent in 1970."

This country has a Labour movement that is numerically strong, but weak in the important field of theory. Britain has a history of struggle against the impositions of capitalism that is second to none, but Britain's control over a far-flung empire had a retarding effect on the political thinking of the working class. The Liberal Party had the support of the workers down to the outbreak of the first world war. Although the Labour Party has replaced the Liberal

Party as the rival to the Tories there remains the same indifference to the root problems of society.

The top leaders of the trade unions differ little from those of the Parliamentary Labour Party. The struggles that gave rise to the trade unions have no meaning for them. The unofficial strikes are not seen in the setting of growing resistance by the workers against the conditions of capitalism. That, they think, is impossible without the guidance of leaders. In this regard the points made by the author in this book on the self-activity of the workers during the Paris Commune and the Russian Revolution, apart from everything else it contains, would alone make it worth reading.

Marx once wrote, "The standpoint of the new materialism is human society or social humanity." For Marx, the welfare of humanity rested in the hands of the oppressed workers. Stalin and his colleagues appalled the world by the crimes they committed—in the name of Marx. They riveted the chains of slavery tighter than ever while they posed as the undisputed champions of freedom. When the workers break their shackles they will, at the same time, bring untold benefits to the human race. Marx stands out in contrast to those pygmies who make long speeches at Party congresses, allegedly de-Stalinised, first by Khruschev and now by Brezhnev.

The necessity of work under conditions of capitalism has been stamped on the minds of workers over many generations, but those who have never rebelled against these conditions, at one time or another, are comparatively few. The urge for action has always come from below; from those who work with, and are dominated by the means of production outside their control. The worker as a human being has feelings, desires and passions that are thwarted by present conditions. This leads to thought, actions, and then more thought. Therein lies the danger for the rulers of the world in the days ahead.

The human passion for freedom is recognised by the author, who, because of that, chose the apt and proper title for her book. She connects Marx more closely with Hegel than do the hack writers on Socialist philosophy. Freedom is the connecting link. Unlike Hegel, its realisation as seen by Marx will come with the new society through the self-activity of the working class. The worker, by his labour, had to create the conditions of his own enslavement before it became possible for him to lead the whole human race to freedom. Thanks to Hegel, Marx, and the proletariat, we can visualise man as the master of his destiny.

Despite the well-known facts of Marx's activity—from the Chartists to the Workingmen's International Association—in the workers' movement in Britain, there is a popular misconception that the only British institution he appreciated was the British Museum, where he worked on *Capital*. The truth is that before he ever came to Britain he wrote enthusiastically about the Levellers as the predecessors of the modern proletariat and its philosophic conceptions. "We find the first appearance of a really functioning communist party in the bourgeois revolution at the moment when monarchy is removed," he wrote in *The Moralising Criticism And Critical Morality*. "The most consistent republicans—in England, the Levellers; in France, Babeuf, Buonarroti etc.—are the first who proclaim these 'social questions'." While our own pragmatists have overshadowed the characteristic dialectic trend, especially in Scotland, Marx never forgot his debt to Adam Ferguson's *Essay on the History of Civil Society 1767*. It is often quoted in *Capital* as a seminal work on the philosophy of history.

Many obstacles stand in the way of the goal visualised by Marx, and pointed to in this book. The level of struggle reached in 1970, and in 1971, in British industry, and in Northern Ireland, has forced the defenders of reaction to erect new barriers to freedom, but the tide sweeps on. The British workers have defended their living standards by an unprecedented number of unofficial strikes. Their wavering "left" leaders are straggling behind.

The British Army, with all its paraphernalia of war, has failed to crush the spirit of revolt in Northern Ireland. James Connolly, the leader of the Irish Rebellion of 1916, an event that had an influence on Lenin, has more followers now than when he was alive. The call for a United Workers' Republic becomes louder in all parts of Ireland. The names of Marx and Lenin are heard more frequently.

Marxist thought is about the future of man and takes us far beyond the aims of the existing reformist parties. Marxist theory seeks realisation in the self-activity of the masses. The author makes use of the Paris Commune to demonstrate what that means.

There is something thrilling about this chapter which, for reasons of space, can only be referred to briefly. No reader of the book will skip over that chapter. There is a sentence there worth memorising. It reads: "This act of self-defence was also the act of self-government."

What she says about the Paris Commune takes us far away from anything put out by the parliamentarian socialists. It is an exposure of the pretensions of Mao tse-tung about whom there is a special chapter in this edition of the book. Mao is now faced with opposition calling itself the Sheng-wu-lieu of Hunan. In English that is Hunan Provincial Proletarian Revolutionaries Great Alliance. This body has issued a manifesto headed "Whither China" in which it is confidently stated that the victory of the broad masses is inevitable.

This, taken together with the 1956 rising in Hungary, events in Czechoslovakia and Paris, confirms the desire of the masses for freedom. The setback caused by the failure of the European revolution and the rise of Stalinism in Russia is in the process of being overcome. The revolutionary cause is now in the hands of a whole new generation. Those who, like the writer of this Preface, were among the revolutionaries of an earlier generation should be appreciative of the new young revolutionaries. The future of mankind is in their hands.

This book, by its theoretical approach, performs a service in the present situation. It raises the banner of theory without letting us forget that the working-class struggle is the source of all theory. Let us hope that this book will lead to a new flow of Marxist literature to counteract those publications that distort the meaning of Marxism. The British Prime Minister told us, recently, that we are all dependent on the production of profits. He may never see this book, but he may be hit when the principles enunciated here are put into practice by those who produce the profits. We should be grateful to Raya Dunayevskaya for writing the book, and to the Pluto Press for publishing the British edition.

Harry McShane

INTRODUCTION TO THE SECOND EDITION

> "Only that which is an object of freedom can be called an idea."—Hegel

The first edition of MARXISM AND FREEDOM went to press as Sputnik No. 1 went into orbit. That same year, 1957, the Little Rock riots shared headlines with the scientific phenomenon. In 1962, two different events were again held in unison in men's consciousness. This time James Meredith's courageous entry into the University of Mississippi took the lustre out of Walter Schirra's spectacular six-orbital entry into space. An age in which "a little thing," like school desegregation, can hold in tow such scientific milestones is an age in which men's consciousness is preoccupied, not with scientific conquest, but with human freedom.

This new edition appears when our life and times impart an urgency to the task of working out a new relationship of philosophy to reality. Thought and deed cannot forever stand apart. Somewhere, some time, they must meet. Throughout history the forces that have produced great social revolutions have also generated great philosophic revolutions. It was true when Rainsborough expressed the motive power of the English Revolution of 1648 as: ". . . the poorest he in England hath a life to live as the greatest he." It is true when, in 1963, James Baldwin speaks of "a glimpse of another world. . . . I speak of change not on the surface but in the depths—change in the sense of renewal." 17th century English Leveller fighting for equality, or 20th century Negro fighting for freedom *now*, pull strenuously at the intellectual tendency to resist the compulsion to original thought on the very eve of social revolutions that demand philosophic reconstructions.

The two features which characterize great periods of upheaval are, one, that a new *subject* is born to respond to the objective pull of history by making freedom and reason the reality of the day.

And, two, a new relationship between theory and practice is forged. This is true for the past—Levellers in 17th century England; the *sans culottes* in the French Revolution of 1789-1793; the runaway slaves impelling the United States to the Civil War of 1861-1865; the St. Petersburg proletariat in the 1905 and 1917 Russian Revolutions. This is true for the present—in the Hungarian Revolution against Russian totalitarianism, no less than in the African Revolutions against Western imperialism. This does not mean that each of these historic periods has given birth to a totally new philosophy. An original philosophy is a rare creation, born after much travail only when called forth by a new stage in world consciousness of freedom. It does mean that a viable philosophy must be capable of meeting the challenge of human experience, of the new revolts symbolic of the lack of specific freedoms.

To this author it meant that, no matter what the reasons were that caused the transformation of the Marxian theory of liberation into its opposite after the Russian Revolutions failed to realize, that is to say, put into practice this philosophy of freedom (see Chapters XII and XIII), a return to the original form of the Humanism of Marxism became imperative. Because Marx's Humanist Essays were not available in English at the time MARXISM AND FREEDOM came off the press in 1958, I included these writings as an Appendix.* Since that time there have been several English translations of these Essays as well as many commentaries on them. It soon became evident, however, that this was done, not to re-establish the integral unity of Marxian economics with his philosophical humanism, but only in order to exorcise the ghost of Karl Marx and then rebury him, this time as a Humanist.

------

* That appendix has been dropped from this new edition because the Essays are now easily available in English. The official Moscow publication (1959) is marred by footnotes which flagrantly violate Marx's content and intent. The preferable translation is T. B. Bottomore which, with other primary materials, is included in *Marx's Concept of Man* by Erich Fromm. (Frederick Ungar Publishing Co., New York 1961.) My original Appendix B, the first English translation of Lenin on *Hegel's Science of Logic,* has likewise been dropped since the material is finally available in English translation (V. I. Lenin, Collected Works, vol. 38, Philosophical Notebooks, Foreign Languages Publishing House, Moscow, 1961).

It cannot be done. Marxist Humanism will remain alive so long as a new world on truly new, human beginnings has not been established.

Totalitarian Communism understands this so well that the counter-revolutionary suppression of the Hungarian Revolution went hand-in-hand with the suppression of thought. The subsequent Khrushchev-Mao designation of Marxist Humanists as "revisionists" and the denunciation of "revisionism" as the "main danger" did not, however, deter the American "ideology specialists" from taking over the term, "revisionism," and similarly using it against the *opponents* of the ruling bureaucracies who had not only revised, but vitiated, Marxism. The very intellectuals who had lost their collective tongue during the period of McCarthyism now found their individual tongues to attempt to fragmentize Marx.

The debate around the Essays degenerated into a question of first-edness as if it were a college debate held for scoring points. As I stated during the discussion in 1961: "The dispute over who was the first to translate Marx's 1844 Economic-Philosophic Manuscripts into English is a meaningful controversy only if it has a substantive relationship to the spirit of those Essays and of our times. I was *compelled* to be the first to publish these Essays in 1958 because for the fifteen years previous I had tried, in vain, to convince other scholars, writers, and publishers of the cogency of these Essays. When in the period between the East German Revolt and the Hungarian Revolution, the Russian Communists openly attacked those Essays (*Voprosy Filosofii*, #3, 1955), I once again began my round of publishers. This time the Essays were part of my book. I held that the Russian Communist attack on them was not academic, but a foreboding of revolutions to come. The following year the great Hungarian Revolution raised the Humanist flag clearly. Because Marxist Humanism, to me, is the only genuine ground from which to oppose Communist totalitarianism, I felt the compulsion to show that Humanism is not something invented by me, but came directly from Marx who fought what he called " 'vulgar Communism,' writing that 'communism, as such, is not the goal of human development, the form of human society.' "

Skepticism also greeted my statement in the first edition, that the road to a new society, opened by the Hungarian Revolution, was no less illumined by the Montgomery Bus Boycott. Since then the Negro struggle has become all-rounded and so engulfed the North, as well as the South, that the phrase, "Negro Revolution," has become almost a cliché. Yet the fact that a revolution can be treated as a mere journalistic phrase only further reveals the failure to grapple with the truth that the American Negro has always been the touchstone of American civilization which had an ever expanding frontier but no unifying philosophy. Nor has the challenge been met when the call for a unifying philosophy came from an altogether new source: the scientist (Dr. William E. Pickering) who first succeeded in sending the American Explorer into orbit. In speaking of the fact that mankind was now "only one-half hour away from total annihilation," Dr. Pickering said that mankind was in need, not of more destructive weapons that the scientists invent, but of "a new, unifying philosophy."

This same period saw the emergence of the African Revolutions under their own Humanist banner.* It was indeed the birth of this new world independent of the Communist orbit that both led to the Communist discovery of this "third world" and to the rift within its own orbit. (On the Sino-Soviet Rift see Chapter XVII.) Because the dynamism of ideas escapes American "ideology specialists," they do not pick up the gauntlet for the struggle for the minds of men. Instead, they act as if any ideological battle, if even it concerns the very survival of humanity, is only rhetoric. It is not that they do not know as well as anybody that, far from rhetoric, this is the overriding fact in a world of H-bombs and ICBMs. Nor is it that they held their breath any less than the rest of us when, in October, 1962, J. F. Kennedy told N. S. Khrushchev that the United States was ready to unloose a nuclear holocaust unless Russia removed its missiles from Cuba. It is rather due to their belief that their aging views toward ideas would somehow magically dissipate the class struggle, and the racial struggle would thereby become bite size.

---

* See my pamphlet, *Nationalism, Communism, Marxist-Humanism and the Afro-Asian Revolutions.* (News & Letters, Detroit, 1959; Cambridge, England, 1961.)

Where some reviewers wished to return Marx's Humanist Essays to the archives, others questioned my theory of state-capitalism, saying that I had paid insufficient attention to the changed conditions in Russia since the ascent of Khrushchev to power. They pointed especially to "the abolition of the forced labor camps." Curiously enough, this criticism came, in large measure, from those who denied the very existence of the camps until Khrushchev declared them abolished. That the worst of the concentration camps have been eliminated does not mean that there are none. It only means that "corrective labor" has taken a different, a milder form. Neither United States "free enterprise," nor Russian "communism," has changed the fundamental Marxian theory of value and surplus value, or capitalism as an exploitative relationship of capital to labor. After the Russian admission, in 1943, that the law of value operates in Russia, there was no further point to continue the detailed analysis of their State Plans. My analysis of the Five Year Plans, therefore, stopped with World War II, and thereafter focused on the Russian assault on Marx's CAPITAL and his ECONOMIC-PHILOSOPHIC MANUSCRIPTS (see Chapters III and XII). There is no reason to revise my analysis.

What is fundamentally new now are the developments in the Sino-Soviet orbit. My analysis of the rift was originally elaborated in 1961 as part of a new book I am writing on world ideologies and the technologically underdeveloped countries. Because "The Challenge of Mao" has a special urgency for today I brought it up to date when Japanese friends asked to include it in the edition of MARXISM AND FREEDOM they are preparing for publication in Tokyo. It is included as Chapter XVII in this new American edition as well. Both editions are going to press as we approach the one hundredth anniversary of the founding of the International Working Men's Association in London, in 1864.

Raya Dunayevskaya

November 1, 1963
Detroit, Michigan

INTRODUCTION TO THE FIRST EDITION

Today, in the face of the constant struggle of man for full freedom on both sides of the Iron Curtain, there is a veritable conspiracy to identify Marxism, a theory of liberation, with its opposite, Communism, the theory and practice of enslavement. This book aims to re-establish Marxism in its original form, which Marx called "a thoroughgoing Naturalism, or Humanism."

Hitherto, the American roots of Marxism have remained hidden. It is known, although not widely, that Marx aided the North during the Civil War in the United States. Less well-known is the fact that the paths of the Abolitionists and Marx crossed at that time. What is not known at all is that under the impact of the Civil War, and the subsequent struggles for the eight-hour day, Marx completely reorganized the structure of his greatest theoretical work, CAPITAL. This is analyzed here for the first time.

Our epoch has been characterized by "a struggle for the minds of men." Unless this struggle begins with a concept of totally new relations of men to labor and man to man, it is hollow. The today-ness of Marxism flows from this: no philosopher has ever had a grander concept of humanity than did Marx, and yet no philosophic conception was ever rooted more deeply in the first necessity of human society—labor and production. The fact that the H-bomb has put a question mark over the very survival of civilization does not change this. The answer to that problem is not in today's headlines. It is in production. That is what makes Marx so contemporary. The problems he posed 100 years ago are battled out today as concrete matters in the factory and in society as a whole.

Until the development of the totalitarian state the philosophic foundation of Marxism was not fully understood. Only today is it possible to comprehend that Marx's rejection of the Communism of his day was not a nineteenth century humanitarian adjunct to his scientific economic theories. Far from being a vulgar materialist, Marx based his perspectives, of the inevitable collapse of capitalism and the rise of a new human order, on a realization that workers would seek universality and completeness in their actual social lives as producers. Because Communism was a mere rejection of private property, Communism to Marx was "not the goal of human development, the form of human society."

Marxism is a theory of liberation or it is nothing. Whereas Marx was concerned with the freedom of humanity, and with the inevitable waste of human life which is the absolute general law of capitalist development, Russian Communism rests on the mainspring of capitalism—paying the worker the minimum and extracting from him the maximum. They dub this "the Plan." Marx called it the law of value and surplus value. He predicted that its unhindered development would lead to the concentration of capital "in the hands of a single capitalist or a single capitalist corporation."

Marx foresaw the present trend toward state capitalism not because he was a prophet but because of his dialectical method of tracing through to the end all trends of social development. It is impossible to understand Marx's major theoretical works if one begins by thinking that the particular method, Hegelian dialectics, is an absurdity. The absurdity would be if the method were the proof. The proof can only be in practice, in the actual development of society itself. This book therefore covers the modern machine age from its birth in the Industrial Revolution to its present-day development in Automation.

Three leading strands of thought are developed here: (1) The evolution of English political economy, French revolutionary doctrines, and German idealist (Hegelian) philosophy, in relation to the actual social development of the period of 1776 to 1831. (2) The development of Marxism in Marx's day and since, in relation to the actual class struggles in the epoch of the Civil War in the United States and the Paris Commune, as well as World War I and the Russian Revolution. (3) The methodology of Marxism applied to the problems that arise from the trend towards state capitalism, on the one hand, and a movement for total freedom, on the other. The unity of theory and practice, which characterized the forty years of Marx's maturity (1843-1883), is the compelling need of our own epoch as well.

The impulse for writing this book came from two sources: (1) the American workers, and (2) the East German workers. It was the period of 1950-1953, the period of the Korean War and of Stalin's death. During those years, the American workers, specifically the miners and auto workers began to come to grips with the realities of Automation by moving the question of productivity from one dealing with the fruits of labor—wages—to one dealing with the conditions of labor and the need for a totally new way of life. It was the period when the East German workers challenged the Communist regime in their Revolt of June 17, 1953. A revolt in the slave labor camps of Vorkuta, inside Russia itself, followed within a few weeks. Thus, in the wilds of Siberia as well as in the heart of Europe the tocsin had sounded for the beginning of the end of Russian totalitarianism.

From the philosopher in the ivory tower to the man on the street, the world is preoccupied with this question: *Can* man be free in this age of totalitarianism? We leaped generations ahead to the affirmative answer with the 1953 Revolts and again with the Hungarian Revolution of 1956. The road to a new society was no less illumined by the Negro struggles of 1956-57. At the same time, the "little war" over Suez brought us close to the brink of World War III. Nevertheless, out of the totality of the world crisis there emerged a search for a new philosophy on both sides of the Atlantic.

No theoretician, today more than ever before, can write out of his own head. Theory requires a constant shaping and reshaping of ideas on the basis of what the workers themselves are doing and thinking. The research for this book, for example, on the transformation of Russia from a workers' state into its opposite, a state capitalist society, began at the outbreak of World War II. Scholars, some who did, and some who did not, agree with my conclusions, took part. In its beginning, this work was a Marxist analysis of state capitalism. But it did not take its present form of MARXISM AND FREEDOM until the new stage of production and of revolts was reached in 1950-53. Because we live in an age of absolutes—on the threshold of absolute freedom out of the struggle against absolute tyranny—the compelling need for a new unity of theory and practice dictates a new method of writing. At least, it dictated the method by which this book was written.

A tour was undertaken to present orally the ideas of the book to groups of auto workers, miners, steelworkers and student youth. In their own words and out of their own lives they contributed a *new* understanding. A West Virginia miner, for example, modest about his own understanding of "Marxism," took freedom out of its abstraction and gave it concrete meaning.

"I've listened to you discussing that fellow Marx," he said. "I can't word it like him but I know exactly what he means. I lay there this morning about a quarter of six. I looked out the window. I said to myself, 'You just got to get up there and go down, whether you feel like it or not.' I didn't even speak it to my wife. I just said to myself, 'Now you call that a free man?' "

After these discussions, the first draft of the book was written. The manuscript was then submitted to some of these groups for study and, over a period of three months, their discussions were taped. Again, the author studied the discussions carefully, revised the first draft, and undertook a second tour for extensive personal discussions some of which are reproduced in the text. Only after these extensive discussions was the book in its present form finally written.

This work is therefore dedicated to the auto workers, miners, steelworkers and student youth who have participated so fully in the writing of this book. They are its co-authors.

                                                    Raya Dunayevskaya

Detroit, Michigan
May, 1957

Postscript: In reading the galley proofs, the author took the liberty of adding a few footnotes on events (such as Mao Tse-Tung's speech "On Contradiction") that happened between this book's going to press and its actual publication.

                                                              R. D.

September, 1957

PART I

FROM PRACTICE TO THEORY: 1776 TO 1848

CHAPTER ONE

THE AGE OF REVOLUTIONS: INDUSTRIAL, SOCIAL-POLITICAL, INTELLECTUAL

Our modern machine age was born of three eighteenth century revolutions—the Industrial Revolution, the American Revolution and the French Revolution. In embryo, every major question of the modern crisis was posed then. Indeed, we are first now living through the ultimate development of the contradictions that arose with the creation of industrialism. The proof that our age has not resolved the contradictions it faced at birth is as big as life. The One-Party Totalitarian State is the supreme embodiment of these contradictions. The central problem remains: *Can* man be free?

The totality of the world crisis today, and the need for a total change, compels philosophy, a total outlook. We today can better understand the revolutions in thought of that era than any previous period in history. The Industrial Revolution had undermined the old feudal order. The labor of men—under the discipline of the yarn-making and spinning machines, coke-smelted iron and the steam engine—conjured up for the capitalist greater wealth than the discovery of gold and the opening of a virgin American continent to trade. Not even the loss of "the colonies in the new world" could halt the development of industrial capitalism in England. Not so in backward France where royalty and the vested interests of the old feudal order kept the fledgling bourgeoisie in check.

1776 saw the birth of America as a nation. It was the year of publication of Adam Smith's, *The Wealth of Nations,* which marked the birth of classical political economy. The impact that the Industrial Revolution exerted on English political economy, the French Revolution exerted on German idealist philosophy. Under this impact, the greatest of the German idealist philosophers, Georg Wilhelm Friedrich Hegel, reorganized all hitherto existing philosophy. These revolutions in thought can be fully understood only in the light of the revolutions in action, particularly the development of the great French Revolution. There is nothing in thought—not even in the thought of a genius—that has not previously been in the activity of the common man.

1) The French Revolution in Books and in Life

Despite the mountain of books on the French Revolution, there is not, to this day, a full account of the depth and breadth of the activity of the French masses. It is only recently that Daniel Guérin has written a truly pioneering work, *The Class Struggles in the First French Republic*,[1] but this has yet to be translated into English. In 1947 there was published in America the translation of *The Coming of the French Revolution* by Georges Lefebvre, Professor Emeritus of the History of the French Revolution at the University of Paris, but that analysis limits itself to the beginnings of the Revolution.[2]

The French Revolution was marked at once by great daring, continuity and permanence of its revolutionary actions. There were great mass mobilizations not only against the royalists, but against the right wing of the rising bourgeoisie (the Girondists), and *also* against the left wing (the Mountain or the Jacobins) led by that best known of all revolutionary leaders, Robespierre.

It is a popular pastime of liberal historians to say that 1789, which brought the middle class into power, was "a child of eighteenth century philosophy." And they add that 1793 was "only" a "work of circumstance and necessity." The inference seems to be that because the masses had no "theory," they left no real imprint on "history." The truth is that precisely the spontaneity of 1789 and of 1793, *especially 1793*, bears both the stamp and the seal of the demands of the mass movement and the *method* by which the masses meant to construct a new society in place of the old.

It is true that prior to the Revolution the *sans-culottes*, that is, the deepest layers of the mass movement, had no *theory* of direct democracy. Neither did anyone else, least of all the philosophers. It is true that the town poor did not organize themselves as a conscious substitute for parliament. But they spontaneously infused the old institutions, such as the Commune, with a new content. At the same time entirely new forms of association—clubs, societies, committees—sprung up everywhere. By the simple act of not going home after voting but remaining at the polls and talking, the electoral assemblies were transformed into genuine communal assemblies of deliberation and action. The Sections of Paris seethed with life. They remained in *permanent* session. First, they met daily (opening at five or six in the evening). Second, they elected a *bureau of correspondence* to assure contact among the various Sections of the capital, thereby keeping constantly informed of developments and *coordinating* their actions. Third, they watched and tracked down suspects and saw to it that the revolutionary spirit was not controverted.

Thus, on January 1790, they opposed the arrest of Marat and made their views known through actions to *consolidate* the gains of the Revolution. On June 18, 1791, they adopted Robespierre's suggestion for the abolition of all distinctions between "active" citizens, that is, those who could pay the tax for voting, and "passive" citizens or those who could not. Indeed, some Sections had already taken matters into their own hands and had already abolished this distinction. The mass movement thus taught the new bourgeoisie its first lesson in democracy. By July 1792, the Assembly sessions became public: women and young people, who were not eligible to vote, were admitted to the galleries.

In his work, Guérin shows how the *sans-culottes* instinctively felt the necessity to oppose their own direct, supple and clear forms of representation to the indirect, cumbersome and abstract representation of parliamentary democracy. The Sections, Communes and popular societies, day after day, immediately expressed the will of the masses, of the revolutionary vanguard. The feeling that they were the most effective instruments and the most authentic interpreters of the Revolution gave them the boldness to dispute power with the sacrosanct Convention. The people were so little enmeshed in a lifeless, preconceived idea, they were so far removed from all abstract formalism, that the concrete forms of their dual power varied at each instant. But let us begin from the beginning.

2) *The Parisian Masses and the Great French Revolution*

July 14, 1789, signalled the most thoroughgoing bourgeois revolution. In distinction from the American Revolution which had preceded it, the French people were not struggling against a foreign enemy. Their suffering came from their own anointed rulers. The enemy was within. The monarchy, corrupt to the marrow of its royal bones and blue blood, kept the masses in poverty and restricted the movements of the young burghers. The nobility, landlords and clergy lived in wanton luxury on the bent backs of the peasants·held in bondage.

At the very time that science had been set free by the rising commercial and industrial class in England, the regime in France tried to maintain serfdom in thought by prohibiting scientists from overstepping the limits set by superstitious faith.

These contradictions and antagonisms reached a point of explosion and of unity with the storming of the Bastille. Classes fused into a new nation to rid themselves of the old order. On the countryside the peasants refused to pay tithes, sacked chateaux, burned deeds and repossessed the commons. In the cities workers and free burghers organized themselves into committees, clubs, societies and Communes to assure the destruction of the old and the creation of the new social order.

The Revolution began with the storming of the Bastille in 1789, but the feudal monarchy was not finally and completely overthrown until the working masses in the Sections of Paris carried through the insurrection of August 10, 1792. Only then did the legislature decide that the new assembly, the Convention, would be elected by universal suffrage. *Democracy, thus, was not invented by philosophic theory nor by the bourgeois leadership. It was discovered by the masses in their method of action.* There is a double rhythm in destroying the old and creating the new which bears the unmistakable stamp of the *self-activity which is the truly working class way of knowing*. This, in fact, was the greatest of all the achievements of the great French Revolution— the workers' discovery of their own way of knowing.

The masses *did* something. They fought concretely for bread and clothes; for arms to fight the enemy at home and abroad; for price controls. The established leaders opposed. The masses then used the committees they had themselves created to impose their will on the Assembly. They linked their demand for bread and work with their demand for political freedom and full citizenship. Necessity, not theory, forced them to act directly in the shaping of the new society. Their actions not only gained them their demands but taught them who truly represented them. By 1793, it was not Robespierre and the Jacobins, but the *enragés* Jacques Roux, Theophile Leclerc and Jean Varlet. They were the true spokesmen for the mass revolutionary movement.[3]

"Deputies of the Mountain," said Jacques Roux, "it is a pity that you have not climbed from the third to the ninth floor of the houses of this revolutionary town; you would have been softened by the tears and groans of the vast masses, lacking bread and without clothes, reduced to this state of distress and misfortune by the gambling on the Stock Exchange and speculation in food."

Theophile Leclerc invited the legislators to rise at three in the morning and to take their place among the citizens who besieged the doors of the bakers: "Three hours of his time passed at the door of a bakery would do more to train a legislator than four years spent on the benches of the Convention."

To Robespierre, Reason was the "Supreme Being." But Reason, said Jean Varlet, lived among the masses: "During four years, constantly on the public square among groups of the people, among the *sans-culottes*, among the people whom I love, I have learned how naively, and just by saying what they think, the poor devils of the garrets reasoned more surely, more boldly than the fine gentlemen, the great talkers, the bumbling men of learning; if they wish to gain scientific knowledge let them go and move about like me among the people."[4]

The working class of France, in 1789, was numerically weak. Yet these approximately six hundred thousand, out of a population of some twenty-five million, had accomplished miracles in the thorough destruction of the old order. They did not, and could not, at this birth-stage of capitalist development, separate themselves completely from the revolutionary bourgeois leadership. They had learned that only by their own mass mobilizations and constant activity could they obtain their demands. Robespierre, who had learned so effectively to mobilize those enormous energies against feudal and royal reaction, worked to confine the Revolution. In the material and historic circumstances of the time, the Revolution could not, in any case, have realized the equalitarian principles for which the true representatives of the Parisian masses fought. We cannot follow Robespierre in the course he charted. For our purpose it is sufficient to note that he opened the door to the White Terror which took his life as it prepared the ground for Napoleon.

The great French Revolution, begun for "Liberty, Equality and Fraternity" emblazoned on its Declaration of the Rights of Man —even as the American Revolution, fought under the banner of the Declaration of Independence—ended in the consolidation of power by a new ruling class. This was a new exploitative class which, nevertheless, had a wider popular support than the feudal predecessor it so thoroughly destroyed: (1) Without temporizing, the new ruling class gave legal sanction to, and participated in, the extermination of feudal tithes without indemnification. (2) Where the peasants had seized the land to which they were formerly bound as serfs, this property of Church and emigré nobility was nationalized. (3) The King was deposed and universal male suffrage was established for the first time in the first modern Republic in Europe.

The Industrial Revolution *and* the definitive taking of the land by the peasants formed the solid economic foundation of the new ruling class.[5] This foundation assured the capitalists of remaining the ruling class, whether the form of political power was Republic or Empire.

Half a century later, the young Marx drew from the French Revolution, from the *mass* movement, the principles of revolutionary socialism. Before Marx's birth, however, Hegel had already met the challenge of the French Revolution to reorganize completely the premises of philosophy.

3) The Philosophers and the Revolution: Freedom and the Hegelian Dialectic

Hegel did not examine the French Revolution directly. He criticized the philosophers. All of philosophy before Hegel—from Bacon and Descartes through the Encyclopaedists, Rousseau, and Kant—was certain that it had worked out all fundamental problems, and that, unencumbered by the feudal order and the authority of the Church which trespassed the rights of science, the millenium would bring itself.

Rousseau and Kant did doubt that happiness would automatically result from the progress of science (industry). They sensed inherent contradiction and appealed to *human* emotions and powers. But they could go no further than an attempt to reconcile opposites through an *outside* force, that is, the practical reason of men behaving according to a universal law—"the general will."

Kant had written his *Critique of Practical Reason* the year *before* the French Revolution. Though his enthusiasm for the Revolution never wavered, he could not meet the new, unprecedented, living challenge to his philosophical premises. Hegel alone met the challenge.

There can be no question of the impact of the French Revolution upon Hegel. Nor can there be any question of the impact upon him of the division of labor and the subjugation of the worker to the machine which had been given such an impetus by the industrial development following the Revolution.

In his First System (1801) Hegel *himself* boldly faced this great new negative phenomenon—alienated labor: "The more mechanized labor becomes, the less value it has and the more the individual must toil." "The value of labor decreases in the same proportion as the productivity of labor increases . . . The faculties of the individual are infinitely restricted, and the consciousness of the factory worker is degraded to the lowest level of dullness."[6]

Hegel's description here is reminiscent of Marx's works, but he did not see the positive elements of alienated labor. Nor could he have seen them. It was to be some forty years before the factory worker would reveal all his great creative energies and be ready to challenge the new order of capitalism. All Hegel saw was a wild animal. There is no more dramatic moment in the history of thought, than when the young Hegel, describing the conditions of workers in capitalist production, breaks off the manuscript of his First System, which forever remained unfinished.

As he retired to his ivory tower, away from the realities of the day, his central theme of alienation was abstracted from the productive system. So profound, however, was the impact of what he himself called a "birth-time and a period of organization," that labor remained integral to his philosophy. We can see this in "Lordship and Bondage," that section in the *Phenomenology* where Hegel shows that the bondsman gains "a mind of his own"[7] and stands higher than the lord who lives in luxury, does not labor, and therefore cannot really gain true freedom.

Marx did not know Hegel's early writings, which were not published until the twentieth century, but he caught the critical impact from the *Phenomenology*, which he summed up as follows: "Thus the greatness of the Hegelian philosophy of its final result —the dialectic of negativity as the moving and creative principle— lies in the first place in the circumstances that Hegel . . . grasps the essence of labor . . . the true active relating of man to himself . . . as human essence is only possible . . . through the collective action of man, only as a result of history."[8]

Marx pointed out that insofar as the Hegelian philosophy "holds fast the alienation of man, even if man appears only in the form of spirit, all elements of criticism lie hidden in it and are often already prepared and worked out in a manner extending far beyond the Hegelian standpoint."[8]

What remained integral to the older, as to the younger, Hegel was the French Revolution. It had revealed that the overcoming of opposites is not a single act but a constantly developing process, a development through contradiction. He called it dialectics. It is through the struggle of opposites that the movement of humanity is propelled forward. As Hegel formulated it, in his

Philosophy of History, it was not so much *from* as *through* slavery that man acquired freedom. Hegel was not content merely to affirm the dialectical principle of self-movement and self-activity through opposition. He examined all of human history in this light. His patient tracing of the specific forms of the creating and over-coming of opposites is a landmark that has never been equalled.

"In my view," Hegel wrote, "everything depends on grasp-ing and expressing the ultimate truth not as Substance but as Subject as well."[9] Freedom is the animating spirit, the "Subject" of Hegel's greatest works. All of history, to Hegel, is a series of historical stages in the development of freedom. This is what makes him so contemporary. *Phenomenology of Mind, Science of Logic,* and *Philosophy of Mind* have to be considered *as a whole.* Freedom is not only Hegel's point of departure. It is his point of return: "When individuals and nations have once got in their heads the abstract concept of full-blown liberty, there is nothing like it in its uncontrollable strength, just because it is the very essence of mind, and that as its very actuality. Whole continents, Africa and the East, have never had this idea, and are without it still. The Greeks and Romans, Plato and Aristotle, even the Stoics, did not have it. On the contrary, they saw that it is only by birth (as e.g. an Athenian or Spartan citizen), or by strength of charac-ter, education or philosophy (—the sage is free even as a slave and in chains) that the human being is actually free. It was through Christianity that this idea came into the world."[10]

The young Hegel may or may not have had reservations on the point that it was through Christianity that the idea of freedom was born. But whether Christianity is taken as the point of depar-ture, or whether—as with Marx—the point of departure is the *material* condition for freedom created by the Industrial Revolu-tion, the essential element is this: man has *to fight* to gain freedom; thereby is revealed "the negative character" of modern society. As Marx's collaborator, Frederick Engels, pointed out: IF man were in fact free, there would be no problem, no *Phenomenology*, no *Logic*. What is crucial to both Hegel and Marx is that there are barriers in contemporary society, which prevent the full develop-ment of man's potentialities, of man's "universality."

Hegel was tracing the development of philosophic thought and used some head-cracking terms, abstractions, but the applicability of his method and his ideas go beyond his own use of them. Brought out of their abstractions, Hegel's "Absolutes" have applicability and meaning for every epoch, ours most of all. Despite the fact that Hegel is tracing the dialectic of "pure thought," the dialectic of "Absolute Knowledge," "the Absolute Idea" and "Absolute Mind" are not confined to thought processes alone, and Hegel did not separate his philosophy from actual history. For every stage of development of thought there is a corresponding stage in the development of the world.[11]

This genius achieved the seemingly impossible. Because to him there was one Reason, and one Reason only—whether he *called* it "World Spirit" or "Absolute Mind," it was the *actuality of freedom*—he succeeded in breaking down the division between the finite and infinite, the human and divine. His LOGIC *moves*. Each of the previously inseparable divisions between opposites—between thought and reality—is in constant process of change, disappearance and reappearance, coming into head-on collision with its opposite and developing thereby. It is thus, and thus alone, that man finally achieves true freedom, not as a possession, but as a dimension of his being: "If to be aware of the idea—to be aware, i.e., that men are aware of freedom as their essence, aim, and object—is matter of *speculation*, still this very idea itself is the actuality of men—not something which they *have*, as men, but which they *are*."[12]

Hegel's *presupposition*, that human capacity has infinite possibility of expansion, enabled him to present, even if only in thought, the stages of development of mankind as stages in the struggle for freedom. Thus, he could present the past and the present as a continuous development to the future, from lower to ever higher stages. This bond of continuity with the past is the lifeblood of the dialectic. Hegel envisions a society where man realizes all of his human potentialities and thus achieves consciously what the realm of nature achieves through blind necessity. "The Truth," that is, freedom as part of man's very nature, is not something "added" by Hegel. It is of the grandeur of his vision and flows from the very nature of the *Absolute Method*, dialectical philosophy: "To hold fast the positive in its negative, and the content of the presupposition in the result, is the most important part of rational cognition."[13]

When Marx said that the Ideal is nothing but the reflection of the real, translated into thought, he was not departing either from Hegel's dialectic *method or* from his Absolutes. We shall see this when we come to Marx's 'CAPITAL and *his* Absolute—the "new passions and forces" for a new society.

"To hold fast the positive in the negative," meant for Marx to hold fast to the concept of the self-activity of the proletariat creating a new social order out of the old, miserable, negative capitalist society which is in existence.

Hegel did not see the creativity of the factory worker—nor could he have at that infant stage of development. He worked out all the contradictions *in thought alone.* In life all contradictions remained, multiplied, intensified. It would however be a complete misreading of his philosophy were we to think that because he resolved the contradictions of life in thought alone that, therefore, his Absolute is either a mere reflection of the separation between the intellectual world and the world of material production, *or* that he thereby remained sealed off from the world in a closed, ontological system. Quite the reverse. Hegel broke with the whole tendency of introversion which characterized German idealist philosophy. Where all other philosophers put the realization of truth and freedom in the soul, or in heaven, Hegel drew history into philosophy.

4) Hegel's Absolutes and Our Age of Absolutes

Every epoch has had something to learn from this most original thinker. Every epoch has had something to contribute. Ours most of all. As we shall see better in the final part of this book dealing with Automation and the new Humanism, the workers have been *acting out* Hegel's Absolute Idea and have thus concretized and deepened the movement *from* practice *to* theory. On the other hand, the movement from *theory* is nearly at a standstill because it blinds itself to the movement from practice. Paradoxical as it may sound, the greatest impediment in the way of the intellectuals discerning the new society in Hegel's "Absolute Mind" is their isolation from the working people in whose lives the elements of the new society are present. This isolation from new impulses makes them ask the old question over and over again: If Hegel went so far as to pose what is, in reality, the logic of a new society, why did he end by sponsoring the German bureaucratic State? He himself tells us the *political* reasons. (We are not concerned with his personal reconciliation.) Society, says Hegel, is broken down into opposing classes and interests. The State is not sufficient to maintain authority. It is necessary, therefore, to have a caste whose only function is to rule and mediate between "the government in general on the one hand, and the nation broken up into particulars (people and associations) on the other."

Marx tells us the *philosophical* reasons. In the Hegelian system, humanity appears only through the back door, so to speak, since the core of self-development is not man, but only his "consciousness," that is, the self-development of the Idea. It is this *dehumanization* of the Idea, as if thoughts float between heaven and earth instead of out of the human brain, which Marx castigates mercilessly: "In place of human actuality Hegel has placed Absolute Knowledge."

It is here that Marx took Hegel—who was thus standing on his head—and stood him on his feet, thereby creating the Marxian world view of history, dialectical materialism. Because Hegel could not conceive the *masses* as "Subject" creating the new society, the Hegelian philosophy—though it had replaced the viewing of things as "things in themselves," as dead impenetrable matter—was compelled to return to Kant's idea of an *external* unifier of opposites. Hegel had destroyed all dogmatisms except the dogmatism of "the backwardness of the masses."

On this class barrier Hegel foundered. He fell back into the rationalist trap from which he had so magnificently sought to extricate European thought. Bourgeois thought had reached its highest point in the development of the Hegelian dialectic and, to use a Hegelian expression, "perished."

Herbert Marcuse is absolutely right when he says that the historical heritage of Hegel's philosophy did not pass to the "Hegelians."[14] There is a dynamism and a contemporary ring to

Hegel's philosophy which breaks through his abstruse language. Marx, in his time, acknowledged Hegelian philosophy as the necessary prerequisite to the *proletarian* view of world history. It is more than that now. It concerns all of humanity. For in Hegel's Absolute there is imbedded, though in abstract form, the full development of the *social* individual, or what Hegel would call individuality "purified of all that interferes with its universalism, i.e., freedom itself."[15] Here are the objective and subjective means whereby a new society is going to be born. That new society, struggling to be born, is the concern of our age.

Our age has seen a successful workers' revolution—the Russian Revolution of November, 1917—which seemed to open up an entirely new epoch in the free development of humanity only to end in the counter-revolution of state capitalism. It is therefore our age that is preoccupied with the question of man's destiny: What happens *after* a revolution succeeds? Are we always to be confronted with a new form of State tyranny against the individual's freedom? Are our struggles for freedom to end in a new despotism as the French Revolution, which Hegel witnessed, ended in the reign of Napoleon, and the Russian Revolution, which we witnessed, in the barbarism of Stalin? In asking ourselves: *How* did the first workers' state in history become transformed into its opposite? and: *Can* man be free? we are groping for a total, an absolute answer. It is the *totality* of the present world crisis which compels us to turn to Hegel and his Absolutes, even as it is the *solid ground* under the most abstract part of Hegel's philosophy which compels the Russian theoreticians to deny him.

As recently as 1947, the Russian Communists felt the blows this dialectical historical method delivered to their barbarous methodology of assuming what they should prove—that theirs is a "classless, socialist society." In the name of the Central Committee of the Communist Party of the USSR, Andrei Zhdanov, Stalin's right hand man, addressed a specially convened congress of "philosophical workers." He told them that "The question of Hegel was settled long ago. There is no reason whatsoever to pose it anew . . . when we speak of the philosophical front, it immediately suggests an organized detachment of militant philosophers . . . waging a determined offensive. . . . But does our philosophical front resemble a real front? It resembles rather a stagnant creek, or a bivouac at some distance from the battlefield. The field has not yet been conquered, for the most part contact has not been established with the enemy, there is no reconnaissance, the weapons are rusting, the soldiers are fighting at their own risk and peril. . . ."[16]

Having thus laid down the line of what he called "the Party character of philosophy," he then claimed nothing less than the discovery of a "new dialectical law": "Criticism and Self-Criticism." Having substituted the subjectivity of well-ordered "criticism and self-criticism" for the objective dialectical law of development through contradiction, he then proclaimed: "In our Soviet society, where antagonistic classes have been liquidated, the struggle between the old and the new, and consequently the development from the lower to the higher, proceeds not in the form of struggle between antagonistic classes and of cataclysms, as is the case under capitalism, but in the form of criticism and self-criticism, which is the real motive force of our development, a powerful instrument in the hands of the Communist Party. This is incontestably a new aspect of movement, a new type of development, a new dialectical law."[17]

By 1955 "the new dialectical law" of criticism and self-criticism had still not laid Hegel to rest, much less the live contradictions in their totalitarian system. Hegel remains so alive and worrisome to the Russian rulers because they correctly sense that his concept of the Absolute and the international struggle for freedom are not as far apart as it would seem on the surface. The Russian theoreticians think, or at any rate they would like us to think, that the historical struggles for freedom stopped with the Russian Revolution of 1917. Under the pretense of separating "the materialism" of Marx from "the idealism" of Hegel, they proceed to mutilate Marx's *Economic-Philosophic Manuscripts* and turn Hegelian dialectics into gibberish.[18] Thereby they hope theoretically to stifle the new society striving to be born. They keep feeling the blows this dialectical historical method delivers them even as the continuous revolt of the Russian workers keeps undermining the bureaucratic power in actual life.

Today we live in an age of absolutes, that is to say, in an age where the contradictions are so total that the counter-revolution is in the very innards of the revolution. In seeking to overcome this total, this absolute contradiction, we are on the threshold of true freedom and therefore can understand better than any previous age Hegel's most abstract concepts.

In Hegel the Absolute is the vision of the future. Whether one accepts it as the new society, or thinks of it only as the ontological unity of the human and the divine, the simple truth is that *this* unity of the human and divine is not up in heaven but here on earth. His Absolute is directed against what he himself called the "emptiness" of the Absolute of previous philosophy. It is true that the categories of his *Logic*, such as, "Being and Becoming," "Essence and Appearance," "Necessity and Freedom," do not, as Hegel imagined, have eternal existence independent of man. They are, in actuality, the reflection in man's mind of processes going on in the material world. It is equally true that the *summation* of Hegel's own analysis is that actuality, the true form of reality, requires freedom, requires man *to be* free. His doctrine of the Notion develops these categories of freedom, and the true potentialities of mankind are thus counterposed to the apparent reality. It is this which gives the material ring to Hegel's idealist philosophy. In fact, the *Science of Logic* may be said to be the *philosophy of history established by the French Revolution,* namely, that man in temporal history, that is, on this earth, can achieve freedom.

Though Hegel deals only with thought, practice is of the essence. Indeed, the "Practical Idea" stands *higher* than the "Idea of Cognition" in the Hegelian system because it has not only "the dignity of the universal, but is the simply actual." While all of Hegel's works end in the Absolute, it is not, as we saw, an Absolute "abstracted" from life. In the *Phenomenology* Hegel begins with the sphere of daily experience, and when he ends with "Absolute Knowledge," he explains it as the unity of history and science.

Hegel's *Science of Logic* begins where the *Phenomenology* ended. Absolute Knowledge, that is to say, history and the science of knowledge, once again undertakes the search for Truth. In a word, history and the philosophic mastery of the forms of organization which history unfolded have reached an absolute only on the surface of society. First now they go from the world of appearance to the world of logic where they reach the unity of theory and practice as "The Absolute Idea." Hegel then shows in the *Philosophy of Nature* that Nature has gone through the same dialectical development as the Idea. Translated materialistically, what Hegel is saying is that there is a movement from practice to theory as well as from theory to practice. In the *Philosophy of Mind* he unites the two movements—nature and the logical principle—on a higher plane but admits that "philosophy appears as a subjective cognition, of which liberty is the aim, and which is itself the way to produce it."[19] He shows how Mind itself becomes "the mediating agent in the process" and adds that "it is the nature of the fact, the notion, which causes the movement and development, yet this same movement is equally the action of cognition."[19] With his Absolute Mind, Hegel has reached the climax of his system.

Marx *did not* reject idealism. "Thoroughgoing Naturalism or Humanism," as the young Marx designated his own philosophic outlook, "distinguishes itself from idealism and from materialism and is at the same time the truth uniting both."[20] Marxism may be said to be the most idealistic of all materialistic philosophy, and Hegelianism the most materialistic of all idealistic philosophy. Hegel, said Marx, could not carry out his dialectical logic consistently because he remained from first to last a philosopher seeking to trace the logical movement, not of the worker, but of the intellectual. Hegel had established the principles. He had discovered them out of the devastating critique which the French Revolution made of all previous philosophy. But the philosopher, working only with ideas in his head and in the heads of others, cannot solve the problems of society. He cannot create new unities. He can only summarize those already reached. He is always standing apart from the real process of nature—which is human nature working on nature—and constantly transforming it into a new unity with himself.

The development of the dialectical method on new beginnings is to be found in Marxism. To develop the dialectical movement further, it was necessary to turn to the real world and its labor process. This is what Marx did.

Official Marxism has repeated *ad nauseum* that Marx stood Hegel right side up, that is, on his feet. As Lenin discovered during World War I, to pay lip service to the dialectic while at the same time to repeat tirelessly that Hegel is gibberish without Marx is to transform Marx into a vulgar materialist. If this was a baited trap during World War I, today it is the greatest perversion of *all* that Marx stood for. Russian Communism is a past master of such total perversion of history. But what is one to think of the way in which most academic Hegelians have aided this perversion by barring an approach to Hegel through their insistence on keeping "the secret" of Hegel?

The manner in which radical intellectuals have joined this twosome in transforming the dialectic into sheer sophistry almost assumes the proportions of a conspiracy. These intellectual cynics have learned to manipulate the dialectic to fit arguments both *pro* and *con* on any subject. They maintain, for example, that Hegel is the theorist of both the counter-revolution and of the "permanent revolution." Hegel himself dealt with these types of philosophical lawyers who, with equal ease, can argue either side of a case: "Sophistry has nothing to do with what is taught:—that may very possibly be true. Sophistry lies in the formal circumstance of teaching it by grounds which are as available for attack as for defence."[21]

To declare, in our day and age, that Hegel's Absolute means nothing but the "knowing" of the whole past of human culture is to make a mockery of the dialectical development of the world and of thought, and absolutely to bar a rational approach to Hegel. What is far worse, such sophistry is a self-paralyzing barrier against a sober theoretical approach to the world itself.

It is necessary to divest Hegelian philosophy of the deadweight of academic tradition as well as of radical intellectual snobbery and cynicism or we will lay ourselves wide open to the putrescent smog of Communism.

CHAPTER TWO

CLASSICAL POLITICAL ECONOMY, THE
REVOLTS OF THE WORKERS, AND
THE UTOPIAN SOCIALISTS

The industrial revolution had uprooted the masses from the land; the industrial capitalist separated them from their instruments of labor and their homes. It was as if a tornado had swept over them and the only thing left in sight was the factory which was sucking them in as "a collection of hands." They had to bow to it because it was now their only means of making a livelihood. Our modern world was born. Production and more production became the theory because it was the life of the new mechanism. The industrial capitalist took command of society.[22]

The chaotic state of economic inquiry was transformed into the system of classical political economy at the very time when the Industrial Revolution undermined the foundations on which the merchant capitalist as well as the small master manufacturer stood. Classical political economy which was born in 1776 with the publication of Adam Smith's *Wealth of Nations,* reached its height—and end—in 1821, with the publication of David Ricardo's *Political Economy and Taxation.*

The classical theory proclaimed that the wealth of nations was not something *outside* of men—like precious metals or land or foreign trade—but in man's *activity itself.* Man should stop looking for gold and busy himself with *production.* That is what is decisive. *The* greatest force of production is *labor.* It is the source of *all* value.

The labor theory of value created as great a revolution in man's thinking as the industrial revolution had in man's conditions of living. Heretofore the dominant theory had been that of the mercantilists—merchant capitalists—who had argued that wealth results from "buying cheap and selling dear." Therefore, they contended, a great market, such as the American colonies, could not be given up without England itself falling. Preceding the mercantilists was the physiocratic school, which argued that *agricultural* labor was the source of wealth. Just as the successful American Revolution gave the final blow to mercantilist theory, so the Industrial Revolution delivered the final blow to the physiocratic theory. Production and more production—the wedding of science and industry—said classical political economy, would lead the world to ever increased happiness and development.

The bourgeoisie embraced the philosophy of classical political economy: production for production's sake. They embraced it all the more readily because the labor theory of value was a single law and as compelling a phenomenon as the outward forms of regulation of feudalism. At one and the same time it gave an integrated view of the economic system and assigned labor its place in society—at the point of production. Somehow, order had emerged from the seeming anarchy brought on by the Industrial Revolution in which each industrialist produced for himself without State regulation and without knowing his market. Economic man, it was asserted, would henceforward work for his *individual* interests and somehow this would prove to be best for society as a whole. Free competition would fully cleanse justice and equality of feudal privileges and inequalities. The possessors of equal rights would exchange freely according to the quantity of labor embodied in their commodities.

Classical political economy worked within a *given* class society, capitalism, which it took for the eternal natural order. Its great merit was that it revealed the *innermost* law of bourgeois production: *the laborer is paid at value*. It is true that these classicists substituted the labor*er* for labor and looked at the working man as a commodity, as a thing. But, thereby, they discovered labor's cost of production, namely, the means of subsistence necessary to enable the labor*er* to work and reproduce his kind. Thus, also, a glaring capitalist contradiction was revealed. The laborer was getting only what was *necessary* to produce him, and all the *surplus* he produced was appropriated by the capitalist. From the *equality* of exchange *in general* arose the *inequality* of exchange of the *particular* "commodity"—labor.

Ricardo never doubted that unhampered production would somehow eliminate all evils and right all things in this integrated, natural world of his. He continued to attribute the irrationalities in his rational system either to feudal vestiges or to governmental interference.

The theories of the Enlightenment had asserted that knowledge and science, released from feudal, aristocratic despotism, would bring about a harmonious world. This concept was smashed to smithereens by the social-political revolution in France. Not only did industry and science break up the feudal order—they revealed new antagonisms from the very start. As we saw, that greatest bourgeois philosopher, Hegel, sensed the irreconcilable contradictions of modern society. Though he did not accept Ricardo's "natural order," he too stood on the basis of classical economics and he too looked at labor, not the labor*er*. Or, more precisely, having once looked at the laborer, he turned quickly away never to look at him again. Nor, for that matter, was classical political economy unaware of the sufferings of the people, but these sufferings seemed a small price to pay for the birth pangs of the "natural order" of society freed at last from all feudal restrictions and state interference.

1) The Continuous Revolts of the Workers and the End of Classical Political Economy

The labor*er*, who had been left out of Ricardo's analysis, loomed very large in the actual development of capitalist society. From the very birth of industrial capitalism the laborer has been in constant revolt. At first he could see no reason at all to crowd into the towns and give up his *personal freedom*. The revulsion against going into the factory, with its prison discipline, was so strong that laws were enacted against "vagabondage" to *force* him into the factory. Once brought into the factory, their oppression forced the workers to uprisings against the instrument of labor, the machine. The first laws against the break-up of machines were passed in 1769. What amazed the bourgeois ideologists was the workers' seemingly abject submission to the machine, on the one hand, and the violent strikes, on the other hand.

The new factory workers—who had been compelled to sign away their personal freedom to become one of a "collection of hands" working under conditions common to all—evolved a new method of revolt. *Combinations,* or the first form of trade unions, emerged. The bourgeoisie retaliated immediately by passing the Anti-Combination Acts of 1799 and 1800. This time, however, the laws were unsuccessful. The factory workers had discovered a *new power*—that of being together at a place forced upon them by the industrial capitalist. Thus, they were united and disciplined by the very instrument of production which coerced them. They continued to form their combinations despite the harsh laws and prison terms. Uprisings continued and were put down in blood—from the Luddite riots in 1811 and 1812 to the Lyons uprisings in 1834. But they had won the repeal of the Anti-Combination Acts in 1824. In 1844 the Silesian weavers, in their revolt, signalled a new stage in their development. They not only broke the machines, they tore up the titles to the machines and burned the deeds.

Trade unions sprung up everywhere and strikes were on the order of the day. Now, however, the workers were striking not against the machine but against the *uncontrolled power of capital.* They questioned the capitalist principle of a "certain quantity of money for a certain quantity of labor." They questioned the conditions of labor. They questioned the hours of labor. They demanded certain wages, factory inspection, a limit on the hours of labor. Then they turned against the legislators. Along with the fight of the trade unions for the Ten Hours Bill, the English workers also organized the Chartist movement and demanded universal suffrage.

Meanwhile, the first great, general capitalist crisis had broken upon an unsuspecting world in 1825. Another crisis erupted in 1837. Overproduction and depression—phenomena quite unknown before—now became normal.

The Ricardian school was battered, on the one side, by recurring crises and, on the other side, by the revolts of labor. Why should he who creates all the wealth, asked the laborer, become poorer the more values he creates? Why, asked the capitalist, should his system of production be wrecked by crises although production was unhampered? What about the integrated whole society run by a single economic law? Where Ricardo had been unable to solve the contradictions in his theory of labor value, his followers could make no headway. That was not because they were merely followers and he was an original thinker. The *objective conditions* developed the contradictions further. Crises and class struggles wrought havoc with a school of thought that had been scientific enough to *pose* contradictions but bourgeois enough to *reject* the laborer who would develop these contradictions to the end.

The failure of the Ricardian theory to explain the exchange between capital and labor on the basis of its own primary law of labor value meant the disintegration of that school. Nassau Senior's infamous theory of the "Eleventh Hour"—the theory that all profit was created only in the eleventh hour and that "therefore" any reduction of the working day to ten hours would mean the end of the whole productive system—sounded the death knell of bourgeois economics as a science. Bourgeois economists became transformed into what Marx called "hired prize-fighters in the interests of the capitalist class."

The greater the crises, the more numerous and violent the strikes, the more machines were introduced. The whole capitalist philosophy of production was reduced "to training human beings to renounce their desultory habits of work and to identify themselves with the unvarying regularity of the complex automaton."[23]

2) *The Utopian Socialists and Pierre Proudhon: a Case of Mental Juggling*[24]

The classicists' philosophy of "production and more production," which Marx called "production for the sake of production," gave modern industry the needed scope in which to develop. The actual development disclosed the conditions of modern production and demonstrated that the welfare of the masses, the producers, does not at all flow from the growth of wealth. The crying inequalities of distribution, arising from this method of production, could not but arouse the sympathy of the intellectual for the proletariat. Being *outside* of production, however, the intellectual could not see that the working class had *power* to overthrow the contradictory conditions of production. For the intellectual, the proletariat existed only as a suffering class.

The utopian socialist had the excuse that in its infancy the industrial working class did not, on the morrow of the bourgeois revolution, form an independent mass movement. The petty-bourgeois intellectual continued to remain outside the mass movement even when the actions of the proletariat had crystallized into organizational forms on both the economic and political fronts. Proudhon, our most typical and most important example, opposed strikes and combinations because they only "made all things dear." He opposed political movements because they did not follow the pattern his mind had conceived.

While classical political economy suffered disintegration as a bourgeois school of thought, a crop of utopian socialists arose who wanted to "use" the classical theory of labor as the source of value "for" the working class.

The utopian socialists based themselves on the Ricardian theory of value which they claimed to be "socialist" and required only cleansing of its capitalistic "conclusions." If, went the argument, labor is the source of all value, it must therefore be the source of all surplus value *and* the "fruits of labor" "rightfully" belong to labor. As Marx put it, the significance of the utopian socialists was that they corresponded to the first instinctive desires of the masses to *reorganize* society. Their continued existence, when the masses moved in another direction, could mean nothing but a reactionary movement *in opposition* to the actual movement of the proletariat.

The utopian socialists stayed away from the living movement of the working class. In England, there were the trade unions and the Chartist movement. But Robert Owen, who had done much in revealing the actual conditions in the factories of England, held himself apart from this real movement of the proletariat. Although it was the suffering of the masses that broke the bourgeois intellectuals from their own class and brought them near

the proletariat, they believed not one iota in the creative initiative
of the masses.

Nothing surprised Owen so much as when he returned to
England, after having built the New Harmony colony in America,
to find that the trade unions, one million strong, were ready to
adopt his schemes. Being proletarians, however, they knew the way
to do that seriously was through a revolutionary mass movement.
They were ready to get rid of the employer class. They were prepared to call a general strike and reorganize industry on a cooperative basis. At first, Owen appeared to be with them. Then he
backed away and, while the real movement collapsed under the
extreme persecution of the government, his own organization became more and more "ethical."

Pierre Proudhon was the most important figure of these
utopian sects. He opposed trade unions in England and strikes
everywhere. At the very moment that Marx was predicting that
Germany was on the eve of revolution, Proudhon "proved" that
the masses had "outgrown" revolution. He no sooner wrote that,
when the revolutions burst out in France and Germany. It was
not a theoretical question. The question was not whether Proudhon
did or did not predict correctly. The question was: *what to do?*
Where Marx was always with the revolutionary working class,
these intellectuals, including the self-made ones like Proudhon,
in action always opposed it.

> Marx wrote: "In place of the great historic movement aris-
> ing from the conflict between the productive forces already
> acquired by man and their social relations, which no longer
> correspond to these productive forces; . . . in place of the
> practical and violent action of the masses by which alone these
> conflicts can be resolved—in place of this vast, prolonged and
> complicated movement Monsieur Proudhon supplies the evac-
> uating motion of his own head."[25]

Instead of analyzing or aligning himself with the actual historical development of the masses, Proudhon had evolved the
development of a "Universal Reason," the "absolute truth," which
gave birth to a few "classless" moral ideas such as "justice" and
"equality." Were political economy infused with these, he argued,

value would come into its own and the Ricardian theory would be righted by granting everyone titles to property.

Proudhon's final discovery was to have "people's banks." The "people's bank," "free credit" and "organization of exchange" came naturally to Proudhon for his whole conception of value was that it was something *quantitative,* a matter of such and such a *proportion* of the products of national wealth. He found no fault with the existing production relations that couldn't be solved simply by changing the legal titles to property. If, in addition, money were made only a circulating medium, all would be righted in his world. He therefore proposed that, instead of money being loaned at interest, it should be "sold and bought at cost like any other commodity." To his mind, the evil seemed to stem from the fact that upon gold was conferred an "economic privilege by the sovereignty of the state." All the evils of capitalism seemed to be a malicious perversion on the part of the governments rather than a result of the method of commodity production.

As though the class struggle were a mere abstraction in his mind, like his "System of Contradictions," this intellectual anarchist conceived the conflict soluble by the "right idea." Proudhon's "right idea" was the "synthesis" of the "good sides" of the opposing forces brought about by "reunited labor and property" *within the present system of production,* which was to remain intact. Where Marx placed the proletariat in the center of all his thinking, Proudhon placed the small producer. His goal was to remove the middleman from between the capitalist -and the worker; parcel out the land and industry; and establish "a society of equal producers." His conception was that "exchange could be organized equitably" if only the merchant and the banker did not have monopolistic power granted them by the government. This good petty-bourgeois mistook *his* weaving between the two major classes of modern society—the workers and the capitalists— for the discovery of the point of equilibrium between these two great opposing forces.

Proudhon elaborated his phantasy in *Philosophy of Poverty.*[26] Marx hit back with *Poverty of Philosophy.* Marx argued that to try "to organize exchange," to try to bring order into the anarchy of the market in a society based on factory production, *must* mean its organization according to the division of labor in the factory where the authority of the capitalist is undisputed. To try to bring that "principle of authority" into society as a whole could only mean subjecting society to one *single master*.

This profound prediction of the totalitarianism to which abstract planning would inevitably lead had no effect on the Proudhonist movement in France, where retarded industrial development made idealization of the small producer natural.

The small peasant, the petty industrialist, the semi-proletarian—these, Proudhon enthroned in his "socialism." Not being subjected to the despotism of the labor process under capitalism, Proudhon thought to solve all problems by leaving commodity production intact and creating "money for all" with his schemes for free credit. A decade later, in the United States, that is exactly what Vanderbilt had too much of, when watered railroad stocks came crashing over his head. Where labor had created no value, not the Vanderbilts nor the Goulds nor the Government could fabricate it. This, Proudhon could not imagine. He had already decided that the workers could save up small shares, set up workshops and, by giving up "interest and profit," soon "buy" all the capital of France from the bourgeoisie. That would indeed make a piker of Peter Minuit, who bought the island of Manhattan from the Indians for a reputed $25. The year 1848 swept away the pretensions of the radical intellectuals. It was necessary however, to expose the *theoretical* root of the error of "organizing exchange"—and Marx turned to it in his economic works.

CHAPTER THREE

A NEW HUMANISM: MARX'S EARLY
ECONOMIC-PHILOSOPHIC WRITINGS

In 1843 the young Marx broke with bourgeois society. From the start Marx's vision was one of total freedom. He was concerned with the freedom of humanity and, against that, the inevitable misery and waste of life which characterizes contemporary society. The late eighteenth century had been marked by great revolutions—American and French—but each of these had ended in a new form of class domination for which the Industrial Revolution had laid the basis. We must not be afraid, Marx wrote his Young Hegelian friend Arnold Ruge, with whom he was to found a new magazine,[27] "to criticize the existing world ruthlessly. I mean ruthlessly in the sense that we must not be afraid of our own conclusions and equally unafraid of coming into conflict with the prevailing powers. . . . The world has long had the dream of something and must only possess the consciousness of it in order to possess it actually."

It was Marx's aim to help the age come to a realization of itself. Even before his break from bourgeois society, when the young man, fresh from the university campus, had first faced the real world and its material interests as editor of the *Neue Rheinische Zeitung,* he was at once embattled with Prussian censorship. "Freedom is so much the essence of man," he wrote, "that even its opponents realize it in that they fight its reality . . . No man fights freedom; he fights at most the freedom of others. Every kind of freedom has therefore always existed, only at one time as a special privilege, another time as a universal right." He fought for the freedom of the press and the right of a newspaper to deal with all questions which interest the public. The point was that all questions—material, religious, political, philosophical—that have become "newspaper questions, have become questions of the time."

1) Dialectical Materialism and the Class Struggle, or What Kind of Labor?

Marx had mastered the Hegelian dialectic as a university student. After his battle with the Prussian censors—his first experience with the vested interests of the world outside the university—Marx turned to a criticism of Hegel's *Philosophy of Right*. Later, he described how, through these studies, he had come "to the conclusion that the legal relations as well as forms of state could neither be understood by themselves, nor explained by the so-called progress of the human mind, but that they are rooted in material conditions of life . . . It is not the consciousness of man that determines their existence, but, on the contrary, their social existence that determines their consciousness."[28]

With this new dialectical materialist view of history, the epoch of proletarian consciousness reached a new world stage. There was nothing mechanical about Marx's new materialist outlook. Social existence determines consciousness but it is not a confining wall that prevents one from sensing and even seeing the elements of a new society. Marx himself turned at once to the living movement of the workers. Where the other Young Hegelians —who had criticized the still existing semi-feudal state of Prussia —had recoiled from the actual uprising of the Silesian weavers that faced them in August, 1844, the young Marx wrote enthusiastically: "The wisdom of the German poor stands in inverse ratio to the wisdom of poor Germany. . . . The Silesian uprisings began where the French and English insurrections ended, with the consciousness of the proletariat as a class."[29]

The year 1844 saw new proletarian impulses literally reach up from the earth of the turbulent 1840's. These new impulses were soon to culminate in the 1848 revolutions which engulfed Europe. It was that same year of 1844 when Marx wrote his *Economic-Philosophic Manuscripts*. Here Marx posed dialectically the fundamental problem—what *kind* of labor—which is today being battled out the world over. Automation has made this question urgent in the United States. In 1844 Marx made this self-same question pivotal, *the* new theoretical response to the workers' revolt against the tyranny of factory labor.

Even as a Young Hegelian, Marx had tried to draw a sharp division between the *revolutionary method* of thought, which analyzed objective development through inherent contradictions, and the *reactionary conclusions* which Hegel drew, and which therefore made it possible for Prussian absolutism to adopt the Hegelian philosophy as the official State philosophy. During the turbulent forties, when he broke from bourgeois society, Marx could see the full significance of the class struggle: that proletarian revolt is the motive force of modern history. It was first now, therefore, that he could rid the dialectical philosophy of its mystical enclosure.

Where Hegel saw objective history as the successive manifestations of a world spirit, Marx placed the objective movement in the process of production. He now saw the core of the Hegelian *method*—the self-movement which is internally necessary because it is the way of the organism's own development—in the self-activity of the proletariat. From the start, therefore, he began with the proletarian activity at the point of producion. He separated labor from product and from property, and looked for the contradiction within labor itself. It is through this contradiction that the laborer would develop, that is, would overcome the contradictions in the capitalist method of production. He was thus able to transcend classical political economy. In essence what he said to Smith and Ricardo was: Your discovery was indeed epoch-making. But you yourselves are doing with private property what the mercantilists did with precious metals. You are treating it as a fact *outside* man. You thought your task was done with the discovery of labor as the source of value. In reality, it had just begun. If that theory means anything at all, it means that you must deal with man, the laborer, directly. Production is not a relationship of man to machine. It is a relationship of man to man through the instrumentality of the machine. The exchange of things, of commodities, not only reflects but also befuddles this relationship of men at the point of production. Your error lies in turning away from the laborer whose function, labor, you hailed to the skies.

That, of course, is no accident since it is the worker who consistently and persistently develops all the contradictions in capitalistic private property by being subjected to its power. It is still labor, but it turns out to be an *alien* power because the labor process which extracts his labor from him is a process that has transformed the machine into an accumulated dead weight resting upon him, the living worker.

Labor *is* first of all the function of man. But labor *under capitalism* is the very specific function of man working at machines to which he becomes a mere appendage. His labor, therefore, is not the *self*-activity, the creative function it was under primitive communism where, in mastering nature, man had also developed his own natural capacities and talents. Labor in the factory is *alienated labor*. Private property arises not because the *products* of labor are alienated from the laborers. That is only the *consequence* of the fact that his very activity is an alien activity. It is as much. a product of the Industrial Revolution as is the machine itself.

When the division of labor, characteristic of all class societies, has reached the monstrous proportions where all science, all intellect, all skill goes into the machine, while the labor of man becomes a simple, monotonous grind, then the labor of man can produce nothing but its opposite, capital. All concrete labors have been reduced to one abstract, congealed mass. Dead, accumulated, materialized labor now turns to oppress the living labor*er*. This mastery of dead over living labor is a *class* relationship. The previous feudal distinctions between the propertied and the property-less, and among the various estates, has now become a full-blown contradiction which is *within* the method of production itself, within labor itself. The relationship of capital to labor is more antagonistic, therefore, than had been the relationships among estates under feudalism. This method of production is neither a natural order, nor an eternal one as you had visioned. Like other social orders, it is historic and transitory.

Where all the charm of work has gone out of work, "simple labor" is by no means lightened. On the contrary. The burden and agony of toil has increased. Witness the prolongation of the working day, the increase in the speed of work, the prison-like discipline.

The factory has turned the laborers into an industrial army under a hierarchy of officers and sergeants. That is why the technical revolution has meant not *harmonious* development as you had visioned, but the accumulation of capital at one pole and the accumulation of misery at the other pole. Labor and capital are such absolute opposites that the class struggle is developing into a veritable civil war. All you have to do, to see in theory what is a truth in life, is to include the wage laborer himself in the study of the production of capitalistic wealth.

Lest anyone think that Marx's use of the term "alienation" was merely a question of philosophic language which he quickly discarded when he worked out his "scientific economic theories," it is necessary to state at once that Marx was *organically* a dialectician.[30] In his "Critique of the Hegelian Dialectic," Marx criticizes Hegel's idealism, that is to say, his exclusive concern with ideas and thoughts, and his solving of all contradictions in thought alone, while in *life* they remain and wreck society. But Marx praises, takes over, develops, the dialectic method. The concept of alienation is basic to what Hegel calls "the dialectic of negativity" which, to Marx, is "the moving and creative principle." Marx attacks Hegel, not for seeing development *through* contradiction, but for seeing this process of development *and yet* making it a question of "Absolute Knowledge" instead of a question of the new society which the revolutionary practice of the proletariat—not some abstract negativity—would bring about. Marx put this most clearly in another of his writings of this period: "He (Hegel) stands the world *on its head* and can therefore dissolve *in the head* all the limitations which naturally remain in existence for *evil sensuousness*, for real man."[31]

Marx absorbed and recreated the principle of "the negation of the negation"—or the revolutionary overcoming of real contradictions, that is to say, opposing class forces—not only in his early writings, but in CAPITAL itself and throughout his life as thinker, as organizer, as writer, as revolutionary. While he criticized Hegel's *limitation* of transcendence because it is achieved only "insofar as it is thought," Marx, as we saw, stressed "the greatness of the Hegelian *Phenomenology* and of its final result —the dialectic of negativity as the moving and creating principle"

and concluded, "the positive moments of the Hegelian dialectic
. . . transcendence as objective movement. This is insight. . . ."[32]

So profound, in fact, was Hegel's development of transcendence
as *objective* movement, that Marx straightaway draws the parallel
between this and the conception of communism: "Communism is
humanism mediated by the transcendence of private property."
He then proceeds to include in that objective movement the second
negation, or "the negation of negation." He drew the line so
sharply between "vulgar communism" and even "positive communism," on the one hand, and his own philosophy of *humanism,*
on the other hand, that it stands to this day as the dividing line
between Marxism as the doctrine of liberation, and all who claim
the name of "Marxism," "socialism," or "communism" while they
pursue an entirely different course, both in thought and in practice, from all that Marx stood for.

"Not until the transcendence of this mediation (abolition
of private property) which is nevertheless a necessary presuppost-
tion does there arise positive Humanism, beginning from itself,"
said Marx. In a word, another transcendence, *after* the abolition
of private property is needed to achieve a truly new, *human* society which differs from private property not alone as an "economic
system," but as a different way of *life* altogether. It is as *free*
individuals developing all their natural and acquired talents that
we first leap from what Marx called the *pre*-history of humanity
into its true history, the "leap from necessity to freedom."

There is no doubt that the mature Marx—who elaborated
his views fully in writings and in actions over the next thirty-nine
years—departed from the strictly Hegelian language of his early
writings, where he described the development of man's true potentialities in the Hegelian terms of "unity of thought and being."
But even when he used the Hegelian language, Marx was never
an idealist in the sense of thinking that contradictions in society
can be solved in thought. "Philosophy cannot solve them," he
writes, "precisely because philosophy grasps them only as theoretical
problems." And in these early essays he says, in no uncertain terms,
that only the revolutionary activity of the masses will do away
with the alienation of labor, *the* contradiction of capitalist society.

The point is, however, that for Marx, as for us today, nothing short of a philosophy, a total outlook—which Marx first called, *not* "Communism" but "Humanism," can answer the manifold needs of the proletariat. Man will not again be alienated. He will not again be fragmented. He must again become whole with the re-unification of mental and manual labor in the living worker whose self-activity will first then develop all his human poten-tialities: "Communism is the necessary form and the energetic principle of the immediate future, but communism is not as such the goal of human development, the form of human society."

2) Private Property and Communism

It was not only Hegel that Marx stood on his feet. It was also the "quite vulgar and unthinking communism" which "com-pletely negates the personality of man." Marx did not know the totalitarian Communists of our day, but he put his finger on all that was essential when he criticized the utopian communists of his day for their total preoccupation with the question of private property. Despite their opposition to it, Marx said, their view was "merely the logical expression of private property."[33] That is to say, there was really no fundamental difference between the exponents of private property and those who were opposed to it *but* were willing to let the mode of labor remain what it was. Of course, said Marx, the product the worker creates is alienated from him, becomes the property of another, the capitalist. Of course, the worker himself becomes poorer the more wealth he creates.

The basic contradictions of capitalism cannot be overcome until what is most degrading of all, and the cause of all other contradictions—alienated labor—is overcome: "In the alienation of the object of labor is only crystallized the alienation, the estrange-ment, in the very activity of labor." *This* is the essence of *all* that is perverse in capitalism.

"Political economy," writes Marx, "proceeds from labor as the real soul of production and nevertheless attributes nothing to labor, everything to private property. Proudhon has concluded from this contradiction in favor of labor against private property. We have seen, however, that this apparent contradiction is the

contradiction of labor alienated from itself, and political economy
has only expressed this law of alienated labor. . . . Even the
equality of wages, proposed by Proudhon, only transforms the relation of today's workers to their labor to that of all men to their
labor. Society would then appear as an abstract capitalist."

So opposed is Marx to anyone who thinks that the ills of capitalism can be overcome by changes in the sphere of distribution,
instead of reorganization in the sphere of production, that he shows
the Communists to be only the other side of the private property
exponents. No other generation can understand the early Marx as
we can, for only our generation bears on its back the fully capitalistic nature of this type of "anti-capitalism" known as Communism,
or One-Party State totalitarianism. Marx warned, back in 1844, "We
should especially avoid establishing society as an abstraction opposed to the individual. The individual *is* the social entity."

Marx's analysis of labor—and that is what distinguishes him
from all other Socialists and Communists of his day *and* of ours—
goes much further than the economic structure of society. His
analysis goes to the actual *human* relations. "To have one basis for
life and another for science," he wrote, "is *a priori* a lie."

Production is no longer limited by a crude instrument, nor
does a crude instrument restrict the activity of man, as it did in
pre-capitalist societies, even when it was his property. Were
man to appropriate the modern machines of production, that would
open up limitless vistas for the development of man himself,
for it would be on such a high material base that the intellect
of the masses could combine with their powers and lay the basis
for a truly new way of life. Thus, the appropriation of the *totality*
of the instruments of production "is nothing more than the development of the individual capacities corresponding to the material instruments of production. The development of a totality
of instruments is for this very reason the development of a
totality of capacities in the individuals themselves."

That is the heart of the problem. The development of man's
capacities means the re-establishment of *self-activity* on a gigan-
tically higher historical scale. So hostile was Marx to labor under
capitalism, that at first he called, not for the "emancipation" of
labor, but for its *"abolition."* That is why, at first, he termed

man's function not "labor," but "self-activity." When he changed from the *expression* "abolition of labor" to "emancipation of labor," it was only because the working class showed in its revolts how it can *through* alienated labor achieve emancipation. It was this "need for universality," man's need to be a whole man, that guided Marx throughout his life. No matter how the language changed, the point remained that labor, in a new society, would in no manner whatever be the type of activity it is under capitalism where man's labor is limited to the exercise of his physical labor power. The division between mental and manual labor would be abolished and what would assert itself under those circumstances would be "the free individuality of the laborer himself."[34]

"When man speaks of private property, he believes he has only to deal with a fact outside of man," Marx wrote. "When man speaks of labor, he has to deal directly with man. This new posing of the question already includes the resolution." But that formulation included the solution *only when* the new world view of history, which Marx called "Humanism," tackled the problem— *not* when the bourgeois economists dealt with it, *nor* when the utopian communists introduced the question of "right" into the question of economics. Marx's point is that it is impossible to disassociate property forms from production relations, that is, the relations of men at the point of production. For Marx the abolition of private property was a *means* toward the abolition of alienated labor, not an end in itself. He did not separate one from the other. He never tired of stressing that what is of primary importance is *not* the form of property, but the mode of production. Every mode of production, he said, creates a corresponding form of property: "But to see mystery in the origin of property; that is to say, to transform the relations of production into a mystery, is that not," asks Marx of Proudhon, "to renounce all pretensions to economic science? In each historic epoch property is differently developed and in a series of social relations entirely different. Thus to define bourgeois property is nothing other than to explain all the social relations of production."[35]

As Marx put it in his earlier writings, *as long as* there exist "powers *over* individuals," "private property must exist."[36] To Marx, private property is *the power to dispose of the labor of others*. That is why he so adamantly insisted that to make "society" the owner, but to leave the alienated labor alone, is to create "an abstract capitalist." Again, our generation can see more in this than other generations could, for private property has developed so diversely under capitalism that one's property is only a "bundle of expectations," as Berle and Means so aptly put it when they spoke of stocks and bonds.[37] Yet what is essential is that it is *power*, power to dispose, or share in the disposal, of the labor of others.

Thirty years before Marx developed his economic theories in full, and could see in dim outline that the growth of capital might lead to its concentration in the "hands of one single capitalist," Marx insisted that the abolition of private property means a new way of life, a new social order *only if* "freely associated individuals," and not abstract "society," become the masters of the socialized means of production.

3) Communism's Perversion of Marx's Economic-Philosophic Manuscripts

In 1955, the leading philosophic journal in Russia suddenly carried a long-winded, fifteen-page article entitled, "Marx's Working Out of the Materialist Dialectics in the Economic-Philosophic Manuscripts of the Year 1844," by one V. A. Karpushin.[38] As Zhdanov had done in 1947, Mr. Karpushin now moved into the field of Marxian philosophy under the pretense of separating "the materialism of Marx" from "the idealism" of Hegel. As if he were merely stating the obvious, he attempts a total perversion of Marxian philosophy. "From Marx's viewpoint," he writes with a straight face, "the problem of the negation is *subordinate* to the basic law of the dialectic—the law of the unity and struggle of opposites. . . . Just as decisively did Marx come out against the mysticism of the Hegelian schema of the first and second negation, against drawing the conclusion of a struggle of opposites from *some kind of negativity* which allegedly inherently clings to things, as Hegel put it."[39]

Where Marx saw "the greatness of the positive moment" of the Hegelian dialectic as "the dialectic of negativity as the moving and creating principle," Karpushin, with his perverse sense of history, referred to this principle as "some kind of negativity which allegedly" inheres in things. Where Marx saw the negation of the negation, the Hegelian transcendence, as an *objective* movement, Karpushin made it "mystic" and "subordinate" to the struggle of opposites. Where Marx writes how "thoroughgoing Naturalism or Humanism distinguishes itself from both Idealism and from Materialism and is at the same time the truth uniting both," Karpushin tried to turn Marx into a vulgar materialist, a practical man concerned with "practical problems." Karpushin then magnanimously concluded: "Marx was the first philosopher who went beyond the confines of philosophy and from the point of view of practical life and practical needs of the proletariat analyzed the basic question of philosophy as a truly scientific method of revolutionary change and knowledge of the actual world."

It is that actual world of Russia with its forced labor camps that compels this Russian attack against Marxism. It is not the idealism of Hegel that worries them. It is the revolutionary method of the dialectic and the Humanism of Marx that threatens their existence in theory even as the working class does in life. The deeper the crisis in Russia, the greater the need for an ideology to keep the workers at work. Just as, in the very midst of World War II, the theoreticians under Stalin's heel laid their brutal hands on CAPITAL,[40] so the theoreticians under Khrushchev's thumb have laid theirs on the early works of Marx. With every new crisis Marx comes to life again. Communism continues to spend incredible time and energy and vigilance to imprison Marx within the bounds of the private property vs. State property concept. The Communists will not succeed. Even the "empiricism of a machine gun," as Trotsky so brilliantly phrased it, cannot win against the dialectics and social vision of the early Marx. It is a strange reflection of our times that this conception—that the solution of the economic contradictions of capitalism is the human solution— is opposed nowhere so bitterly as in the so-called "Vanguard Parties." They are Planners, one and all, and that is why they are so close to the totalitarian rulers in Russia who *must* destroy the Humanism of Marx if they are to maintain themselves in power.

The critical question today—which the Communists must avoid like the plague—is *what happens after?* Is the power achieved in a successful revolution to go, not to the proletariat, but to a new bureaucracy? Although Marx was faced with no such question, he anticipated precisely such a situation resulting from a *mere* abolition of private property.

Marx, the Hegelian, had a conception of labor and freedom as *activity*, completely different from the utilitarian conception of the economists who, *at best*, could see freedom only as satisfied hunger and "culture." These—and they include the scientists of our age who see the break-up of the atom, but not the totality of the person—see free time only as "enjoyment." Marx saw the free time liberated from capitalist exploitation as time for the free development of the individual's power, of his natural and acquired talents.

He did not consider that Utopia. It was not the hereafter. It was the road to be taken, on the morrow of capitalism's fall, *if* the nationalized means of production were to serve any better end than the privately owned means of production. This too our age can understand more than any previous age, and it is this conception which hangs over the Russian theoreticians like the Sword of Damocles.

Marx must have had them in mind when he criticized classical political economy for wanting to keep the industrial workers' eyes riveted *not* on the vision of total freedom, but on their "freedom from feudal blemishes." Marx wrote, "For them there was history, but history is no more." For the Russian totalitarians, the Russian Revolution stopped in 1917, and history stopped with the triumph of the One-Party State.

In broad outline, what Marx expressed in the early writings is the essence of Marxism as it was to remain and develop through the remaining thirty-nine years of his life. Marxism became richer, of course, that is to say, the theory became more concrete as Marx *and* the proletarian struggles developed. Marxism became an ideology as he worked out his economic theories. Never for a moment did he separate his economics from his politics or from his philosophy. Nothing from his early Humanism was ever jettisoned by him when, at another period, he called it communism. It was the very bones and marrow of his *Communist Manifesto*, which first unfurled the banner not only of a new organization of workers and intellectuals called the Communist League, but of the world proletariat. On one and the same banner was inscribed: "Workers of the world, unite!" *and* "The free development of each is the condition for the free development of all." That "individualistic" element is the soul of Marxism. That is why from the start Marx warned, "We must above all avoid setting up 'the society' as an abstraction opposed to the individual. The individual *is* the social entity. The expression of his life . . . is therefore the expression and verification of the life of society." He was always watching what he called the "spontaneous class organizations of the proletariat." With these he aligned himself. This did not stop the development of his theory. Quite the contrary. We will see later, in the development of the structure of CAPITAL, how the proletariat helped him break from the bourgeois concept of theory. The point here that needs stressing, in the development of Marx himself, is that with Marx we touch a new intellectual dimension—an intellectual whose whole intellectual, social, political activity and creativity become the expression of precise social forces.

In every period of crisis, which Hegel called the birth of history, there have been intellectuals who have "gone to the people," from the Utopians in England, to the Narodniki (Populists) in Russia. But in each case, not only has the separation between these intellectuals as leaders, and the people, been maintained, but what is of far greater importance, at the critical juncture in the development of the movement, they fell behind and were an actual hindrance to the people's forward movement. Marx alone did not. It was no accident that his *Communist Manifesto* was published on the eve of the 1848 Revolutions. He could do this because of his idea of theory as the generalization of the instinctive striving of the proletariat for a new social order, a truly human society—a striving that arises out of the dialectic of the economic process which, at each stage, produces what Marx called the "new passions and forces" for the next social order. Although no one can see the concrete form of the new society until it actually appears, Marx's vision did anticipate the future society. He was not "left behind," not because of his individual genius, but because of his dialectical method of uniting theory and practice. He thereby gave the intellectuals who aligned themselves with the proletariat

as a "political tendency" that new human dimension to enable
each to become as tall as the proletariat straightened up to its
full height in the creation of a new society.

Nothing changed Marx's social vision: the vision of the future which Hegel called the Absolute and which Marx first called
"real Humanism" and later "communism." The road to both is by
way of "the negation of the negation," that is to say, the destruction of the existing system which had destroyed the previous system. That is what the Russian ruling class trembles at, as well
it may, for it knows this movement *not* by the name of "negation
of the negation," but by the reality of the revolution against it.
The struggle of the working people against the Communist overlordship in the factory is not without its impact on intellectual
monolithism. The Russian theoreticians suddenly decided "to
accept" the struggle of opposites—*after* they denuded it of its class
struggle content and transformed it into a harmless fight between
"the old" and "the new." Life, however, is a much harder taskmaster than even the theory of dialectics. History refused to turn
at the turning point marked by the Russian theoreticians. The
"new dialectical law" went nowhere. They turned against "the
Hegelian mystical Absolute, "the negation of the negation." The
undercurrent of revolt, however, is merciless and will not give
them a respite.

PART II

WORKER AND INTELLECTUAL AT A TURNING POINT IN HISTORY: 1848 TO 1861

CHAPTER FOUR

WORKER, INTELLECTUAL, AND THE STATE

1) The 1848 Revolutions and the Radical Intellectual

The 1848 Revolutions covered Europe from end to end. As the absolutist regimes fell and democracy seemed within reach of the masses, the middle class leaders turned and ran. Today, it is admitted: "There would have been no revolutions in 1848 if it had depended on the revolutionary leaders. The revolutions made themselves; and the true heroes of 1848 were the masses. The radical intellectuals had supposed that, once tradition was overthrown, the masses would acknowledge instead the claims of intellect. Nietzsche expressed later this great illusion of 1848: 'Dead are all Gods. Now the superman shall live.' The masses never responded to the ambitions of the intellectuals. . . ."[41]

One of the most astute bourgeois minds of the nineteenth century, Alexis de Tocqueville, who left us a classic book, *Democracy in America,* revealed sharply the crossroads which the French bourgeoisie had reached in 1848. A few weeks before the outbreak of the February Revolution he seemed to predict it: "Do you not feel the revolution in the air!" he said in his famous speech before the Assembly. Yet, when it broke out and he was given credit for this prediction, he denied it: "I did not expect a revolution like the one we had."

He was right both times. He foresaw that the hunger and restlessness of the masses, against the background of restored monarchical spending and debauchery, would burst forth in revolt *if* concessions were not made to them by the absolutist regime. But he thought electoral reform to be the need of the hour. His mind did not conceive that the workers would take to the streets, set up barricades, and present an *economic program in their own right,* not only against the king but against the bourgeoisie. "I do not believe the people," wrote this good bourgeois mistaking his class for "the people," "were ever so frightened at any stage of the Great Revolution and I think their terror can only be compared with that of the civilized communities of the Roman Empire when they saw themselves in the hands of the Goths and the Vandals." The "Goths and the Vandals," for de Tocqueville, were the Parisian workers bearing arms!

The discovery of irreconcilable class antagonisms made 1848 a turning point in modern history. Today, even bourgeois writers can see that 1848 opened the era of mass proletarian revolutions. But in 1848 only Marx saw. The *Communist Manifesto,* which reached the publishers just a few weeks before the outbreak of the February Revolutions, proclaimed all hitherto existing history to be "the history of class struggles," and, it continued, while "the bourgeoisie cannot live without revolutionizing methods of production and relations of production," its greatest accomplishment was the forging of "the revolutionary working class itself" which would put an end to all class struggle: "The proletariat, the lowest stratum of our present society, cannot raise itself without the whole super-incumbent strata of official society being broken up into the air. . . . Workingmen of the world, unite! You have nothing to lose but your chains. You have a world to gain."

Not only had the bourgeoisie not conceived of a revolt against them. Neither had the radical intellectuals who had aligned themselves with the masses before the revolution, but were caught by surprise by the actual revolutionary uprising.

Blanqui had conceived a small, well-organized, conspiratorial coup led by himself. Louis Blanc had talked of "National Workshops," but not of any revolution to achieve these. Proudhon had declaimed against the "brazen law of wages," but most certainly did not advocate revolution to overcome wage slavery.

Had the workers listened to their leaders there would have been no revolutions in 1848. But with no parties, in the modern sense of the word, to lead or mislead, the revolutions made themselves. Thousands of workers and students appeared on the streets of Paris demanding universal suffrage and "organization of labor." This mass uprising, that was without arms, suddenly found it had arms when events took another unexpected turn and the National Guard, instead of firing upon them, joined them!

The king had no sooner fled, and a Provisional Government set up, when the bourgeoisie, who up to this point had not opposed the masses, counselled against setting up a Republic by barricade might. The masses forced the proclamation of a Republic. The creative energies of the masses, disciplined and united, which had created the Republic, now demanded of that Republic that it be a *social* Republic and create work for all.

Marche, a worker, dictated the decree and now the masses were demanding the formation of a Labor Ministry. They took seriously their role in the revolution *and* in the reconstruction of society. In a few weeks, 171 newspapers appeared. Although the workers believed in this coalition provisional government, revolutionary workers' clubs sprung up all over Paris—145 of them in the first month.

Lamartine, the poet who joined the revolutionaries at the first outburst, did so, as he himself put it quite bluntly, "To harness the storm." That defined the character and the limits of the Provisional Government. This newly-created bourgeois government now turned against the economic demands of their proletarian allies. Lamartine conceived the idea that it was the government's function "to remove the misunderstanding which exists between the classes." Socialist Louis Blanc, the workers' representative, accepted the compromise that a "Commission of Labor" be set up.

The Parliament became a talking shop and the National Workshops which were set up had alloted to them such a picayune sum that they were no more than the charity workshops which England had long before experienced. Still, the unemployment and starvation were so severe in this year of crisis, that no less than 110,000 workers streamed into these shops. The Government hoped to turn this pitiable labor army into an army against labor. They badly underestimated the modern working class. When Parliament voted to expel the unmarried men from the shops and foree them to join the army, they found this labor army an army of mutiny. The true essence of the 1848 revolutions was now revealed: it was the emancipation of labor.

On June 23rd, the workers took up the challenge. Barricades were once again set up. The slogan now heard was, "Down with the bourgeoisie!" We have Marx's description of this first great battle between the two classes, how the workers, "with unexampled bravery and talent, without chiefs, without a common plan, without means, and, for the most part, lacking weapons, held in check for five days the army, the Mobile Guard, the Parisian National Guard, and the National Guard that streamed in from the provinces."[42] So vast was the massacre and brutality committed by the *bourgeois* Republic. But the bloodletting could not erase the accomplishments of those few months: 1) abolition of slavery in the colonies; 2) abolition of the death penalty; 3) abolition of imprisonment for debt; 4) universal suffrage; 5) the ten-hour day.

Neither could the defeat erase the greatest lesson: it is not the political form of the state that is decisive, but the rule of capital. Parliamentary democracy became synonymous, not with proletarian freedom, but with bourgeois butchery and wage-slavery. Whereas universal suffrage proved to be no panacea, it did have the great merit of unleashing the class struggle and robbing the bourgeois democrat of his hypocritical mask of "liberty, equality and fraternity."

Marx hailed these revolutionaries and contrasted them to "the socialist doctrinaires who begged at the doors of the bourgeoisie on behalf of the people and were allowed to preach long sermons and to compromise themselves as long as the proletarian lion had to be lulled to sleep." Even where he criticized their slogan, "Organization of Labour,"—because "wage labor is the existing bourgeois organization of labor" and that thereby they would only continue the form of wage slavery from which they were already suffering—he realized that what the workers meant, essentially, was the overthrow of this bourgeois regime. Indeed, this became evident in June. In fact, that was the greatest lesson of June. Whereas, in February, the masses followed the bourgeoisie because what they were after was the overthrow of the *form* of state power—absolutism—in June they fought the bourgeoisie, the capitalistic order and fought it by *their own great combined re-*

sources. Marx caught the essence and the spirit of the creative energies of the masses when he recognized that the workers had declared the revolution *permanent,* that is to say, not to stop at the bourgeois democratic phase but to continue to full proletarian democracy: "They placed themselves in violent contradiction with the very conditions of existence of bourgeois society by declaring the revolution permanent."[43]

Marx's discovery—that the objective movement itself produces the subjective force for its overthrow—transformed utopian socialism into scientific socialism. It drew a sharp class line between the intellectuals (utopians) who would continue with their schemes and the proletariat itself which had now separated itself from these sects and was creating movements of its own. He warned later against any "narrow-minded notion" of the petty-bourgeois leaders of this revolution as of the subsequent reaction. We must not "imagine that the democratic representatives are all shopkeepers or enthusiastic champions of shopkeepers. According to their education and their individual position they may be separated from them as widely as heaven from earth. What makes them representatives of the petty-bourgeoisie is the fact that in their minds they do not go beyond the limits which the latter do not go beyond in life, that they are consequently driven theoretically to the same tasks and solutions to which material interests and social position practically drive the latter. This is in general the relationship of the *political and literary representatives* of a class to the class that they represent."[44]

The division between the creative energies of the masses, on the one hand, and the plans of the radical intellectuals, on the other, widened and deepened in the 1848 revolutions because the proletariat had gained consciousness of itself as a class. On this independent road the intellectuals would not follow. The radical intellectuals were forever planning to do something "for" the worker, substituting *their* activity, or at least planning, for the self-activity of the working class. At one point in history, following the French Revolution, this type of planning had the heroic proportions of Babeuf's "Conspiracy of the Equals." By the 1840's it had the pathetic shape of Proudhon's "organization of exchange" while in the actual revolution of 1848 it had the anti-

revolutionary stamp of Lamartine's joining "to harness the storm."
Whatever the forms they plan—and they will be myriad as we
progress to our age—the radical intellectuals are blind to the
creative energies of the masses. In opposing them and keeping his
eyes glued instead to the activity of the masses, Marx was able to
generalize their creative activities into a *theory* of liberation never
fooling himself that theory is otherwise than ever "grey while the
tree of life is ever green."

2) *Ferdinand Lassalle, State Socialist*

After the defeat of the 1848 Revolutions Marx returned to
his economic studies. He kept away from the emigré circles. The
quiescent 1850's ended in the financial crisis of 1857 and his
work, *A Contribution to the Critique of Political Economy,* was
published in 1859. During this period some younger men came to
"scientific socialism" (Marxism). Ferdinand Lassalle was the most
important of these. Lassalle was born, in a political sense, at the
turning point in modern history—1848—when, for a brief historic
moment, the fight against absolutism united the bourgeois democrat and the proletarian revolutionary. The 1848 revolutions un-
derlined, in rivers of blood, the irreconcilability of these two
class forces. Lassalle appealed directly to the working class to form
its own independent political party. Nevertheless, Marx had to
separate himself sharply from this perverse progeny of his, even
as he had separated himself from the anarchist socialism of Proudhon. This was necessitated by the fact that where Proudhon tried
for a compromise between the two classes, Lassalle tried for a
short-cut to socialism through the State—through the Prussian
landowners' absolutist State with the Iron Chancellor, Bismarck, at
its head.

It is not that Lassalle misunderstood the class nature of the
State. But he could not rid himself of the concept of the "backwardness" of labor, despite the glorious pages it wrote in nineteenth
century history. When the class struggles once again assumed open
and violent shape, Lassalle conceived it to be his duty to "bridge
the gulf between the thinkers and the masses." From his attitude,
one would guess that all the science of the age was incorporated

in him and he would have to bring that science to the "ignorant."
In his defense, when on trial for inciting the masses, he revealed
his special conception of the role of the intellectuals: "How is it
that the middle classes have come to be so frightened of the common people? Look back to March and April of 1848. Have you
forgotten how things were then? The police force impotent. The
common people swarming along the streets. The streets and the
people themselves under the sway of unthinking agitators . . .
rough ignorant men thrown up by the storm. . . . Where were
the intellectuals then? Where were you, Gentlemen? . . . You
should thank those who are working to bridge the gulf between
the thinkers and the masses who are pulling down the barriers
between the bourgeoisie and the people."[45]

Because this was his conception of the masses, Lassalle's
theoretical concept of labor moved no further than the Proud-
honian concept of the workers "buying up" all capital from the
bourgeoisie. Lassalle proposed that the workers establish producers'
cooperatives with "State aid." Although this meant treating the
Prussian absolutist State as if it were a classless animal, it isn't
true that Lassalle actually thought so. However, once he did
not believe in the masses' ability to overcome their conditions
of labor—and once he convinced himself that Marx was "too abstract" and failed to understand "real politics" because he *did*
believe in the workers' historic creativity—it was easy for Lassalle
to convince himself that *he* could force Bismarck to accede.

Lassalle's sense of "real politics"[46] also led him to search
for a collaborator in the royal Prussian governmental "socialist"
and economic theoretician, Karl Rodbertus. He did at first actually get Rodbertus' approval for his plan of producers' cooperatives with State aid, although the latter's concept of how long
the socialist transformation would take numbered no less than
five hundred years. Lassalle, on the other hand, wanted socialism
"quick"—within the year if possible. Yet so strong are the organic
ties between intellectuals who have a certain concept of labor,
that the impatient Lassalle and the overly patient Rodbertus were
collaborators for a brief period.

This representative of labor, however, was no armchair socialist. He was an activist. Nor did he restrict himself to writing.

He was instrumental in building the first great independent political party of the German proletariat. Lassalle's plan to bring pressure to bear upon the absolutist Prussian State, to force it to give economic aid to the workers who would establish their own factories, meant active agitation among the workers. He issued this appeal: "The working class must establish itself as an independent political party and make its slogan and banner—Universal, Equal and Direct Suffrage. . . . To make the working class its own employer, that is the way, the only way, by which this cruel and iron law (of unchangeable minimum wages) can be set aside. Once the working class is its own employer, the contrast between wages and profit disappears. It is therefore the task of the State to facilitate the great cause."

Thousands of workers responded to the call and the General German Workers Association was formally organized in May 1863. In June, unbeknownst to the workers it need hardly be added, Lassalle sent the statutes adopted to Bismarck with the following note: ". . . this will be enough to show you how true it is that the working class is instinctively inclined to dictatorship if it feels that such will be exercised in the working class interests."

Lassalle was no "traitor." He could not have been bought. He fought for his principles, went to prison for them and would have been ready to die for them. But he simply was incapable of thinking that *they* (the workers) could rule. To him, they were a "mob." He thought so in 1844 when the Silesian weavers revolted. He was only a student then, but already he felt that the State should restore "order." He did not change his concept when, in 1848, the workers were breaking up, not the machines, but the bourgeois order. He defended the working class victories, yet he continued to think of them as a "mob" under the sway of "unthinking agitators . . . thrown up by the storm." Things did not change in 1862 when he himself called upon the masses to organize an independent political party of their own. His call was, however, inseparable from his aim "to put myself at its head." The workers were a suffering mass and weak, whereas the State was strong and could achieve "for each one of us what none of us could achieve for himself." He therefore felt called upon to rule "for" the masses. *He* would lead. *They* would continue to work, and, in the meanwhile, be so good as to send him to Parliament.

"His attitude," wrote Marx, "is that of a future workers' dictator. He resolves the question between labor and capital as easily as play. The workers are to agitate for universal suffrage and then send people like himself armed with the shining sword of science into Parliament. They will establish workers' factories, for which the state will put up capital, and by and by these institutions will embrace the whole country . . ."[47]

Marx wrote this, not because he knew of Lassalle's machinations with Bismarck, but because he knew of Lassalle's concept of the backwardness of labor. Lassalle suffered from the illusion of the age: that science is "classless." Such an attitude made it natural for him to think that he represented "science and the worker," for science was surely incorporated *in the intellectual, the leader*. Marx, on the other hand, rejected this "puerile stuff." As he rejected the bourgeois conception that this was the age of "science and democracy," so he rejected the abstraction of "science and the worker." Concretely, he stressed, science was incorporated in the *machine,* and democracy in the bourgeois *parliament*. Lassalle's conception of the workers' leader had this in common with the bourgeoisie: *the workers remained in the factory*.

Between Lassalle and Marx there was as deep a division in thought and in practice as in life there is between the petty bourgeois and the worker. The illumination that the 1848-61 period sheds on the relationship of the worker and intellectual is to disclose the administrative *type* long before the administrators are armed with power. Where Proudhon showed the separation between petty bourgeois and worker before the revolutionary outburst, Lassalle revealed the type after the revolutionary defeat. Lassalle was the living proof that *within* the revolutionary movement itself the radical intellectual solution waits to strangle the theoretician who is blind to the creative energies of the masses. Lassalle was the anticipation of the State Socialist administrator of our day.

PART III

MARXISM: THE UNITY OF THEORY AND PRACTICE

CHAPTER FIVE

THE IMPACT OF THE CIVIL WAR IN THE UNITED STATES ON THE STRUCTURE OF *CAPITAL*

The decade of the 1860's was decisive for the structure of Marx's greatest theoretical work, CAPITAL. No one is more blind to the greatness of Marx's contributions than those who praise him to the skies for his genius as if that genius matured outside of the actual struggles of the historic period in which he lived. As if he gained the impulses from the sheer development of his own thoughts instead of from living workers changing living reality by their actions. We shall see in a moment that Marx's *Critique of Political Economy* is proof of the limitations of a theoretical work when the workers themselves are not in motion. CAPITAL, on the other hand, is proof of the creative impact of masses in motion on theory. The historic circumstances in which this greatest theoretical work of Marxism takes final shape were not simply "background" for a genius who coincidentally "happened" to complete his theoretical studies of more than two decades. A glance at the objective events that made him, as he put it, "turn everything around," will show us *how* he reconstructed his own work.

1) The Abolitionists, the Civil War, and the First International

On January 11, 1860, Marx wrote to Engels: "In my opinion, the biggest things that are happening in the world today are on the one hand the movement of the slaves in America started by the death of John Brown and, on the other, the movement of the serfs in Russia. . . . I have just seen in the *Tribune* that there has been a fresh rising of slaves in Missouri, naturally suppressed. But the signal has now been given."

From now on he will not only keep his eyes glued to the mass movement; he will participate in it. The decade of the Civil War in the United States is also the decade of the Polish Insurrection, the strikes in France, and the mass demonstrations in England which culminate in the creation of the International Working Men's Association headed by Marx.

The Civil War was the first modern war of mass armies and total involvement.[48] It lasted four years and cost the lives of a million men. The cost in lives was so frightful and the duration so long because Lincoln sought to confine the conflict as a white man's war. Though slavery was the root, and the creative energies of the runaway slaves the vital force, Lincoln's main strategic concern was to conciliate the so-called "moderate" border slave states which remained in the Union. Consequently, he wanted neither to free the slaves nor to allow them to participate in the war as soldiers. As Marx put it in letters to Engels: "All Lincoln's acts appear like the mean pettifogging conditions which one lawyer puts to his opposing lawyer. But this does not alter their historic content. . . . The events over there are a world upheaval. . . ."

Even from the narrowest military point of view, Marx knew that Lincoln would *have* to move towards emancipation of the slaves. "I do not think that all is up. . . ," he wrote Engels. "A single Negro regiment would have a remarkable effect on Southern nerves. . . . A war of this kind must be conducted on revolutionary lines while the Yankees have thus far been trying to conduct it constitutionally." Long before sheer military necessity forced Lincoln to bow to the inevitable and issue the Emancipation Proclamation, Marx recorded the views of the Abolitionists.[49] In one of his columns for the *Vienna Presse,* at the very time that both the American and English press were attacking Wendell Phillips he summarized a speech by him. This is the introduction Marx gave his summary: "Together with Garrison and G. Smith, Wendell Phillips is the leader of the Abolitionists in New England. For thirty years he has without intermission and at the risk of his life proclaimed the emancipation of the slaves as his battle-cry, regardless alike of the persiflage of the press, the enraged howls of paid rowdies and the conciliatory representations of solicitous friends. . . . In the present state of affairs Wendell Phillips' speech is of greater importance than a battle bulletin."

The movement of the runaway slaves,[50] who followed the North Star to freedom, brought on the Civil War. But Lincoln's generals fought to maintain slavery and therefore they fought in vain. "I do not say," Marx quoted Wendell Phillips, "that McClellan is a traitor; but I say that if he were a traitor, he must have acted exactly as he has done. . . . The President has not put the Confiscation Act into operation. He may be honest, but what has his honesty to do with the matter? He has neither insight nor foresight. . . . I know Lincoln. I have taken his measure in Washington. He is a first-rate *second-rate* man."[51]

Marx was watching the impact which the Civil War was having upon the European working class. As the foreign correspondent for the newspapers he represented—the *New York Tribune* and *Die Vienna Presse*—Marx reported the mammoth meeting of the English workers which prevented the government's intervention on the side of the South. It was under the impact of the Civil War and the response of the European workers as well as the Polish insurrection, that the International Working Men's Association, known as the First International, was born. In the name of the International Marx wrote to Lincoln: "From the commencement of the titanic American strife the workingmen of Europe felt instinctively that the star-spangled banner carried the destiny of their class. . . . Everywhere they bore therefore patiently the hardships imposed upon them by the cotton crisis, opposed enthusiastically the pro-slavery intervention, importunities of their 'betters,' and from most parts of Europe contributed their quota of blood to the good cause.

"While the workingmen, the true political power of the North, allowed slavery to defile their own republic; while before the Negro, mastered and sold without his concurrence, they boasted it the highest prerogative of the white-skinned laborer to sell himself and choose his own master; they were unable to attain the true freedom of labor or to support their European brethren in their struggle for emancipation, but this barrier to progress has been swept off by the red sea of civil war."[52]

We can see from the very contents of CAPITAL that this was by no means sheer "diplomacy." Marx separated himself from the self-styled American Marxists who evaded the whole issue of the Civil War by saying they were opposed to "all slavery, wage and chattel."[53] His analysis of the struggle for the shortening of the working day comes to a climax, as we shall see later, when he writes of the relationship of the end of slavery to the struggle for the eight hour day: "In the United States of North America, every independent movement of the workers was paralyzed so long as slavery disfigured a part of the Republic. Labor cannot emancipate itself in the white skin where in the black it is branded. But out of the death of slavery a new life at once arose. The first fruit of the Civil War was the eight hours' agitation, that ran with the seven-leagued boots of the locomotive from the Atlantic to the Pacific, from New England to California. The General Congress of Labor at Baltimore (August 16, 1866) declared: 'The first and great necessity of the present, to free the labor of this country from capitalistic slavery, is the passing of a law by which eight hours shall be the normal working-day in all States of the American Union. We are resolved to put forth all our strength until this glorious result is attained.' "[54]

The impact of the Civil War on the European revolution (the Paris Commune) is stated succinctly enough right at the start of CAPITAL. Its preface states: "As in the eighteenth century the American war of independence sounded the tocsin for the European middle-class, so in the nineteenth century the American Civil War sounded it for the European working class." We now turn to the impact it had on the structure of CAPITAL.

2) The Relationship of History to Theory

In contrast to the actions of the European masses, the arrogant insensitivity of European intellectuals to the Civil War in the United States is best exemplified by Lassalle. Where Marx turned his attention to the world-shaking event, Lassalle dismissed it. In a letter to Engels, dated July 30, 1862, Marx reports Lasalle's views: "The Yankees have no 'ideas.' 'Individual liberty' is merely a 'negative idea,' etc., and more of this old, decayed, speculative rubbish."[55]

Under the impact of the Civil War, Marx, on the other hand, gave an entirely new structure to his theoretical work. He had long since dismissed Lassalle's pretense of being a dialectician: "He will learn to his cost," Marx wrote on February 1, 1858, "that to bring a science by criticism to the point where it can be dialectically presented is an altogether different thing from applying an abstract ready-made system of logic to mere inklings of such a system." The result of Marx's own study, at that time, was called *A Contribution to the Critique of Political Economy*.[56]

a) *Critique of Political Economy*: The Limits of an Intellectual Work

Marx begins with that everyday thing, the commodity, and immediately points to the *duality* of this thing which is a use-value and an exchange-value all at once. Hence, it is not just a thing, not just a utility, but a value. It could not have this two-fold nature as a product of labor if the *labor itself* did not have that character. The commodity in embryo contains all the contradictions of capitalism precisely because of the contradictory nature of labor. That is the key to *all* contradiction. That, Marx will point out again in CAPITAL, is his original contribution to political economy. Without that, it is impossible to comprehend political economy.

Exchange value, Marx continues, only *appears* to be a quantitative relation, that is, a given proportion of time embodied in wheat being exchanged for a given proportion of time embodied in linen. But the question is: what *kind of labor* creates value? It cannot be concrete labor: "Tailoring, e.g., in its material manifestation as a distinct productive activity produces a coat, but not the exchange value of a coat. The latter is produced not by the labor of the tailor as such but by abstract universal labor that belongs to a certain organization of society which has not been brought about by the tailor."[57]

This *organization of society*, which has not been brought about by the tailor, is the capitalistic organization where all labor, no matter what its concrete nature, is timed according to what is socially necessary. It becomes one mass of abstract labor precisely because the *laborer himself* is paid at value, that is, the necessities of life needed to sustain him. "Thus relative value measured by labor time is fatally the formula of modern slavery of the worker instead of being, as M. Proudhon would have it, the revolutionary formula of the emancipation of the proletariat."

The very duality of the labor, the very duality *within* the commodity, is what has made it necessary for one single commodity, money, to act as the value measure of the commodity. For his commodity, the capitalist wants to buy not another use-value, but money, which buys "all things." The division of commodities and money makes that possible. Money, like any other commodity, is equal to the labor time that it took to produce, to mine it and mint it; but unlike any other commodity, it is universally recognized to be just that and hence acts as a "natural" measure. But that measure is natural to it only because it is the recognized representative of labor in its abstract form. In other words, like labor, it is not a thing, but a *social relationship*.

The very fact that Proudhon wants it to be "no more than" a circulating medium, which is precisely its function, shows that even he recognizes that it hides an exploitative production relationship. Only he thinks not to break up that production relationship which is the cause of it, but only to alter its appearance in money. Under capitalism, money can no more be made available to everyone than classes can be abolished by fiat—from Proudhon or from the government.

In this work, Marx limits himself to the question of exchange. He does no more than point to the fact that behind the exchange of things there is a relationship of production. Only comparatively recently, (1939), have we seen the publication of his immense intellectual labors and writings for the year 1857-1858.[58] They show a tremendous dialectical and original economic development. Marx himself allowed only the first chapters to be published as the *Critique*. In the preface to that he states why he omits "a general introduction which I had prepared as on second thought any anticipation of results that are still to be proven seemed to be objectionable, and the reader who wishes to follow me at all must make up his mind to pass from the special to the general." The truth is that the work, both in its special and in its general aspects, lacks a structure, a shape that can come only out of the developing class itself. That is why Marx started "all over" in CAPITAL.

It is not that labor had not been central to Marx. But in the period of the 1850's, following the defeat of the 1848 Revolutions, the workers were quiescent. What happens to a theoretician, to any theoretician, even to a Marx, when the proletarian revolutions are crushed, is that he must watch the laws of economic development of the old social order without being able to see the *specific* form of revolt with which the workers mean to meet the new stage of production.

The *Critique* turned out to be an intellectual, that is, a remote work; a theoretical answer to an actual problem. Or, to put it differently, it was an *application* of dialectics to political economy, instead of the *creation* of the dialectic that would arise out of the workers' struggles themselves.

Marx had no sooner finished the work than he became dissatisfied with it. Although his *Critique* was by no means mere "inklings of a system" but the whole of classical political economy subjected to a profound criticism, Marx decided not to continue with it. The great historic events of the 1860's wrought basic changes in society, in politics, in thinking. As the proletariat began to move positively towards its own emancipation, they illuminated all the studies Marx had undertaken in the previous period, and gave new insights into the development of capitalist production.

b) *The Working Day and the Break with the Concept of Theory*

Between 1861 and 1867 the manuscript of the *Critique,* now become CAPITAL, underwent two fundamental changes, one in 1863, and the other in 1866. We can trace the changes both by comparing CAPITAL to the state the manuscripts were left in, which Engels describes in the Preface to Volume II of CAPITAL, as well as from Marx's own letters. As he puts it in the letter to

Engels on August 15, 1863, he has had "to turn everything around":
". . . when I look at this compilation (the manuscripts of the
Critique, which he is now re-working under the title of CAPITAL)
and see how I have had to turn everything around and how I had
to make even the *historical* part out of material of which some
was quite unknown, then he (Lassalle) does seem funny with '*his*'
economy already in his pocket. . . ." By the time, three years
later, that he has finally prepared everything for the printer, he
informs Engels about yet a new addition: "Historically I developed
a part about *the working day* which did not enter into my first
plan." (February 10, 1866)

It sounds fantastic to say that until 1866 Marx had not
worked out the seventy pages on the Working Day. Yet so inherent
in theory itself is its own limitation that even when Marx turned
the monographs for the *Critique* entirely around, and wrote the
first draft of his new work, CAPITAL, even this work at first
had no section on the Working Day. That Ricardo didn't concern himself with the working day is understandable because
he evaded the whole problem of the *origin* of surplus value. That
socialists, from the utopians through Proudhon to Lassalle, were
not weighted down by this problem is explained easily enough
since they were too busy with their plans ever to study the real
workers' movement. But for Marx, who had never once taken
his eyes off the proletarian movement, not to have had a section
on the Working Day in his major theoretical work seems incomprehensible.

It seems even more incomprehensible when we realize that
Marx had already written the "Primitive Accumulation" of CAP-
ITAL, which describes the "Bloody Legislation against the Expropriated," in which he dealt with laws that made the lengthening of the working day compulsory. The concept of the theory of
surplus value includes the division of the working day into paid
and unpaid labor. But that still leaves the exact analysis of the
working day, for the most part, undetermined. As he was to put it
later about his adversary, Dühring: "One thing in his account
has struck me very much. Namely, so long as the determination of
value by working time is itself left 'undetermined,' as it is by
Ricardo, it does not make people shaky. But as soon as it is brought

into exact connection with the working day and its variations, a very unpleasant light dawns upon them."[59]

"The establishment of a normal working day," he wrote, "is the result of centuries of struggle between capitalist and laborer."[60] Marx's method of analysis was revolutionized thereby. Where, in his *Critique,* history and theory are separated, with a historical explanation attached to each theoretical chapter; in CAPITAL, history and theory are inseparable. Where, in *Critique,* history is the history of theory; in CAPITAL, history is the history of the class struggle.

He who glorifies theory and genius but fails to recognize the *limits* of a theoretical work, fails likewise to recognize the *indispensability of the theoretician.* All of history is the history of the struggle for freedom. If, as a theoretician, one's ears are attuned to the new impulses from the workers, new "categories" will be created, a new way of thinking, a step forward in philosophic cognition.

Marx's shift from the history of *theory* to the history of *production relations* gives flesh and blood to the generalization that Marxism is the theoretical expression of the instinctive strivings of the proletariat for liberation. More than that. He says that ultimately the fundamental abolition of inequality lies in the shortening of the working day. In 1866, he made *this* the historical framework of capitalism itself. The struggles of the workers over the working day develop capitalist production. The ultimate creation of freedom rests upon the shortening of the working day. The philosophy of the shortening of the working day, which arose out of the actual struggles, embraces all concepts inside and outside of it. Thus, the thinking of the theoretician is constantly filled with more and more content, filled by workers' struggles and workers' thoughts.

Beginning in 1866, Marx had been developing the section on the Working Day. By the time CAPITAL is published in 1867, we read this tribute to the workers' own thinking: "In place of the pompous catalogue of the 'inalienable rights of man' comes the modest Magna Charta of a legally limited working day which shall make clear when the time which the worker sells is ended, and when his own begins. *Quantum mutatus ab illo.*"[61]

The real movement of the proletariat, at this specific stage of capitalist development, revealed not only the negative aspects in the fight for the working day—the struggle against unlimited capitalist exploitation—but the positive aspects—a road to freedom. This then, was a *new philosophy, the philosophy* of labor, arrived at naturally out of its own concrete struggles. We see *why* Marx had "to turn everything around." Now let us look at *how* he did it. Engels tells us the original manuscripts consisted of 1472 pages, as follows:[62]

(1) Pages one to 220 and again pages 1159 to 1472 are the first draft of Volume I, beginning with transformation of money into capital and continuing to the end of the volume. Note that this does *not* account for pages 220 to 1159. The skipped pages turn out to have dealt with the question of the history of theory and the decline in the rate of profit, thus:

(2) Pages 978 to 1158 comprise the first draft of the subject material of capital, profit and rate of profit. Ultimately that formed the subject matter of Volume III. Originally, however, he intended to include, as part of Volume I, the subject matter dealt with on these pages. This type of procedure was later castigated by Marx: "We shall show in Book III that the rate of profit is no mystery so soon as we know the laws of surplus value. If we reverse the process we cannot comprehend either the one or the other."[63]

(3) Now then, pages 220 to 972 constitute what Marx later considered to be Book IV of CAPITAL, and entitled "History of Theory."[64] In this first draft, however, these 750 pages would have followed directly after the buying and selling of labor power. A look at the published *Critique* will reveal what this first plan meant in the actual structure. After each chapter of the *Critique* —Commodities; Money—there follows an excursus on the history of the theory of the same subject, somewhat on the order of Hegel's "Observations" in the *Logic*. Marx meant to follow that same procedure for the rest of the work. That is to say, as soon as he would state his theory on any subject he would have followed it up with arguments against *other theorists*. Somewhere he says that this is the natural procedure as one works something out for himself. It is an ordinary procedure *for an intellectual* to study the history of other theories and to separate himself from them on

their ground. It is the method which Marx discarded when he decided "to turn everything around."

Once he decides to do this, he separates the material dealing with the phenomena of profit and rate of profit, or *"forms* of the process of production as a whole," from the process of production itself. At the same time, he takes out the voluminous material on the "History of Theory," and relegates it to the very end of all three volumes, as Book IV. *He is breaking with the whole concept of theory as something intellectual, a dispute between theoreticians.*

Instead of keeping up a running argument with theorists, he goes directly into the labor process itself, and thence to the Working Day. He no sooner relegated the history of theory to the end of the whole work, and began to look at the history of production relations, than he of necessity *created* a new dialectic instead of *applying* one. Or, more precisely, a new dialectic flowed out of the labor process. This new dialectic led him to meet, theoretically, the workers' resistance inside the factory and outside of it. The result is the new section in CAPITAL, "The Working Day."

Marx, the theoretician, created new categories out of the impulses from the workers. It wasn't he, however, who decided that the Civil War in the United States was a holy war of labor. It was the working class of England, the very ones who suffered most, who decided that.

From start to finish, Marx is concerned with the revolutionary actions of the proletariat. The concept of theory now is something unified with action. Or, more correctly, theory is not something the intellectual works out alone. Rather, the actions of the proletariat create the possibility for the intellectual to work out theory. Here then, we have the really fundamental break with Hegel. It is in this that CAPITAL is distinguished from the *Logic* and yet contains it, for CAPITAL is the dialectic of bourgeois society, its development and downfall. As Lenin was to put it in 1915: "If Marx did not leave a Logic (with a capital letter), he left the *logic* of CAPITAL. . . . In CAPITAL the logic, dialectic and theory of knowledge of materialism (three words are not necessary: they are one and the same) are applied to one science, taking all of value in Hegel and moving this value forward."[65]

CHAPTER SIX

THE PARIS COMMUNE ILLUMINATES AND DEEPENS THE CONTENT OF *CAPITAL*

1) The Despotic Plan of Capital vs. the Cooperation of Freely Associated Labor

Marx had begun his analysis of capitalism some three decades before the establishment of the Paris commune in 1871. Labor was the pivot of his theory from the start. It was the concept of alienated labor that enabled him to dig deep into the inner mechanism of capitalist production. The first edition of CAPITAL, published in 1867, disclosed that what appeared, ideally, as plan, revealed itself, in reality, in the labor process, to be but the undisputed authority of the capitalist. For Marx, the theoretical axis of CAPITAL—the central core around which all else develops —is the question of plan: the despotic plan of capital against the cooperative plan of freely associated labor.

The despotic plan inherent in capitalist production reveals itself in a form all its own—*the hierarchic structure of control over social labor*. To keep production going on an ever-expanding scale, to extract the greatest amount of surplus or unpaid labor, requires a whole army of foremen, managers, superintendents. These all work for the capitalist with one aim and purpose: to force labor out of the many laborers. The attempt to control cooperative labor within capitalist confines must of necessity assume a despotic form. Planned despotism arises out of the *antagonistic* relationship between the workers, on the one hand, and the capitalist and his bureaucracy on the other hand.

Cooperation under the mastership of the capitalist is in direct opposition to the cooperating laborers. The worker had lost his individual skill to the machine. But he gained a new power in cooperating with his fellow workers. From the start this is a *mass power*. The opposition is between the *nature* of the cooperative form of labor and the capitalistic *form* of value production.

Cooperation is in itself a productive power, the power of social labor. Under capitalistic control, this cooperative labor is not allowed to develop freely. Its function is confined to the production of value. It cannot release its new, social, human energies so long as the old mode of production continues. Thus the *nature* of the cooperative form of labor power is in opposition to the capitalist integument, the *value-form*. At the same time the monstrous creation of monotony, speed-up, uniformity, military regularity and more speed-up robs science also of its self-development, confining it to the single purpose of extracting ever greater amounts of surplus, unpaid labor from the workers.

This develops into the *absolute contradiction* between the *nature* of machine industry and the value-form of its *operation*. Technological writing had analyzed the few main fundamental motions. There it stopped. It could go no further because there is no such thing as an abstract, remote, classless development of machinery. Technology is an integral part of the development of the productive forces. To exclude from it the greatest productive force—living labor—cripples and emasculates science itself. Under capitalism, the separation of the intellectual powers of production from manual labor, the incorporation of all science into the machine, means the transformation of intellectual power into the might of capital over labor, the engineer and technician against the worker. In a word, it means the transformation of man into a mere fragment of a man, just when the narrow technical needs of the machine itself demand variation in labor, fluidity, and mobility—all rounded, fully developed human beings using all of their human talents, both natural and acquired.

This is what Marx announced to the whole world in 1867. Before this theoretic onslaught, so total as to include both history and the actuality of the class struggle, bourgeois economics lay prostrate. Whereas nearly fifty years earlier, in 1821, Ricardo had at least *posed* the contradiction in machine production, vulgar economy was now, in 1867, reduced to denying this contradiction altogether. The emptiness of bourgeois economic thinking can be seen in their argument: since the contradiction is not inherent in machinery "as such," it is a delusion to think that there are contradictions in machinery under capitalist control. This adding of two and two and coming up with zero did not stop the bourgeois economist, however, from declaiming against the "backwardness" and stupidity of the worker who broke up the machinery. The capitalist ideologist tries to argue away the workers' enslavement to capital at the same time that society itself is threatened with the destruction of its human resources.

If the workers are too absorbed in their concrete struggles to indulge in abstract arguments about machinery "as such," the very struggles nevertheless reveal them to be full of new perceptions. True, they fought the machine itself as a competitor. But the first appearance of machinery as a handmaiden of capital was its *true* appearance. Their instinct was right while the economist's thinking was abstract. There is no such thing as machinery "as such." The worker could not possibly regard the machine "as such" —as standing above and apart from the capitalistic mode of production under which the machine was developed to extract relatively greater amounts of unpaid labor from the workers. In the further struggles against capital, the worker learned to fight not the instrument of labor, but the capitalistic employment of it— the conditions of production which transformed him into a mere cog in the machine.

Due to the cooperative form of the labor process the *resistance* of the workers is also a mass power. The workers' revolt develops from their fight against the instruments of labor into their struggle against the capitalistic conditions of labor. *The workers thus at one and same time fight for their emancipation and against the capitalistic limitations of science and technology.* The depth and breadth of the class struggles are a sign that the contradictions of capitalistic production are driving toward a new resolution. The resolution toward which the Paris Commune drove shed such strong illumination on the fetishism of commodities and the law of motion of capitalism that it deepened the very content of CAPITAL.

2) *The Paris Commune—a Form of Workers' Rule*

The social revolution that erupted in Paris on March 18, 1871 was not like anything ever before seen in history. The treason of the ruling class necessitated the saving of French civilization by the proletariat. A few months earlier, Napoleon III had suffered defeat in the Franco-Prussian war. The bourgeois republic which took over the reins of government was more afraid of revolutionary Paris than of Bismarck's army. With the flight of this government to Versailles, the revolutionary proletariat reached the greatest turning point in history—the remolding of itself as the ruling class.

Louis Blanqui, famous revolutionary and head of a secret armed force, had been plotting insurrection, seriously and unremittingly, for years. He tried again when the Republic of France showed itself ready to sell out to Bismarck. Without mass support, the insurrectionary plan of his elite group failed of necessity. In real life, the insurrection came at the peak of ascending revolution, not vice versa, and not as a plot.

On March 18th, the soldiers were ordered by M. Thiers, the head of the reactionary government, to transport the cannon of Paris to Versailles. The milkmaids, who were on the streets before dawn, saw what was afoot and thwarted the treacherous plans of the reactionary government. They surrounded the soldiers and prevented them from carrying out Thiers' orders. Although the men had not yet come into the streets on this early morning, and although the women were not armed, they held their own. As in every real peoples' revolution, new strata of the population were awakened. This time it was the women who were to act first. When reveille was sounded, all of Paris was in the streets. Thiers' spies barely escaped with the information that it was impossible to inform on who the leaders of the uprising were, since the *entire* population was involved.

This act of self-defense by the Parisian masses was also the act of self-government. Just as the Second Empire was the natural offspring of the parliamentary government which had crushed the 1848 Revolution, so the parliamentary government that had succeeded Napoleon III had but one function—to be the engine of class despotism.

The first act of the Revolution was to arm itself. The armed people struck out against the everywhere present state organs —the army, the police, officialdom—which were such a faithful copy of the hierarchic division of labor in the factory. The first workers' state in history, called the Commune of Paris, was born.

The Commune was composed, in the main, of Blanquists and Proudhonists. But the Blanquists became Communards only by giving up their insurrectionary plan and riding on the wave of the peoples' revolution. The Proudhonists likewise had to give up their utopian schemes. The development of large-scale production had already undermined the artisan type who formed the social base for Proudhonism. Now, the 1871 Revolution destroyed entirely the Proudhonist philosophy of "no political activity." The Parisian workers, who had just overthrown bourgeois domination, got down to the task of ruling themselves and setting down the conditions of their labor. All this was being done while the enemy was at the gates.

The first decree of the first workers' state was the abolition of the standing army. The first announcement of the *type* of political rule to be set up is typical: *"All public services are reorganized and simplified."*

The armed people smashed parliamentarianism. The people's assembly was not to be a parliamentary talking-shop but a *working* body. Those who passed the laws were also to execute them. There was thus to be no division between the executive and legislative bodies. The sham independence of the judiciary was similarly eliminated. Judges, as all other representatives, were to be elected and subject to recall. Representatives of the proletariat, however, were not yet the proletariat as a whole. Therefore, to assure control over the elected representatives, they too were subject to recall. *Thus, the power remained always in the hands of the mass as a whole.*

Public service was to be performed at a workman's wage. Thus was laid the basis of inexpensive government. The hierarchic divisions of labor were given further blows. The decree separating church and state abolished religious control of education and kindled intellectual life on all fronts. True to their proletarian spirit, some districts began immediately to clothe and feed their children. Education was to be open and free to all. Even above that, the reorganization of the methods of education was to begin with the fullest participation of the whole people. The first call went out to teachers and parents. The teachers were instructed "to employ exclusively the experimental and scientific method, that which starts from facts, physical, moral and intellectual."

The utopians had been busy inventing political forms of rule; the anarchists had been ignoring all political forms; the petty-bourgeois democrats had been accepting the parliamentary form. But this Commune was what the workers came up with—*smash* the state form of capital's rule; *supercede* it by a commune-type of self-government. This then was "the political form at last discovered to work out the economic emancipation of the proletariat." Marx had deduced from history that the bourgeois state form would disappear and the proletariat, organized as the ruling class, would be the point of transition to a classless society. He hailed the heroism of the Communards. He studied their specific form of proletarian rule and disclosed its secret: "The political rule of the producer cannot coexist with the perpetuation of his social slavery."[66]

The inseparability of politics and economics was established by the Commune, by its own working existence. Its Commission of Labor and Exchange, staffed mainly by members of the International, accomplished its greatest work, not in the decrees it passed, but in the stimulation it gave to workers to take things into their own hands. It began by asking the workers to reopen the works which had been abandoned by their owners and to run them by "the cooperative association of the workers employed in them." The aim was to transform land and means of production into mere instruments of "free and associated labor."

The Commune's workshops were models of proletarian democracy. The workers themselves appointed the directors, shop and bench foremen. These were subject to dismissal by the workers if relations or conditions proved unsatisfactory. Not only were wages, hours, and working conditions set, above all, *a factory committee met every evening to discuss the next day's work.*

Thus, plain working men, under circumstances of unexampled difficulty, governed themselves. The Commune, by being the self-government of the producers, set free all the elements of the future society. Marx described it as "Working, thinking, fighting, bleeding Paris—almost forgetful, in its incubation of a new society, of the cannibals at its gates—radiant in the enthusiasm of its historic initiative!"[67]

The spontaneous mass outburst that took this form of the Commune of Paris lasted only two months before the Parisian workers were massacred in one of the bloodiest terrors in history. But, in those two short months before the blood bath, the workers accomplished more miracles than capitalism had in as many centuries. The greatest miracle was its working existence. It abolished the standing army and armed the people instead. It smashed to smithereens State bureaucratism, placed public officials on a workman's salary and made them subject to recall. It abolished the division of labor between the legislative and the executive and transformed the parliament from a talking to a working body. It created new conditions for labor. On all fronts, the creative initiative of the masses had ensured the maximum activity for the masses and the minimum for their elected representatives. It thus stripped the fetishisms off all forms of rule: economic, political, intellectual.

3) The Fetishism of Commodities and Plan vs. Freely Associated Labor and Control of Production

The *totality* of the reorganization of society by the Communards shed new insight into the perversity of relations under capitalism. By smashing the old State-form and superseding it with the Commune, an end had been put to the hierarchic division of labor, including the division between politics and economics. By exposing the bourgeois State as the public force of social enslavement that it was, the proletariat demonstrated how the *absolutely new form of cooperation*, released from its value-integument, expresses itself. This was so clearly the absolute opposite of the dialectic movement of labor under capitalism, forced into a value-form, that all the fetishisms were stripped off of capitalist production.

Before the Commune, Marx had written that only freely associated labor could strip off the fetishism from commodities. Now that the Communards did precisely that, the concrete *doing* extended the *theory*. In the "Civil War in France," Marx writes. that what has now become clear is this: if cooperative production itself is not to become "a sham and a snare," it must be under the workers' own control. At the same time, he prepares a new, French edition of CAPITAL and there, as he tells us in the afterword,[68] he has changed the section on fetishism of commodities "in a significant manner." Marx asks: "Whence then arises. the enigmatical character of the product of labour, so soon as it. assumes the *form* of commodities?"[69] And he answers simply: "Clearly from this form itself."

Previous to this edition, this was not so clear to anyone,. not even to Marx. The simplicity of expression achieved in 1872 is. worth tracing, especially since the significance has been lost.

There is nothing simple about a commodity. It is a great fetish that makes the despotic *conditions* of capitalist production *appear* as if they were self-evident truths of social production. Nothing could be further from the truth. Just as these conditions were *historically* determined and rest on the servitude of the laborer, so the commodity, from the start of capitalism, is a reflection of the dual character of labor. It is, from the start, a unity of opposites—use-value and value—which, in embryo, contains *all* the contradictions of capitalism.

This simple relationship was beyond the perception of the greatest bourgeois economist, Ricardo, despite the earlier discovery of labor as the source of value. Although classical political economy had reduced value to its labor content, it had never once asked WHY did this *content*, labor, assume this *form*, value?

Long before CAPITAL, Marx had analyzed the duality pervading bourgeois society: "In our days everything seems pregnant. with its contrary; machinery, gifted with the wonderful power of shortening and fructifying human labor, we behold starving and overworking it. The new-fangled sources of wealth, by some strange weird spell, are turned into sources of want. The victories of arms seem bought by the loss of character. At the same pace that mankind masters nature, man seems to become enslaved to other men or to his own infamy. Even the pure light of science seems unable to shine but on a dark background of ignorance. All our inventions and progress seem to result in endowing material forces with intellectual life, and in stultifying human life into a material force. This antagonism between modern industry and science on the one hand, modern misery and dissolution on the other hand; this antagonism between the productive powers and the social relations of our epoch is a fact, palpable, overwhelming, and not to be controverted."[70]

In general, *but only in general,* the logic of content and form of labor was actual to Marx's thinking from the very beginning when he worked out the concept of alienated labor. Nevertheless, insofar as economic *categories* were concerned, he accepted them, more or less, as worked out by classical political economy. That is true as late as the publication of *Critique of Political Economy* in 1859, when he still used exchange-value in the sense of value and not in the sense of value-*form.* He still was "taking for granted" that "everyone knows" that production relations are really involved in the exchange of things.

By 1867, in the first edition of CAPITAL, he singles out the commodity-*form* as the fetish. Even here, the main emphasis is on the *fantastic* form of appearance of production relations as exchange of things. It is only *after* the eruption of the Paris Commune that his French edition shifts the emphasis from the fantastic form of appearance to the *necessity* of that form of appearance because that is, *in truth,* what relations of people *are* at the point of production: "material relations between persons and social relations between things."

Having located the trouble at its source, Marx sees that a product of labor *can have no other form than that of a commodity.* Thus, to the question: whence the fetishism of commodities?—the answer is simple and direct: "Clearly from the form itself."

It is not that Marx did not "know," before the Paris Commune, that everything under capitalism is perverted. He "knew" that the machine dominates man, not man the machine. He "knew" that all science is embodied in the machine rather than in the actual producers. He wrote often enough that all human relations are confined and perverted under capitalism. He stressed that it cannot be otherwise so long as the process of production has mastery over man instead of being controlled by him.

This perverse relation of subject to object is so all-pervading that it has in its grip the oppressor class. That is why classical political economy could not dissolve the mystery. *It met here its historic barrier.*

"The value-form of the product of labor is not only the most abstract, but is also the most universal form, taken by the product in bourgeois production, and stamps that production as a particular species of social production and thereby gives it its special historical character. If then we treat this mode of production as one eternally fixed for every state of society, we necessarily overlook that which is the *differentia specifica* of the value-form, and consequently the commodity-form and of the further developments, money-form, capital-form, etc."[71]

What was *new* was that the Commune, by releasing labor from the confines of value production, showed *how* people associated freely without the despotism of capital or the mediation of things. Contrast the *expansiveness* of that movement with the mutilation of labor under capitalism, which robs the workers of all individuality and reduces them merely to a component of labor *in general*. That is the specific character of labor under capitalism. The *value-form*, which alone contains the *reduction* of the many, varied, concrete labors into one abstract mass, is the necessary result of this *specific* character of capitalist labor.

The Commune transformed the *whole question of form* from a debate among intellectuals to the serious *activity* of workers—"facing with sober senses the conditions of their being and their relations with their kind." By dealing with their social relations openly and directly, they reorganized them completely and thus established a new social order. All existing relations were involved: production, property, the State, the market, the plan, the law of motion of the economy. The full and free development of each individual, once begun in the Commune, had become the condition for the full and free development of all.

The richness of human traits, revealed in the Commune, showed in sharp relief that the fetishism of commodities arises from the commodity form itself. This deepened the meaning of the form of value both as a logical development and as a social phenomenon.

Marx never looked at concrete events one-sidedly to see how they conformed to his previously-established theory. The theory always gained in depth by the processes of history itself. Not alone was the form of value fully illuminated. Important additions were introduced into the final part, on the "Accumulation of Capital." In analyzing the "General Law of Capitalist Accumulation," Marx now poses the question of the *ultimate* development of the law of concentration and centralization of capital: "In a given society, the limit would be reached at the moment when the entire social capital were united in the hands either of a single capitalist or a single capitalist corporation."[72]

Yet the importance of this crucial addition, with which we shall deal in detail when we analyze our own age of state capitalism in Part V, is *not* in the prediction of state capitalism, but in the fact that nothing fundamental is changed in the relations between classes by such an extreme development. On the contrary, all contradictions are pushed to the extreme. What was *new* was the concreteness this gave to Marx's concept of the relationship of the ideal to the real. "They (the Communards) have no ideals to realize," he writes, "but to set free the elements of the new society."[73]

CHAPTER SEVEN

THE HUMANISM AND DIALECTIC OF
CAPITAL, VOLUME I, 1867 TO 1883

1) The Split in the Category of Labor: Abstract and Concrete Labor, Labor and Labor Power

> "*All* understanding of the facts depends upon a comprehension of this dual character of labor."—K. Marx

Marx begins CAPITAL as he began *Critique,* with an analysis of the dual character of the commodity. He moves straightaway from the duality of use-value and value of the commodity to the dual character of labor itself. He considers the analysis of abstract and concrete labor as his original contribution to political economy, "the pivot on which a clear comprehension of political economy turns."[74] He tirelessly reminds us, in his correspondence, that since "*all*" understanding depends upon this, "It is emphasized in the *first* chapter."[75] As we saw from his earlier writings, for Marx the *whole* of human history could be traced through the development of labor. The evolution of man from lower to higher stages takes place by means of the developing process of labor. Labor has transformed the natural conditions of human existence into social conditions. In primitive communism, labor was a mode of self-activity, the creative function of man, which flowed from his natural capacities and developed his natural talents further. In his contact with nature, primitive man, despite the limitations of his knowledge, exercised not only his labor power but his judgment as well. He thus developed himself and nature.

The social division of labor was the necessary prerequisite for moulding nature to man's will and creating new productive forces. However, this undermined the collective nature of production and appropriation. Producers no longer consumed directly what they produced and they lost control over the products of their labor. Man is essentially a tool-making animal and the process of the production of his material life, the process of labor, means the process of the growth of the productive forces and his command over nature. We have seen Marx explain industry as "the real historic relation of nature, and consequently the science of nature, to man."

The Industrial Revolution, the progress of natural science and the general technological advance so revolutionized the mode of production that finally there arose a true basis for freedom. However, with the division of labor—the most monstrous of which is the division between mental and manual labor—class societies arose. The separation of intellectual and physical labor stands in the way of man's full development. Labor in class societies— whether they be slave, feudal or capitalist orders—no longer means the free development of the physical and intellectual energy of man. It has reached its most alienated aspect under capitalism where not only the product of his labor is alienated from the laborer, but his very mode of activity also. It has ceased to be "the first necessity of living" and has become a mere *means* to life. Labor has become a drudgery man must perform to earn a living, and not a mode of activity in which he realizes his physical and mental potentialities. He is no longer interested in the development of the productive forces and, in fact, the productive forces seem to develop independently of him. Labor has become a means of creating wealth and "is no longer grown together with the individual into one particular destination."[76]

What is *new* in CAPITAL, both as compared to the early works where he uses the term alienated labor and calls for "its abolition," and as compared to the *Critique* where it "is no longer grown together with the individual into one particular destination," is that Marx now goes directly to the labor process itself. The analysis of the capitalistic labor process is the cornerstone of the Marxian theory. Here we see what *kind* of labor produces value—abstract labor—and *how* concrete individual labor with specific skills becomes *reduced,* by the discipline of the factory clock, to nothing but a producer of a mass of congealed, abstract labor.

There is no such creature as an "abstract laborer"; one is a miner or a tailor or a steelworker or a baker. Nevertheless, the *perverse* nature of capitalist production is such that man is not master of the machine; the machine is master of the man. Through the instrumentality of the machine, which expresses itself in the ticking of a factory clock, it has indeed become immaterial what the skill of man is so long as each produces a given quantity of products in a given time. *Socially-necessary* labor time is the handmaiden of the machine which accomplishes the fantastic transformation of all concrete labors into one abstract mass. Constant technological revolutions change *how much* labor time is socially necessary. If what took an hour to produce yesterday takes only one-half hour to produce today, that is what the factory clock is now set at. Specific skills do not count. All must subordinate themselves to the newly-set socially necessary time to be expended on commodities. Competition in the market will see that it be done.

Paid or unpaid, all labor is *forced* labor. *Every instant* of it. With his analysis of what kind of labor produces value and surplus value, and how this is done, Marx transcended Ricardo. At one and the same time, he extricated the Ricardian labor theory of value from its contradictions and transformed it into a theory of surplus value.

Some Marxists have treated the phenomenon of alienated labor as if it were a leftover from Marx's Young Hegelian days that stuck to him before he succeeded in working his way out of philosophic jargon into "materialism." The mature Marx, on the other hand, shows *that* to be the very pivot on which turns, not alone the science or literature of political economy, but the productive system itself. There is nothing intellectual or deductive about the worker's individual skills being alienated from him to become social labor whose only specific feature is that it is "human." It is a very real and very degrading labor process which accomplishes this transformation. It is called the factory. Marx's concept of the degraded worker seeking universality, seeking to be a whole man, transformed the science of political economy into the science of human liberation.

As we showed, Marxism is wrongly considered to be "a new political economy." In truth, it is a critique of the very foundations of political economy which is nothing else than the bourgeois mode of *thought* of the bourgeois mode of *production*. By introducing the laborer into political economy, Marx transformed it from a science which deals with *things*, such as commodities, money, wages, profits, into one which analyzes *relations of men* at the point of production. It is true that man's cardinal tie, in this historic, that is, *transitory*, system called capitalism, is exchange and that this makes social relations between men appear as relations between things. But these things belie, instead of manifest, the essence. To separate the essence—the social relations—from the appearance— the exchange of things—required *a new science that was at the same time a philosophy of history. That new phenomenon is Marxism.*

It is characteristic of Marx, known the world over as the creator of the theory of surplus value, to disclaim the honor because the theory was "implicit" in the classical theory of labor value. What he did that was new, he said, was to make this explicit by showing what *type* of labor creates values and *hence* surplus values, and the *process* by which this is done. What kept others from seeing it, is that they had kept a goodly distance away from the factory. They remained in the market place, in the sphere of circulation, and it is this "which furnishes the 'Free-trader Vulgaris' with his views and ideas and the standard by which he judges society based on capital and wages." But once you leave the market place where "alone rule Freedom, Equality, Property and Bentham," you can perceive "a change in the physiognomy of our *dramatis personae*. He who before was the money owner, now strides in front as the capitalist; the possessor of labor power follows as his la- borer. The one with an air of importance, smirking, intent on business; the other, timid and holding back, like the one who is bringing his own hide to market and has nothing to expect but— a hiding."[77]

Ricardo had been unable to extricate his labor theory of value from the contradictions that befell it when it came to this most important exchange between capital and labor. Marx, on the other hand, was able to demonstrate how *inequality* arose out of the *equality* of the market.

That is because, in the millions of commodities exchanged daily, *one and only one,* labor power, is incorporated in a living person. A $5 bill or a piece of cloth has the same value in the market as at home or in the factory or in the pocket. Labor power, on the other hand, has first to be utilized, put to work in the factory. The laborer, therefore, can be, and is, made to work more than it takes to reproduce him. When he finds that out, his voice "stifled in the storm and stress of the process of production," cries out: "That which appears on your side as self-expansion of value, is, on my side, an extra expenditure of labor power."[78] It is too late. His commodity, labor power, no longer belongs to him, but to the one who bought it. He is therefore told unceremoniously that he can quit if he wants to, but so long as he is in the factory he must work under the command of the capitalist. He must subordinate himself to the machine and obey the factory clock.

The capitalist is most righteous about the whole transaction. He hasn't cheated. He has a contract with the laborer, duly executed according to the laws of exchange: so much money for so many hours of labor. The *utility* of a thing, he tells the laborer, belongs to him who has paid the exchange value. He has paid so much money for a day's labor, and he has as much right over it as the laborer over his wages. He, the capitalist, doesn't follow him, the worker, to see whether he is a good provider and brings his $5 bill home to his wife, or whether he goes to the bar to drink it down. Why then can't the laborer be as considerate of the capitalist's right over his product? In any case, the worker can take it or leave it. But so long as he is in the factory—and here the voice of "Mr. Moneybags" is full of unquestioned, military authority—the worker had better know who is boss.

It is too bad that labor power cannot be disembodied from the laborer. If it could, he would let the laborer go and use only the commodity—labor power—which rightfully belongs to him since he has paid for it. Thus he concludes quite piously that he hasn't violated any laws including the Ricardian law of value.

This is true. The law does hold in the factory. But in the factory "it" is no longer a commodity—"it" is the *activity* itself, labor. True, the living laborer is made to work beyond the value of his labor power. His sweat congeals into unpaid labor. That precisely is the "miracle" of surplus value: that labor power is incorporated in the living laborer, who can be, and is, made to produce a greater value than he himself is.

The failure of the Ricardian theory to explain the exchange between capital and labor, on the basis of its own primary law of labor value, meant the disintegration of that school. It was a fatal failure for it could not explain how it is that labor—the source and creator of all values—becomes the poorer the more values the worker creates. Utopian socialism could move nowhere because it remained a prisoner of the economic categories of Ricardo.

Marx broke through the barriers both because he split the categories created by classical political economy, and created new categories. He rejected the concept of labor as a commodity. Labor is an *activity*, not a commodity. It was no accident that Ricardo used one and the same word for the activity and for the commodity. He was a prisoner of his concept of the human laborer as a thing. Marx, on the other hand, showed that what the laborer sold was not his labor, but only his capacity to labor, his *labor power*.

Two principles are involved here, one flowing from theory and the other from practice. By splitting the old category, labor, into (1) labor as activity or function, and (2) ability to labor, or labor power, the commodity, Marx forged a new theoretical weapon with which to investigate the new material forces that developed outside of the old category. The very term, labor *power*, opened all sorts of new doors of comprehension. It enabled him to make a leap in thought to correspond with the new activity of workers.

Proof of this new power on the part of the theoretician, even as the new power in the worker, is to be seen most clearly in the short chapter in CAPITAL on "Cooperation." Its twenty-five pages seem merely to describe how men work together to produce things, but in reality, by analyzing how men work together, Marx described how a new social power is created. He could discover this new social power in production because, first of all, he distinguished between the productivity of machines and the productivity of men. What characterizes CAPITAL from beginning to end is the concern with living human beings. Marx lived in the second half of the nineteenth century when most theoreticians believed that as technology advanced, all of humanity's problems would be solved. Because Marx thought first and foremost of how the workers feel, he could anticipate the key question of our epoch: is productivity to be increased by the expansion of machinery or by the expansion of human capacities?

Capitalists and their ideologists think always of expanding productivity by more perfect machines. What happens to the worker as a result, well, that is just something that "can't be helped." Their governing principle is to keep their eyes on economies and the expansion of machinery. That, said Marx, is "quite in keeping with the spirit of capitalist production."

At the opposite pole from these, Marx was concerned with the worker's "own personal productiveness." That is the *class line* which he draws. Starting from these premises—so strange to the intellectual and so natural to the worker who has worked in large-scale production—Marx was able to discover that what is involved in the cooperation of many workers is a productive force. Marx is not dealing with a simple sum of individuals. No words can substitute for Marx's: "Not only have we here an increase in the productive power of the individual by means of cooperation, but the creation of a new· power, namely, the collective power of masses."[79]

New powers are not easily imagined or created. It requires a revolution in thought to understand them, as it requires a revolution in society to create them. Marx analyzed this new social power. He indicated the new psychological powers that are developed through cooperation: "hands and eyes both before and behind." He insisted that this new capacity must not be explained away merely by calling it a heightening in the mechanical force of labor; nor was it merely an extension of action over a greater space. What is developed is a new social force:

"The special productive power of the combined working day is, under all circumstances, the social productive force of labor, or the productive power of social labor. This power is due to cooperation itself. When the laborer cooperates systematically with others, he strips off the fetters of his individuality and develops the capacities of his species."[80]

Marx has here deepened his earlier concept of the workers' "quest for universality." It is no longer an ideological force alone, it has now become a powerful material force as well. In *Poverty of Philosophy*, Marx wrote: "But from the moment that all special development ceases, the need for universality, the tendency towards an integral development of the individual begins to make itself felt."[81]

In CAPITAL, he shows *how* the stripping off the fetters of individuality and the development of capacities of the human species, discloses what is second nature to workers as the result of years in large-scale production—the vast store of creative energy latent in them.

Capitalism knows this new social power as a rival and an opponent. The capitalist Plan exists to stifle and suppress it. In his chapter on "Cooperation," Marx first develops his concept of capitalist Plan, how to the workers "the connection existing between their various labors appears to them, ideally, in the shape of a preconceived plan of the capitalist, and practically in the shape of the authority of the same capitalist, in the shape of the powerful will of another, who subjects their activity to his aims."[82] Our age sheds a new illumination here since we see that management, whether state capitalist or private corporative, claims its Plan is necessary because the work is complicated and requires direction. The workers are not deceived by these claims. They know from their daily experiences of the wanton waste which goes hand in hand with the tyranny of capitalist Plans. The intellectuals are the ones who are deceived. They say there are two sides of the Capitalist Plan: the "good" side of leadership and foresight, and the "bad" side of domination.

This distinction exists only in their minds. Practically, in the lives of the workers the authority of the capitalists is "the powerful will of another who subjects their activities to his aims." Here, again, because the only reality for Marx is the actual experience of the workers, he cuts through the treacherous illusions about Plan.

Ideology and economy are as integrally connected with the historic movement as are content and form to a work of literature.[83] This shines forth from that most remarkable piece of analysis in the annals of political economy, "The Fetishism of Commodities." In this section, Marx demonstrates that the appearance of capitalist wealth, as an accumulation of commodities, is *not* mere show. The appearance dazzles the sight and makes relations between men seem to partake of "the mystical character of commodities." That a relationship between men appears as a relationship between things is, of course, fantastic. It is characteristic of the narrowness of bourgeois thought which not only created the fetishism, but became its victim. Even classical political economy, which discovered labor as the source of value, could not escape being held a prisoner by this "mystical character of commodities."

Under capitalism, relations between men appear as relations between things because that is what "they really are." The machine is master of man and consequently man is less than a thing. So perverse is the nature of capitalist production that the fantastic fetishism of commodities is its *true* nature. Marx states that only *freely* associated labor will be able to strip the fetishism off of commodities.

By tracing the dialectical development of this fetishism, Marx arrives at the *class nature* of the *value form*. That is when Marx first asks the question: Whence does the fetishism arise?—and answers, "Clearly from the form itself.' The fetishism of commodities is the opiate which passes itself off as the mind,[84] the ideology of capitalistic society. It is false from top to bottom and holds prisoner both the capitalist and his intellectual representative. As far back as in the *Communist Manifesto*, Marx showed that the capitalists are unable to grasp the truth that capitalism is a transitional social order because they and their ideologists transform "into eternal laws of nature and reason the social forms springing from the present mode of production." Because they do not see the future, the next social order, they cannot understand the present. Proletarian knowledge, on the other hand, grasps the truth of the present. Because it is not a passive, but an active force, it at the same time restores the unity of theory and practice.

2) *The Marxian Economic Categories and the Struggle at the Point of Production: Constant and Variable Capital, or the Domination of Dead over Living Labor*

> "The Hegelian contradiction (is) the source of all dialectic."[85]

In analyzing the economic system of capitalism, Marx wrote some five thousand pages, or about two million words. Throughout this gigantic work, he was able to use the categories already established by classical economy. He refined value—and with it surplus value—but he took over the categories themselves from classical economics. In three instances, *and in three instances only,* he had to *create entirely new categories*. These are: labor power, constant capital and variable capital. It cannot be stressed often enough that all the new categories flow from Marx's original contribution to political economy—the analysis of the duality of labor itself—for it is out of the split in the category of labor into concrete and abstract labor that these new categories emerged. Having already dealt with labor power, we now turn to the other two categories.

Heretofore economic science had made a distinction only between fixed and circulating capital. This distinction flowed from the process of circulation, *not* from the process of production. The process of production, however, is what determines all else. Constant and variable capital are of the essence once you try to analyze the process of production itself. Labor power and means of production are of course the main elements of any social system of production but only under capitalism do they unite as "the different modes of existence which the value of the original capital assumed when from being money it was transformed into the various factors of the labor process": variable capital and constant capital.

(1) *Constant capital* comprises the means of production and raw materials, the dead labor. They undergo no change in magnitude in the process of production. Their value has been established by the labor process from which they issued. In whole or in part

they yield their value to the commodities, but they cannot yield more than they have.

(2) *Variable capital* is labor power in the actual process of production. It does undergo a variation in the magnitude since it reproduces not only its own value, but an unpaid surplus. In a word, the laborer cannot quit work when he sees he has already produced the equivalent of his wages because the factory clock says it is only noon, and not quitting time

Marx is most specific and adamant about naming *both* factors of production *capital*.

There was dead labor or machines, or at least tools in pre-capitalist societies but dead labor did not dominate living labor. The savage was the complete master of his bow and arrow It did not dominate him; he dominated it. The serf was without a tractor and had to use a wooden hoe. But that crude instrument did not have a value which asserted its independence in the process of production so that the energy of the living laborer was a mere means for *its* expansion. Automation, however, means that more and more machines need less and less living labor, and more and more efficient machines need less and less skill in the general mass of human labor.

The worker is unable to resist this "process of suction"[86] because he is now but a component part of capital, "a simple, monotonous, productive force that does not have to have either bodily or intellectual faculties." The radio assembler whose line has to produce 75 to 90 radios an hour will not stop to inquire into its mechanics. He will know only that it means making eight connections per radio, and the wires mean to him only blue, red and green colors so that his eye can pick them out without stopping to consider. He will twist about 4800 wires per day, and his hands will handle the pair of pliers with such speed that the chassis do not pile up alongside his bench. That will be proof to the boss that he can keep up with the line, that he is a good means for the expansion of value.

This, Marx calls the real subordination of labor to capital. That is how accumulated labor dominates living labor. It is this domination which turns accumulated labor into capital, a force divorced from the direct producer and exploiting him. Therein is the antagonism between accumulated labor and living labor. Living labor faces dead labor as its mortal enemy. Under capitalism, wrote Marx, all conditions of existence have become so concentrated and sharpened that they have been reduced to two: accumulated labor and living labor, that is to say, constant capital and variable capital.

The antagonism between accumulated labor and living labor becomes personified in the struggle between the capitalist and the worker but the mastery of the capitalist over the worker is "only the mastery of things over man, of dead labor over living labor."[87]

Because the domination of dead over living labor characterizes the whole of modern society, Marx calls capital "value big with value, a live monster that is fruitful and multiplies."[88] Yet at every critical turn in history even Marxists, as we shall see when we deal with Rosa Luxemburg, have tried to denude these categories of their specifically capitalist character which, as Engels put it, gives them their "peculiar distinctness." They have blinded themselves to Marx's methodology which took its point of departure from the real world in which he lived.

The economic reality determined the structure of Marx's work. He no sooner established the two new categories—constant and variable capital—than he departed from the abstraction of theory to the actual struggles of the working class against what he called the capitalist's "werewolf hunger for surplus labor," which expresses itself at first in an unremitting attempt to lengthen the working day. Surplus value produced through the extension of the working day Marx calls *absolute surplus value*.

Whoever thinks that Marx spent sixty-four pages on "sob-story stuff" is totally blind to the fact that society itself would have collapsed had the worker not fought for the shortening of the working day. The section on the "Working Day" is one of the unique contributions to the analysis of human society. Any struggle by the workers to establish a normal working day was met with hostile opposition by the powers of the State as well as by the might of the capitalist. This "protracted civil war"[89] curbed the capitalist's disregard for human life. In three generations, capitalism used up nine generations of spinners. The workers learned labor solidarity and organized themselves against this mass slaughter.

Capitalism fought back with an even more potent factor than the State's extension of the working day. Technological development made possible the extraction of greater surplus value *within the same working day*. By the time we reach Machinofacture, we can see how Marx's new categories—constant and variable capital—illuminate the ever greater contradictions of capitalist production. The constant capital—the machinery—undergoes no change in value, no matter how light or how hard it is worked. The laborer, with his concrete type of labor, can transfer the value of the machine to the new product only to the extent of its original value, that is to say, the socially necessary labor time it took to produce it. As dead matter, machinery is incapable of creating value and gains nothing from the labor process. The capitalist is therefore fully dependent on his other type of capital, variable capital—the labor power of the living laborer, who therefore, must be forced to produce ever more. When this can no longer be done through the lengthening of the working day, it must be done by speed-up. This is where the factory clock plays its part. It is now not merely a sort of counting machine for the quantity of output. It has become a *measure of the intensity* of labor itself. The surplus labor or value thus extracted is related *directly* to the wear and tear of the laborer himself. Where the extraction of surplus value, by lengthening the working day, was the production of absolute surplus value, the extraction of surplus value with a given working day is *the production of relative surplus value*. In machine-ism, capitalism has not merely a *productive* force; it has a *force* to strike down the hand of labor to the right degree of intensity and docility, "a barrack discipline."[90]

When machine-ism is organized into a system, when it becomes the *body* of the factory, its *spirit* is incorporated in the factory clock. The function of the capitalist is to extract as much, and more, surplus value within the *given* working day, as he had previously extracted during an elastic working day. The machine must justify its cost of production by lengthening that part of the working day in which the worker produces the surplus above what is necessary to maintain him and have him reproduce his kind.

Cheaper goods make this possible. That is all the liberals saw. Marx saw the greater exploitation of the worker, the greater contradiction in capitalist production. From the very start Marx noted: "An increase in the quantity of use-values is an increase of material wealth. With two coats two men can be clothed, with one coat only one man. Nevertheless, an increased quantity of material wealth may correspond to a simultaneous fall in the magnitude of its value. The antagonistic movement has its origin in the two-fold character of labor."[91]

At the beginning, the bourgeois ideologists' relation to science was unambiguous. Professor Ure was most frank: "When capitalism enlists science into her service, the refractory hand of labor will always be taught docility."[92] The rejoicing was loud and clear. "One of the most singular advantages we derive from machinery," Marx quotes Barbage, "is in the check it affords against the inattention, idleness and knavery of human agents." If, with Automation, and the experience of a few revolutions, the capitalists and their ideologists boast only of "the magic carpet" of the new industrial revolution which "lightens" work, it is nevertheless true that machinery has not only superseded the skill and strength of the worker, it has put a greater nervous as well as physical strain on him the greater effort per unit of labor time. Marx saw all this one hundred years ago. He described the method whereby millions of specific types of labor are transformed into one abstract mass, and he focused on the domination of capital through the "peculiar distinctness" of his original categories: constant and variable capital.

The role played in the production of absolute surplus value by the struggle for the shortening of the working day is now played by the "Strife between Workman and Machinery." Professional Marxists have too sophisticated an attitude to the revolts which have raged throughout the history of capitalism. They manage to "take the revolts for granted."

They act as if they were ashamed (and many are) of the period when workers broke up machines. They would have "preferred" it if the workers had, instead, fought with "the real enemy" on the political front. Yet these very acts by the workers against the machines Marx called "revolts against this particular form of the means of production as being the material basis of the capitalist mode of production." These professional Marxists thus miss the central point of Marxian theory that *revolt* marks *every* stage of capitalist *progress*. As Marx puts it: "It would be possible to write quite a history of the inventions, made since 1830, for the sole purpose of supplying capital with weapons against the revolts of the working class."[93] The revolt caused the change to advanced methods; the revolt saved the life of the country. In turn, each revolt caused a greater centralization, exploitation, socialization *and* greater organization, both objectively and subjectively, of the proletariat.

There are two movements in CAPITAL: the historical and the logical. The historical includes the origins of capitalism which Marx calls "The Primitive Accumulation of Capital." The power of the State was employed "to hasten, in hothouse fashion, the process of transformation of the feudal mode of production into the capitalist mode." Marx shows, first, that "the expropriation of the agricultural producer, of the peasant, from the soil, is the basis of the whole process,"[94] and then says, of the genesis of the industrial capitalist: "The discovery of gold and silver in America, the extirpation, enslavement and entombment in mines of the aboriginal population, the beginning of the conquest and looting of the East Indies, the turning of Africa into a warren for the commercial hunting of black-skins, signalised the rosy dawn of the era of capitalist production. These idyllic proceedings are the chief momenta of primitive accumulation."[95] But all this is preliminary to the actual development of capitalist production.

The three stages of development of capitalist production itself are: (1) Cooperation; (2) Division of Labor and Manufacture; and (3) Machinofacture. Just as out of the historical development of the expropriated peasant, so out of the logical development of capitalism, we reach the point of no return—concentration and centralization of capital at one end, and the socialization and revolt of labor, at the other end.

The commodity of commodities in capitalist society is labor power. The whole society is governed by the necessity of producing labor power according to the labor time necessary for the production of this commodity. Hence the cost of the laborer is the first consideration of the capitalist. Let us repeat: *it is his first consideration.* He must keep its cost down.

Unless he constantly increases the amount of accumulated labor, expands, or reorganizes his plant or does all three things, the value of his productive system not only declines but disappears altogether. In normal times he loses his market because he cannot sell. In abnormal times he is defeated in battle and his whole productive system is bodily taken away from him. Therefore his main concern must always be to increase the value of such capital as he has. Now—and again we owe this to Marx—the only power of increasing the capital is the amount of living labor which he can apply to the capital which he already has. Therefore his main concern is to augment value, that is, to create surplus value, to gain a value greater than the value which he expends. This is the essence of capitalist production. This is what Marx called "the *characteristic specific nature* of capitalist production."

The modern bourgeoisie has emasculated the word, revolutionary, so that it is equivalent to nothing but a violent overthrow in the dark of night, "a conspiracy." In truth, as compared to every previous social order, capitalism was the most revolutionary *not* because of its violent overthrow of the old, feudal order, but because of its *daily technological* revolutions. In the *Communist Manifesto,* the young Marx had written:

"The bourgeoisie cannot exist without continually revolutionizing the instruments of production, and thereby the relations of production and all the social relations. Conservatism, in an unaltered form, of the old modes of production, was on the contrary the first condition of existence for all earlier industrial classes. Constant revolution in production, uninterrupted disturbance of all social conditions, everlasting uncertainty and agitation, distinguish the bourgeois epoch from all earlier ones. All fixed, fast-frozen relations, with their train of ancient and venerable prejudices and opinions, are swept away, all new formed ones become antiquated before they can ossify. All that is solid melts into air, all that is holy is profaned, and man is at last compelled to face with sober senses his real conditions of life, and his relations with his kind."

The mature Marx quotes precisely this passage when, in his analysis of "Machinery and Modern Industry," he reaches the "absolute contradiction between the technical necessities of Modern Industry and the social character inherent in its capitalistic form," and sees how "this antagonism vents its rage in the creation of that monstrosity, an industrial reserve army," and "the devastation caused by a social anarchy which turns every economical progress into a social calamity."[96]

Marx stresses that this is "the negative side." He shows how the *resistance* of the workers is the positive aspect which compels Modern Industry *"under the penalty of death"* to replace the mere fragment of a man "by the fully developed individual, fit for a variety of labors, ready to face any change in production, and to whom the different social functions he performs, are but so many modes of giving free scope to his own natural and acquired powers."[97]

Having traced the dialectical development of the two opposites, living labor and dead labor, labor and machinery, from *"Cooperation"* through the *"Division of Labor and Manufacture"* to *"Machinery and Modern Industry,"* Marx concludes that there is no other than the *historical* solution to the "revolutionary ferments, the final result of which is the abolition of the old division of labor, diametrically opposed to the capitalistic form of production and to the economic status of the laborer corresponding to that form."[97] The penalty of death hanging over the capitalistic mode of production, and the elements of the socialist society which are imbedded in the old, will clash head-on in *"The Accumulation of Capital,"* the final part of Marx's great work.

3) Accumulation of Capital, and the New Forces and New Passions

> "It is the ultimate aim of this work to lay bare the economic law of motion of modern society." (Preface to CAPITAL)

The historical and logical in CAPITAL are not two separate movements: the dialectic contains them both. It is not that *Marx* has interrelated them. It is the very nature and life of the one to contain the other. What Marx has as his underlying assumption is that history has not discharged theory from the need to transcend the given society. With Marx, theory is not kept above the earth, but rather takes its departure from reality, which is also its point of return. It is the reality out of which the movement comes, and what Marx does is to see that object and subject are kept as one. The two together, theory and practice, make up the truth at any moment. The very first sentence in the chapter which is the climax to the whole of Volume I—"The General Law of Capitalist Accumulation"—states: "In this chapter we consider the influence of the growth of capital on the lot of the working class."[98] This is not mere agitation. It can be and is expressed in the most precise scientific terms yet discovered to discern the law of motion of capitalist society. "The most important factor in this inquiry," Marx's very next sentence reads, "is the composition of capital."

The law of the ever greater growth of machinery at the expense of the working class, which had heretofore been expressed as the growth of constant over variable capital, is now, when viewed as a totality, expressed as the *value* and *technical* composition of capital, which Marx calls "the *organic composition of capital*." That is to say, they are part of the very organism and can no more be separated, one from the other, than can the head from the body and still live.

From the very beginning of CAPITAL we learned of the interdependence of use-value. Value, wrote Marx, may be indifferent to the use-value by which it is borne, but it must be borne by some use-value. This bodily form assumes added significance in the question of accumulation or expanded reproduction: "Surplus value is convertible into capital solely because the surplus product whose value it is, already comprises the material elements of new capital."[99]

Capital, which is "value big with value," deepens the contradiction between use-value and value. This is so because not only are the material and value forms of capital in constant conflict, but so are the *class relations* which "interfere with" the production process. Capital is not a thing but a relation of production established by the instrumentality of things. Expanded production further aggravates this class relationship which is produced and reproduced by capitalist production. Capitalist private property "turns out to be the right on the part of the capitalist to appropriate unpaid labor of others or its product, and to be the impossibility, on the part of the laborer, of appropriating his own product."[100]

Out of the innermost needs of capitalist production, whose motive force is the production of surplus value, comes the drive to pay the laborer the *minimum* and to extract from him the *maximum*. The class struggle produced thereby leads, under certain circumstances, to a rise in wages. But that rise is never so high as to threaten the *foundations* of capitalist production. The law of value, dominating over this mode of production, leads, on the one hand, to the centralization of the means of production and, on the other hand, to the socialization of labor.

Capitalism develops according to these two fundamental laws: the law of centralization of capital, and the law of the socialization of labor. "One capitalist always kills many," writes Marx, adding that, "hand in hand with this centralization, or this expropriation of many capitalists by a few, develop, on an ever-extending scale, the cooperative form of the labor-process, the conscious technical application of science, the methodical cultivation of the soil, the transformation of the instruments of labor into instruments of labor only usable in common, the economizing of all means of production by their use as the means of production of combined socialized labor, the entanglement of all peoples in the net of the world-market, and this, the international character of the capitalist regime."[101]

Note the phrase "the cooperative form of the labor process." Marx has his eyes fixed on what is happening in production, the law of the socialization of labor. Every stage in this process of development of cooperative, socialized labor increases its numbers, unites it, disciplines it, organizes it. When Ford builds the River Rouge plant, needing some 60,000 workers, he has thereby—by the very fact that they work together in one large production unit— organized those 60,000 into a social force. There were no Rouge plants in Marx's day, but, in the workers, trained to cooperative labor by the organization of large-scale production, he saw that capitalism itself "produces its own grave-diggers."

Others, besides Marx, had noticed the cooperative form of labor, and they believed that higher and higher standards of living, more and more democracy, more and more equality would be the consequence. Marx laughed them to scorn. He insisted that it was the *workers* who were being trained to cooperation. It was the cooperative form of the *labor* process which grew continually. The more the workers were knit into huge cooperative units, the more capital had to attack and suppress them. Instead of a continuous growth of equality and democracy, you would have such class struggles as the world had never seen before, and a growing and unceasing revolt of the workers. Here are his own words:

"Along with the constantly diminishing number of the magnates of capital who usurp and monopolize all advantages of this process of transformation, grows the mass of misery, oppression, slavery, degradation, exploitation, but with this too grows the revolt of the working class, a class always increasing in numbers and disciplined, united, organized by the very mechanism of the process of production itself."[102]

Marx wrote this in 1867, ninety years ago. Since that time, the unity, discipline and organization of the working class has grown until today it is the most powerful social class the world has ever seen. As centralization has increased and the number of capitalist magnates diminished, so of necessity has the labor bureaucracy grown. For the magnates by themselves are too few to discipline tens of millions of workers. This bureaucracy is their weapon against the cooperative society. Every worker in large-scale industry recognizes that today; hence the wildcats.

The foreman does not tell the worker *how* to do his work. Neither does the committeeman. They are there to discipline the worker. Every day *that* becomes harder to do. Hence, more bureaucracy, more supervision, more time-study men, more negotiations, more "fact-finders." The ultimate end of all this is what there is in Russia, the completely bureaucratized State of totalitarianism with its slave labor camps. It is the final centralization within a single country. The relations of production in any society determine, shape, put their stamp upon all other relations. As production expands and is bureaucratized, so is it with all other spheres of social activity. All this bureaucratism, ending in the One-Party State, is rooted in the need to discipline workers in production.

Marx foresaw this trend because he carried through to the logical conclusion all the laws of capitalist development. He showed first how the centralization of the means of production ends in trustification and, ultimately, in statification. Whether this ultimate development of the centralization of capital would be accompanied by "the violent means of annexation" or the "smooth road of forming stock companies"—the results are the same: "With the advance of accumulation, therefore, the proportion of constant to variable capital changes. If it was originally, say, 1:1, it now becomes successively 2:1, 3:1, 4:1, 5:1, 7:1, etc., so that, as the capital increases, instead of $1/2$ of its total value, only 1/3, 1/4, 1/5, 1/7, etc., is transformed into labor power and, on the other hand, 2/3, 3/4, 4/5, 5/6, 7/8 into means of production."[103]

The end result of this relationship of capital to the lot of the working class is the great, the insoluble contradiction which is wrecking the entire system—the unemployed army. Marx calls this *"the absolute general law of capitalist accumulation."* The greater the use of machinery, or constant capital, the lesser *relatively* the need for variable or living labor power. There may now be 30 million workers where formerly there were half as many, but the investment of capital is sevenfold. And with it will always come unemployment. Thus, on the one hand, capitalism keeps reproducing the wage laborer; on the other hand, he throws him into unemployment.

This failure to give "full employment" to labor shakes the whole structure of capitalist society. Marx emphasizes that "every special historic mode of production has its own special laws of population, historically valid within its limits alone."[104] For capitalist production, as we saw, that law is the law of the surplus army, surplus, that is to the capitalist mode of production.

The incapacity of capitalism to reproduce its own value-creating substance—labor power in the shape of the living, employed laborer—signals the doom of capitalism. Marx defines this doom in the final part—Part VIII[105]—where he deals with the historical genesis and then with the historical tendency of capitalistic accumulation.

The historic beginnings of capitalism, described under "The So-Called Primitive Accumulation of Capital," has, as we saw, highly-charged agitation material. The fact that Marx relegates this material to the end, instead of the beginning of CAPITAL, cannot be overestimated. It means that Marx wished, above all, to analyze the *law of development* of capitalism. For, no matter what its beginnings were, the contradictions arise not from its origin but from its *inherent nature*, which "begets with the inexorability of a law of Nature, its own negation."[106]

The law of motion of capitalistic society is therefore the law of its collapse. Marx discerned this law through the application of dialectical materialism to the developmental laws of capitalist production.

"All means for the development of production transform themselves into means of domination over, and exploitation of, the producers; they mutilate the laborer into a fragment of a man, degrade him to the level of an appendage of a machine, destroy every remnant of charm in his work and turn it into a hated toil; they estrange from him the intellectual potentialities of the labor process in the same proportion as science is incorporated in it as an independent power, they distort the conditions under which he works, subject him during the labor process to a despotism the more hateful for its meanness; they transform his life-time into workingtime, and drag his wife and child beneath the wheels of the Juggernaut of capital."[107]

How many have, at this point, stopped and bemoaned that nevertheless the worker is out only for higher wages, and that once he gets it, he is satisfied "because he is better off." *Marx says the exact opposite.* As he continues, Marx stresses that whether *"his payment is high or low"* his lot is worse:

"It follows therefore that in proportion as capital is accumulated, the lot of the laborer, be his payment high or low, must grow worse. The law, finally, that always equilibrates the relative surplus population, or industrial reserve army, to the extent and energy of accumulation, this law rivets the laborer to capital more firmly than the sledges of Vulcan did Prometheus to the rock. It establishes an accumulation of misery, corresponding with accumulation of capital. Accumulation of wealth at one pole is, therefore, at the same time accumulation of misery, agony of toil, slavery, ignorance, brutality, mental degradation, at the opposite pole, i.e., on the side of the class that produces its own product in the form of capital."[108]

"Centralization of the means of production and socialization of labor at last reach a point where they become incompatible with their capitalist integument. The integument is burst asunder. The knell of capitalist private property sounds. The expropriators are expropriated."[109]

The positive side of all this is that "it brings forth the material agencies for its own dissolution. From that moment new forces and new passions spring up in the bosom of society; but the old social organization fetters them and keeps them down. It must be annihilated. It is annihilated."[110]

Thus the development of capitalism itself creates the basis of a new Humanism—the "new forces and new passions" which will reconstruct society on new, truly human beginnings, "a society in which the full and free development of every individual is the ruling principle."[111] It is because Marx based himself on this Humanism, more popularly called "the inevitability of socialism," that he could discern the law of motion of capitalist society, the inevitability of its collapse. The Humanism of CAPITAL runs like a red thread throughout the work. This gives it both its profundity and its force and direction.

CHAPTER EIGHT

THE LOGIC AND SCOPE OF *CAPITAL*, VOLUMES II AND III

> "All science would be superfluous if the appearance, the form and the nature of things were wholly indentical." (CAPITAL, Vol. III).

Political economy has produced two theories between which it oscillated: (1) that production creates its own market; and (2) that it is impossible for the worker "to buy back" the products he himself produced. Marx's great contribution consisted in dialectically combining these. The dominant feature remained the fact that production did create its own market. But this did not negate the existence of under-consumption. It merely showed that within capitalistic production there resides a disregard for the limits of consumption.

The outstanding characteristic of Volume II, whose subject is the process of circulation, is its demonstration that "realizing surplus value," that is, selling, is *not* the problem. The significance of the first two parts dealing with the metamorphoses and turnover of capital lies in the analysis that the very *continuity* of the process of circulation involves the sphere of *reproduction*. Thus, even when Marx's point of departure is the market, reproduction is of the essence.

Reproduction, he states, must be posed "in its fundamental simplicity," that is to say, it is necessary not to get lost in "a vicious circle of prerequisites"—of constantly going to market with the products produced and returning from market with commodities bought.

1) The Two Departments of Social Production: Means of Production and Means of Consumption

To cut through the tangle of markets, Marx divides the entire social product into two, *and only two,* main departments: Department I produces means of production, and Department II produces means of consumption.[118] The division is symptomatic of the class division in society. Marx categorically refused to divide social production into more than two departments, for example, a third department for the production of gold, although gold is neither a means of production nor a means of consumption, but rather a means of circulation. That is an entirely subordinate question, however, to the basic postulate of a closed society in which there are only two classes and *hence* only two decisive divisions of social production. It is the premise that decides the boundaries of the problem. The relationship between the two branches is not merely a technical one. It is rooted in the class relationship between the worker and the capitalist.

Surplus value is not some disembodied spirit floating between heaven and earth, but is embodied *within* means of production and *within* means of consumption. To try to separate surplus value *from* means of production and *from* means of consumption is to fall into the petty-bourgeois quagmire of underconsumptionism. It is impossible to have the slightest comprehension of the economic laws of capitalistic production without being oppressively aware of the role of the material form of constant capital. The material elements of simple production and reproduction-- labor power, raw materials and means of production—are the elements of expanded reproduction. In order to produce ever greater quantities of products, more means of production are necessary. That, and not the "market," is the *differentia specifica* of expanded reproduction.

Marx established that the social product cannot be "either" means of production "or" means of consumption. There is a *preponderance* of means of production *over* means of consumption. Marx's point here is that the *bodily* form of value predetermines the *destination* of commodities: iron is not consumed by people but by steel; sugar is not consumed by machines but by people. Value may be indifferent to the useful form which holds it, but it must be incorporated in some use-value to be realized. Just because the capitalist is only interested in surplus value (profit) doesn't mean that he can disembody it from the article in which it is embodied.

The division of the whole product into but two departments is not a hypothesis. It is a fact. It not only is so. It *must* be so, for the use-values produced are not those used by workers, nor even by capitalists, *but by capital*. We can see this most clearly in this country, for example, where ninety per cent of pig iron is "consumed" by the companies which produce it; fifty per cent of the "market" for the products of the steel industry is the transportation industry. Where all utilitarian economists were floundering in talking of use-values because they were talking of articles for consumption, Marx shows that the *use-value of the means of production* shows how important is "the determination of use-value in the determination of economic orders."[114] *Under capitalism*, the means of production form the greater part of the two departments of social production and, *therefore,* also of the "market." That is what Marx called "the real being of capital," and that is why the market was not the problem.

The consumption market is limited to the luxuries of the capitalists, and the needs of the workers, paid at value. *It cannot be larger*. The only market that can expand beyond the limits of the workers paid at value is the capital goods market. Means of production literally shoot up to the sky. To illustrate this for both simple and expanded reproduction, Marx devised his famous formulas which show constant capital to be greater than variable capital and surplus value.

To understand the formulas one must comprehend the premise upon which they are built: a closed *capitalist* society, that is, an isolated society dominated by the law of value. For Marx, the fundamental conflict in a capitalist society is that between capital and labor; all other elements are subordinate. If this is so in life, then the first necessity in theory is to pose the problem as one between the capitalist and the worker, purely and simply. Hence, the assumption of a society consisting only of workers and capitalists. Hence, the exclusion of "third groups" and, as he states repeatedly, the exclusion of foreign trade as having nothing to do fundamentally with the conflict between the worker and the capitalist.

A capitalist society is distinguished from all previous societies by being a value-producing society. The law of value has nothing in common with the fact that in other class societies the worker was paid his means of subsistence. Under capitalism the thirst for unpaid hours of labor comes from the very nature of production and is not limited by the gluttony of the master. Value, the socially necessary labor time needed to produce commodities, is constantly changing due to the unceasing technological revolutions in production. This is a never-ending source of disturbance in the conditions of production as well as in the social relations, and distinguishes capitalism from all other modes of production. Marx's isolated capitalist society is dominated by this law of value, and Marx does not let us forget that this law is a law of the world market. "The industrialist always has the world market before him, compares and must continually compare his cost prices with those of the whole world, and not only with those of his home market."[115]

Thus, while Marx excludes foreign trade, he nevertheless places his society in the *environment* of the world market. These are the conditions of the problem.

Marx's formulas were designed to serve two purposes: (1) on the one hand, he wished to expose the "incredible aberration" of Adam Smith, who "spirited away" the constant portion of capital by asserting that "in the final analysis" it dissolved itself into wages; (2) on the other hand, Marx wanted to answer the underconsumptionist argument that continued capital accumulation was impossible because of inability to sell, that is, because of "overproduction."

Smith's "fundamentally perverted analysis"[116] became part of the dogma of political economy because it dovetailed with the *class* interests of the capitalists to have that error retained. If, as Smith maintained, the constant portion of capital "in the final analysis" dissolved itself into wages, then the workers need not struggle against a "temporary" appropriation of the unpaid hours of labor. They need merely wait for the product of their labor to "dissolve" itself into wages. Marx proved the contrary to be true. Not only did the constant portion of capital not "dissolve" itself into wages, but it became the very instrumentality through which the capitalist gained the mastery over the living worker. Utopian socialists who didn't grasp *this* freed themselves of the actualities of the class struggle.

Each of the two departments of social production comprises three elements: (1) constant capital; (2) variable capital; and (3) surplus value. Just as the division of social production into two main departments was not merely technical, so this was not a merely technical division. It was rooted in the relationship of worker to capitalist, and was inseparable from the inherent laws of capitalist production. "It is purely a tautology to say that crises are caused by the scarcity of solvent consumers, or of a paying consumption. The capitalist system does not know any other modes of consumption but a paying one, except that of the pauper or of the thief . . . . But if one were to attempt to clothe this tautology with a semblance of profounder justification by saying that the working class received too small a portion of their own product, and the evil would be remedied by giving them a larger share of it, or raising their wages, we should reply that crises are precisely always preceded by a period in which wages rise generally and the working class actually get a larger share of the annual product intended for consumption. From the point of view of the advocates of 'simple' (!) common sense, such a period should rather remove a crisis."[117]

Marx spent a seemingly interminable time in exposing the error of Smith. This was so because this was the great divide *not alone* between bourgeois economics and Marxism, *but also* between petty-bourgeois criticism, or utopian socialism, and scientific socialism. There is not the wealth of statistical and historical material in Volume II, which Marx did not live to complete for publication, that there is in Volume I, which he prepared for the printer himself. This has given rise to as many misrepresentations among Marxists as among anti-Marxists. The chief objection is directed against Marx's thesis that production creates its own market. The objectors say that this implies a "balance" between production and consumption. The truth is that the proportional relationship between Departments I and II, in the Marxian formula, means the *exact opposite*. Marx based himself on the laws of accumulation which he analyzed in Volume I when he showed that constant capital keeps on expanding. The exact relationship to variable capital that he gives it is seven to one. It should therefore have been clear that the "balance" that exists in the formulas— which were built on the most extreme assumptions of "an isolated nation" with no foreign trade, nor with the ordinary headaches of sales—exists *solely* because of the production relations under capitalism which resulted in this fantastic proportion of seven to one. That is why Marx's categories are so immutable for capitalism and apply to no other society. They assume that what is produced is consumed because it is *capitalist* production, and capitalist production is the production of capital and hence is *consumed by capital*. Marx built his theory of capitalist breakdown on this. To deduce from the formulas that there was "no disproportion" in an ideal capitalism with no market troubles, is enough to make Marx turn in his grave.

What Marx did, in disproving the underconsumption theory was to demonstrate that there is no direct connection between production and consumption. As Lenin phrased it, in the most profound analysis that Volume II ever received: "The difference in view of the petty-bourgeois economists from the views of Marx does not consist in the fact that the first realize in general the connection between production and consumption in capitalist society, and the second do not. (This would be absurd.) The distinction consists in this, that the petty-bourgeois economists considered this tie between production and consumption to be a *direct* one, thought that *production follows consumption*. Marx shows that the connection is only an *indirect* one, that it is connected *only in the final instance,* because in capitalist society *consumption follows production*."[118]

The preponderance of production over consumption was considered to mean the "automatic" collapse of capitalist society. Where the classicists saw *only* the tendency *toward* equilibrium, the petty-bourgeois critics saw *only* the tendency *away* from equilibrium. Marx demonstrated that *both* tendencies were there, inextricably connected. Volume II is both a critique of bourgeois and petty-bourgeois thought, and an analysis of the actual movement of capitalist production. As Trotsky put it, when Stalin suddenly "discovered" that the formulas also "apply to a socialist society," "Marx's formulas," Trotsky wrote, "deal with a chemically pure capitalism which never existed and does not exist anywhere now. Precisely because of this, they revealed the basic tendency of *every* capitalism but precisely of *capitalism* and *only* of capitalism."

2) *Appearance and Reality*

Volume II of CAPITAL was published posthumously, in 1885, by Marx's lifelong collaborator, Frederick Engels. This posthumous publication hit a blank wall in the Second International. It seemed to pass by *both* the reformists *and* the revolutionaries within the International. In fact, the greatest revision came from the revolutionary martyr, Rosa Luxemburg. As for Karl Kautsky, the theoretical leader of the Second International, he wrote sophomoric essays on Volume II. The sole exception to this common obtuseness was Lenin. It was not because Lenin was "smarter" than Kautsky that he knew how "to apply" the concepts Marx developed in Volume II to the actual development of the Russian economy. In Russia, the question whether capitalism could develop without foreign markets was not the theoretical question it was in Germany, where imperialist expansion was conquering new markets daily. In backward Russia, which could not successfully compete for the world market, there arose a whole school of theoreticians, the Narodniki (Populists) who maintained that "since" capitalism could not exist without a market, and "since" Russia had come too late on the historic scene to secure one, Russia could "therefore" skip capitalism and go directly from the *mir* (peasant commune) to communism. Lenin hit out against them theoretically and practically. He combined both attacks in a most profound study of *The Development of Capitalism in Russia*. It cleared the ground for Marxism.

The main burden of Luxemburg's critique of Marx's theory of accumulation was directed against his assumption of a closed

THE LOGIC AND SCOPE OF *CAPITAL*

capitalist society. She gave this assumption a twofold meaning: (1) a society composed solely of workers and capitalists; and (2) "the rule of capitalism in the entire world."

Marx, however, did not pose the rule of capital in the *entire world*, but its rule in a *single* isolated nation. When Luxemburg's critics[119] pointed this out to her, she poured vitriolic scorn upon them. To speak of a single capitalist society, wrote Luxemburg in her *Anticritique*,[120] was a "fantastic absurdity" characteristic of the "crassest epigonism." Marx, she insisted, could have had no such stratospheric conception in mind. Nevertheless, as Bukharin pointed out, Luxemburg was not only misinterpreting Marx's *concept*, but misreading the simple *fact*, which Marx had most clearly put on paper: "In order to simplify the question (of expanded reproduction) we abstract foreign trade and examine an isolated nation."[121]

Rosa Luxemburg falsely counterposed reality to theory. She argued that a "precise demonstration" from history would show that expanded reproduction has never taken place in a "closed society," i.e., in isolation from the world market, but rather through distribution to, and expropriation of "non-capitalistic strata and non-capitalist societies." Her critique flowed theoretically from this one fundamental error of falsely counterposing reality to theory. She was betrayed by the powerful historical development of imperialism that was taking place, to substitute the relationship of capitalism to non-capitalism for the relationship of capital to labor. This led her to deny Marx's assumption of a closed society. Once she had given up this basic premise of the whole of Marxist theory, there was no place for her to go but to the sphere of exchange and consumption.

This is most clearly revealed by Luxemburg herself. Some of her best writing in *Accumulation*, occurs where she describes the "real" process of accumulation through the conquest of Algeria, India, the Anglo-Boer war, the carving up of Africa, the opium wars against China, the extermination of the American Indian, the growing trade with non-capitalist societies, and her analysis of protective tariff and militarism. Marx gave at least as graphic a description of primitive accumulation as Rosa did of imperialist exploitation of backward lands. Though "capital comes dripping from hand to foot, from every pore with blood and dirt," nevertheless, primitive accumulation created only the *conditions* for real capitalism. It now had a certain accumulation of capital, propertyless workers, and a lot of subordination of labor to capital. However, it still remained merely "formal." As Marx put it, *so long as* "variable capital preponderated greatly over constant," there was "as yet no specific capitalist character."[122]

Luxemburg denied that this preponderance of constant over variable capital was inherently capitalistic. To her it was merely "capitalistic language" for the essential elements of production in any society. She offered to demonstrate this by taking up the relations of capitalism to non-capitalist lands. She began by supplementing CAPITAL. She ended by revising it.

Where Luxemburg maintained that Marx's formulas of expanded reproduction were incorrect in theory and did not correspond to real life in any one living nation, Lenin said they held in life and were correct in theory. Russia, even as America, however, seems to have the perfect soil for all sorts of theories of "exceptionalism" from "skipping capitalism" to having "communism" under totalitarianism. When Lenin argued theoretically, his critics said he didn't know *Russia*. When he showed from exhaustive Russian statistics that capitalism was indeed coming to Tsarist Russia, they said he didn't understand *theory*. When he both won on the theoretical front and routed the Narodniki on the organizational front as well, the ideological children of the Narodniki, present-day economists, state that it wasn't, after all, such a great feat for it was not Marxism but irrefutable economic facts which won out. Precisely. That is the logic of Volume II.

It is necessary to bear in mind, that the passage, in Volume I of CAPITAL, which deals with the ultimate development of the centralization of capital in the hands of a single capitalist or single capitalist corporation, did *not* appear in the early edition of the work. He added this passage only after the Paris Commune, which was the period when he discussed with Engels the concentration of all capital in the hands of the State.[123] Volume I, on which Marx never stopped working until the day of his death in 1883, is the one complete volume we have from his own hand. In a note to the French edition, and in all subsequent editions incorporating these changes, he asked the readers to acquaint themselves with these additions because they "possessed scientific value independent of the original."[124]

Because our epoch has had concretely to face the problems posed only theoretically by Marx, we can see the reason why Marx built Volume II on what, in the 1870's was certainly a non-existent, fantastic society. Under such a society, he was saying, we would expect to see the following:

(1) *The worker will be paid at value. Well-intentioned* planners may, during the Depression, have wondered whether it wouldn't be possible to raise the standard of living of the workers —not of some Stakhanovites, but of the working class as a whole —if all capital were concentrated in the hands of the State and thus easily planned. But Russian totalitarianism is with us to puncture that grand illusion. For, the moment that working standards are raised, the cost of production of a commodity goes up above the cost of the surrounding world market and then the production inside the country is undersold by the product from a value-producing society, which means that the society cannot indefinitely continue. The jet plane would cost so much more to build that the competing countries on the world market would be able to defeat the particular country in the present form of capitalist competition, which is total war. It is not a question of simple competition or sale.[125] If the United States has the H-bomb and atomic energy and Automation, Russia had better discover them too, or be destroyed. She discovered these soon enough.

(2) *The means of production will far outdistance the means of consumption.* Because value production automatically limits the consumption goods of a community to the luxuries of the capitalist class plus the amount which the worker can buy when paid at value, and because the material form of production the world over shows that means of production outdistance means of consumption, Marx assumed the capitalist world as "one nation." It will be impossible, over a historic period, to avoid unemployment because the society will be straining every nerve to bring its plants to the level of the more advanced productive system. The only way "to stay in the race" is to pay the worker as little as possible and to have him produce as much as possible.

The fundamental error of those who cannot understand that a single capitalist society is governed by the same laws as a society composed of individual capitalists is that they simply will not understand that what happens in the market is merely the result and the consequence of the inherent difficulties in the process of production itself. Where Marx kept us in the process of production throughout Volume I, and there reached the ultimate limit of capitalist development into a closed, single capitalist company controlling everything, they seem to think that a single capitalist society will have a limitless market. The single capitalist —call him "Collective Leadership under Khrushchev, Inc.," if you will—will have, at a certain stage, a magnificent plant, completely automatized, or a jet bomber, but he cannot stop to raise the standard of the masses of workers. He may be able to avoid the more extreme forms of ordinary commercial crises, but even within the community itself he cannot escape the internal crisis of production. The Plan at no stage can stop to improve the conditions of the masses. Capital does not allow it. That is why Marx, throughout CAPITAL, insists that either you have the self-activity of the workers, the plan of *freely* associated labor, or you have the hierarchic structure of relations in the factory and the despotic Plan. *There is no in-between.*

The only possibility of avoiding capitalist crises is the abrogation of the law of value. That is to say, planning must be done according to the needs of the productive system as a *human* system. A system where human needs are *not* governed by the necessity to pay the laborer at *minimum* and to extract the *maximum* abstract labor for the purpose of keeping the productive system, as far as possible, within the lawless laws of the world market, dominated by the law of value.

It may seem that all this would not apply to a capitalist society of a "really" advanced stage of development, like the United States. If, for the sake of argument, we were to imagine the United States becoming a single capitalist society, even this, far from improving the conditions of the workers, would worsen them. It would then be a *given* capitalist society, which means the rest of the world market would exist. Thereupon, Europe and the Far East would probably combine against it, and the struggle for the capitalist world market would result in a war which would either end in (1) a single capitalist state; (2) socialism; or (3) the destruction of civilization altogether. Backward country or advanced, the absolute law of capitalism, as analyzed by Marx, would hold good even if all capital were concentrated in the hands of one single capitalist or one single capitalist corporation. What to Marx was theory is a most concrete problem now. Russia is proof of the fact that the logic and scope of Marxian theory are as integrally connected as are appearance and reality in life.

The "mystic" Hegel saw clearer the relationship of the dialectic to life than our present pragmatists who laugh at the dialectic and meet each fact of life as an "unforeseen" phenomenon. "Wherever there is movement, wherever there is life, wherever anything is carried into effect in the practical world, there Dialectic is at work. It is also the soul of all knowledge which is truly scientific."[126]

3) *The Breakdown of Capitalism: Crises, Human Freedom, and Volume III of CAPITAL*

> "At last we have arrived at the *forms of appearance* which serve as the *starting point* in the vulgar conception: ground rent, coming from the earth, profit (interest) from capital, wages from labor. . . . Finally, since these three (wages, ground rent, profit (interest)) constitute the respective sources of income of the three classes of landowners, capitalists, and wage laborers, we have in conclusion the *class struggle,* into which the movement of the whole *Scheisse* is resolved."—Marx to Engels[127]

Marxist textbooks, for generations, have repeated the following truisms: (1) Capitalism is a form of society in which the means of production and the land are the private property of the capitalists. (2) The worker is compelled to sell his labor power at the cost of his production and reproduction in order to be able to live. (3) The motive force of this mode of production is the desire of the capitalist for profit. This profit is gained in the following manner: capitalist production produces commodities; commodities are sold for money. The money contains what the capitalist spent plus a surplus, part of which is his profit.

In order that the society may be looked upon as capitalist, it seems essential to have this process of money in the pocket of the private capitalist; the buying of labor power and means of production; the production of commodities; the selling of the commodities on the market for more money; etc. All this is true, but it is not the whole truth. Marx did not have to spend forty years to prove that.

Marx's primary theory is a theory of what he first called "alienated labor" and then "abstract" or "value-producing" labor. He analyzed commodities and showed that the exchange of commodities is an exchange of certain quantities of labor. Commodities in general had been exchanged more or less sporadically for centuries before capitalism. Capitalism begins when the capacity to labor becomes a commodity. As we saw in Volume I, production becomes capitalist commodity production from the moment when the direct producer must "instead of a commodity, sell his own capacity to labor, as a commodity."[128] Hence, it is more correct to call the Marxist theory of capital not a labor theory of value, but a value theory of labor.

Marx repudiated entirely the idea that the sale and purchase of labor power is the essential mark of capitalist society. In Volume I he showed how this pertained only on the surface; that it was only "an apparent exchange. . . . The relation of exchange subsisting between the capitalist and the laborer becomes a mere semblance pertaining to the circulation, a mere form, foreign to the real nature of the transaction and only to mystify it. The ever-repeated purchase and sale of labor power is now mere form; what really takes place is this—the capitalist again and again appropriates without equivalent, a portion of the previously materialized labor of others and exchanges it for a greater quantity of living labor."[129]

In Volume II, he wrote: "The peculiar characteristic is not that the commodity, labor power, is saleable, but that labor power appears in the shape of a commodity." This perversity is due to the perverse nature of capitalism where dead labor dominates over living labor and where relations between men appear as if they were relations between things: "It is, however, quite characteristic of the bourgeois horizon, which is entirely bounded by the craze for making money, not to see in the character of the mode of production the basis of the corresponding mode of circulation, but vice versa."[180]

In Volume III he stated: "The way in which surplus value is transformed into profit via the rate of profit is but a continued development of the perversion of subject and object taking place in the process of production."[181]

And again: "We have the complete mystification of the capitalist mode of production, the transformation of social conditions into things, the indiscriminate amalgamation of the material conditions of production with their historical and social forms. It is an enchanted, perverted, topsy-turvy world, in which Mister Capital and Mistress Land carry on their goblin tricks as social characters and at the same time as mere things."[182]

Indeed he says these same things in a thousand different ways throughout his work. That is the content and form, the essence *and* the absolute of the whole analysis.

It is obvious from the very nomenclature that the primary feature of commodities in general is that they are sold on the market. It should be equally obvious that the fundamental feature of labor power as a commodity is *not* that it is bought or sold on the market, but the specific function it performs in the process of production, where it is *"a source not only of value, but of more value than it has itself."* This is the issue. This is the hub around which all Marxist economic theory—"production" (Volume I), "circulation" (Volume II), and "forms of the process as a whole" (Volume III)—revolves.

Marx develops his analysis of capitalism on different levels of abstraction and each level has its own dialectic. In Volume I, the categories which enabled us to comprehend the realities of production were: constant and variable capital (labor power).

In Volume II, where we are on the surface of society, the categories which disclose the inner mechanism are: *means of production and means of consumption.* In Volume III, it is the decline in the rate of profit, "the general contradiction of capitalistic production that reveals its law of motion and points to its collapse."

It took the crash of 1929 to open the skulls of the academic economists to Marx's analysis of the breakdown of capitalism. It then became a popular pastime to say that if Marx had only shed his "Hegelianism," taken off the "mysticism" with which he enveloped the concept of value, and begun instead with Volume III where he deals with "real life," that is to say the surface phenomena of competition, profit, rent, etc., his "prophecies" of Big Business and cyclical crises would have been easy to see and they would have learned "much" from him. Marx dealt with that type of argumentation a half century before. That is why he pointed out that: "The annual process of reproduction is easily understood so long as we keep in view merely the sum total of the year's production. But every single component of this product must be brought into the market as a commodity, and there the difficulty begins. The movement of the individual capital, and of the personal revenue, cross and intermingle and are lost in the general change of places, in the circulation of wealth and society; this dazes the sight and propounds very complicated problems for solution."[133] He not only pointed to the difficulty. We find that he warned against the easy way out, such as beginning with the surface phenomena of profit rather than the production reality of surplus value: "We shall show in Book III that the rate of profit is no mystery so soon as we know the laws of surplus value. If we reverse the process we cannot comprehend either the one or the other."[134]

The third volume, which presumably best meets the taste of the academic economists, analyzed life in the capitalist market as it really is. We learn that commodities sell, not at value, but at price of production; that surplus value is not an abstraction, congealed unpaid labor, but that its real form is threefold: (1) profit for the industrialist; (2) rent for the landlord; and (3) interest for the banker; that capital is not only a *social* relation of production, but that it has a *bodily* form of money-capital. Here we study the role of credit and even get some glimpses into swindling.

And what is the grand result of learning all the facts of life? How have they changed the laws that arise from the strict process of production which the academic economists call "abstract"? Not at all. *Not at all.* At the end of all these intricate transformations of surplus value into ground rent, interest and profit, as well as the conversion of values into prices, rate of surplus value into rate of profit, etc.—at the end of it all, Marx takes us back to that on which it is based: production of value and surplus value. He shows us that in the final analysis the sum of all prices is equal to the sum of all values. Where the worker has created nothing, the capitalist manipulator can get nothing. Profit, even as surplus value, comes not from "ownership" but from production. To get at the real cause of crises Marx makes an abstraction of "the bogus transactions and speculations which the credit system favors."[135]

Nothing fundamental has changed; nothing whatever. Labor power, which is the supreme commodity of capitalist production because *it* alone creates capital, is still a commodity, sold at value, and—still *in* the process of production and *not* in the process of exchange or the market—creates a greater value than it itself is.

Note the far-reaching insight of Marx into the doom *of value production out of its* own inherent laws of development: "In order to produce the same rate of profit, when the constant capital set in motion by one laborer increases ten-fold, the surplus labor time would have to increase ten-fold, and soon the total labor time, and finally the fully twenty-four hours a day would not suffice, even if wholly appropriated by capital." (Vol. III, p. 468)

Even the concept of a single capitalist society pales before the concept of appropriating the value of "fully twenty-four hours a day." Marx makes this extreme assumption because in no other way can he express the fundamental movement. What Marx is saying is that even if the worker learned to live on air and could work all twenty-four hours a day, this ever-expanding monster of machine production could not keep on expanding without collapsing, since *living labor* is the only source of this value and surplus value. Since that is exactly what is constantly being cut *relatively* to the ever greater machines that are being made and used, there just wouldn't be sufficient surplus value to keep the thing going.

"*The real barrier of capitalist production,*" Marx concludes, "*is capital itself.* It is the fact that capital and its self-expansion appear as the starting and closing point, as the motive and aim of production; that production is merely production for *capital,* and not vice versa, the means of production mere means for an ever expanding system of the life process for the benefit of the *society* of producers."[136] In opposition to this he points to the fact that "the realm of freedom does not commence until the point is passed where labor under the compulsion of necessity and external utility is required. In the very nature of things it lies beyond the sphere of material production in the strict meaning of the term."[137]

The constant revolutions in production, and the constant expansion of constant capital, writes Marx once again, necessitate, of course, an extension of the market. But as he has explained over and over again, both theoretically and practically, the enlargement of the market in a capitalist nation is limited by the fact that the worker is paid at value. This is the supreme manifestation of his simplifying assumption that the worker is paid at value. In Volume III, we see that this is the innermost cause of crisis— that in production, not in the market, labor creates a value greater than it is itself. The worker is a producer of overproduction. *It cannot be otherwise in a value-producing society,* where the means of consumption, being but a moment in the reproduction of labor power, *cannot be bigger than the needs of capital for labor power. That is the fatal defect of capitalist production. On the one hand, the capitalist must increase his market. On the other hand, it cannot be larger.*

The crisis that follows is not caused by a shortage in "effective demand." On the contrary, it is the crisis that causes a shortage in "effective demand." The worker employed yesterday is unemployed today. A crisis occurs not because there has been a scarcity of markets. As we saw in theory, and as 1929 showed in practice, the market is largest just before a crisis. *From the capitalist viewpoint,* however, there is occurring an unsatisfactory distribution of "income" between recipients of wages and those of surplus value or profits. The capitalist decreases his investments and the

THE LOGIC AND SCOPE OF *CAPITAL*

resulting *stagnation* of production *appears* as overproduction. Of course, there is a contradiction between production and consumption. Of course, there is "inability to sell." But the inability to sell manifests itself as such *because of the fundamental antecedent decline in the rate of profit, which has nothing whatever to do with inability to sell.*

Marx considered the theory of the declining rate of profit to be the *"pons asini"* of the whole political economy, that which divides one theoretic system from another. The classical political economists *felt* it, but they couldn't understand it, because they could not conceive that the capitalist system, which they considered not a historical, transitory system, but a permanent one, had something in its vitals that would doom it. When Marx showed that decline in the *rate* of profit was due to the fact of the relative ever-smaller use of living labor, which is the only source of surplus value, to ever-greater use of machines, the capitalist pointed instead to the mass of products and hence the *mass of profits*. They thought thereby to forget the fall of the *rate*. Even some Marxists considered that the tendency for the decline in the rate of profit had so·many counteracting tendencies in the mass of profits from mass production and in imperialist expansion that it was central to no one's, not even Lenin's, thinking before 1929. Only then people began to see that this was not theory but reality. They then begun to look for solutions everywhere *except in the reorganization of the process of production itself by the laborer himself.*

What Marx is describing, in his analysis of what he calls "the general contradiction of capitalism," is (1) the degradation of the worker to an appendage of a machine; (2) the constant growth of the unemployed army; and (3) capitalism's own downfall because of its inability to give greater employment to labor. Since labor power is the supreme commodity of capitalist production, the only source of its value and surplus value, capitalism's inability to reproduce it dooms capitalism itself. As we saw from the beginning, Marx's critique of capitalist society was based primarily on the perverse, inverted relation of dead to living labor at the point of production, and extended to the surface of society where the fetishism of commodities made the relations between

people assume "the fantastic form of the relations between things."
Now, in Volume III, he says the very existence of commodities,
and especially of commodities as products of capital, "implies the
externalization of the conditions of social production and the per-
sonification of the material foundation of production, which characterize the entire capitalist mode of production." Over and over
again, Marx categorically asserts that since *all* labor under capitalism is *forced labor,* Plan can be nothing but the organization of
production under the domination of the machine. As he told
Proudhon from the first, to try to bring order into the anarchy of
the market of a society based on the *factory* Plan, could only
mean subjecting society to "one single master." Marx warned
then: not to see the plan inherent in the activity of the revolutionary proletariat *must* force one to pose an *external* factor to do
the planning. He dismissed, with great contempt, Proudhon's
Plan to do away with exchange. In "Unravelling the Inner Contradiction," Marx shows that in capitalism's "disorder is its order."

Proudhon was neither the first nor the last of the Planners,
as our age knows much better than Marx's. Planning is not limited
to idealists. The *abstract* materialist who views technological development *outside* of the class relationship also slips back into
considering the *capitalistic* factors of production as mere factors
of any social form of production. That is why Marx created new
categories to describe *the manner in which* machines and labor
unite under a capitalistic economy. Marx developed his analysis
of capitalist production in opposition to all Planners—abstract materialist as well as idealist.

In Volume I of CAPITAL, the nature of the cooperative form
of the labor process is held out in sharp contrast to the hierarchic
structure of capitalist control. In Volume II, Marx isolates the
capitalist nation and analyses it as a *unit*: ". . . we must not
follow the manner copied by Proudhon from bourgeois economics,
which looks upon this matter as though a society with a capitalist
mode of production would lose its specific historical and economic
characteristics by being taken as a unit. Not at all. We have in
that case to deal with the aggregate capitalist."[138]

As we saw, the whole of Volume II is built, not on individual,
private capital, but on aggregate, national capital. In Volume III,

Marx returns to the creative plan of the workers as the plan "most adequate to their human nature and most worthy of it": "Just as the savage must wrestle with nature in order to satisfy his wants, in order to maintain his life and reproduce it, so civilized man has to do it, and he must do it in all forms of society and all possible modes of production. With his development the realm of natural necessity expands, because his wants increase; but at the same time the forces of production increase by which these wants are satisfied. The freedom in this field cannot consist of anything else but of the fact that socialized man, the associated producers, regulate their interchange with nature rationally, bring it under their common control, instead of being ruled by it as by some blind power; that they accomplish their task with the least expenditure of energy under conditions most adequate to their human nature and most worthy of it. But it always remains a realm of necessity.

"Beyond it begins that development of human power which is its own end, the true realm of freedom, which, however, can flourish only upon the realm of necessity as its basis. The shortening of the working day is its fundamental premise."[139]

Thus we see that it isn't only the young Marx but the mature Marx to whom the creative role of labor is the key to all else. It isn't only that this creative plan of the workers, in opposition to the authoritarian Plan of the capitalist, permeates all three volumes of CAPITAL. It is that the actual necessity of revolt will arise out of the fact that capitalism, as conditions, activity, and purpose, is destroying society. The only force which can overcome this necessity therefore is a freedom which in itself and for itself inseparably combines objective conditions, subjective activity and purpose. In the *Grundrisse* Marx said that, once the productive process "is stripped of its antagonistic form," "the measure of wealth will then no longer be labor time, but leisure time."[140] The free time liberated from capitalist exploitation would be for the free development of the *individual's powers*. The conception of freedom that the young Marx had when he broke from bourgeois society as a revolutionary Hegelian remained with him throughout his life.

Essentially Marx said what he wanted to say. This is true not only of Volumes II and III, which Engels edited with scrupulous care and presented exactly as Marx had written, but even Book IV, with the structure of which Karl Kautsky did tamper when he published it as *Theories of Surplus Value*. The reason is that Volume I, published by Marx is not only, as he put it, a whole in itself. *It is the whole.*

He reorganized[141] the last part, "Accumulation of Capital," in order to show (1) *where* Volumes II and III (including *Theories of Surplus Value* as Book IV of Volume III) belong logically; (2) *how* they are dialectically connected with Volume I; and (3) *what* is the law of motion of capitalism in general and the dialectic of his analysis in particular. The "Historical Tendency of Capitalist Accumulation" thus ends with the two absolute opposites—capital accumulation and the revolt of the workers headed for a clash and at the same time going in opposite directions—the first to its collapse, the second creating "the new passions and forces" for reconstructing society on new, socialist-humanist beginnings.

There are theoreticians who are willing to say that the analysis holds for Russia, but not in the exceptional soil of America. If it wasn't the American frontier that made America different, it was the American pragmatic character; and if not that, it is that the American workers "aren't class conscious." Be that as it may, the economists now do give Marx credit for understanding "history." Some even admit that economic theory has indeed been running a losing race with history, except in the case of Marx. One has even gone so far as to "admire" Marx for his "idea of theory" and his ability to transform historic narrative into "historic *raisonne*."[142] But none have the slightest conception that Marx's "idea of theory" is as profound as it is *only because* he had broken with the bourgeois conception of theory and placed the worker in the center of *all* his thinking. *There is no other source for social theory.*

It isn't that Marx "glorified" workers. It is that he knew what is their role in production. Just as history has not discharged theory from its mission of criticizing *existing* society, so the workers, on whose back all the exploitation occurs *must*—to straighten up to the height of men—throw all this off their backs and *therefore* can criticize it and overcome it and see ahead.

It isn't that Marx vilified capitalists and their ideologists. It is that he knew *their* role in production and how limited, therefore, their outlook. Because they were satisfied, they couldn't grasp all of reality, and *therefore* their ideology was false.

Marx, when he began, *didn't* know all the implications of his materialistic conception of history. Thus, although he saw the mode of production as determinant for ideology, he thought all that needs to be done to demonstrate the bankruptcy of bourgeois thought is to show that the bourgeoisie can no longer be scientific and that with the development of the class struggle their economic science has become "vulgar" and their ideologists "prize fighters." He, on the other hand, would show the decline, and then the workers as changing the world which had long had its interpreters. It was only in the 1860's, that he changed the very structure of CAPITAL and placed theories at the end of all volumes. As we saw, it was in that period that he gave the explanation that what was written first was put last because that is the ordinary way a theoretical work develops. That is to say, as an intellectual he needed to clear his own mind first. Only then comes the creative part with the workers themselves not only as activists but as thinkers. Thus, in the same way in which the "Primitive Accumulation of Capital," was placed at the *end* of Volume I, so the "History of Theory" (or, *Theories of Surplus Value*, as Kautsky renamed it) was put at the *end* of Volume III, that is to say, at the end of the entire work.

This is the outline of work as Marx set it down when Volume I was going to press:

Book I: Process of Production

Book II: Process of Circulation (both of these books were intended as Volume I, but only Book I was published by Marx during his lifetime)

Book III: Forms of the Process as a Whole

Book IV: History of Theory

The *entire* work had been completed when the first Volume went to press. After the second edition of CAPITAL, Volume I, Marx reworked Volume II. It is the last piece of work we have from his pen. If there is any truth at all to the incomplete state in which Volumes II and III were published, it is the exact opposite of what is implied by those who are so anxious to stress the incomplete state of the manuscripts. Marx himself tells us how he intended to change the manuscripts, or rather the extent to which he would have changed them, had he lived to edit them himself. He says, in his letter to Danielson, the Russian translator of Volume I, not to wait for Volume II:[143] *"First of all* I would under no circumstances consent to publish the second volume before the present English industrial crisis has reached its limit . . . it is necessary scrupulously to follow the present development of events to their full maturity before you are in a position to utilize' these facts 'productively,' I mean 'theoretically'. . . .

"Meanwhile—strikes and disturbances everywhere.

"*Secondly* a tremendous mass of material received by me not only from *Russia* but also from the *United States,* etc., gives me a pleasant excuse to continue research instead of definitively working over for publication.

"The United States at present have overtaken England in the rapidity of economical progress, though they lag behind in the extent of acquired wealth; but at the same time the masses are quicker and have greater political means in their hands to resent the form of a progress accomplished at their expense. I need not prolong the antitheses."

It is clear that Russia and America were to play the role in Volumes II and III that England played in Volume I. Lenin filled it out for Russia. In their attitude to Automation, the American workers are concretizing this for America.

Marx removed the question of value from a dispute among intellectuals and transformed it into a question of the struggle of the proletariat for a new society. The material and the ideal were never too far apart.[144] He best summarized his own social vision when he defined the new social order as a society in which "the free development of each is the condition for the free development of all," and that never again would the rights of the State be counterposed to that of the individual. Human freedom is the principle toward which he worked and his philosophy can be most fittingly called a *New Humanism.*

There was no difference between Marx the Hegelian and Marx the revolutionary, nor between Marx the theoretician and

Marx the practical organizer. He finished CAPITAL and turned to the Paris Commune not merely as "activist" and "materialist" but as *idealist*. As we saw, he himself summed up most profoundly the fact that the ideal is never far from the real when he wrote that the Communards "have no ideals to realize but to set free the elements of the new society."

ORGANIZATIONAL INTERLUDE

CHAPTER NINE

THE SECOND INTERNATIONAL, 1889 TO 1914

> "Kant's *results* are made the immediate beginning of these philosophies, so that the preceding exposition, from which these results are derived, and which is philosophic cognition, is cut away beforehand. Thus the Kantian philosophy becomes a pillow for intellectual sloth, which soothes itself with the idea that everything has already been proved and done with."—Hegel[145]

The death of the First International came soon after the defeat of the Paris Commune. The years of the "Great Depression" that set in seemed to spell the doom of all working class organizations. In America, for instance, the severe 1873 crisis signified the collapse of the Eight-Hour Leagues. In the 1880's, however, the working class in Europe and America began to act in an organized manner on both the economic and political fronts. At its St. Louis Congress in December, 1888, the A. F. of L. decided to launch a campaign for simultaneous strikes to take place all over the country on May 1, 1890. The plan was to strike a single industry, with workers in all other industries giving it financial aid until the struggle was won. Each industry would have its turn until the eight-hour day was won for all. Delegations went abroad to see what could be done to make this an international struggle.

Those American beginnings of the formation of the Second International have been forgotten[146] not only because the A. F. of L. later became the advocate of "business unionism" rather than international class struggle. When, in 1905, the very militant Industrial Workers of the World was organized it hardly got any more attention from the Second International. This happened not alone to America, where there was no established Marxist party. The Russian Social Democracy, which adhered fully to the International's program, played a completely insignificant role. It was small. When the great 1905 Revolution broke out and involved hundreds of thousands it was not on the agenda as a separate point. It had happened between Congresses. In a word, the Second International was from the beginning to the end a West European organization. It was headed by the German Social Democracy, which was the largest political mass organization of workers in the world. Bigness counted.

The Second International was established on July 14, 1889, on the occasion of the One Hundredth Anniversary of the fall of the Bastille which had opened the great French Revolution. For a quarter of a century the Second International was to experience unprecedented growth, be respected as a powerful organization and stand for established Marxism. Suddenly, and against the basis of its very existence as an opponent of capitalism, it collapsed in the face of Western Civilization's plunge into the chaos of the first World War.

Its voting of war credits certainly was a total change of front from its previous anti-militarist and anti-war manifestoes. Yet the breakup of the Second International came as the logical conclusion to strong objective forces.

With hindsight, and much systematic study of the new stage of capitalistic development, Lenin traced the double transformation into opposites: (1) of competition into monopoly; and (2) of a *stratum* of the working-class into the aristocrats of labor who gained by the super-profits of imperialism.[147] We will deal with this in Part IV, "The Great Divide in Marxism." The point here is that the slow poisoning of Marxism, *long before* the collapse, is to this day overlooked by people claiming to be Marxists. Karl Kautsky's works, written when he was a "good revolutionary theoretician," are used as textbooks by so-called revolutionary theoreticians as well as by reformists to this day. The *methodology* of presenting the *results* of Marx's studies as if they were something to be learned by rote, and disregarding the *process,* the relationship of theory to history, past and present, in the development of Marxism, still permeates what is left of the Marxist movement.[148] Yet without the relationship of theory to actuality Marxism is meaningless. Learning by rote becomes, to use a Hegelian expression, "a pillow for intellectual sloth." Nowhere is that intellectual sloth more deep than among self-avowed Marxist theoreticians. The truth is that what has happened to the Second International was only the first link in a continuous chain that is by no means limited to reformists and betrayers. It is time, therefore, to begin at the beginning, even though the "Organizational Interlude" must of necessity be sketchy.

Engels was still alive when the Second International was founded, and at its birth, predicted its end. "You (Karl Kautsky) put abstract political questions in the foreground and hide thereby the most immediate concrete questions, the questions which the first great events, the first political crisis itself places on the order of the day."[149] This was true not only politically of the *Erfurt Program* but theoretically. In his correspondence with Kautsky on his books, the *Economic Doctrines of Karl Marx,* and on the *Erfurt Program,* Engels put his finger on the Achilles' heel. He wrote in his criticism of Kautsky's identification of planlessness with capitalism: "When we go over to trusts which monopolize and rule over whole branches of industry, then not only private production but also planlessness ceases." There, in a nutshell, was the theory that dominated the Second International, revolutionary and reformist alike, throughout the span of its life. Engels could do no more than criticize and wait for events to bear out his criticism. Meanwhile, what was on the order of the day was the organization of the working-class—trade union organization and political organization. In this, the German Social Democracy could show enough gains to impress Engels in his last days.

1) Achievements of the Second International: Trade Union and Political Organization of the Proletariat

The German Social Democracy was the greatest party of the Second International, both numerically and in theoretical stature. It was the first modern mass organization in the world. It was founded in 1875, led by Wilhelm Liebknecht and August Bebel in a merger between the Lassalleans and the Marxists.[150] Karl Kautsky became its outstanding theoretician. In 1887, two years before the formation of the Second International, Kautsky published the *Economic Doctrines of Karl Marx*, which became the standard popularization of Marxism. If the reduction of Marx's "economic principles" to a catechism was done without any of the underlying philosophic concepts, it made up for this lack in sufficient lip service to "the dialectic." The Second International became the titular heirs of the Marx-Engels writings. They never published Marx's *Economic-Philosophic Manuscripts*. But Kautsky's heavy standardization of Marxism became the foundation for all sorts of "concrete studies" on slums, juvenile delinquency, and other "crimes of capitalism." In 1892, Kautsky wrote the *Erfurt Program*, and this also became the model for all Social Democratic Parties on the political, programmatic front.

The key word, in theory as well as in practice, was: Organization, organization, organization. It lived entirely in the realm of the difference between immediate demands and the ultimate goals of socialism. The ultimate goals of socialism could wait. Meanwhile, there was the "practical" struggle and in that they could show phenomenal gains.

During the twelve years of their existence, the German Social Democracy had to work under the handicap of Bismarck's Anti-Socialist Laws. Their meetings and publications were prohibited. Their leaders were harried and often thrown into jail. The publications were published abroad and smuggled into Germany. Bismarck tried to win the workers away from socialism by some welfare-state features such as old-age and sickness insurance. The workers, on the other hand, were determined to build up their own organizations with their own aims and methods. They struggled for a shorter workday and better wages; for popular education and freedom for the press. They kept growing despite the persecutions. By 1890, when the Anti-Socialist Laws expired, it was the Iron Chancellor who had to resign. In the very first free election, the German Social Democracy received 1,427,000 votes, or fully twenty per cent of the vote. By 1903, twenty-five per cent of the German population voted Socialist and sent eighty-one Social-Democratic deputies to the Reichstag (Parliament). By 1914 the Party had a million members and another three million trade union members were under its control.

This was indeed the most elaborately organized socialist movement the world had ever seen, not alone in its mass political party and trade union organizations, but in cooperatives, among the youth, among women. They published an impressive array of newspapers, journals, books, and pamphlets. They were a world unto themselves, even having "socialist" rituals for births, weddings, funerals, as well as sponsoring organized sport, travel, recreation. They began to believe that their organized strength, in and of itself, would make capitalistic war impossible, and would assure Social-Democratic power. When capitalism "inevitably" and "automatically" fell, they fully expected their ruling cadre to be ready to replace the capitalist managers who were "mismanaging" the productive forces and embarking upon colonialism and burdening the population with military expenditures.

This belief in organizational strength, which would "automatically" insure the world against war, became characteristic not alone of the German Social Democracy, but of the whole International. Keir Hardie, for example, the founder of the Independent Labor Party of Britain, and a left winger at all the sessions discussing militarism, stated: "A strike of British coal miners would suffice by itself to bring warlike activities to a stand." The Austrian, Adler, spoke of how the "crime of war" would "automatically" bring the downfall of capitalism. No words were more popular in the Second International's lexicon than "inevitable" and "automatic." All this was possible because of organization, organization, organization.

No word was used with greater contempt than "unorganized."

As one German study[151] put it, "the unorganized worker became a low species of human."

Monopoly was "organized capitalism" and looked upon as "the necessary stage to socialism." They had contempt not alone for small scale enterprisers but for the great mass of peasantry, and not only for the artisans but for the great mass of unorganized workers. Even "colonialism," which was fought officially, was not looked upon with such revulsion as anything or anybody that was "unorganized." The conception seemed to be: the trade unions would organize the proletariat on the economic field; the Party would organize it on the political field; and the youth would be organized on an anti-militaristic basis.[152] Then, when they had won sufficient votes, the world could be theirs.

At the highest point of the International's development, in 1907, the Congress voted for the anti-war amendment of Luxemburg-Lenin. Yet it is at this high point that we can discern the beginning of the end of the International. This Congress of 1907 was the first to take place after the 1905 Russian Revolution. That great event, however, was not on its agenda, much less did it make a point of departure for theory.

The left revolutionaries (Lenin, Luxemburg, Trotsky) who did make this event a new departure for their theory did not ask the Congress to do the same. None challenged the *West European* character of the international gathering at a time when the Russian working-class had "stormed the heavens." None asked that the point be put on the agenda. None challenged the dominance of the German leadership in theory as well as in practice. Luxemburg, Lenin, and Trotsky[153] differed quite fundamentally among themselves. Their failure to draw a sharp line between themselves and other political tendencies was, however, not due to their differences. They were all more conscious of the similarity of views *with* those of the International than of the dissimilarity.

The spirit of 1905 entered the Congress only insofar as it was an outgrowth of the Russo-Japanese war. Luxemburg and Lenin moved an amendment to the anti-war resolution to the following effect: (1) that they were duty-bound to do everything to prevent war by all means; and (2) in case of war "to intervene in order to bring it promptly to an end, and with all their strength to make use of the economic and political crisis created by the war to stir up the deepest strata of the people and precipitate the fall of capitalist domination." That was general enough to gain unanimous acceptance.

There is no such thing as Marxist theory that does not link the *specific* stage of workers' *revolt* to the *specific* stage of capitalist development. The 1905 Revolution gave birth to an unheard-of new form of workers' organization called the Soviet (Council). If such a new phenomenon was not even put on the agenda it could mean only one thing—the theoreticians were not receiving the impulses from these deepest layers of the revolutionary proletariat. The whole concept of theory as Marx *lived* it flowed from the proletariat as its source. The *concrete* struggles of the workers in his day produced the break in Marx's concept of theory. It isn't that intellectuals must work out "ideas." But, as we saw, the actions of the workers created the conditions for Marx to work out theory. No such thing happened as a result of the 1905 Revolution. 1905 did not do for the theoreticians of the Second International what 1861-71 did for Marx's theory. In that could be seen the fact that the Second International *as an organization* was beginning to go off the Marxist rails. Despite their adherence to Marxist "language," *there was no organization of Marxist thought.*

2) The Beginning of the End of the Second International: New Form of Workers' Organization: the Soviet

The very first Soviet in Russia seems to have arisen in May during a general strike in Ivanovo-Voznesensk, the great textile center two hundred miles south of Moscow. It was made up of workers' delegates from factories and similar informal groups, drawn from all types of industry. None of the socialist underground groups paid any attention to it. Trotsky, who was soon to head the most famous of these Soviets, the St. Petersburg Soviet, was then in Finland. He was busy writing about the possible development of the Russian revolution, and his theory of permanent revolution which he then elaborated certainly paved the way for his tremendous activity later. But the Soviet, as the specific form of workers' rule that was so totally new, did not fructify that theory.

In June, after the Cossacks fired on a workers' demonstration in Lodz, Poland, and put down an attempted insurrection, the great strikes spread to Odessa and the enlisted sailors aboard the battleship *Potemkin* mutinied. In August, there was a general strike in Warsaw where martial law was proclaimed. In that same month, there was a printers' strike in Moscow, which spread to the railways and postal workers. It was October before the strike movement spread to St. Petersburg, where a Soviet of Workers' Deputies was formed to direct and coordinate the strikes. It was this Soviet which Trotsky came to head. But Trotsky joined it; he did not create it. The workers created it. The workers went searching for socialist organizations with which to collaborate.

The strike *began* with the printers' demand for shorter hours and higher wages. The strike spread. The nucleus of the Soviet was formed by fifty printing shops which elected delegates and instructed them to form a council. They were soon joined by other trades. This was the first elective body of the heretofore disfranchised Russian working class and it immediately assumed an authority which overshadowed the centuries-old autocratic Tsarist regime. In fact, the Tsar seriously considered fleeing. The power and authority and political character of this new council came from the fact that the deputies represented no fewer than 200,000 workers. That is to say, fifty per cent of all workers in the capital had taken part in the elections. After further elections, the number of deputies grew to 560 and the Soviet decided to publish its own paper, *Izvestia*.

The workers demanded constitutional freedom as well as better wages and shorter hours. It was clear that the Soviet of Workers' Deputies was something never before seen in Russian history; and it was on a higher historic scale than the Paris Commune. No one then knew it was the dress rehearsal for 1917. It was considered a form of trade union federation.

The general strike had reached its peak in October. The principal slogan was for the eight hour day and for the convocation of a Constituent Assembly. The workers were joined by the sailors. *Kronstadt* mutinied. On October 17th, the Tsar was sufficiently shaken to issue a Manifesto promising a constitution, civil liberties, and universal suffrage. But, while the liberal Prime Minister, Count

Witte, composed that Manifesto, General Trepov gave police orders to "spare no bullets." It was then that Trotsky addressed the crowds: "Citizens, now that we have put our foot on the neck of the ruling clique, they promise us freedom. . . . Is a promise of freedom the same as freedom? Our strength is in ourselves."

The workers, through the Soviet, had indeed instituted freedom of the press by requisitioning printing offices to print their own papers and those of the Socialist parties and groups. They acted as if indeed they were an alternative government. They issued permits for indispensible work to be done; they countersigned municipal orders and maintained their own discipline. The Soviet asked the workers to enforce the eight-hour day on their ships. It was strong enough to prevent the summary execution of leaders of the *Kronstadt* mutiny and, before that, to secure amnesty for many political prisoners who were simply released from jail. Only in mid-December did the Autocracy dare to hit back and arrest the Executives of the St. Petersburg Soviet.

The St. Petersburg Soviet lasted fifty days. During that time it (1) took charge of the general political strike; (2) proclaimed freedom of the press; (3) proclaimed the eight-hour day and called upon the workers to institute it by refusing to work more; (4) organized the November strike in defense of the arrested *Kronstadt* sailors and of revolutionary Poland where martial law had been declared; (5) assisted in the creation of trade unions and took the initiative in organizing and supporting the unemployed; (6) issued the Finance Manifesto in which it called upon the population not to pay taxes; (7) called for a Constituent Assembly and autonomy for national minorities, as well as a peoples' militia instead of the standing army. In the general tide of revolution it was joined by waves of liberation movements of oppressed nationalities.

It was the only democracy and civilization that Russia had ever known. The brutality and ferocity with which it was put down was because it had, in such a short time, done so much to undermine the hated Tsarist regime. Indeed, when the members of the St. Petersburg Soviet were arrested in mid-December, the Moscow Soviet first reached its climax. It called for a general strike and the Socialists[154] were determined to make this the actual beginning of an insurrection. Barricades were erected and pitched battles took place in the streets. The whole city of Moscow was in the hands of revolutionaries for several days before it was put down in blood.

There are philistines who are now busy explaining the definition of the word "Soviet," or "Council," after which they go on to draw the conclusion that "if" the Russian workers had had unions (and thus a Labor and Trades Council) the word "Soviet" would never have been charged with all the political and revolutionary overtones. They forget only one thing—the stubborn facts: (1) No "vanguard groupings" "invented" these councils nor embellished them with revolutionary phraseology. Quite the contrary. The Socialist underground was caught completely by surprise. The Bolsheviks were suspicious of these new forms of organizations as rivals to their Marxist party. (2) These councils were spontaneous outbursts of the broad masses of people. No one had told the workers to build such organizations. No one had seen the role they would play. The Mensheviks may have joined them faster than the Bolsheviks, but *they joined what had already been created spontaneously by the proletariat.* (3) The Soviets of Workers' Deputies were *not* just a "name" for a Labor or Trades Council, though they had grown out of the need to coordinate the strikes that spread all over Russia toward the end of the Russo-Japanese war. The revolutionary "overtones" expressed the natural revolutionary content that dared not only to challenge the Tsarist Autocracy, but to act as if they were indeed an alternative government. Years later Lenin first summed up the significance of the Soviets:

"These organs were created exclusively by the *revolutionary* strata of the population, without laws or norms, in an entirely revolutionary manner, as the product of the inborn creativeness of the people, which had freed itself or was freeing itself from the old police shackles. These were precisely organs of *power*, notwithstanding their embryonic, spontaneous, informal and diffuse character as regards composition and method of functioning. . . .[155]

"They (philistines) shout about the disappearance of sense and reason, when the picking to pieces of parliamentary bills by all sorts of bureaucrats and liberal 'penny-a-liners' give way to a period of direct political activity of the 'common people' who in their simple way directly and immediately destroy the organs of oppression of the people, seize power, appropriate for themselves what was considered to be the property of all sorts of plunderers of the people—in a word, precisely when the sense and reason of millions of downtrodden people is awakening, not only for reading books, but for action, for living human action, for historical creativeness."[156]

But this "sense and reason of millions of downtrodden people" not only was no part of the theory of philistines; it was no part of the theory of the German Social Democracy.

The 1905 Revolution had the "misfortune" of having taken place between Congresses. "Therefore" it was not germane to the agenda of 1907. No one gave any serious consideration to the phenomenon of the soviet. Luxemburg spoke of the general strike and tried to build her theory on that phenomenon. Lenin did no more than join Luxemburg in an amendment to the anti-war Resolution.

Revolutionary theory is a hard taskmaster. It does not evolve out of good will. It has no source but that of the proletariat in revolt—the ever deeper and lower layers of the proletariat that remain true to its revolutionary being. "The proletariat is revolutionary or it is nothing," said Marx to Lassalle. The theoretician who is not permeated with this concept to the very marrow of his being is fatally drawn to the "solution" posed by the radical intellectual which, in essence, is the *bourgeois* solution. Lassalle was neither the first nor the last of the Marxists who was willing to settle for much less than this concept. When the Second International did not steep itself in the new impulses from the Russian working class revolt, it of necessity left itself open to impulses from the opposing force—capitalist production. That was so in 1907. It was so in 1914. Indeed, the proof is not limited to the phenomenon of betrayal but includes the revolutionary Bukharin who wanted to blame the working class *as a class* for that betrayal. He thus anticipated the next stage of development, the development of bureaucracy *after* the Revolution, 1917-23. For the period after Lenin's death Trotskyism is the phenomenon to watch. Trotsky was compelled to create a forced identification between workers' state and statified property that did violence to the very concept of socialism. Abstractions have ever been the refuge of ultra-leftists as for idealists. As a result, they can no more penetrate the dialectic in *action* than they can penetrate it *in thought*. Instead, these theoreticians create "new Notions" out of their own brain waves, freed from the dialectic of the objective movement and subjective proletarian aspirations. (We will return to this subject later.)

3) The End of the Second International: New Stage of Capitalist Production and Stratification of the Proletariat

The twentieth century opened with the first billion dollar trust (United States Steel). The age of steel followed the age of steam. Heavy industry preponderated over light industry. Large-scale production began to take on new forms: cartels and trusts. Free competition was being transformed into its opposite, monopoly. With cartels and trusts came imperialism; and with imperialist superprofits a stratification took place in the working class itself, between the aristocrats of labor (the craftsmen) and the great mass of poorly paid and unorganized workers.

Once the Second International cut itself off from the new impulses arising from the year 1905—not alone the Russian Revolution but the I. W. W., not alone the "advanced" countries but backward Africa and the Zulu Rebellion—whose impulses could they attune to but those of the aristocrats of labor?

No one was in the least mistaken about the rapid transformation of the American Federation of Labor from a militant fighting organization to undiluted "business unionism." *Everyone, including Lenin,* was led astray when the same happened to the German unions "under Socialist influence" because the manifestoes and pronunciamentos kept coming in full force and in "traditional" language. In truth, it was not the German Social Democracy that "set the line" which permeated them through and through, but the labor aristocracy. It could not have been otherwise since only the latter had an *objective* base. The upper stratum of the working class began to have a stake in the super-profits of German imperialism.

Where Marx spoke about the "bourgeoisification" of part of the British proletariat and the need to go to "lower and deeper" layers of the working class, the leaders of the Second International said: "Since" there is only one proletariat, "therefore" there must be only one Social Democracy in each country. Where Marx wrote, "the proletariat is revolutionary or it is nothing," Bernstein wrote that to him "the movement," (that is to say, the Socialist *Party*,) was everything, "socialism nothing."

That was a harsh statement, and "revisionist." Nevertheless it characterized not only the Revisionists, who were a minority, but "the orthodox" Marxists who were in the majority. Indeed, the German Social Democracy was never able to make as sharp a line against the right as against the ultra-left. Anarchists were expelled in 1896; not only were the Revisionists not expelled, but the "censure" of them meant nothing since they were allowed to remain as authoritative leaders. They corrupted the whole Party.[157] When Bernstein criticized and revised Marx's analysis of the law of motion of capitalist society, he was only the open example of what was corrupting the inner core of the German Social Democracy in its adaptation to the capitalist milieu.

Not only Bernstein, but the orthodox theoreticians—from Kautsky, who wrote "pure" theory, to Hilferding, who made the concrete study, *Finance Capital*—gave expression precisely to this new stratification in the working class. This passed for "Marxist theory." Yet Rudolf Hilferding's, *Finance Capital*, is hardly distinguishable from the liberal study of *Imperialism* by Hobson. They are equally pedantic and filled with statistics. Hobson's book is a pioneer work in its field. It was written in 1902. Hilferding's, written in 1910, is a follow-up, with "Socialist conclusions" tacked on. Hilferding is "for" the dictatorship of the proletariat. *But the proletariat in both studies is just an inert mass*. Indeed, Hilferding's book describes monopolistic control as if it overcame anarchy instead of deepening the contradictions of *both* "control" *and* "anarchy of the market." His theoretical conceptions are of a smooth, well-oiled mechanism of events. Contradiction has been eliminated. As monopoly capitalism brought "order" into the national market, he argues, so the workers will "take over" and bring order out of the anarchy of the international market.

All, in fact, would be *organized*. The unions would manage industry while the political party would take over the State apparatus. There is no longer any sense of breaking the chains of the ubiquitous capitalist machine, nor is there the faintest glimmer of the idea that "the dictatorship of the proletariat" or "the workers organized as the ruling class" means the total reorganization of the relations of men at the point of production *by the men themselves*. The underlying assumption seems to be that a ruling cadre—the labor organizers—would replace the financial oligarchy and do on an international scale what the bourgeoisie did only on the national level.

Missing from their picture of organized capitalism and no "great wars" was the dialectic of the minor "incidents," from the imperialistic carving up of Africa to the Balkan cauldron. They were blind to the inner necessity and drive toward imperialist expansion, and the irreconcilable breakdown of Western Civilization.

It could not have been otherwise for what was missing from the "trustified" concept of "socialization of production" was the *fragmentation* of the worker to a cog in a machine, the actuality of capitalist progress as *dehumanization*. The German Social Democracy had become part of the very organism of "progressive capitalism" and was bound to fall with it.

PART IV

WORLD WAR I AND THE GREAT DIVIDE IN MARXISM

CHAPTER TEN

THE COLLAPSE OF THE SECOND
INTERNATIONAL AND THE BREAK
IN LENIN'S THOUGHT

The holocaust of World War I, erupting after a century
of near peace and general optimism, shook the world to its
foundations. It brought about the fall of the world Socialist organization known as the Second International. The German So-
cial-Democracy had voted war credits to the Kaiser. So incredible
did this appear, so completely unexpected, that the *Vorwärts,* which
announced this fact, was thought by Lenin to be a forgery of the
German Imperial Office. When it was proved to be true, the
theoretical ground on which he had stood, and which he had
thought so impregnable, gave way under him.

Prior to August 1914, all Marxists agreed that material conditions create the basis for the creation of a new society; that
the more advanced the material conditions, the better prepared
the proletariat would be for taking power. Now, these same mass
labor parties—in the most advanced countries, where technology
was most fully developed and the proletariat most highly organized—took an action which hurled masses of workers across
national boundaries to slaughter each other "in defense of the Fa-
therland." Germany was only the first. The Marxists of the other
warring European countries soon followed suit. The German
Social Democracy was not an organization of bourgeois liberals
or of deviating reformists. It was, in the main, an organization of
avowed revolutionary Marxists. Before the outbreak of war, they
had taken an unambiguous stand against any imperialist war

that might break out. The war no sooner broke out than they were part of that mobilization for destruction. *Why?* They betrayed, yes, but betrayal wasn't merely "selling out." What were the *objective* causes for such total *ideological* collapse? The fact was overwhelming, totally unforeseen, incontrovertible. Confronted with the appearance of counter-revolution *within* the revolutionary movement, Lenin was driven to search for a philosophy that would reconstitute his own reason.

He began reading Hegel's *Science of Logic*. It formed the philosophic foundation for the great divide in Marxism.[158] His *Philosophic Notebooks* show how completely he reorganized his conception of the relationship between the materialistic or economic forces, and the human, subjective forces, the relationship between science and human activity.

1) Lenin and the Dialectic: A Mind in Action

> "All revolutions, in the sciences no less than in general history, originate only in this, that the spirit of man, for the understanding and comprehension of himself, for the possessing of himself, has now altered his categories, uniting himself in a truer, deeper, more intrinsic relation with himself."—Hegel

Krupskaya, Lenin's wife and closest collaborator, in her *Memories of Lenin*, tells us that Lenin began his study of Hegel for the "Essay on Marxism," commissioned by the *Encyclopaedia Granat*. He thereupon placed the philosophical question in the forefront, as is evident from the first section of the essay. She adds: "This was not the usual way of presenting Marx's teaching."

This is true. Scores of "popularizations" of Marxian economics had been written. Lenin's *Essay* is the first, since the death of Marx and Engels, to show the primacy of a philosophical approach. There is no doubt that as soon as Lenin opened the *Science of Logic*, he grasped the importance of dialectics, the *movement* of thought:

"Movement and self-movement (this NB! independent, spontaneous internally necessary movement), 'change,' 'movement and life,' 'the principle of every self-movement,' 'impulse' to 'movement' and to 'activity'—opposite of 'dead-being'—Who would believe that this is the core of 'Hegelianism,' of abstract and abstruse (difficult, absurd?) Hegelianism? We must disclose this core, grasp it, save, shell it out, purify it—which is precisely what Marx and Engels have done."[159]

When Lenin *began* his study of Hegel, as his *Philosophic Notebooks* show, he still felt compelled to emphasize that he is reading Hegel materialistically, instead of taking that for granted, and going on to what was *new*. By the *end* of the Hegelian studies, he wrote:

"Intelligent idealism is nearer to intelligent materialism than is stupid materialism.

"Dialectic idealism instead of intelligent; metaphysical, undeveloped, dead, vulgar, stationary instead of stupid."

With his characteristic precision, Lenin himself tells when he first fully grasped the dialectic. He wrote the *Essay on Marxism* between July, and November, 1914, the period when he began his study of the "Larger Logic." On January 4, 1915, having already forwarded the *Essay* to the *Encyclopaedia Granat,* he wrote: "By the way, will there not still be time for certain corrections in the section on dialectics? Perhaps you will be good enough to write and say when exactly it is to go to the printers and what the last date is for receiving corrections. I have been studying this question of dialectics for the last month and a half and I think I could add something to it if there was time . . ."

Six weeks. That is the time it took him to reach the book on "Subjectivity," in the "Doctrine of the Notion." The *Notebooks* carry the date, December 17, 1914. It is under the section on "Syllogisms," where Hegel destroys the opposition between subjectivity and objectivity, that Lenin bursts forth with the aphorisms that reveal how decisive was his break with *his own philosophic past.*

Heretofore, to Lenin, as to everybody else in the Second International, the Hegelian dialectic had been important mainly as a reference point in internal polemics. If an opponent was

obscure, he was accused of dialectical sophistry and reminded that
Marx had turned Hegel around and stood him right side up. Reformist and evolutionary theorists of socialist development were
fought by citing Hegel's "dialectic." It was generally agreed that
Hegel stood for development and revolution, rather than standing
still and evolution. The conception of contradiction was that of
two units existing *alongside of* one another. The conception of opposition had not gone beyond Kant's dualism—as if Hegel had never
destroyed it with the conception that every single thing is itself
a contradiction, is the basis of all movement. Hence, that all
movement is self-movement.

Having broken with this philosophic past, Lenin now moved
boldly to sum up the essence of the dialectic: "Briefly, the dialectic
can be defined as the doctrine of the unity of opposites. Thereby
is the kernel of the dialectic grasped, but that demands explanation and development."

For the first time he was no longer satisfied with Hilferding's
Finance Capital, the standard, accepted study of the latest stage
of capitalist development. He embarked on an independent analysis. His voluminous notebooks, filling 693 pages, were his preparation for the small volume that was published as *Imperialism*.
These preparatory notes show how, in the concrete economic study,
he holds tight to the dialectic. The published work itself was a
demonstration in economics of the dialectic as the unity of opposites.

Prior to 1914, Marxists had treated cartels, trusts, syndicates,
as mere "forms" of large-scale production, as part of a continuous
development of capitalism. Capitalism seemed to be "organizing
the economy," removing "planlessness," and thus making it easier
for the workers "to take over"—as if it were merely a matter of
replacing one set of office holders with another. Now, however,
Lenin treats monopoly not so much as a part of a continuous
development, but as a development through contradiction, through
transformation into opposite.

Competition was transformed into its opposite, monopoly.
But monopoly didn't transcend competition. It coexists with it. It
multiplies contradictions; it deepens the crisis. Imperialism arose,
not out of capitalism in general, but out of capitalism at a specific

stage "when its essential qualities became transformed into their opposites." Just as competition was transformed into its opposite, monopoly, a part of the proletariat was transformed into *its* opposite, the aristocracy of labor. That was the bulwark of the Second International. That caused its collapse.

Lenin's study of monopoly capitalism followed his *Philosophic Notebooks* and outside of that context cannot be fully understood. Once Lenin saw the counter-revolution within the revolutionary movement, he felt compelled to break with his former conception of the relationship between materialism and idealism. The keynote of his *Philosophic Notebooks* is nothing short of a restoration of truth to philosophic idealism against vulgar materialism to which he had given the green light in 1908 with his work on *Materialism and Empirio-Criticism*.[160] Necessary as that book may have been for the specific purposes of Russia—only Russia was so backward that in 1908 one still had to fight clericalism in the Marxist movement—he now includes himself among the Marxists who "criticized the Kantians . . . more in a Feuerbachian than in a Hegelian manner."

Of his former teacher, Plekhanov, respected as such, Lenin now writes: "Plekhanov wrote on philosophy (dialectic) probably nearly 1,000 pages (Beltov+ against Bogdanov+ against Kantians+ basic questions, etc., etc. on philosophy (dialectic). There is nil in them about the Larger Logic, about it, *its* thoughts (i.e., the dialectic *proper*, as a philosophic science) nil! !"

With himself, he is as merciless, giving no quarter, not even in the economic field:

"It is impossible completely to grasp Marx's CAPITAL, and especially its first chapter, if you have not studied through and understood the *whole* of Hegel's *Logic*. Consequently, none of the Marxists for the past half a century have understood Marx! !"

Before 1914, Lenin had one view of CAPITAL and philosophy. War and the collapse of the Second International made him turn to the dialectic and changed his views. But he didn't face either event with a blank mind. He had been a practicing revolutionary in Russia and was molded by the sharpness of the contradictions of that backward country. There is no study of Volume II of CAPITAL more profound than that which Lenin had made at

the turn of the century. There is no more profound grasp of
the dialectic in action, that is to say, *"masses as reason,"* than that
which he made of the 1905 revolution. No matter where Lenin
resided, however, he *lived* in Russia. He was a *Russian Marxist.* He
was unprepared for the International's collapse. But having faced
it both in actuality and in philosophy, he became politically more
irreconcilable than ever. It was not a "mood." His attitude was
not only against those who betrayed. The collapse of the Second
International meant the breakdown of all previous thought and
method of thought which called itself Marxist, i.e., *all* established
Marxism.

2) *The Irish Revolution and the Dialectic of History*

There is no major work of Lenin's, from the *Philosophic
Notebooks* until his death, that is not permeated with the dialectic.
It is the very warp and woof of all his works from *Imperialism* to
the *Split in the International;* from the *National Question* to
State and Revolution; from the famous *Trade Union Debate* to
his *Will.* It is in the *Will* that Lenin says he thinks Bukharin never
quite grasped the dialectic and, *therefore,* cannot be considered
"fully a Marxist." Thus we see that the great divide in Marxism,
that set an unbridgeable gulf between the Second International
and the tendency that would become the new Third International,
did not exhaust itself there. On the contrary, the new philosophic
foundations already contained in germ the *next* division of Marxism. For this is the battle of reason and if one hasn't changed his
method of thought, he can be sure to collapse at the next great
crisis. The supreme example of that, during the war, was one
who would become a leader of the Russian Revolution—Nikolai
Bukharin. The question was that of Self-Determination of Nations
on which Lenin suddenly found himself isolated even among the
Bolsheviks.

Prior to World War I there was no difference among the
Bolsheviks on the question of the self-determination of nations.
All agreed to the liberation of nations "in principle." But where,
with the outbreak of war, Lenin saw a new urgency in the question, Bukharin elaborated an entirely new thesis: "The imperialist

epoch is an epoch of the absorption of small states. . . ." he wrote. "It is therefore impossible to struggle against the enslavement of nations otherwise than by struggling against imperialism . . . *ergo* against *capitalism* in general. Any deviation from that road, any advancement of 'partial' tasks, of the 'liberation of nations' *within* the realm of capitalist civilization, means diverting of proletarian forces from the actual solution of the problem. . . . The slogan of 'self-determination' is first of all *utopian* and *harmful* . . . . as a slogan which *disseminates illusions.*"[161] And, blaming the masses, he also wrote: "The collapse of the Second International is recognized as a fact. This collapse is explained not so much by the treason of the leaders as by the objective causes of chauvinist conduct of the masses."[162]

Lenin called this nothing short of "Imperialist Economism," saying it is clear Bukharin had permitted the war "to *suppress*" his thinking: "The scornful attitude of 'imperialist economism' toward *democracy* constitutes one of these forms of *depression,* or *suppression,* of human reasoning by the war."[163]

Lenin hit as hard against Bukharin's co-leader, Pyatakov: "The real source of all his curious errors in logic is that his thinking *has been depressed* by the war and because of this depression the position of Marxism toward democracy in general has been basically distorted."[164]

It is true, Lenin continued, that "capitalism in general and imperialism in particular transforms democracy into an illusion." But it "at the same time generates democratic tendencies among the masses. . . ."[165] As opposed to Bukharin's and Pyatakov's counterposing the existence of imperialism and the non-existence of democracy, Lenin stressed the *co-existence* of imperialism and the democratic tendencies among the masses.

On Easter Day, 1916, the Irish masses acted. The shortage of food which was being used for military needs, the threat to conscript Irishmen for service in the British Army, the heavy taxation, the jailing of thousands under the "Defense of the Realm Act," all brought to a fever pitch the anger of the Irish people.

The insurrection began with the proclaiming of the Irish Republic at the foot of Nelson's Column in Dublin. Detachments of Irish Volunteers seized important positions throughout Dublin:

the General Post Office, the park called St. Stevens Green, the Four Courts, many bridges and roof-top vantage points.

The military force was the Irish Volunteers, first organized in 1913 as an aftermath of the heroic strike of the Irish Transport Workers Union to defend its constitutional rights.

At Jacobs Factory, the poor workers of the district formed themselves as an unarmed human barrier around the factory, protecting their means of making a living from destruction by the British Army.

Women and girls carried food and ammunition to the barricades; fought alongside their men; carried dispatches between points held by the rebels. The teen-age girls—organized as Cuman Na Ban; the Boy Scouts—organized by Countess de Markievicz —were everywhere in the fighting and dispatch-carrying.

The worker and intellectual, the clergyman, the shopkeeper and the manufacturer, all were determined to rid themselves of British domination. As one journalist, Maurice Joy, wrote: "There were no intellectual boundary lines—poets wrote treatises on wireless telegraphy and wireless telegraphers wrote dramas, above all there were no dilettantes among them."

On the first day, the British were stunned by the activity and success of the Irish. The conduct of the Irish during these events was above reproach as even the most bitter English enemy had to admit. There was no looting, rapine or brutality. Captives received the same treatment as those defending the barricades.

The slogan of the men was, " 'Tis better to have fought and lost than never to have fought at all."

It not only delivered a powerful blow to the British Empire. It gave a signal to the world that man's struggle for freedom was not alone an ideological, but a material force. The revolt was not crushed until all forces were completely out of ammunition and isolated from all support. It raised a flame that would continue to burn until independence was finally won.

Lenin hailed the rebellion and accepted it as the real test of his thesis. In summing up the discussion on self-determination he concluded:[166] "The dialectics of history is such that small nations, powerless as an *independent* factor in the struggle against imperialism, play a part as one of the ferments, one of the bacilli, which help the *real* power against imperialism to come on the scene, namely, the socialist proletariat."

"To imagine that social revolution is *conceivable* without revolts by small nations in the colonies and in Europe . . . means *repudiating social revolution.*"[167]

Bukharin was entirely blind to the fact that the dialectics of the revolution itself was at stake in the theoretical debate. Where he was looking for some integral picture of the collapse of imperialism and capitalism, *Lenin was searching for new beginnings which would determine the end,* and he found these in two directions: (1) the struggle of national groupings for independence, and (2) the very stratification of the working class. Far from finding the working class *as a class* "chauvinist," he was searching for lower and deeper strata in it to release the creative energies of millions.

If Hegelian phraseology may be permitted, what Lenin was saying to Bukharin was that he who does not see a new "subject" emerge out of a great crisis is compelled to run to the "Absolute" (read: Socialism) like a bolt out of the blue, instead of living through the birth-throes of an actually developing revolution or living history. Long ago Marx had castigated the "abstract materialist" for not seeing "the processes of history." Now Lenin became intolerant of the "economist." The *logic* of self-determination, in theory as in fact, showed that *just when* there was the growing "internationalization," i.e., imperialist suppression, *that is when* there was also the revolt. He was asking Bukharin to get away from "causality" to explain the relation between the ideal and the real, and instead to be where the "notion" of freedom and subjectivity are, that is to say, the free creative power of the masses.

Thus, the great divide in Marxism was not alone with those who betrayed, but with those who, in thought, are near the dialectic, but never quite make it and thus cannot be considered "fully Marxist." The slightest slip off the dialectic of revolution—that is, the strictest *relationship* of the revolutionary activity of the mass to the specific economic epoch—and the Marxist theoretician ends by anticipating the next stage of *bourgeois* development. What Bukharin only theorized about, Stalin was ruthless enough to put into effect. We shall see, when we deal with Stalin, how prophetic Lenin was when he wrote: "The necessity of solidarity of forces against the international West which defends the capitalist world is one thing. . . . It is another thing when we ourselves fall into something like imperialistic relations toward the oppressed nationalities."[168]

It remains the most devastating commentary on present-day Russia.

CHAPTER ELEVEN

FORMS OF ORGANIZATION: THE RELATIONSHIP OF THE SPONTANEOUS SELF-ORGANIZATION OF THE PROLETARIAT TO THE "VANGUARD PARTY"

> "The transformation of the ideal into the real is *profound*. Very important for history. . . . Against vulgar materialism. NB. The difference of the ideal from the material is also not unconditional, not excessive."
>
> "At the end of Volume II of the *Logic*, before the transition to the Notion a definition is given: 'the Notion, the realm of Subjectivity or of Freedom':
>
> *NB*:
>
> Freedom=subjectivity ("or") goal, consciousness, striving. *NB*"—Lenin

Marxism is a philosophy of human activity. The core of all of Marxism begins with and centers around the activity of labor in the process of production itself. It is here that the living laborer revolts against the domination of dead labor, against being made an appendage to a machine. Marx did not entertain any illusion that any one can know the *forms* this revolt will assume before it actually bursts forth. No one's *objective* view, however, was more *sensuous*—that is, using *all* senses—than Marx's, as witness his anticipation of the 1848 revolutions in the *Communist Manifesto*.

No one followed the spontaneous self-organization of the proletariat with greater vigilance than Marx. Whether in trade union form, Chartism, the First International or the Paris Commune, they were the foundations for all his theory. He followed their development like a hawk and based himself exclusively on the intellectual development of the working class whom he considered the only true inheritors of all the achievements of civilization, including Hegelian philosophy. But despite the close connection of his theory with the organizational activity of the proletariat, *he never elaborated a theory of organization.*

Lenin did. In 1902 he wrote *What Is to Be Done?* In 1903 the Russian Social Democracy split into Bolshevik (Majority) and Menshevik (Minority) tendencies. By 1912 these two tendencies became two parties. The book, followed by all his uncompromising organizational activity, earned Lenin every epithet, from "splitter" to that of the alleged theoretician of Russian Communist totalitarianism.

No one is more anxious, spends more money and time to perpetuate this perversion of history, than the totalitarian bureaucracy now ruling Russia. It has at its disposal the whole power of the State. The "Big Lie" reached its most poisonous application at the moment when the Khrushchev bureaucracy destroyed the Stalin myth, only to perpetuate the more heinous slander of Lenin as the precursor of *their* Party, thus in fact maintaining and strengthening Stalin's elite Party intact. There is no question that is more germane, not alone to the Marxist movement, but to the whole future of mankind, than that of the relationship of a Marxist Party to the spontaneous movement of the working class.

The phenomenon of the One-Party State, which hangs over our age like a Damocles sword with H-bomb power, appears to be the only alternative to bourgeois democracy. It is so pervasive a phenomenon, so full of tension and shock, or purgation and death, that it very nearly suppresses all rational thinking on the subject. All the more reason not to permit easy answers to soothe us back to complacency. What is needed here, in place of our famous pragmatism, is some Hegelian "labor, patience, and suffering of the negative" with which to trace the historical development of the Bolshevik party through every step of the way, from the time it was

just an "idea" that an obscure revolutionary exile in Siberia was
mulling over in his head, to the time when it was the Party in
power ruling over one-sixth of the earth's surface, and the obscure
revolutionist was now the famous Lenin writing his *Will*, and
warning of the ominous shadow of the rude and disloyal Stalin
who had accumulated too much power in his hands and "did not
always know what to do with it." Only then can we face the modern
phenomenon of the One-Party State in both Fascist and Communist
countries.

1) What Was at Stake in 1902-03: *the Activity of the Workers, and the Discipline of the Intellectuals*

Lenin is rightly known as the founder of the theory of "the
vanguard party." Not that this was the first such party. The underlying conception of what has been called "vanguardism" belonged
to the theoretician of the German Social Democracy and of the
Second International, Karl Kautsky. Although, on paper, the
German Social Democracy was not a Lassallean but a Marxian
party, in its organizational practice it was Lassallean through and
through. Karl Kautsky, without due acknowledgment it might be
added, developed Lassalle's idea of the need "to bridge the gulf
between thinkers and the masses" to its logical conclusion. In
turn, Lenin brought to its logical culmination Karl Kautsky's
conception that "the vehicles of science were not the proletariat,
but the bourgeois intellectual." This permeates Lenin's statement
that, by themselves, the workers could only reach trade union consciousness, that socialism must be introduced to them "from the
outside." Lenin quoted Kautsky approvingly and at length: "Socialist consciousness is represented as a necessary and direct result
of the proletarian class struggle. But this is absolutely untrue.
Of course, Socialism, as a theory, has its roots in modern economic
relationships in the same way as the latter emerges from the
struggle against the capitalist-created poverty and misery of the
masses. But Socialism and the class struggle arise side by side
and not one out of the other; each arises out of different premises.
Modern socialist consciousness can arise only on the basis of profound scientific knowledge. . . . The vehicles of science are not

the proletariat, but the *bourgeois intelligentsia*. It was out of the hearts of members of this stratum that modern Socialism originated. . . . Thus Socialist consciousness is something introduced into the proletarian class struggle from without, and not something that arose within it spontaneously."[169] This guided Lenin in his fight against the economists who wanted to limit the proletarian struggle to economic demands, that is, to building unions. On this both Bolshevik and Menshevik agreed. Nevertheless the split took place. The blame was placed on the two differing conceptions—Martov's and Lenin's—of what constitutes party membership: whether it is sufficient to "agree" with party principles, or whether one must be "under the discipline of a local." But Martov's formulation had already passed despite Lenin's objections when the split into Bolshevik and Menshevik took place. Clearly something else must have been at issue. And it was.

What is true—and it is this which modern students of the Russian party couldn't avoid sensing—is that there was an element in Lenin's theory on organization which was *not* borrowed from the German Social Democracy, which was *specifically Leninist*—the conception of what constitutes membership in a Russian Marxist group. Indeed, the definition did not merely rest on a "phrase"—that only he is a member who puts himself "under the discipline of the local organization." The disciplining by the local was so crucial to Lenin's conception that it held primacy over verbal adherence to Marxist theory, propagandizing Marxist views, and holding a membership card. Undoubtedly you have something in your head that is at sharp variance with the prevailing Social Democratic conception when you are that stubborn about a "phrase."

To Lenin, activity was different in each economic epoch. In 1894, when Marxism won over the Russian Populists, capitalist production disciplined the worker and laid the foundation for the bourgeois revolution to come. It did not discipline the intellectual. It was precisely this roving petty-bourgeois who needed the discipline. There was nothing personal or subjective or even just organizational about this. Lenin insisted that the Marxist intellectual needed the *ideological* discipline of the proletarians in the local because otherwise he was resisting not only local discipline but also resisting being theoretically disciplined by the *economic content* of the Russian revolution.

From the start, therefore, it was not really a "mere" organizational question. To the Mensheviks who accused him of acting dictatorially when all were "united politically," Lenin answered:[170] It is not I, but you who have to answer how it happened that you voted the main political resolutions and yet could not accept the organizational conclusions flowing from them. Do not ask *me* what happened. Ask *yourselves.* Ask yourselves, objectively, politically: what happened at the turn of the century in Russia when capitalist production in that semi-feudal land laid the basis for the bourgeois revolution but found the bourgeoisie utterly incapable of overthrowing Tsarism? Didn't that signify that to this "backward" Russian proletariat befell the greatest revolutionary democratic task in the world: the overthrow of Tsarism? Doesn't that, in turn, signify that, while the *economic content* of the revolution will be capitalistic, *the method will be proletarian?* Isn't it that duality of content and method that set you veering in all directions at once, but pretty steadily *away* from the proletarian responsibility? You *need* the discipline of the proletariat.

It was these two contradictory aspects of the content and method of the revolution that Lenin emphasized over and over again. *Before* 1905 it was just a theory, and the organizational conclusions may have seemed irrational. What was theory in 1903, however, became fact in 1905. Fact that had a living subject, a living *self-developing* subject—the Russian proletariat. This working class would soon appear on the historic stage with the creation of the unheard-of Soviets, "peculiar organizations" which no theoretician thought of in his wildest flights of fancy. These peculiar organizations, without even covering the whole of Russia, shook Tsarism to its very foundations. Mensheviks and Bolsheviks were together in the Revolution and for a brief moment afterward attempted a unity congress.

2) *The 1905 Revolution, and Political Tendencies in Russia after 1905*

The 1905 Revolution smashed to smithereens the monstrous conception of the backwardness of the workers and their inability to reach socialism without the "vanguard." The "backward" Russian proletariat, *in action,* went far beyond the most daring conceptions of the most advanced theoreticians. Lenin hailed the appearance of "the masses as reason." Where, in 1902, Lenin wrote that the workers, by their own instincts, could only reach trade union consciousness, he wrote, in 1905, "The working-class is instinctively, spontaneously, Social Democratic."[171] Where, in 1902, Lenin wrote that Socialism could only be brought to the proletariat from the outside, he, in 1905, wrote: "The special condition of the proletariat in capitalistic society leads to a striving of workers for socialism; a union of them with the Socialist Party bursts forth with spontaneous force in the very early stages of the movement." Where, in 1902, Lenin wanted the party to be a tight, closely-knit, small grouping with very exclusive standards for membership, he, in 1905, wrote that workers should be incorporated "into the ranks of the Party organizations by the hundreds of thousands."

The defeat of the Revolution brought the grimmest period of reaction in history up to that time. Organizationally it was once again necessary to go underground, to work in small, highly disciplined groups. It is this which has given some students the impression that Lenin reverted to the previous conception of the 1902 variety of "vanguardism." Those who think so only prove that they cannot distinguish between the conditions under which reactionary Tsarism *forced any democratic* grouping to live, and the underlying assumptions and aims which permeate the Marxist grouping and give it the conviction to carry on under the most adverse conditions, knowing that when the workers rise again the Marxists will find their way to them.[172]

It was not abstract logic nor personal venom, but the vicious offensive of the capitalist class *and* the adaptation by the petty bourgeois intellectual to the objective necessity of the *opposing* class that *compelled* the proletariat to find, once and for all, its own native proletarian mode of being—revolutionary activity. From his very birth, at the time of the great French Revolution, the factory worker found that his own proletarian way of knowing was through his self-activity. By the turn of the century the workers' own way of knowing *concretized* itself in political practice, *a party*.

This is what the German Social Democracy and the Second International seemed to represent. When Lenin fought the Economists, saying—No, not economic action but political practice, a party—he *seemed* to be in full Social Democratic, that is, established Marxist, tradition. Indeed, it seemed a rather belated statement that needed repitition only because Russia was so backward. However, the fact that Russia was so backward that no independent trade unions were allowed, much less a Marxist political party, meant that *therefore* what was involved in political practice was *not* parliamentary but underground activity. This transformed the question entirely.

Even as an ordinary person, a genius does many things unconsciously, impelled to them by strong, objective forces, and by new impulses from yet undefined, deep strata of the population. Thus was Lenin moving empirically to the construction of a Marxist party under Russian conditions. In 1902, what had not been clear even to Lenin, was that his organizational formulations were giving expression to the instinctive striving, the new, elemental, proletarian urge for political practice, which was revolutionary activity itself, and not a parliamentary shadow. But what was not clear in 1902, when he wrote *What Is to Be Done?*, was made obvious by the Russian working class itself when it burst forth in the 1905 Revolution. Lenin never lost sight of the highest point reached by that Revolution. But many other intellectuals, under the whip of the counter-revolution, took flight into everything from God-seeking to "liquidationism."[173]

Lenin hit back with everything he had, sometimes quite crudely, as in *Materialism and Empirio-Criticism;* sometimes very profoundly, as in his strict relating of political tendencies to the objective movement; always uncompromisingly. In 1910, he summed up the historical significance of that internal party struggle in Russia. He took issue with Trotsky's statement that "It is an illusion to imagine that Mensheviks and Bolsheviks struck deep roots in the depths of the proletariat" because that was not the question at all. Trotsky's "philosophy of history" is summed up in his own analysis of the differences between these two tendencies (he was a member of neither). He insisted that it was all *"a struggle for influence over the politically immature proletariat."* Lenin replied: "This is a specimen of the sonorous but empty phrases of which Trotsky is master. The roots of the divergence between Menshevism and Bolshevism lie, not in the depths of the proletariat but in the *economic content* of the Russian revolution. By ignoring this content, Martov and Trotsky deprived themselves of the possibility of understanding the historic meaning of the internal party struggle in Russia. The crux of the matter is not whether the theoretical formulation of differences have penetrated deep into this or that stratum of the proletariat, but the fact that the economic conditions of the Revolution of 1905 *brought* the proletariat into hostile relations with the liberal bourgeoisie—not only over the question of improving the conditions of life of the workers, but also over the agrarian question, over all the political questions of the revolution, etc. To speak of the struggle of the trends in the Russian revolution and to distribute labels such as 'sectarianism,' 'lack of culture,' etc., not to utter a word about the fundamental, economic interests of the proletariat, of the liberal bourgeoisie and of the democratic peasantry is tantamount to stooping to the level of vulgar journalists."[174]

Where many—and there were among them Bolsheviks as well as Mensheviks, non-factionalists and non-parliamentarians—where many took flight under the whip of the counter-revolution, Lenin was steeled by it *because* he took the *highest* point reached by the Revolution and built *from there.* Therefore, from that time on, to consider any serious progressive role for the liberal bourgeoisie was utopian and reactionary. It was the role of the proletariat and its relationship to the peasantry that had to gain ever greater precision. He called it "the revolutionary democratic dictatorship of the proletariat and peasantry." The Mensheviks, on the other hand, held that since it was a bourgeois revolution "therefore" the bourgeoisie must lead it. For Lenin, not only were such "practical" views good for nothing; but so was Trotsky's "permanent revolution."

That was the theory that the revolution would not stop at the bourgeois phase but continue straight on to socialism and "the dictatorship of the proletariat." It was not the role of the proletariat in a socialist revolution that was in question, argued Lenin, but its role in a bourgeois revolution *in a country that is overwhelmingly peasant*: "Whoever wants to approach socialism by any other path than that of political democracy will inevitably arrive at absurd and reactionary conclusions, both economic and political."[175]

Whoever hides the fact that the economic content of the revolution in Russia is bourgeois, Lenin wrote, helps the bourgeoisie. Whoever evades the fact that its method nevertheless will be proletarian cannot define the Marxist party's relationship to it. Whoever fails to see that it cannot be other than democratic, the widest, broadest, deepest democracy such as the bourgeoisie can never realize, involving millions, dooms the Marxist party to isolation and dooms the revolution to defeat as well.

Just as the 1905 Revolution *and* counter-revolution prepared the Russian masses for the successful Revolution of 1917, so it shaped Lenin's mind. What runs through it like a red thread is this closeness to the Russian masses. He never at any time had any conception of the party as an elite in the sense in which our age uses the term.

3) What Was New on the Party Question in the Great Divide and After: the Relationship of the Masses to the Party

> "Actuality and thought (or the Idea) are often absurdly opposed. . . . Thought in such a case is, on the one hand, the synonym for a subjective conception, plan, intention or the like, just as actuality, on the other, is made synonymous with external and sensible existence. . . .
>
> "For on the one hand ideas are not confined to our heads merely, nor is the Idea, upon the whole, so feeble as

to leave the question of its actualization
or non-actualization dependent on our
will. The Idea is rather absolutely active
as well as actual. And, on the other
hand, actuality is not so bad and irrational as it is supposed to be by the
practical men, who are either without
thought altogether or have quarrelled
with thought and have been worsted in
the contest."—Hegel[176]

Prior to 1914, the contradiction in Lenin between the practicing revolutionary dialectician and the thinking Kautskyan reflects the contradiction in Russian society whose singular development from the feudal monarchy to the bourgeois monarchy was
through proletarian methods of struggle. It was the extreme contradiction in the development of the Russian economy, and the
manifold but *concrete* struggles of political tendencies, which prepared Lenin for the break in thought which the collapse of the
Second International signified in life. As he returned to the philosophic foundations of Marx and Hegel, he went there with all
this rich and contradictory experience behind him.

The break in thought, the battle of reason, now was to break
up the rigidity to which Kautskyan understanding had reduced
everything. Prior to 1914, Lenin had accepted a series of abstractions—party, mass, revolution. *Except for Russia,* he never contrasted these with the struggles of the revolutionary masses, even
as he had previously failed to analyze the latest phase of world
capitalism and had failed to see the connection of the Second
International with it. It is only now that he saw that not only
had capitalism changed. So had the labor organization *because* so
had the labor living off the super-profits of capitalist imperialism.
Now that he fully analyzed the objective reasons for the collapse
of the International, he questioned the Social Democratic Party's
very use of the phrase—mass organization. He denied it was a
mass organization.

On a much higher, that is, more complex, historical scale,
Lenin's problems and views here parellel the position of Marx

in his struggle with the British trade unions whose leadership began to take flight from the First International during the Paris Commune. According to the protocol of Marin, during the September 20, 1871 conference on trade unions, Marx stated "that the trade union represents an aristocratic minority. The poorly paid worker cannot belong to it; the great mass of workers whom the economic development daily drives from the country to the city remain outside of the trade union for a long time, and the most poverty-stricken mass does not go into it at all. The same is true of workers born (and raised) on the East End of London, among whom only one out of ten belongs to the trade union. The peasants never join these societies.

"Trade Unions by themselves are impotent; they remain a minority. They have no authority over the mass of the proletarians while the International shows a direct influence among these people."[177]

It is first now that Lenin "discovered" Marx's and Engels' analysis of the "bourgeoisification" of the British proletariat. Lenin first now sensed the emphasis on the need to go *"deeper and lower"* into the working class. Although the founders of modern socialism had carried on this fight all the way from 1858 to 1892 he saw it for the first time. He saw it with the eyes of one who had just gone through the collapse of the Second International. He called this, *just this,* going "deeper and lower" into the working class, *"the quintessence* of Marxism."[178]

After questioning the German Social Democracy's claim to being a proletarian mass organization, he concluded that, above all, a Marxist would have to answer: organization of proletariat *for what purpose?*

His mind working dialectically, Lenin now approaches the problem from two levels: (1) the real, and (2) the ideal springing from the real. The betrayal of the proletariat by the Second left no doubt that, far from being an ideal organization, it had become the enemy of the purpose for which it was formed—to organize the revolutionary activity of the masses. No doubt the corruption of the Second was unavoidable under the growth of monopoly capitalism and imperialism. But having traced its objective basis, that is to say, the economic roots, his mind found it all the more necessary to see it philosophically, and to go forward from the *recognition* of the contradiction in every single thing, to its *resolution*: If the unity of opposites is not limited to the two fundamental classes in society, if the duality extends to labor itself, then one must speak out the truth—the labor party itself is *bourgeois*. It is thus necessary to *drive a wedge between the opposites in labor itself*. It was the deeper and lower layers, in *and* outside the party, that would have to restore labor to its revolutionary being. The masses would do more than regain their self-activity when they finally destroyed the *bourgeois labor party*. In overcoming that barrier, the working class will finally find itself undivided against itself. Its "knowing," its consciousness, will be reunited with its "being," its creative activity. The type of party it creates would not shirk *taking power*.

What was still not clear was what type of organization the spontaneous workers' revolt would form. Lenin did not think of the Soviet. It was now January, 1917. He had long since broken with the Second International; he had called for the formation of a new, Third International. He had long since said that the only way out of the war was to turn the imperialist war into a civil war. The imperialist slaughter had now been going on for nearly three years. He did not know that he would live to see the revolution, but he was sure the youth would, and it was the Swiss youth he addressed in January, 1917, on the Russian Revolution of 1905. He singled out, not the Soviet, but the mass strike as the outstanding feature.

The following month, the February (March) Revolution broke out. In eight days, the monarchy which had maintained itself for centuries and had withstood the Revolution of 1905, was overthrown. When he heard of the February Revolution he sent his co-leaders a telegram which showed that his mind was still operating within old categories. Combine legal and illegal work, read his first telegram. The very next day, the *newness*, the truth dawned upon him, finally. The Russian workers had, *on their own*, re-created that "peculiar organization," the Soviet, and now it had spread through the length and breadth of the whole land. There were Soviets of Workers, Soviets of Soldiers, Soviets of Peasants. The Russian workers alone had remembered Not a single theoretician—including Lenin—had thought of Soviets or told the workers to build them. The workers' own creative energies had built this alternative form of government. It continued to stand there challengingly, though the Tsar was overthrown and there was now a Provisional Democratic Government headed by Kerensky, Socialist.

Now that Lenin finally comprehended the Soviet fully he realized that he never had really seen it before, not as *the* form that would supersede the Paris Commune and become the workers' state itself.

Lenin's mind leapt forward with the surge of the spontaneous movement of the workers which revealed what Engels had long since called their "latent socialism." "I'm afraid," Lenin now wrote his colleagues from his exile as he prepared to return to Russia, "that the epidemic of 'sheer' enthusiasm may now spread in Petrograd, without a systematic effort towards the creation of a party of a *new* type, which must *in no way* resemble those of the *Second International*." "*Never again* along the lines of the Second International!" And again: "Our immediate problem is organization, not in the sense of affecting ordinary organization by ordinary methods, but in the sense of drawing in large masses *and* embodying in this organization, military, state, and national economic problems."[179]

What was to become the famous April Thesis was taking shape. Heretofore, the break had been against Kautsky, then against Bukharin. Now, the big break was to be with *his own past*. The contradictions had been *in himself*. The workers had broken out of all old shackles and were creating a truly new way of life for millions. He must now break with all that stood in the way of this elemental surge for freedom, for peace, for bread, for land.

The first thing he did was to discard the old slogan, "the democratic dictatorship of the proletariat and peasantry." The democratic revolution, he now said, *has been completed*. An entirely new, unforseen situation has arisen, that of a *Dual Power*: on the one hand stood the Provisional Government which was still carrying on the war; on the other, stood the Soviets themselves which wanted peace. Had the creative impulse of the Russian masses not created the Soviets, the Russian Revolution would have been hopeless. But now, with "socialism looking out of all windows," *all* politics stemmed from that. Only the Soviets could create a new order.

What was needed now was the arming of the proletariat, strengthening and broadening and developing the role *and* power of the Soviets: "All the rest is mere phrases and lies and the self deception of politicians of the liberal and radical stamp." It was not that the workers must support the Government. It was that the Provisional Government must support the workers. "All Power to the Soviets!"

His Bolshevik colleagues, no less than the Mensheviks, thought that Lenin had come home from another planet altogether, and *Pravda* published his thesis as an "individual" viewpoint.

Where to the others it seemed as if he forgot about "the role of the party," to Lenin a vanguard party now was such *only because* in April, 1917, it represented the revolutionary masses. As he was to tell his co-leaders and his party in the next few months as he mobilized them for just this purpose of reflecting the will of the revolutionary masses, the ranks of the party are ten times more revolutionary than the leaders, and the masses *outside* are ten times more revolutionary than the ranks. He told them if they would not place the question of *workers' power* on the order of the day, he would "go to the sailors!" "I am compelled *to tender my resignation from the Central Committee* which I hereby do, reserving for myself the freedom to agitate among the rank and file of the Party and at the Party congress."[180] But he didn't have to go to that extreme before the party finally did become "the vanguard," that is to say when they finally saw that without the spontaneity, the creative energies of millions, the "masses as reason," which meant *concretely* their form of organization to have *power*, the Marxist party would indeed be nothing but an elite.

The method of winning his party was this total concept which he now had. Not only were economics, politics and philosophy *not* three separate constituent parts. The point was that unless all, as a totality, are taken *in strict relationship to the actual class struggle, the activity of the masses themselves,* it would be nothing but "project-hatching."

The foundation was, of course, economics, and the *new*, the *concretely* new was that "Monopoly had evolved into state-monopoly." That meant that planlessness has ceased. There is no such thing, however, as "pure plan"; the *class* character of the plan must now be fought relentlessly. To the Government's Plan he counterposed "Workers' Control." Control and accounting by workers, he warned, "must not be confused with the question of a scientific educated staff of engineers and agronomists, etc." Nationalization without workers' control meant nothing: "The workers must sweep aside high-sounding phrases, promises, declarations, projects evolved in the center by bureaucrats, who are always ready to draw up the most ostentatious plans, rules, regulations, and standards. Down with all this lying! Down with all this hullabaloo of the bureaucratic and bourgeois project-mongering that has everywhere collapsed with a crash. Down with this habit of procrastination! The workers must demand *immediate* establishment of control *in fact* to be exercised by the *workers themselves*."

The workers became the center of everything in Lenin's mind. Everything else was subordinate to it: "I 'calculate' *solely* and *exclusively* on the workers, soldiers, and peasants able to tackle better than the officials, better than the police, the *practical* and difficult problems of increasing the production of foodstuffs and their better distribution, the better provisions of soldiers, etc. etc."

Lenin now sat down to work out his theory. As he had "lived" with the *Science of Logic* in the writing of *Imperialism, so now he re-created Marx's Civil War in France, for his country and his epoch, as State and Revolution.* Basing himself on Marx's concept that "centralised state power, with its ubiquitous organs of standing army, police, bureaucracy, clergy and judicature—are organs wrought after the plan of a systematic and hierarchic division of labor,"[181] Lenin now saw that the need of his time was *to destroy bureaucratism.* There is no other way to wither away The State. Even the workers' State cannot wither away *unless* the workers, "organized as the ruling class," *are* to become the basis for the end of all class rule. That now became the key to his theory and his practice. It was a new organization of thought in the true Hegelian-Marxian manner.

In his book, Lenin writes against Kautsky's conceptions, *not only in the period when he became a traitor to the workers' cause, but when he was the established Marxist theoretician.* He explains that even in his most "revolutionary" works, *Social Revolution,* and *The Road To Power,* Kautsky had developed ideas that "certain enterprises cannot do without a bureaucratic organization," and even Marxists could not do "without officials in the Party and the trade unions."

This, Lenin now says, "is the *essence* of bureaucracy and until the capitalists are expropriated *even* proletarian officials will be bureaucratised to some extent." For Lenin, democracy under capitalism is mutilated by wage slavery. "This is why, and the only reason why. . . . This is the essence of bureaucracy." The only way to have genuine democracy is to have proletarian democracy, to suppress bureaucracy and give all powers to the workers.

That is why it is important to establish from the start "immediate introduction of control and superintendence by *all* so that *all* shall become 'bureaucrats'." The essence of a commune-type of government is that "the *mass* of the population will rise to *independent* participation, not only in voting and elections, *but also in the everyday administration of affairs.*"

The population *"to a man"* must manage production and the state. That is the Ideal which must become the reality.

There have been self-avowed Marxists whose own narrow vision led them to the conclusion that Lenin's *State and Revolution* was "nothing but a re-write" of Marx's *Civil War in France.* They fail to see that "to re-write" *Civil War in France,* on the eve of a Revolution in Russia, is a creative act. It meant cleansing the concept of superseding the bourgeois State of its Second Internationalist perversion, which was not a literary perversion but a perversion of a working class movement and aspiration. In counterposition, Lenin put his theoretical emphasis on the concept of all, "to a man" to run their own lives. *"No police, no army, no officialdom. Every* worker, *every* peasant, *every* toiler, *every one* who is exploited, the whole population to a man."

That was Lenin's vision and that is what he aimed at in practice. The masses, to Lenin, were not a "means" to reach an "end," socialism. Their self-activity *is* socialism. All of this sharpened sense of self-movement as the inner core of the dialectic; all of this sharpened sense of the opposition of dialectics to eclectics as the central philosophic concept of revolution was, of course, not a "study" of past revolutions. It was the preparation for the coming one in Russia. As Lenin approached the section of the book which was to deal with the Russian scene, the actual November Revolution broke out. Such an "interruption," he wrote in the Postscript to the unfinished *State and Revolution*, "can only be welcomed." And, having led the first proletarian revolution to victory, Lenin addressed the Congress of Soviets on January 24, 1918: "In introducing workers' control we knew it would take some time before it spread to the whole of Russia, but we wanted to show that we recognized only one road—changes from below; we wanted the workers themselves to draw up, from below, the new principle of economic conditions."[182]

The greatest test of all was now at hand: practice.

CHAPTER TWELVE

WHAT HAPPENS AFTER?

The November, 1917 Revolution was the first historical instance where the workers not only gained power, but held it. In contrast to the Paris Commune, which was bloodily put down after but two short months of existence, the new workers' state, called the dictatorship of the proletariat or the Soviet State, survived the protracted civil wars launched against it by national and international capitalism. It left a ruined country facing starvation but there was no doubt at all that "the dictatorship of the proletariat" was there to stay. The two biggest tasks it faced theoretically were: (1) *how* would labor assert its mastery over the economy and the state? and (2) since the dictatorship is supposed to be a transitional state—transitional to socialism—*how* would it achieve its own "withering away"? On these hinged the long-range aim of establishing a truly classless society where the free and full development of each individual was the condition of development of all, and thus, once for all, to end what Marx considered the pre-history of man.

The re-integration of man's manual and mental abilities in the producer himself would first open the real history of humanity. As Lenin put it, the overthrow of the exploiter class is the easiest part of the social revolution. Now comes the prosaic, daily, hard, and more important work of abolishing "the distinction between manual workers and brain workers." The difficulty is that workers are *"shy"* and do not know all the organizing talent in them, while the intellectuals are full of conceit and yet are "lackadaisical":

"This lackadaisicalness, carelessness, slovenliness, untidiness, nervous haste, the inclination to substitute discussion for action, talk for work, the inclination to undertake everything under the

sun without finishing anything is one of the characteristics of the
'educated'; and this is not due to the fact that they are bad by
nature, still less is it due to malice; it is due to their habits of
life, the conditions of their work, to fatigue, to the abnormal separation of mental from manual labor, and so on and so forth. . . .

"The workers and peasants are still 'shy'; they must get rid
of this shyness, and they *certainly will* get rid of it. . . . 'It is not
the gods who make pots'—this is the motto that the workers and
peasants should get well drilled into their minds. They must
understand that the whole thing now is *practice*, that the historical
moment has arrived when theory is being transformed into practice, is vitalized by practice, corrected by practice, tested by practice. . . .

"The Paris Commune gave a great example of how to combine initiative, independence, freedom of action and vigour from
below with voluntary centralism free from stereotyped forms. Our
Soviets are following the example. But they are still 'shy'. . . .
There is a great deal of this talent among the people. It is merely
suppressed. It must be given an opportunity to display itself. It
and it alone, with the support of the masses, can save Russia and
the cause of Socialism."[183]

The point was that the Communist Party, now that it was
in power, was *not* eliciting this talent. On the contrary, it was
displaying "a passion for bossing." The main enemy was the
bureaucracy which was springing up.

It is true the workers on their own moved quickly from
control of production to the spontaneous seizure of the factories.
It is true the peasants took the land. It is true the Soviets were
now organs of state power. It is true the new Soviet State's Declaration of the Rights of Toilers, and the New Program of the newly-
formed (or more correctly, newly-named) Communist (Bolshevik)
Party incorporated as theory and practice the principle that eventually the population "to a man" should manage production and the
state.

It is no less true that the protracted civil war right on the
heels of the World War and the two Revolutions left Russia a
ruined economy, and a devastated land. The trade unions were so
young in this country, where Autocratic Tsarism had so recently

been overthrown, that their first national convention was held only *after* the Revolution. They voted "to participate most energetically in all the administrative departments of production, organize labor boards of control, registration and distribution of labor, the exchange of labor between the village and the city; to fight against sabotage and establish complete labor cooperation and discipline."

The Communist Party acknowledged them as "the chief means of struggle against the bureaucratization of the economic apparatus of Soviet power that creates the possibility for the real peoples' control over the results of production." Yet, at the first serious crisis, immediately after the cessation of civil war, the Party was shaken by a violent dispute over the role of these same trade unions in the workers' state. Though all voted for the first resolution, there were three different answers to exactly how workers should participate in the management of the economy: (1) Trotsky said: statify the trade unions. (2) Shlyapnikov demanded: turn the management of the entire economy over to the trade unions; instead of statifying the trade unions, trade unionize the state. (3) Lenin said: while drawing the unions into management of the state, you must at the same time see that they are "schools of communism." Since this is not only the most famous debate during Lenin's lifetime, which tested the relations of party to mass in life, but also anticipated the problems of today, we will go into all the facts.

1) The Famous Trade Union Dispute of 1920-1921: the Positions of Lenin, Trotsky and Shlyapnikov[184]

In the ruined conditions of Russia, railroad transportation was in utter chaos. It goes without saying that no modern country can exist without transportation and here, at the birth of a new society, the railroads weren't running and the whole transportation system was still plagued with sabotage · from the defeated counter-revolutionary forces. Something drastic had to be done. A central executive committee of transportation was established called *Cectran*. It was a merger of the railroad workers and the water transport workers unions, and a non-union man was put at the head of it—Leon Trotsky, Commissar of War. He and his Committee were granted extraordinary military powers in order to cope with the disastrous situation.

Within a year not only were the railroads running again, and on time, but the railroad trackage had been much expanded. The country was beginning to breathe again. It was then that the water workers union spoke up. They said that they had fully approved the granting of extraordinary military powers needed to restore transportation, but now that the job was done, they demanded "our normal trade union democracy be given back to us."

Trotsky reacted violently. He said it wasn't the special commission that had to be abolished. It was the trade union leaders that "had to be shaken up."

That is how the famous trade union debate *began*. Before it *ended,* subjects in dispute ranged far and wide: (1) What is a workers' state? (2) What is the role of trade unions in such a state? (3) What is the relationship between workers at the point of production and the political party in power? (4) What is the relationship between leaders and ranks, party and mass?

The uniqueness of the 1920 debate is that, in the three leading positions are contained, embryonically, the problem we face today as to the relationship among the three major social formations: trade unionists, politicos, masses. What, in 1920, was an almost doctrinaire debate among Communist leaders, is, in 1957, an almost daily problem we face in any strike.

Lenin rose to the defense of the trade unions. "Taken as a whole," he said, "Trotsky's policy is one of bureaucratically nagging the trade unions. . . . There is valuable military experience: heroism, zeal, etc. There is the bad experience of the worst elements of the military: bureaucracy and conceit." Had Trotsky looked at the "reality of the transition," Lenin insisted, and not been "carried away by intellectual talk or abstract arguments" he would have seen the Soviet Union was not a "pure" workers' state, but a state in which, first, the peasantry predominated, and, secondly, it was bureaucratically distorted.

"Our present state is such," continued Lenin realistically, "that the entirely organized proletariat must protect itself and must utilize the workers organizations for the purpose of protecting the workers from their own state and in order that the workers may protect our state."[185] When has anyone ever made a more profound *and* more devastating attack on the Russian workers' state, than to say that the workers *as workers* must protect themselves from the workers *as state*.

Trotsky, on the other hand, contended that since Soviet Russia was a workers' state, the workers had nothing to fear from it and hence the trade unions could be incorporated into the State, and labor could be militarized. He argued for the establishment of "such a regime under which each worker feels himself to be a soldier of labor who cannot freely dispose of himself; if he is ordered transferred, he must execute that order; if he does not do so, he will be a deserter who should be punished. Who will execute this? The trade union. It will create a new regime. That is the militarization of the working class."[186]

Trotsky's callousness to the dissatisfaction of the workers with the functioning of his special commission, the Cectran, showed itself especially clearly in the attention he concentrated upon the trade union leadership who, he said, must be "shaken up." According to him, it was not the extraordinary political commission with its extraordinary military powers that was at the root of the crisis. Rather, it was the trade union leadership which had failed to create a proper "production atmosphere."

Shlyapnikov, the head of the Workers' Opposition, opposed both Lenin and Trotsky. He too began and ended with the abstraction of *a* workers' state. Since that was already established, he asked, what is the necessity for political leadership to hold primacy? It was as if all problems had faded away with the conquest of political power. To him it was a simple matter: all that was needed in the chaotic conditions of 1920 was to turn over industry to the corresponding trade unions. Although he was a Bolshevik leader, he could not see the role of the Communist Party once there was a workers' state. He called for the convocation of a "producers' congress": "The organization of the management of the national economy is the function of the All-Russian Congress of Producers organized in industrial unions which elects bodies to manage the whole of the national economy of the republic."[187]

Lenin was the supreme realist. He asked both Trotsky and Shlyapnikov what was the use of talking about "a" workers' state when the *concrete* reality of the *specific* Russian Soviet State disclosed that the dictatorship of the proletariat existed in a country where the workers were a tiny minority surrounded by a sea of peasants. To talk of "a producers' congress"—a term used by Marx and Engels for a classless society—in the specific circumstances where the defeated counter-revolution was looking for ways and means to get back into power, was to play right into its hands.

At this moment in our history—Lenin turned sharply to Shlyapnikov—you and your "Workers' Opposition" are the greatest danger to our continued existence. Just look at your position, look at the Kronstadt mutiny[188] and see how quickly the White Guards have grabbed on to the anarchistic, syndicalistic talk of "freedom from political leadership," and *with guns in their hands,* are threatening the new workers' state. Under these actual conditions for you to propose a "producers' congress" means for you to ask the workers' state to commit suicide.

Lenin then turned to Trotsky and told him he must never forget that Soviet Russia was a workers' state *with bureaucratic distortions.* Every other word on Lenin's lips those days was *bureaucracy.* Any attempt "to plan," that did not involve the masses themselves, was nothing but "bureaucratic project-hatching." Anyone who desired to "shake up the trade union leadership" displayed "a bureaucratic concentration on the leading strata." In fact, any political tendency, that did not concentrate the whole weight of the argument on the question of working out a new relationship to the masses, betrayed "bureaucratic tendencies."

The whole point, Lenin was most persistent in this, is "the method of approach to be adopted toward the masses, the method of winning the masses, of contact with the masses." When Trotsky pontificated, "Workers democracy knows no fetishism. It knows only revolutionary expediency," Lenin replied uncompromisingly that the workers are right when they say, "We, the ordinary rank and file, the masses, say that we must renovate, we must correct, we must expel the bureaucrats; but you pitch us a yarn about engaging in production. I do not want to engage in production with such and such a bureaucratic board of directors, chief committee, etc., but with another kind."[189]

Marxists have always been acutely aware of the fact that a theoretical position is not accidental. That is why Lenin tried *to correct* Trotsky. "We must not fear to admit the disease"—the disease of bureaucratism, Lenin warned, lest we ourselves develop an administrative mentality. When you come down to rock bottom, there is one way, *only one way*, to arrive at new social relations for ever new millions of toilers, and that is "gradually to draw the whole toiling population to a man in the work of running the state."[190] That is not easy, and there are many "cogwheels" and "transmission belts" from the masses to the vanguard; that is precisely why the vanguard cannot turn the trade unions into organs of force (statify them), but must rather make of them "schools of communism."

Where Trotsky contended, "We suffer not so much from the bad sides of bureaucracy, as chiefly from the fact that we have not assimilated the many good sides."[191] Lenin insisted that the only correct position was that of the trade union thesis itself: "Introduction of genuine labor discipline is conceived only if the whole mass of participants in production take a conscious part in the fulfillment of these tasks. This cannot be achieved *by bureaucratic methods and orders from above.*"[192]

This was a leadership divided against itself on the very basic ground of its relationship to the masses. Objective forces were already pulling in a direction *away from* the full development of the workers themselves. Where Lenin said that what was new, what was shocking, was to discover "a passion for bossing" among the Communists, now that they had power, Trotsky was shadowboxing with "the old trade union concepts"; and Shlyapnikov was flirting with the anarchistic "freedom from political leadership." Where Lenin put the workers' attitude in the center of all his thoughts, Trotsky put the administrative solution. Trotsky refused to recognize the administrator as *the* new enemy. Quite the contrary. He accused Lenin of approaching "very practical questions too much from the propagandist point of view, and forgetting that here we not only have *material* for agitation but a problem which must be solved administratively."

. Lenin, on the other hand, stated loudly and clearly that the bureaucracy was the new *enemy*, and that Trotsky's administrative approach made him weakest where he should have been strongest —as a propagandist. What was wrong with his thesis, Lenin maintained, was that through it "there runs like a red thread the administrative approach." "History knows all sorts of degenerations," Lenin kept hammering away, "to depend upon conviction, devotion and other spiritual qualities in politics, that is not at all a serious thing."

2) *Lenin and His New Concept*: *"Party Work to Be Checked by Non-Party Masses"*

Lenin's enemies are legion nowadays. There is always a lot of talk about his having been a "democrat" and an exponent of "workers management from below" only "in theory," but that as soon as *State and Revolution* was put away as a book, the practice of governing made him a "dictator." Attempts have been made to give the impression that the young workers' state forbade strikes. If it did, it surely failed to enforce the edict. In the year of the trade union debate, Tomsky, the head of the trade unions, reported that there were, in Moscow alone, between thirty and forty strikes a month. Naturally, the Party thought the trade unions ought to function so well that workers' grievances are acted upon as they arise, and not let dissatisfactions accumulate and cause walkouts. But, not only were strikes permitted, Tomsky and other Communist leaders were complaining that Communists were losing influence because some were stupid enough not to walk out when the workers in their shops went on strike!

Tomsky severely rebuked "the *chinovnik* (petty bureaucrat) attitude" underlying the proposals that strikes be allowed only in privately-owned plants, and not in state enterprises. Lenin's insistence on trade unions as "schools of communism" was *not* to enforce discipline, which he insisted only the workers themselves can enforce, but to stress that production problems cannot be solved "for" the workers—*if* the transitional state was to be transitional to socialism and *not* to a "return backwards to capitalism."

One of the "conclusive" proofs of Lenin's "dictatorship," cited by his enemies, is that it was he who introduced the Resolution on Party Unity which forbade factions. It is true that at the Tenth Congress—when the economy lay in ruins, and the Kronstadt mutiny threatened the very existence of the new state, and forced a return backward to limited capitalism (The New Economic Policy)—Lenin asked that all differing positions within the Communist Party be expressed to the Party directly rather than through caucuses. But: (1) this was done after the discussion was over, after delegates had been elected on the differing platforms, and after the duly convoked Congress had come to majority decisions and voted; (2) Shlyapnikov, against whom the Resolution was aimed, was not only *not* removed from his post, but representatives of his position were taken into the Central Committee; (3) the Platform of the Workers' Opposition had appeared in the central organ of the Party in no fewer than 250,000 copies; and (4) even after the elimination of caucuses, a Discussion Sheet was established so that opposing views could continue to be expressed.

The Kronstadt mutiny compelled sharp measures which are certainly no model for a workers' state to follow. But, to draw a parallel between Lenin's Resolution and Stalin's monolithism is to fly in the face of facts as well as of theory, and to make a complete hash of historic periods.

The truth is, precision such as Lenin's, in the 1920 debate, can come only from a man who lives by his theory, or more precisely, by the vision of the future society. To put it dialectically, Lenin had a clear "Notion" in his head—it was the new absolute, *"to a man"*—and he judged the truth of reality *by* its relationship to the truth of the "Notion."

"The toiling population to a man." *To a man.* That is to say, *every single* man, woman, and youth, from cook to bottle washer, from machinist to handyman, from intellectual to washer-woman, *especially* "the unskilled laborers who are living under *ordinary, i.e., very hard* conditions."[193] (Emphasis is Lenin's.) Lenin was most insistent, in his writings in those early years, that, just as Marx, in CAPITAL counterposed the workers' struggle for the shortening of the working day to all the grandiloquent and empty phrases of the "Declaration of Rights," so must they now, in Russia, have "fewer pompous phrases, more plain, *everyday* work, concern for the pood of grain and the pood of coal!"[194] Genuine communism, he wrote, differs from phrasemongering in that it *"reduces everything to the conditions of labor."* (Emphasis is Lenin's.) This total conception—that only the masses, *from below,* "to a man," can create a new way of life for millions—he elaborated in *State and Revolution* as theory. It was the guiding line in his every-day practical work.

The tragedy of the Russian Revolution is that this was *not* achieved. Even with a correct approach to the masses, as exemplified in the trade union resolution incorporating Lenin's views, the young workers' state could not lift itself by its own bootstraps, particularly as it didn't have any boots. A retreat to the N.E.P. (the New Economic Policy which permitted operation of certain capitalist enterprises) had to be undertaken. None of the Bolshevik leaders thought they could hold out for long in isolated backward Russia without the aid of the European revolution. In explaining the policy of the NEP to the Third Congress of the Communist International, Lenin stressed their dependence on the international revolution: "We quite openly admit, we do not conceal the fact that concessions in the system of state capitalism mean paying tribute to capitalism. But we gain time and gaining time means gaining everything, particularly in the epoch of equilibrium when our foreign comrades are preparing thoroughly for their revolution."

With the defeat of the German Revolution of 1923 (after the beheading of the German Revolution of 1919) the proletarian revolution in Russia was completely isolated. Lenin, who made no fetish of the workers' state, watched like a hawk the further development of the NEP *and* of his party. He knew very well that the dictatorship of the proletariat was a transitional state which could be transitional "either to socialism or to a return backward to capitalism," depending upon the historic initiative of the masses and the international situation. He knew that the Party, especially now that it had power, was not immune to the circumstances under which it operated. The whole 1920-1921 debate showed that the same great formations in society—trade unionists, politicos, masses—

were reflected in the leadership of the party. He depended on the ranks, who were closest to the masses outside, to set the party straight.

Party work must be checked by the *non-party* masses. He wrote: "Of course we shall not submit to everything the masses say, for the masses also yield to sentiments that are not in the least advanced, particularly in years of exceptional weariness and exhaustion resulting from excessive burdens and suffering. But in appraising persons, in determining our attitude to those . . . who have become 'commissarised,' 'bureaucratised,' the suggestions of non-party proletarian masses and in many cases of the non-party peasant masses, are extremely valuable. The toiling masses have a fine instinct for the difference between honest and devoted Communists and those who arouse revulsion of feeling in one who obtains his bread by the sweat of his brow, who enjoys no privileges, and who has no 'open door to the chief.' "[195]

This "Party man," in his last appearance before the Communist Party Congress,[196] spoke about how "mortally sick" he was of "Communlies"[197] (Communist lies). This Communist leader *invented* words to express his severe criticism of the young workers' state and of the Party that led the Revolution. Precisely because he *stood on the great achievements of this Revolution,* his criticism was more devastating than that of any of its enemies. "History proceeds in devious ways," he kept warning. Making no fetishism out of the workers' state, he spoke of "the simple class truth of the class enemy" who say that the Soviet state "has taken the road that will lead to the ordinary bourgeois state." "It is very useful to read this sort of thing, which is written not because the Communist state allows you to write some things and does not allow you to write others, but because it really is the class truth, bluntly and frankly uttered by the class enemy."[198]

What he warned about, in a word, is of the inevitable coming of state capitalism if the bureaucratization and isolation of the Soviet state continued: "If we take that huge bureaucratic machine, that huge pile, we must ask: Who is leading whom? I doubt very much whether it could be said that the Communists were guiding this pile. To tell the truth, it is not they who are leading, they are being led."[199]

Just as he made no fetishism out of the workers' state, neither did he of the Bolshevik Party which he founded. We have followed the development of his views on that since 1902, and especially the period of 1917, when he told his Party that if they would not put the question of workers' power on the agenda, he would "go to the sailors." He, at all times, not only said so but *acted* on the principle that in revolutionary situations the masses are far in advance of the Party, and the Party ranks far in advance of the Party leadership. Of course, that did not mean that he did not assign a very fundamental role to the Party he founded; but it was *in strict relationship* to the actual spontaneous movement of the masses. *Outside of that relationship* the Party would become anything its worst enemies could think of. It did.

3) Lenin's Will

There is no greater indictment of the Party leadership that led the only successful revolution in history than Lenin's *Will*. In it he was concerned with his own colleagues, leaders of the Bolshevik Revolution in Russia in November 1917, who had themselves given birth to a new bureaucracy.

There is no more amazing document in the annals of politics than this brief, two-page *Will*.[200] It deals, in the concrete, with the leaders of the Russian Communist Party in a manner which leaves no division between politics and economics, history and philosophy, theory and practice, revolution and counter-revolution.

Lenin states boldly that, if the *dual* nature of the Russian state—that of being a state of workers and peasants—is at the root of the dispute between the principal combatants—Trotsky and Stalin—then no force on earth could stop the class division from bringing down the workers' state. Its fall is inevitable. However, the trends implicit in the dispute are *not yet* a reality. With that in mind, says Lenin, let's take a look at the general staff which made the revolution:

(1) *Stalin.* He is "rude and disloyal." *He must be removed.*

(2) Trotsky. His "non-Bolshevism," writes Lenin, does not in any way detract from the fact that he is "the most able man

in the present Central Committee," but he is *far too much attracted by the purely administrative side of affairs.*" (My emphasis.)

(3) Zinoviev and Kamenev. They publicized the date of revolution in the capitalist press, at the very moment when the workers were trying to take power. This was "no accident," Lenin reminds us. That is to say, at every critical moment, they can be expected to do the same.

What stands out in the rest of the *Will* is that it was not alone the older men who would look for administrative, instead of human, solutions to complex problems, but the younger men. Take Bukharin:

(4) "Bukharin is not only the most valuable and biggest theoretician of the party, but also may legitimately be considered the favorite of the whole party; but his theoretical views can only with the very greatest doubt be regarded as fully Marxian, for there is something scholastic in him (he never learned, and I think never fully understood, the dialectic)."

Lenin once said that the one word which could characterize the whole of the Marx-Engels Correspondence was "dialectics." This is no less true of Lenin in the period since his *Philosophic Notebooks*. This, again, is the central feature of all of Lenin's disputes with Bukharin, beginning with the National Question during World War I and ending with the *Will.* That was so not only in his public debates but in his commentary on Bukharin's theoretical works which Lenin did not publicly criticize. We have Lenin's Notebooks of 1920[201] in which he commented on Bukharin's *Economics of the Transition Period*.[202] The book puts forward the theory of an allegedly classless force, "a third group," (neither capitalist nor worker that is) which Bukharin calls "the technical intelligensia," whose mission it seems to be to establish "economic equilibrium." According to Bukharin, the "technical intelligentsia" was born "to replace the blind laws of the market." The development from industrial to finance capital was a development from an unorganized, anarchic commodity economy "to an organized, planned economy." The organizing force of that is the technical intelligentsia. This is the new absolute for state capitalism *and* for the dictatorship of the proletariat, "the transition period." No wonder Bukharin found himself alongside Trotsky in the Trade Union debate. As Lenin put it, in his "Remarks on Bukharin's *Economics of the Transition Period*," when he reached a passage where Bukharin finally remembered the two fundamental laws of capitalist production—centralization of capital and socialization of labor—"Finally, thank god! Human language instead of 'organized' babbling. All is well that ends well."[203] But two pages later he is hitting out against Bukharin again. He quotes Bukharin: "Once the destruction of capitalist production relations is really given and once the theoretic impossibility of their restoration is proven." Then Lenin comments: " 'Impossibility' is demonstrated only practically. The author does not pose *dialectically* the relationship of theory to practice."[204]

Now, in his *Will*, Lenin is summing up his analysis of Bukharin the theoretician, and again, the criticism is all concentrated in the word, "dialectic." It is evident that, to Lenin, one cannot be regarded as a Marxist though one is "the biggest theoretician of the party" *if* one has "never fully understood the dialectic."

Far from making the *Will* a new point of departure, the whole leadership of the Bolshevik Party agreed not to publish the founder's *Will*.

After Trotsky was exiled he published it. His commentary does not shed much illumation on it. Because Trotsky was closest to Lenin in that year, he tried to play down the seriousness of the 1920-21 debate, although it is clear Lenin had that debate in mind when he spoke of Trotsky's administrative attitude. Far from admitting his error, Trotsky insisted in all his later writings that "the mistake was not in the demand for statification, but in the fact that the economic policy did not correspond to the economic conditions."[205] He maintained that it was the economic conditions which made him propose free trade a year before the NEP and when the Political Bureau rejected his proposal, then he proposed statification of the union and "in the end" Lenin and he agreed. The truth, however, is that though all did vote for the NEP, Trotsky did so administratively once again and *therefore* he spoke of the concrete conditions which now "excluded the possibility of practical inclusion of trade unionists in the management of the economy."

It was not the economic conditions, neither in 1920, nor in 1921, nor in 1923, that made Trotsky write as he did. It was his attitude to the broad masses. Whether his program was for "free trade" or for the "Single Plan," his attitude to the masses was the same. The proof is in his theories *after* he was expelled from Russia and his arch-enemy, Stalin, put into operation the Five Year Plan which moved to its own gory conclusion in 1932. Trotsky still spoke the same language: "The role of factory committees remains important, of course, but in the sphere of the management of industry it has no longer a leading but an auxiliary position."

If Trotsky did not "mean" what he wrote, this great revolutionary wrote for two decades without finding the words to express what he did mean. Yet he always found words, thousands and thousands of words, to express the *opposite* of what he "did mean." It is impossible to arrive at any other conclusion than the fact that even Lenin's closest colleagues—and none was closer than Trotsky in that last period when Lenin appealed to him for a joint struggle against Stalin—had been treating Lenin's philosophic concepts as the Marxists before World War I had treated Marxian philosophy—as some rhetorical adjunct to "the great economic theories."

Nothing could be further from the truth. Without the Humanism of Marx, and later, of Lenin, the economic theories of both are meaningless. Leaders are not classless creatures floating between heaven and earth. They are very much earth men. When they lose close connection with the working class, they begin to represent the only *other* fundamental class in society—the capitalist class.

What was not yet a reality when Lenin wrote this, became a reality very soon when Stalin consolidated his power and introduced the Plan. It is true that even Lenin did not see Stalin as representing an alien class. But he was prophetic in this: he stated that *if* the differences within the leadership *did* reflect outright class differences, then nothing could save the workers' state. Nothing did. It became transformed into a State Capitalist society.

As we shall see later, once a new class. that of state capitalism, emerged in Russia, not only did the Russian Communist Party become its victim, so too did the Third International. Where Lenin, with characteristic precision, moved from the strict conditions he laid down for joining the International to an admission that the "language" of its Resolutions was "too Russian," Stalin imposed monolithism upon the Russian Communist Party and made it the ukase for the entire International.

The totalitarian dictators who now rule Russia have, after more than a quarter of a century of silence, during which the State and the Party have been entirely transformed, and all the people mentioned in the *Will* are dead, "suddenly" decided to admit its existence, subordinating it to their contrived myth of "the cult of personality." Nothing could have been stranger to Lenin. The "rude and disloyal" characterization of Stalin had nothing to do with any "cult of personality." What Lenin was saying was: it is the masses and only they who can smash the old and create the new, while the leaders who made such great contributions to the success of the Revolution, are, *as individuals* impotent to change the course of history. *Worse yet*, there is nothing in the philosophy and politics of the leaders that can keep the passions that stirred in their breasts from being as "base and mean" as those that stirred the capitalists to their mission.

What was not a reality in January, 1924, soon became a reality. It is not alone Stalin whom Lenin characterized, it is his progeny, the present rulers whom Stalin brought up in his own image. The one and only way for them to carry out Lenin's *Will* is to remove themselves from power.

Lenin *summed up* a lifetime spent in the revolutionary movement and concluded that if the Party dispute reflected actual class lines, nothing on earth can close up those divisive lines. The proletarian state would collapse. *So it did.*

PART V

THE PROBLEM OF OUR AGE: STATE CAPITALISM VS. FREEDOM

SECTION ONE

THE RUSSIAN SCENE

In the background of the 1920-21 trade union debate hovered the question of "planning." Despite Trotsky's later claim, it is not true that he had been the first to propose "a single national economic plan." The "necessity of a single national plan" appeared in The New Program, that is to say, the first program of the newly reorganized Communist Party following the successful 1917 Revolution. However, it is true that the whole question of planning, with the exception of that for the critical electric industry—GOELRO—was unreal when the working class was the soldiery defending the country. Trotsky was the first to reintroduce the idea of "the single national plan" as something concrete. In his speech to the Ninth Congress of the Russian Communist Party, March 1920, he said: "If we are seriously talking about planned economy which is planned from the center with a single thought, then manpower is distributed in accordance with a national economic plan on a given stage of development, then the working mass cannot be wandering Russians. It must be moved about, appointed, commanded, exactly like soldiers." This conception permeated all of Trotsky's speeches during the entire trade union debate. It is this which Lenin continued to oppose to his dying day.[206]

On December 22, 1920, Trotsky addressed the Eighth Congress of Soviets. In his speech—"The Road to a Single Economic Plan"—his administrative conception came out clearly enough in the formulation, "It is necessary to guarantee the unity of leadership in all economic commissariats." This administrative conception had been in Trotsky's propositions from the start when he first introduced into the leadership the idea of both planning and free trade. When Lenin "came around" to the idea of a single national plan, he repeated his objection: "but not administratively, not in uniting the commissariats"; rather in "drawing in the broadest possible masses." Even during the Kronstadt mutiny and the introduction of the NEP, the Resolution of the Tenth Congress considers necessary the realization of the following organizational measures: (1) *participation of the trade unions in the working out of a single economic plan and production program* and equal participation in the practical leadership by the realization and execution of these programs. (2) *The formation of economic organizations.* The organization of management of industry is formed by agreement between the trade union and the corresponding economic organs on the basis of proposals of the trade unions."

In a word, the two opposing conceptions of plan—which Marx in CAPITAL had first analyzed as the despotic plan of capital and the plan of cooperative labor—were being fought out in life rather than in theory in the most unusual circumstances of a workers' state with bureaucratic distortions allowing private trade. After the death of Lenin, the development of the NEP proceeded according to its own dialectic. Begun as a limited measure to allow the workers' state a breather, it ended in the usual growth of capital and the worsening of the conditions of the workers. Trotsky then introduced the question of Plan, this time to curb private trade and give a greater role to the workers, or at least, the workers' *state*. Stalin's opposition was purely factional. He was with Bukharin who had maintained that Russia could reach socialism "at a snail's pace." But Trotsky was no sooner expelled than the Plan, with a capital "P," was introduced. Stalin became the Planner extraordinary. To the extent that Trotsky clung to "the Plan," to that extent—despite his constant criticisms of "the tempo"—he was in actuality a prisoner of Stalin's Plan. In the process the very concept of socialism was reduced to the concept of Plan.

At the same time, on a world scale, the 1929 crash brought forth a flood of Plans from New Deal alphabetical agencies to Japan's Co-Prosperity Sphere. The theoretical problems Marx had posed, nearly a century ago, of the centralization of capital "into the hands of one capitalist or one capitalist corporation," the unemployed army, and the breakdown of capitalism had become concrete and crucial.

During the long Depression, thousands of American intellectuals turned toward Marxism and Leninism. They met Stalinist Communism which spent an incredible amount of time, care, energy and vigilance to confine Marx and Lenin within the bounds of its warped philosophy that private property equals capitalism, and State property equals socialism. Because Trotsky's conception, that workers' state equals state property, was not fundamentally different from the Stalinist thesis, it could not become an independent polarizing force despite his continuous struggle against the Stalinist bureaucracy. The result was that Russia continued to parade as if it were something different from capitalism, as if state capitalism was the new society of socialism rather than the ultimate development of capitalism.

Indeed, the analysis of the Russian Five Year Plans, and therefore of the law of motion of the Russian economy, originally made by this author to prove state capitalism in Russia, was disregarded by academic economists and Trotskyists alike. It is only with the cold war since the end of World War II that the academic economists took a second look at Russia and the phrase, "state capitalism," has suddenly become almost a journalistic cliché. Economics, however, is once again running a losing race against history, for by now it is not the "economics" of Marx, but his Humanism, which has assumed concreteness. This is *the* crucial question which Russian Communism must avoid like the plague. A concrete study of the actual development of the Plans *and* of the unplanned revolts against them will show why.

CHAPTER THIRTEEN

RUSSIAN STATE CAPITALISM VS. WORKERS' REVOLT

A. *The First Five Year Plan: Relations Between Planners and Workers, 1928-32.*

The First Five Year Plan was introduced in October 1928, shortly after Stalin emerged as the complete victor over all competing tendencies in the Russian Communist Party. The internal struggle had been unloosed with Lenin's death, and ended for a time with the exile of Trotsky and the imprisonment of his Left Opposition.

For a brief moment—the first few months of the Plan—the Russian workers welcomed the end of the New Economic Policy and the beginning of what they thought would be socialist planning. They were indeed so enthusiastic that they overfulfilled all "norms" (quotas of production) set by the State Plan.

The workers had gained the seven-hour day. Workers' Conflict Commissions were still functioning and, in general, favored workers in their fight with management. On January 5, 1929, for example, *Economic Life,* organ of the Council of Labor and Defense, emphasized that piece-work rates were subject to the approval of the Workers' Conflict Commission. The responsibility for fulfilling the financial program on the other hand, rested exclusively with management. That issue of the publication also reported that it was an ordinary occurrence for workers who were dismissed by management to be reinstated by the labor inspector. A new decree on January 24th, made workers responsible for damaged goods. The State Planners ordered the Five Year Plan to be completed in four. This speed-up became the sharp point of division between Planner and worker.

The State Planners called 1929 "the year of decision and transformation." That was certainly fact. From then on, the execution of the State Plan turned into an endless battle between the State Planners and the workers. The *two* antagonist plans inherent in capitalistic production, that of the workers and that of the management hierarchy, came to the fore. The Planners struck out against the workers' resistance to Plan. They eliminated workers' production conferences with their Conflict Commissions. Instead, production conferences were instituted between engineers and managers presided over by the politicians. At the same time, trials of professionals began. A number of State Plan officials were charged with "wrecking." This was the preview of that distinctive feature of state capitalism—confessions and recantations. It was lost upon the world because of the 1929 crash.

The world crisis, in turn, adversely affected the price Russian wheat could command on the world market. Money was short for the purchase of tractors. This was crucial for the Plan since tractors were not manufactured rapidly enough in Russia to take the place of draft animals. The peasants, in their resistance to collectivization, carried out such mass slaughter of animals that Russia has not recovered to this day.

The vast extent of this slaughter of animals was first revealed in Stalin's Report to the Seventeenth Congress of the Russian Communist Party, in 1934:

Millions of Head	1928	1932
Horses	33.9	19.6
Large Horned Cattle	70.5	40.7
Sheep and Goats	146.7	52.0
Pigs	26.0	11.6

There was such havoc on the countryside that the grain harvest declined from 83.5 million tons in 1930 to 70 million in 1931. The Planners never admitted the terrible famine of 1932-1933. They destroyed the census rather than reveal the number who perished.

In this "year of decision and transformation," the Russian workers grew increasingly restless. Beginning with 1930, the State hit back and instructed labor exchanges to put workers who leave jobs on their own initiative on a "special list." That blacklist deprived the worker of unemployment compensation. By October 9th, unemployment was declared "abolished." Unemployment compensation was stopped altogether. It became obligatory for factory directors to insert into the worker's paybook the reasons for his dismissal. But nothing could stop the labor turnover. By the end of the First Five Year Plan the labor turnover had reached the staggering figure of 152 per cent. Thereupon, Russia passed a new decree ". . . to order that a worker be dismissed from the services of a factory establishment even in the case of one day's absenteeism from work without sufficient reasons, and be deprived of the food-and-goods card issued to him as a member of the staff of the factory or establishment, and also of the use of the lodgings which were allowed to him in the houses belonging to the factory or establishment."

Planner and worker had reached opposite sides of the production perspective. As if stage-directed, the Soviet theoretician-politicians followed in the footsteps of classical political economy whose theory, Marx stated, was to "Accumulate, accumulate! That is Moses and the prophets! . . . . Accumulation for accumulation's sake, production for production's sake; by this formula classical economy expressed the historical mission of the bourgeoisie and did not for a single instant deceive itself over the birth-throes of wealth."[207]

Stalin did not deceive himself either. He was more ruthless because we live in the age of state capitalism. While the basic problem, everywhere in the world now, is labor productivity—how to get workers to work more—nowhere is it more urgent than in a totalitarian State. That is why it is totalitarian.

1) The Turnover Tax

There is a parallel between the functioning of a totalitarian State and the origins of private capitalism. In tracing the history of primitive accumulation, Marx concluded that "The only part of the so-called national wealth that actually enters into the collective possessions of modern peoples is their national debt."[208] Never was this more true than in Russia where the whole cost of industrialization and militarization has been borne by the people through that ingenious scheme known as the "turnover tax."

The manner of raising the State Treasury to pay for the Plan appeared in an innocent enough guise. On December 5, 1929, the Central Committee of the Russian Communist Party passed the following resolution: "To instruct the Peoples' Commissariat of Finance and Supreme Council of National Economy to draw up a system of taxation and government on the principle of a single tax on profits."

The "single tax on profits" turned out to have two sections: (1) a tax on profits which comprised nine to twelve per cent of the State budget; and (2) a turnover tax which comprised sixty to eighty per cent of the budget. Added to the compulsory deliveries by the collective farms, the turnover tax suffices to finance all industrialization and militarization.

The turnover tax is unevenly applied. It is lightest on heavy industry and heaviest on bread and agricultural produce. Contrary to the usual sales tax, which is a fixed percentage of the base price of the commodity, the turnover tax is a fixed percentage of the total sales value of merchandise including the amount of tax. In plain language this means that whereas a ninety per cent sales tax raises the price of merchandise ninety per cent, a ninety per cent turnover tax increases the sales price *tenfold*.

Take bread, which is the staff of life for a Russian worker. In paying a ruble for his kilo of black bread, he pays twenty-five kopeks for the actual cost of the bread, including production, distribution and delivery. The remaining seventy-five kopeks of that ruble go to the State as turnover tax. Prices skyrocketed so that the worker was faced with actual starvation. Rationing had to be introduced to assure the manual laborers of getting at least enough food.

The dividing line between Planners and workers was reaching the breaking point. Stalin, as usual, didn't flinch from his headlong march to capitalistic relations. Far from halting, or even slowing down the unbearable tempo of industrialization the slogan was: "the Five Year Plan in Four." Stalin called for the creation of a new "industrial and technical intelligentsia." He was very specific and tirelessly repetitious as to what the "New Conditions, New Tasks" were:

(1) It was necessary "to end depersonalization" by displaying "the maximum care for the specialists, engineers and technicians."

(2) It was necessary to be done with the foolishness of "equalitarianism." "Better Pay for Better Work."

(3) It was necessary to stop the "instability of labor in industry." A greater differentiation must be made between skilled and unskilled. "Wages must be organized in a new way."

(4) Business accounting must be introduced in order that an increase in accumulation and a lowering of production costs be achieved.

"Such," continued Stalin, in his address to the Conference of Industrial Managers on June 23, 1931, "are the new conditions of the development of industry, demanding new methods of work and new methods of leadership in our economic construction."

Although this was being done with great deliberation and consciousness, let no one assign omniscience to Stalin. There is no doubt that he was making a conscious effort to create "leaders," "managers," "organizers"—in a word, bosses. However it took another four years before an aristocracy of labor could be created. *His iron will was the manifestation of the objective drive of the industrial development.*

The First Five Year Plan ended with: (1) actual famine conditions on the countryside where Stalin was busy "liquidating the kulak as a class"; (2) a 152 per cent labor turnover in cities; and (3) the beginnings of a new class called "the industrial and technical intelligentsia."

The country had certainly achieved a rapid degree of industrialization, although we can dismiss the fantastic claims of accomplishments. (See Statistical Abstract at end of chapter.) More unplanned-for events occurred than those which were planned. The one thing that was certain beyond the peradventure of a doubt was the *direction* in which the economy was developing: there was a continuous preponderance of means of production over means of consumption. What Marx had shown as the principle of *capitalist* development turned out to be the exact direction of Russian economic development. The Planners proudly paraded the *relationship* achieved between the two major departments of production:

	1928	1932
Means of Production	44.3	52.3
Means of Consumption	55.7	46.7

On the horizon now appeared the social psysiognomy of the new ruling class which, in 1930, Christian Rakovsky, a leader of the Left Opposition, characterized as follows: "A ruling class other than the proletariat is crystallizing before our very eyes. The motive force of this singular class is the singular form of private property, state power."[209] Its *specific* contribution to capitalist production in general is forced labor. Forced labor camps appeared at the outset of the Second Five Year Plan.

B. *The Second Five Year Plan: The One-Party State Takes Full Totalitarian Form and Completes the Counter-Revolution*

1) *Forced Labor Camps*

Thus far the movement of the Russian economy was along the traditional direction of *any* capitalism. What greets us, however, in the Second Five Year Plan is *new*. That frightful companion of state capitalism—forced labor camps—made its first appearance in a modern industrial society in 1933.

In June of that year, the Commissariat of Labor was abolished and the trade unions were incorporated as part of the State machinery. Five weeks later, on August 1, 1933, under the euphemistic title of the "Labor Corrective Code," we find listed as "places of detention": "Corrective colonies, factory colonies, agricultural colonies, colonies of mass work and penalty colonies." The purpose? "Factory colonies are organized for the purpose of inculcating labor habits." By July 10, 1934, the Commissariat of Internal Affairs (NKVD) was created to take the place of the OGPU (secret police). It was given the additional duty of forming a "Department of Correctional and Labor Camps and Labor Settlements."

On October 27, 1934, this was supplemented by a Resolution of the Central Executive Committee and Council of Peoples' Commissars as follows: "All correction institutions (prisons, isolators, correction colonies and the bureaus of correction work without deprivation of freedom), which are at present managed by the Peoples' Commissariat of Justice of each constituent Republic, are to be transferred to the competence of the Peoples' Commissariat for Internal Affairs and its local organs."[210]

The "Commissariat of Justice" is nothing but a tool of the GPU which had been transformed into the NKVD so that from now on, Party purges, arrests, exile as well as inculcating "labor habits" are all "coordinated."[211] The image of the One-Party State Ruling Class now loomed inside every factory and hamlet and school. Not even minors were spared. The death penalty was introduced for "minors from twelve years of age."

2) Stakhanovite Speed Demons

The first year of the Second Five Year Plan had begun, on April 28, 1933, with the ordering of a Party purge. The purge lasted no less than two years and completely transformed what was left of the Bolshevik Party. The trade unions, as we saw, had already been abolished. They were blamed for the resistance of the workers to the norms set by the Plan. The terrible famine on the countryside drove millions of peasants to the city, creating a considerable army of "surplus labor." In an effort to halt this disrupting flow of peasants into the city, the Planners introduced the system of internal passports. At the same time they looked to this army of "surplus labor" to offset the low productivity in the factories. On March 16, 1933, *Industry,* the organ of the Commissariat of Heavy Industry, advised managers that they now have "a trump card: there are *more workers* in the shops than is necessary according to plans." (Emphasis in original.) The advice wasn't lost. The struggle between management and workers intensified.

Stalin's slogan of 1931, "End Depersonalization," or "Better Pay for Better Work," had lain dormant because it could not gain momentum until a piece-work system was introduced. Marx had declared the piece-work system to be best suited for the capitalist mode of production. In 1935, Stalin hailed such a system as "a gift from heaven." V. Mezhlauk (then chairman of the State Planning Commission) thus explained the "gift from heaven": "A plain miner, the Donets Basin hewer, Alexei Stakhanov, in response to Stalin's speech of May 4, 1935, the keynote of which was the care of the human being and which marked a new stage of development of the USSR, produced a new system of labor organization for the extraction of coal. The very first day his method was applied, he cut 102 tons of coal in one shift of six hours instead of the established rate of seven tons."

In the four months that elapsed between Stalin's speech of May 4th and Stakhanov's achievement of August 31st, the State did not miss a single publicity trick in setting up this "miracle." The press, photographers, the wires of the world, all immediately heard of the "gift from heaven." What they did *not* hear about were the hothouse conditions that were created to enable Stakhanov to become a speed demon: (1) He, and subsequent Stakhanovites, received the finest tools and ruined them at the fastest pace without having to pay for them. *The average production worker, on the other hand, must pay for all goods he damages.* (2) A brigade of helpers do all the detail work. They get no extra money. (3) Above everything, those record-breakers for a day do not repeat their records. They retire to swivel chairs. The mass of workers are now told that the "miracle" must be the *"norm."*

Armed with Stakhanovism, the State was able to revive the 1931 slogan, "End Depersonalization," or "train the recalcitrant factory hands," as the capitalist philosopher, Ure, expressed it more honestly in the day of the Industrial Revolution. Piece-work was made the prevailing system of work.

In the early workers' state, the pay differential, from the lowest paid worker to the highest, ranged from one to three. With Stakhanovism, the range became one to twenty.

"Ending depersonalization" and creating this extreme differentiation in pay would, however, mean nothing *if* rationing was still in effect and the Stakhanovites could buy nothing with their money. Thereupon, rationing was ended and the production of luxury goods extended:

	1932	1936
Watches	65,000	558,000
Gramaphones	58,000	337,000
Cameras	30,000	557,000
Silk (million meters)	21.5	51,220

The average worker continued to eat black bread and have his *kipyatok* (hot water). Given this base, *and with the given aim,* it was impossible simultaneously to extend production of the means of production as well as production of the means of consumption. One or the other had to be sacrificed. It was so under competitive, "market" capitalism. It proved to be so under autarchic, statified production. The constant necessity to expand in order to "catch up with and outdistance the capitalist lands"; the high organic composition of capital in the advanced capitalist world which imposed the same technical composition upon the Russian economy—all these demanded sacrifice in the sphere of producing. articles for mass consumption. Distribution of articles for mass consumption had to be brought into conformity with the reality of the stage of production. It was not a question, as Trotsky thought, of "bourgeois norms of distribution."[212] It was a matter of the *bourgeois method of production.* In his Preface to CAPITAL, Marx explained that he did not paint the capitalist and landlord in *"couleur de rose"* not because, as individuals, they were necessarily evil, "But here individuals are dealt with only insofar as they are the personifications of economic categories, embodiments of particular class-relationships and class-interests."

3) Stalin's Constitution on the "Classless" Intelligentsia

The mid-thirties saw the emergence of a "new type of Soviet man"—the type of executive-administrator familiar enough in the Western world as "the Man in the Grey Flannel Suit." He made clear by his everyday behavior how different he was from the workers. As if giving bodily form to what Marx called "the strictly regulating authority of the social mechanism of the labor process graduated into a complete hierarchy,"[213] this gentleman of the "intelligentsia" acted the part as if it were made for him.

In this hierarchic structure of the labor process, the "intelligentsia" serve the Plan. The norms are to be fulfilled *by others*— the great mass of the population. The compelling needs of capitalist value production made them of the mould of all rulers. They bear as little resemblance to the men and women who led the Revolution as Napoleon bore to the *sans-culottes*. The Russian workers know that the job of factory director is not, as the Planners put it, merely "functional." The extreme income differentials of 1 to 20 *are a starter*. The "mass" base of the present regime is wider than that under the Tsars. But the top echelons constitute, as we shall see in a moment, a bare 2.05 per cent of the total population.

In 1937, Molotov boasted that there were 1,751,000 "leading positions" in the Soviet Union, and "250,000 engineers and architects without personal responsibility for enterprises or projects." By 1939, Molotov achieved a precision that can come only from extreme *class* (ruling class) consciousness. The specificity in enumerating the hierarchy of skills and responsibility is a reflection of the class structure as enshrined in the Constitution of the land, which differentiates between workers and peasants, on the one hand, and "the intelligentsia," on the other hand:

Aristocracy of Labor (*thousands*) [214]

Heads of Tractor Brigades	97.6
Heads of Field Brigades	549.6
Heads of Livestock Brigades	103.1
Tractor Drivers)	803.1
Combine Operators)	
Skilled Laborers in Industry	5374.4
(including metal workers, lathe operators, welders and molders)	
Total	6927.8

"Employees" (*thousands*)

Economists and Statisticians	822
Legal Personnel (judges, attorneys)	46
Engineers, Architects (excluding those acting as directors)	250
Doctors and Middle Medical Personnel	762
Middle Technical Personnel	836
Agro-Technical Personnel	96
Teachers	1207
Cultural and Technical Workers (journalists, librarians, club directors)	495
Art Workers	46
Bookkeepers, Accountants, etc.	1769
Total	6329

"The Advanced Intelligentsia"[214]
(*thousands*)

Factory Directors and Managers, Kolkhoz, Sovkhoz & MTS Presidents	1751
Agronomists	80
Scientific Workers (including supervisors, professors)	93
Others (including army intelligentsia)	1550
Total	3474

We see revealed here that approximately 16.7 million, or less than ten per cent of the total population, are considered to be the "classless intelligentsia" in the broadest sense of the word. The "most advanced" of the intelligentsia, "the genuine creators of a new life," as Molotov called them—those who are the real bosses over the economy—constitute a mere 3.4 million or 2.05 per cent of the total population. The remaining eight per cent share in the surplus value and sing the praises of the rulers, to whom they leave the running of the economy and the State, setting policy and making Plans. Even without marking this "advanced" section, "exploiters," the social physiognomy of the ruling class is clear enough.

The "classless intelligentsia" had now to be given legitimacy. In 1936, the "Stalin Constitution" did just that. It is in direct opposition to the early Constitution which bore witness to the transitional character of the dictatorship of the proletariat in the following words: "The principal object of the constitution of the RSFSR, which is adapted to the present transition period, consists in the establishment of the dictatorship of the urban and rural proletariat and the poorest peasantry in the form of the strong All-Russian power with the aim of securing the complete suppression of the bourgeoisie, the abolition of exploitation of man by man, and the establishment of socialism under which there shall be neither class division nor *state* authority."

The new "Stalin Constitution," on the other hand, while claiming that "socialism was irrevocably established," nevertheless strengthened the State authority in the form of complete totalitarianism. It established piece-work as the reigning system ("From each according to his abilities, to each according to his work"). It decreed the protection of State property and personal property from "thieves and misappropriators." Far from the withering away of this State, this octopus will first gorge itself on what is left of the Revolution and on the workers who dare to resist. The Moscow Trials will liquidate, literally liquidate, the "general staff" who led the Revolution.

The ruling bureaucracy let loose with a series of macabre trials, the like of which had not been seen since the Spanish Inquisition and the hunt for witches. These trials had all the added terrorism, violence and shamelessness that only a totalitarian State can produce. First was the Zinoviev-Kamenev Trial; then the Radek-Piatakov and Bukharin-Rykov Trials; then the trial, en camera, of the military staff, headed by Tukhachevsky; and finally, the trial of the Yagodas who staged the first set of trials. The fantastic confessions and debasement of the "general staff of the Revolution" (who had long since capitulated and recapitulated and been isolated and imprisoned and were without stature or dignity) added up to the extermination of the memory of Revolution in *some* men, and helped complete the rewriting of history. But it was not for "history" that all this was staged. The full totalitarian State had taken shape. It was throwing its weight around. It needed that bloodletting in order to install firmly the *new* class created by the "new" method of production. Nor was the greatest frameup in history limited to the men who led the Revolution. Quite the contrary. Its *full* fury was unloosed against the workers. The *mass graves* discovered at the end of the war bear terrifying witness to that.[215] The millions who filled, and fill, the concentration camps show that the Moscow Trials did not change the workers' attitudes to the totalitarian State.

The Moscow Trials were the culmination of the counter-revolution that we saw developing early in the changed relations of production. A hangman's noose, rather than a full army, sufficed because only one of the parties to this conflict was armed. Whatever had been left of the October Revolution was exterminated and the proletarian state overthrown, not so much by the execution of the Old Bolsheviks (although that is always a manifestation of counter-revolution) *but by clearing a place in the process of production for the new class*. That place could have been cleared for the "classless intelligentsia" only where such a full-blown class had already come into existence, only where the *method of production itself* called it forth.

The production relations established by the Revolution had long become incompatible with this new method of production. That is why the blood-bath came at the end of the Second Five Year Plan. The Russian worker knows that the production relations of State-property demand his sweat and degradation. That State bears as much resemblance to a workers' state as the President of the United States Steel Corporation does to a steel worker just because they are both "employees" of the same corporation.

The counter-revolution of 1935-1937 was the culmination of what began with the introduction of the Plan. The Plan brought worker and manager into immediate conflict. The liquidation of the trade unions into the State apparatus symbolized the unbridgeable gulf between Planner and worker. Stakhanovites, engineers and administrators in production, and officers in the Army, joined those in the State to form the bulwark of the new ruling class which was given juridical status, that is, legitimacy, in the Soviet Constitution of 1936. *The experience of Russia since 1936 has exploded the idea that planning by any other class than the proletariat can ever reverse the law of motion of capitalist society.*

C. The Third Five Year Plan and a Summation of All the Plans at the Outbreak of War

Russia has achieved great industrial growth. The claims made by the Russians however are very questionable. The agricultural collapse in 1932, e.g., is listed as the Plan 93.7 per cent fulfilled. Since it did not figure as part of the Plan, the Planners simply ignored the drastic slaughter of livestock (greater than the decrease between 1914 and 1920, due to the war, Revolution, civil war and famine!). Since there were always more unplanned things occurring than planned ones, the Planners simply took the "average" of a basic industry which had overshot its mark "103 per cent" plus an uncompleted house which could not be lived in at all. It was thus easy for them to declare all sorts of "accomplishments." Two plus two equals anything they want it to equal.

Prior to World War II, however, criticism of the Russian method of measuring industrial growth was not widely believed because Russia alone seemed to be growing while the rest of the world was unable to get out of the throes of the long Depression.

The Russian economists referred to the purported 650 per cent achievements of Soviet industrialization, but an index of total industrial production which carefully weights each element in the economy in order to arrive at a statistically valid index of the volume of production, has never been prepared by the Russian economists. This task, never easy under ordinary circumstances, is especially difficult in the case of Soviet statistics, which are concealed or perverted to prove the correctness of the "general line." Under these circumstances, the best available gauge is to compare physical output of selected sections of both heavy and light industry, as well as agricultural production, against a background of statistics on population and national income. Below is an abstract of the USSR, prepared by this author, to illustrate the course of development for the whole economy from Tsarist times through 1940. Figures for the year 1922 have been included in order to show the accelerated pace of the growth of production, from the year of ruin following the end of counter-revolution and famine, to the eve of the First Five Year Plan. All data are from official State documents in the original Russian: 1913, 1922 and 1928 figures from *Gosplan: State Planning Commission for the Development of the National Economy of the USSR: The Five Year Plan*; 1932 and 1937 figures from *Gosplan: Results* (of respective Plans); 1940 figures from reports to the eighteenth conference of the Russian Communist Party, appearing in *Pravda*, February 18-21, 1941:

STATISTICAL ABSTRACT, 1913-1940*

Item	Unit	1913	1922	1928	1932	1937	1940
HEAVY INDUSTRY							
Electricity	Billion Kwt. Hrs.	1.9	1.0	5.0	13.0	36.4	39.6[1]
Coal	Million Tons	28.9	11.0	35.5	65.4	127.9	164.6
Petroleum	"	9.3	5.0	11.7	21.3	30.4	38.0
Pig Iron	"	4.2		3.3	6.2	14.5	14.9
Steel	"	4.2		4.0	5.9	17.7	18.4
Metal-Working							
Lathes	Thousands	1.5	.	3.8	18.1	36.1	53.9[1]
Tractors	"	0.0	0.0	1.3	48.9	51.0	31.1
Combines	"	0.0	0.0	0.0	10.0	43.9	
Length of Rail-							
roads	Thousand Kms.	59.0	71.0	77.0	83.4	84.9	93.0
Freight Traffic	Million Tons	132.4	58.0	156.2	267.9	517.3	536.6
LIGHT INDUSTRY							
Cottons	Million Meters	2224.0	0.6	2742.0	2417.0	3447.0	3491.0[1]
Woolens	"	95.0	22.0	96.6	88.7	108.3	114.0
Linen	Million Sq. Mtrs	219.0	93.0	165.0	135.0	285.2	272.2
Paper	Thousand Tons	197.0		284.5	479.0	831.6	834.0
Sugar	"	1290.0	211.0	1340.0	828.2	2421.0	2530.0
Leather Footwear	Million Prs.	60.	29.6	60.0	84.7	164.3	
AGRICULTURE & LIVESTOCK							
Total Area Sown	Million Hectares	105.0	77.7	112.9	134.4	135.3	141.2
Grain Harvested	Million Quintals	801.0	503.1	733.2	698.7	1202.9[2]	
Yield of Crop	Per Hectare	8.5	7.6	7.9	7.9	10.4[2]	
Horses	Million Head	35.8	24.1	35.9	19.6	16.7	17.5[3]
Cattle	"	60.6	45.8	70.5	40.7	57.0	64.6[3]
Sheep & Goats	"	121.2	91.1	146.7	52.0	81.3	111.6[3]
Pigs	"	20.9	12.1	16.0	11.6	22.8	32.5[3]
POPULATION & NATIONAL INCOME							
Total Population	Millions	139.3	133.3	152.3	165.7		170.5[3]
Workers & Em-							
ployees[5]	"	11.2		11.5	22.8	27.0	30.4
National Income							
of which:	Rubles pr Capita	52.0		56.0	95.0	198.0	30.4
Nominal Wages	Rubles pr Wk.	6.0		14.0			78.0[6]
Real Wkly Wages							
% of 1913[7]	"			125.0			62.4

* for footnotes consult following page (p. 231)

The value of gross industrial production (in billions of rubles, fixed 1926-1927 prices) reveals the following proportional development of the means of production (Group A) to the means of consumption (Group B) since the initiation of the First Five Year Plan:

	1928		1932		1937		1940	
	Value	%	Value	%	Value	%	Value	%
Group A	7.0	44.3	23.1	52.3	55.2	57.5	83.9	61.0
Group B	8.7	55.7	20.3	46.7	40.3	42.5	53.6	39.0

The statistical measurement of the Russian economy is presented here not in order to enter the field of dispute as to the phenomenal or non-phenomenal development of Russian industrialization. Nor, as important as that may be, is the author interested in the correct weighting of the official figures.[216] The fundamental purpose of this table of Russian industrialization, rather, was to show the *direction* in which the Russian economy moved, during the years of the Plans, before World War II wrought its devastation. It is clear from this that the direction of its growth—the preponderance of means of production over means of consumption, the high organic composition of capital, and the rapid deteriora-

---

1. 1938 figure.

2. This is not based on the unit which was used for previous years since, in 1933, for reasons best known to the Russian State and unrevealed to the public, a measure known as the "biological yield" was adopted. This standard of measurement meant that the grain was estimated on the stalks in the field before harvesting and a ten per cent deduction allowed for waste. All agricultural economists, with the exception of the Communists, agree that such an estimate does not account for actual waste. Some discount twenty per cent, others as high as thirty to forty per cent. However, this abstract reports official figures only.

3. 1939 figure.

4. 1937 census was destroyed and data were not made available to public.

5. Russian statistics lump workers and employees into one category; or when they separate them into two categories they lump rural and urban workers into one category and rural and urban employees into another; the above figures represent urban workers and employees.

6. Approximate, computed from eighteenth Party conference report.

7. Author's estimate. See next table on cost of food.

tion of the living standards of the masses—is neither merely accidental nor due to "war conditions" but was the inevitable consequence of the law of motion of that economy which, like any other capitalist economy, rests on paying the worker at minimum and extracting from him the maximum.[217]

From the statistical table it was seen that this author's estimate of the real weekly wages of the average Russian worker, in 1940, was only 62.4 per cent that of 1913. This point can be made more graphic by showing what food, which takes most of his pay, costs a Russian worker. An official 1926 study provided the information as to the foods an average Moscow worker consumed. The publication of the food index in Russia was stopped in 1930. However, with the abolition of rationing, the prices of the main commodities were published. Further data in regard to the rise in retail prices, in government stores in Moscow, 1939 and 1940, were gathered by the American Embassy and published in the November, 1939, and May, and August, 1940, issues of the *Monthly Labor Review*. From the food prices, against wages, a true picture of the conditions of the Russian workers will emerge:

COST OF FOOD IN TSARIST TIMES, AND BEFORE AND AFTER THE FIVE YEAR PLANS[218]

(In rubles per kilo, except milk in liters and eggs in units.)

Foodstuffs consumed in Moscow in 1926	Weekly Quan.	1913 Price	1913 Cost	1928 Price	1928 Cost	1940 Price	1940 Cost
Black bread	2.46	0.07	.1722	0.08	.1968	0.85	2.0910
Wheat flour	0.79	0.12	.0948	0.22	.1738	2.90	2.2910
Potatoes	3.04	0.05	.1520	0.09	.2736	1.20	3.6480
Beef	0.92	0.46	.4232	0.87	.8004	12.00	11.0400
Mutton	0.17	0.34	.0578	0.79	.1343	14.00	2.0080
Sugar	0.45	0.34	.1530	0.62	.2790	3.80	1.7100
Milk	1.24	0.11	.1364	0.06	.0744	2.10	2.6040
Butter	0.11	1.15	.1265	2.43	.2673	17.50	1.9250
Eggs	1.60	0.03	.0480	0.20	.3200	0.85	1.3600
Sunflower oil	0.12	0.15	.0180	0.53	.0636	15.65	1.8780
Totals			1.3819		2.5832		30.6270

Using 1913 as 100, the index of the cost of food for 1928 is 187, and for 1940 is 2,248. The weekly wages for those years were: 1913, six rubles; 1928, fourteen rubles; and 1940, 83 rubles. Again using 1913 as our base year for nominal weekly wages, we have an index for 1928 of 233, and for 1940 of 1,383. We can now construct our index of real wages by dividing the nominal weekly wage into the real cost of food, thus obtaining 125 *as the index of real wages* in 1928 and 62.4 per cent for 1940, when compared to Tsarist times.[219] Had we considered the further rise in food prices by October, 1940, it would have been a mere 55 per cent of 1913! And even that appallingly low figure, which so glaringly proves the deterioration in the worker's standard of living, does not picture the situation at its worst, for we have considered the single uniform price in 1940 and not the open market price (to which the worker sometimes had to resort because few foods were available in State stores). On the average, the open market prices were 78 per cent higher than the State store prices! There is supposed to be no black market in Russia but in the officially recognized free market beefsteak sold for seventeen rubles a kilo when the State stores sold the same commodity at ten and a half rubles!

At the same time, industrial development has *not* brought Russia out of its backwardness when judged by *per capita* production. These comparative figures cited by Molotov in 1937 make the point:

PER CAPITA WORLD PRODUCTION IN 1937

	Unit	USSR	USA	Germany	Japan
Electricity	kwt. hr	215	1160	735	421
Coal	kilo	757	3429	3313	643
Pig Iron	"	86	292	234	30
Steel	"	105	397	251	62
Cement	"	32	156	173	60
Soap	"	3	12	7	—
Sugar	"	14	12	29	17
Cottons	sq. meter	16	58	—	39
Paper	kilo	5	48	42	8
Leather ftwr.	pair	16	2.6	1.1	—

In presenting the Third Five Year Plan, therefore, Molotov made *per capita* production the key word: "People here and there forgot that economically, that is from the point of view of the volume of industrial output *per capita* of the population, we are still behind some capitalist countries. . . . Socialism has. been built in the USSR but only in the main. We have still a very great deal to do before the USSR is properly supplied with all that is necessary . . . before we raise our country economically as well as technically to the level not only as high as that of the foremost capitalist countries but considerably higher."

The slogan of the First Five Year Plan—"to catch up with and outdistance the capitalist lands"—held for the Second Plan and remained for the Third Plan. Again, the unpardonable sin was the Russian workers' attitude to work under the Plan. Molotov knows better than anyone that to accomplish what they did in the First Plan they were forced to use 22.8 million workers whereas the Plan called only for 15.7 million. He knows that the low labor productivity of the Russian worker is not a sign of his backwardness but a *sign of his continuous revolt against the conditions of production.*

1) Crises and Purges

The fundamental error of those who assume that a single capitalist society is not governed by the same laws as a society composed of individual private property-owning capitalists lies in a failure to realize that what happens in the market is not the cause, *but the consequence,* of the inherent contradictions of the process of production. A single capitalist society does not have an unlimited market. The market for consumption goods, as we have shown, is strictly limited to the luxuries of the rulers and the necessaries of the workers when paid at value.

The slogan, "to catch up with and outdistance capitalist lands," was the reflection of the compelling motive of the present world economy—who will rule over the *world* market?[220] Therein lies the secret of the growth of the means of production at the expense of the means of consumption. Therein lies the cause for the living standards of the masses growing worse despite the "State's desire" for what it called "the still better improvement of the conditions of the working class."

Our specific single capitalist society has achieved some highly modern factories, a showy subway, and, as Khrushchev assures us, an H-bomb big enough so that if he dropped it over the polar ice caps it would flood the world, but it has not stopped to raise the living standards of the masses of Russian workers. It cannot. Capital will not allow it. Because of this the economy is in constant crisis.

The value of capital in the surrounding world is constantly depreciating which means that the value of capital inside the capitalist country is constantly depreciating. It may not depreciate fully on the bureaucrats' books. However, since the real *value* of the product can be no greater than the value of the corresponding plant on the world market, the moment the Ford tractor was put alongside the Stalingrad tractor, the State had to reduce the price of its own brand. This was the case in 1931 when Russia, while importing ninety per cent of the world's production of tractors, sold its own below cost.

Of greater importance—and therein lies the essence of Marx's analysis of all economic categories as social categories—is the fact that no matter what figures may appear on the books, the means of production *in the process of production* reveal their true value in their relationship to the worker. That is to say, if an obsolescent machine was not destroyed but continued to be used in production, the worker suffers the more since the manager of production still expects him to produce articles at the socially-necessary labor time set by the time clock of the *world* market.

As long as planning is governed by the necessity to pay the laborer the *minimum* necessary for his existence, and to extract from him the *maximum* surplus value, in order to maintain the productive system as far as possible within the lawless laws of the world market, governed by the law of value, that is how long capitalist relations of production exist, no matter what you *name* the social order. It has thus been absolutely impossible for Stalin, as for his heirs, to guide the productive system without sudden stagnation and crises due to the constant necessity of adjusting the individual components of total capital to one another and to the world market. They have avoided the ordinary type of commercial crises. But on the other hand, when the crises came, they were more violent and destructive. Such was the case in 1932 and again in 1937. In 1932 it took the form of complete chaos on the countryside; in 1937 it took the form of the spectacular Moscow trials and the *en camera* military trials. In both cases, industrial production as planned was as far apart from industrial production as accomplished, as heaven is from earth.

Purges are not due to a state of mind but to a state of production.[221] They have never ceased in Russia and will never cease under that regime because the crises never cease. The crises never cease because the revolt of the working class is continuous.

2) *Labor Before the Law*

The Party bureaucracy, armed with full State power, began to wreak their vengeance in a new set of anti-labor "labor legislation"—the most oppressive ever recorded in the history of modern times.

The 1940 laws forbid a worker to leave his job. Any infraction of factory discipline, such as coming fifteen minutes late, is made punishable by six months at "corrective labor," that is, labor in the factory at twenty-five per cent reduction in pay. If this law is violated, the worker is sent to forced labor camps.

From the workers, the totalitarian bureaucracy moved over to take their vengeance on the youth. Teen-agers were taken out of school and given six months to two years "free vocational training," at the end of which they were to work where the State directed, for two and up to four years at "the prevailing rate of pay."

On December 26, 1940, *Pravda* reported that, particularly in the coal mines, truancies were greater in the first six months of the operation of the law than in the previous period. At the 1941 Party Conference, held just a few months before the Nazi attack and after the European war had already been going on for nearly two years, the report stated that workers "were constantly absenting themselves, particularly after pay day," and that fully a third did not accomplish their "norms."

This Draconian anti-labor legislation records the terror of the ruling bureaucracy in the face of the revolt of the workers. The revolt had begun soon after the inauguration of the First Five Year Plan. The workers perform miracles of ingenuity and endurance in resisting the totalitarian stranglehold over production. The peasants do the same on the countryside.

The millions in forced labor camps are the true measure of the never-ending resistance of the Russian masses to the Russian rulers in the State, in the factory, and in the fields. Had the *revolt* not been so persistent, the terror would not have been so violent.

D. *The War and the Assault on Marx's CAPITAL*

In 1939, Hitler—with his own Three Year Plans, his own "end to unemployment," his gas chambers and concentration camps—was poised, ready to centralize all of European capital. He got the go-sign from Stalin and, with the Nazi-Soviet Pact, launched the war against Poland which the two dictators carved up between themselves. By 1941, the dictators fell out. Stalin's full imperialist ambitions were not to be met until he joined with the Allies and got what he couldn't get from Hitler: Eastern Europe. In June 1941, Nazi Germany launched its attack against Russia. So deep are the antagonisms within Russia, that Hitler marched up to Stalingrad before the Russian people chose to turn the invaders back rather than suffer the added torment of foreign rule.

But the Russian Planners did not change. Nor did they stop at taking away the workers' seven-hour day and making eight hours the regular working day with obligatory "overtime." In fact, the slogan was, "No distinction between the front and the rear."

The insatiable hunger for "production and more production" lost all bounds, right in the midst of war, when the bureaucracy discovered the conveyor belt system. The year 1943 is officially referred to as "the year of the conveyor belt system." The assembly line technique was used to transform the individual break-neck competition of Stakhanovism into "socialist emulation," that is, factory-to-factory competition.

No Russian worker could see the difference between his "socialist labor" and that which was described by Marx as capitalistic, alienated labor. The questions asked by students were likewise unanswerable, hence the teaching of political economy was stopped altogether.[222] In the year that they discovered the conveyor belt system, the totalitarian theoreticians were emboldened to lay their brutal hands on Marx's CAPITAL. They ordered that the dialectical structure of CAPITAL no longer be followed. They now said that the law of value functions in "the land of socialism."

Heretofore, everyone—friend and foe, Marxist and non-Marxist alike—had agreed that Marx's law of value was the characteristic mark of the capitalist society. For that very reason, Russian theoreticians, until the publication of this 1943 article, claimed that the law of value did not operate in their country which they declared to be "the land of socialism." Now, they found themselves in the dilemma of refusing to depart from the claim that Russia is "socialist," yet at the same time suddenly admitting that the law of value does operate in Russia. For a Marxist that would be an impossible situation. For a Russian Communist, however, it was a blessing for Russian theory was thus finally squared with Russian reality. As I wrote in my commentary then: "The ideas and methodology of the article are not accidental. They are the methodology of an 'intelligentsia' concerned with the acquisition of 'surplus products'. What is important is that this departure from 'past teaching of political economy' actually mirrors economic reality. The Soviet Union has entered the period of 'applied economics'. Instead of theory, the article presents an administrative formula for minimum costs and maximum production. It is the constitution of Russia's post-war economy."

It is true that the theoreticians thought they would solve their main problem of explaining away the functioning of the capitalistic law of value. However, the theoretical change of front is the least important aspect of the startling reversal in theory. Take, for example, the proposal that henceforth the teaching of CAPITAL should not begin with Chapter I which includes the famous section on the "Fetishism of Commodities." The fetishism of commodities is the mystery with which the social relations of production are clothed in bourgeois society. In Russia, where the society is completely state capitalist, the bourgeois fetishism of commodities seems to be overcome. In a sense it is. The Russian bureaucrats are not affected by problems of the market, nor confused by ideas of equal exchange, as are the bourgeois economists. But another aspect of fetishism, *the* critical one that Marx uncovered, was the *perversity* of relations between machine and man where dead labor dominates over living labor. That is why Marx is so insistent in saying that the *form* of the commodity is fantastic, not because it is not true, but because it correctly reflects the *real* relations at the point of production. This fetishism not only has not been overcome in Russia, the Plan has perfected it and become a prisoner of it.

They have substituted for fetishism of commodities the fetishism of the Plan. But their Plan turns out to be no more than a disguise for the actual relations of production in the factory. They are no more able to overcome *this* fetishism than are the bourgeois economists. In other words, far from the Plan bringing light into the relations of production in the factory the State Planners express in the Plan the total domination of the workers by the machine. In reality, therefore, the State Plan is nothing but the organization of the proletariat to produce under the domination of the machine.[223] The need to square theory with reality meant one thing for the theoreticians and something else for the Russian workers. The former searched for the proper quotations. The latter knew that nothing at all would be changed for them with the end of the war. The teaching of CAPITAL would undergo the change. They would have to continue to produce more and more. At the same time the theoretical revision served notice to the Allies that Russia was "in the market" for world domination. The theoretic foundation for the cold war was laid.

Never before has so gigantic a State mobilized itself with such murderous vigilance to keep the proletariat at work while the leaders plan. The Russian totalitarian bureaucracy is the most deadly, the most insidious, the most dangerous enemy because it springs from the proletariat and cloaks itself in Marxist terminology.

CHAPTER FOURTEEN

STALIN

Upon what meat hath this our Caesar
fed
That he has grown so great.—Shakespeare

Stalin had once been a revolutionary, a Bolshevik, which meant an uncompromising fighter for the overthrow of Tsarism. There was a time when Bolshevism was a doctrine of liberation. Today, everyone knows Russian Communism as the greatest barbarism on earth. Stalin is the name which symbolizes this.

It was this one-time revolutionary who initiated, and carried through, with unmatched brutality, the greatest *counter-revolution* in all history. But Stalin is only the Russian name for a phenomenon that is *world-wide.*

Two questions stand out: (1) Why does any individual behave like that? *What objective movement in the economy, what class impulses, necessitate such brutality?* (2) What specific characteristics in a man enable him to become the receptacle and the executor of class impulses from an alien class—the very one he either challenged or actually helped overthrow?

When the energies of the million-headed masses smashed the old and created the new, those who led the Russian Revolution could and did make great contributions to the greatest single fact of world history: the creation of the workers' state.

However, when the Russian working-class was itself in a crisis, these intellectual leaders, as individuals, did not stack up very high. At a critical juncture in world history their will reflected the movement of the working-class. But, as Lenin pointed out in his *WILL*, "A seriously false turn at that juncture could unloose the disintegrative forces at work in a dual worker-peasant state which is surrounded by world capitalism, from which it cannot fully free itself without the help of the advanced European working-class."

As Lenin lay dying, the German Revolution failed, and in Russia's exhaustion Stalin flourished.

Stalin's outstanding trait was a bureaucratic attitude to the masses. He claimed to be a leader of the workers, but to him it meant to make the workers do as the leader wanted and told them to do. He spoke of the party as "the vanguard of the proletariat," but to him this meant that just as the leaders of the party were *to tell the ranks* what to do, so the party was *to order the masses about*. This was true of him as an individual even when he was a revolutionary fighting in the underground. Once the Communist Party got into power his passion for bossing came out in full bloom. It showed itself clearest of all in his attitude to the many nationalities which constitute the Soviet Union.

In overthrowing the Tsarist monarchy, the Russian workers had fought not only to overthrow the capitalists and the landlords, but to overthrow as well the Great Russian overlordship of the many nationalities in Russia. One of their first acts upon getting into power was to grant freedom to all the different nationalities that lived in Russia. But Stalin, though himself a Georgian, ran roughshod over the aspirations of his native Georgia, displaying a chauvinism and a national arrogance that was as rabid as that of any Tsarist official.

Lenin drew back in horror. "Scratch a Bolshevik," he wrote, "and you will find a Great Russian chauvinist." It remains the most precise commentary of the totalitarian personality-in-the-making.

Lenin's last appeal to Trotsky reads: "I am declaring war on Great Russian chauvinism."[224] His last theoretical contribution on the National Question continued: "It is said we need a single apparatus. From where come such assertions? Is it not from the same Russian apparatus, which, as I have pointed out in one of the previous numbers of my diary, was borrowed from Tsarism and only barely annointed with the Soviet chrism?"

When Stalin began his struggle for power, as Lenin lay dying, he moved quite empirically. The road to power seemed obvious: it was to get control of the Party which was the State which was the Economy. To get the Party which was *in power* meant to get control of its functionaries, those people who displayed a "passion for bossing," and whom Lenin had fought. These, Stalin embraced. He knew them and knew how to talk to them. Where Lenin appealed to the *non-party masses* to help him expose the vain Communist bureaucrat, Stalin was later to appeal to the *non-party careerists* to flood the Party and help defeat Trotsky. It wasn't, as Trotsky thought, because the new members didn't know the *issues* in dispute. It was that they *chose* what Stalin represented.

No one, however, at that time conceived Stalin as a *class* enemy, not even Lenin who had asked for his removal from the post of General Secretary. Although Stalin was crafty enough, there is no point to assigning omniscience to him either. He didn't know what strong objective forces were pulling for him. He didn't have a *theory* about that. He let Bukharin carry the ball here while he shied away from fundamental theoretical questions. That does *not* mean that theory didn't matter to him, but as yet he didn't know *what* theory he would espouse. He was nowhere the mediocrity Trotsky made him out to be—he was capable enough when he wanted to win that way. It was *he* who made Trotsky argue on *his* ground, *his* fantastic notion of "socialism in one country." It was *he* who made Trotsky's "permanent revolution" appear as an immediate adventuristic scheme that was out of all bounds for exhausted Russia in the 1920's. He wasn't playing intellectual games. He was playing for power. He maneuvered with one faction, then with another. He played the modest man who didn't hunger for Lenin's mantle and portrayed Trotsky as one who did. Thus he defeated both the Left and Right Oppositions and became the undisputed leader of the Party.

The first problem that confronted him when he won the victory of Party power was that the kulak refused to turn grain over to the Soviet State. That decided the sudden zigzag for the abolition of "the kulak as a class," just as the resulting chaos made him turn backwards with his "Dizzy With Success" speech.

There wasn't a zigzag, however, that didn't rhyme with the strong pull of an objective force.

Once the Russian people, "to a man," did not run the economy and the state; once the German Revolution too was defeated; once world capitalism regained its breath and the vortex of the world market had full sway, the logic of the Russian development was startling, unforeseen, but inevitable. The Revolution then found the really serious counter-revolution *inside itself*. Stalin was the perfect representative of that counter-revolution, not only because his personality suited the task so well, but, above all, because he did come *from* the Revolutionary Party and did have command of the Marxist "language." So corrupt and outlived is capitalism that it cannot hope to win except by pretending to be other than it is. Hitler too knew how to call his fascism National *Socialism*. Stalin was Hitler's superior by far, because his functionaries came from the working-class.

In Stalin's zigzags and lack of theoretical acumen was the straight line of development of the newly-emergent world phenomenon of state capitalism. It now had a personality, a totalitarian personality, armed with a theory of totalitarianism called "the monolithic Party."

Nor was the "liquidation of the kulak as a class" as ludicrous as Trotsky made it appear. It is true a class cannot be liquidated by fiat. A class is such by virtue of its role in production and production would have to be entirely differently motivated to overcome a class. That is certainly not a job to be done in a day or a year. But, *objectively*, this is not what Stalin meant. Objectively, the kulak couldn't stand up to the *combined* might of State and industry. That was true even under "ordinary capitalism" —agriculture lost out to industry in the long run. Stalin saw that it happened in an enormously accelerated fashion. State power enforced collectivization so rapidly that he could dream of "liquidating the kulaks as a class." He first now became conscious of representing a new force—*State* power, the *State* Plan, the *State* economy, the *State* Party. There was going to be no "withering away" of *his* State. His rule was absolute and so was his theory and ideology.

In 1931, Stalin's slogan, "End Depersonalization," got nowhere. By 1934, however, when there was sufficient means of production built up, and insufficient means of consumption to go around, there were enough opportunists to create a "mass" base for the ruling bureaucracy. Again, the creation of Stakhanovism was done in hothouse fashion. This time, however, as opposed to the time of liquidating kulak resistance, there was but one purpose—to appropriate the wealth created by the workers. No ghost come from the grave was needed to tell him of this. Stalin concluded it was time to legitimize the new class called "the classless intelligentsia." The new Stalin Constitution likewise had no need for ghosts from the past. It was then that he planned the macabre Moscow Trials to kill off, at one and the same time, what was left of the "General Staff of the Revolution," *and* the workers who resisted the norms set by the Plan.

Stalin acted that way to the Russian *people*. He acted that way to *Hitler*. He, Stalin, set the conditions for the Nazi-Soviet pact. His share of Poland was one, *only one,* of the territories he wanted. What he didn't get from Hitler, namely, all of Eastern Europe, he got from the *Allies*. When the war was over in 1945, and he was victor over his immediate enemy, he wanted to move straightway toward world conquest—especially if he could get others, Chinese and North Koreans, to do the fighting.

Hitler used to rave and rant to his lieutenants of his envy and appreciation of the genius of Stalin who had the perspicacity and audacity to get rid of the general staff of the Red Army before launching a world war. He knew whereof he spoke, for totalitarian economics has no room for a command divided between political and military needs.

But by 1948, after two decades of undisputed power, topped by a military victory, Stalin, to use a phrase of his own on another occasion, was "dizzy with success." This is not used here as a psychological epithet. His exhilaration from success was a sign that he no longer was responsive to the *objective needs* requisite for a struggle for world power. The bureaucracy whom Stalin had so long and so fully represented began to find him inadequate to the new situation created by the end of a world war which no one really won but which left each of the two state capitalist giants so exhausted that a halt had to be called. Stalin failed to grasp the new situation. He had won a war, a mighty one, over Nazi Germany, yes. But he had yet to face the real contender for world power—the United States.

Economists like Varga[225] were saying that if Plan means "no general crisis," then there will be no general crisis in the private capitalist world. Plan, said Varga, is no longer a monopoly of "socialism." The war showed that the Allies also planned and meant to continue to plan, and not to let a depression follow the war.

One top economist, Maria Natanovna Smit, spoke of state capitalism in the spirit in which Lenin had analyzed it. "The book," she began, referring to Varga's work, "lacks an analysis of the great new changes connected with the transition from simple monopoly capitalism to state monopoly capitalism, as Lenin understood this transition. . . . During the war, world capitalism took a step forward not only toward concentration in general, but also toward state capitalism in even a greater degree than formerly." (Lenin's *Collected Works*, Russian edition, Vol. XXX, p. 300.) "Where Lenin unites the concept of 'state' and of monopoly, Com. Varga seems to separate them: each exists by itself, and meanwhile in fact the process of coalescence of state with monopolists manifests itself quite sharply at the present time in such countries as the U.S.A. and England."

This, for Stalin, was "dangerous cosmopolitanism." It had to be fought—not in Varga nor in Maria Natanovna Smit, who had no power and could easily be made to sing another song—but among those closest to him, the Politburo members who were "deviating." The first to go was Voznessensky, Chairman of the State Planning Commission.

How pyrrhic was Stalin's victory could be seen in the unrest in the national republics which constitute Russia. By a ukase of the Supreme Soviet, five autonomous republics were liquidated. Russia had suffered the greatest devastation and was in crying need for a labor force to rebuild the country. It could not hope to have that force enlarged by the return of slave laborers in Hitler's Germany—too many had willingly escaped from the prison which was Stalin's Russia. Anyone who was in Germany at the end of the war knows that long before Koje, the Korean War and the massacre of P.O.W.'s, a veritable civil war was going on in the Russian displaced persons camps. But the Allies forced the Russians to return to their "homeland."

The restlessness of the Russian masses knew no bounds. If they were merely to go on in the same old way, keeping their noses to the grindstone, then at least it would not be in the god-forsaken Urals. The totalitarian Russian bureaucracy had all the power and all the force and all the laws it needed to enforce labor discipline, but absolutely nothing could stem the tide of resistance of returning Russians. The tide invalidated all laws. To have a labor force at all, the Planners were compelled to make an unplanned declaration—an amnesty for all labor offenses committed during the war.

So catastrophic, however, had been the decline of the labor force during the war years (a drop from 31.2 million in 1940 to 27.2 million in 1945 with more than a third of these unskilled new women workers) that even the amnesty was insufficient to create the labor force necessary. Thereupon occurred one of the speediest demobilizations of an army anywhere in the world; no fewer than ten million were demobilized between 1945 and 1947.

By 1948, Stalin had only one colleague fully with him in the headlong rush to World War III and he, Zhdanov, was assassinated without the "Great Leader" knowing. This was the beginning of the end of Stalin's power.

By 1950, the Russian economy had about got back to normal when Stalin had a brainstorm. It was known as the "Stalin Plan for the Transformation of Nature." To put the scheme into effect Stalin brought to Moscow one N. Khrushchev from the Ukraine, where he had been Premier. This man had been ruthless enough to put down actual armed insurrection, and now he was given the job to announce the most fantastic scheme yet—the creation of *agrogorods* (agricultural towns). Just like that—decree them, and they shall arise, and abolish the centuries old distinction between city and country. Instead of "abolishing" the distinction between city and country, this scheme brought such chaos to the country-side that even in this land of monolithic planning, the idea had to be shelved in a few months. It was easy enough to have songs written about this irrigation which would soon produce enough food to feed 100 million people. It was something quite different to convince the peasant to transport, at his own expense and his own time, his little hut in the collective farm to the agro-town which was yet to be created, while the apartment house in which he was to live like a worker had not only not been built, it had not even been planned.

But if Stalin had to be satisfied with something less than the "abolition" of the difference between city and country, he was going full speed ahead towards a head-on collision with the United States—at least where he could get the Koreans and the Chinese to do the fighting for him. There was no breathing spell, let alone peace. Yugoslavia had defected.[226] The iron-fisted Stalin was clearly becoming a millstone around the neck of the bureaucracy which yearned for a truce between wars.

Stalin may have read the handwriting on the wall; he certainly took no chances with his too-eager heirs. Though he let Malenkov read the main address at the nineteenth Congress, he made his greatest bid to remain *the* immortal theoretician with his 1952 magnum opus, "Economic Problems of Socialism."

This, which we may call Stalin's "Last Testament," is the most pathetic document that ever a tyrant left his fighting heirs. After a quarter of a century of Plans, and what he assured them was the actual transition "from socialism to full communism," Stalin's mighty labors brought forth only the need to merge the peasant's private allotment adjoining the collective farm into the collective itself. Upon this private garden, rightly called in this country "an acre and a cow," evidently depends the building of "full communism." This, plus the "gradual abolition" of the collective farm market, and substitution of "products exchange" for money exchange, will bring them to "communism in a single country."

That was little enough of a legacy to leave his bureaucratic heirs. But the Russian masses, who know that Stalin doesn't go in for theory unless he *plans to apply it,* made one grand rush to transform their money into manufactured products (consumer goods), and the peasants at the same time withheld farm products. This does not mean that it was the Stalin thesis and not the actual difficulties, particularly in agriculture and particularly since Korea, that created the crisis. Nevertheless it is true that it was the closest to panic Russia had been since forced collectivization took its toll in 1932.

The minute Stalin was buried, the bureaucracy ran from his last testament like rats from a sinking ship. This absolute tyrant who, when alive, could command the adulation, "Sun of the Himalayas," was forgotten ere a single sundown. This does not mean that his battling heirs fundamentally changed a single part of the state capitalist structure they inherited, either before or after "De-Stalinization." They continue "Communism" as a system of the most sweated labor in a modern industrial society, buttressed by a vast complex of spies and counter-spies. The counter-spies are not "foreign agents." They are "Party men" who spy on the police who spy on the Party men and both spy on the people. This does not mean the death of Stalin brought about the new conflicts in Russia. It would be far more correct to say that the continuous, inner crisis in Russia had produced Stalin's death. It does mean that the death of Stalin symbolizes the beginning of the end of totalitarianism, not on the part of his heirs, but from the forced labor camps in the wilds of Siberia that buttress the Russian regime. But before the challenge from Vorkuta, the bell of freedom sounded in East Berlin in the heart of Europe.

CHAPTER FIFTEEN

THE BEGINNING OF THE END OF
RUSSIAN TOTALITARIANISM

1) East Germany, June 17, 1953

The myth that the Russian totalitarian State is invincible was suddenly and strikingly shattered. On June 17, 1953, the workers in the East German satellite took matters into their own hands on the questions of speed-up. They moved speedily, confidently, courageously and in an unprecedented manner to undermine the puppet state. Heretofore, absenteeism and slowdowns were the only weapons used by the workers against the intolerable conditions in the factories. But the struggle reached a new and higher stage of opposition in late Spring of 1953. Here is a brief chronicle of the events leading up to June 17th and the days that followed:

Beginning with May 18th, the Communist government announced a new increase in work hours. The German workers broke out in open strikes. In one effort to stop the strikes the Communist government, on June 10th, offered concessions on all points *except* speed-up.

On June 16th, construction workers organized a protest march against speed-up from the Stalin Alee housing project. The government sent its supporters to join the marchers, apparently hoping to appear as sponsor. But as the marchers approached the government, joined enroute by swelling numbers of demonstrators, the cry had become, "Down With the Zones—Down With the Government." The government then admitted it had been doing "wrong" and issued an order revoking the speed-up. It was too late.

249

By the evening of June 16th, the workers had turned the streets of East Berlin into political centers. On block after block, hundreds of people assembled and discussed what to do next. Early on the morning of June 17th they acted.

Columns of strikers charged the main government buildings where the government bureaucrats cowered. Reluctant police moved into pre-arranged positions. Youth and workers tore down the symbols of Communist power—flags, posters, pictures of Communist leaders. Despite rifle shots, one young man clambered up the famous Brandenburg Gate and tore down the Communist banner. Dispersing on one street and surging up another, the swelling ranks of strikers chanted, "We will not be slaves." *For four hours the only power in East Berlin belonged to the workers.* They, in fact, overthrew the East German government. They destroyed the police power, burning barracks, throwing policemen out of windows, and forcing them to flee to the West or to come over to the side of the workers.

At 1:00 P.M. the Russian command marched into Berlin with ten thousand troops and decreed martial law. Street gatherings of more than three people were forbidden. The people laughed at the order.

At the same time, in Jena, strikers from the Zeiss optical factory stormed the Communist Party and Communist Youth offices and hurled books, papers, typewriters out of the windows and burned them.

At the Kodak supplies plant, the workers took over and put strikers in charge.

State railway workers walked out, crippling zonal intercommunications and halting the shipment of reparations into Russia.

Construction workers cut power cables of both elevated and subway lines and blocked the tracks.

Twenty-five thousand workers at the Leuna Chemical plant (formerly I.G. Farben) at Halle set the plant afire. The workers at the Buna synthetic rubber plant burned it down. These plants were the chief suppliers of gas and tires to the occupation army.

The hard coal area at Zwickau was damaged beyond estimate. The demonstrators set fire to huge piles of coal between Halle and Magdeburg. They destroyed uranium mining facilities.

They opened prisons and concentration camps to set free the political prisoners. At Gera, an industrial city about the size of Cincinnati, near the Russian-operated uranium mines of Saxony, thousands of workers struck and marched on the city prison demanding release of its political prisoners.

Later in the day, five thousand uranium miners from nearby Ronneburg joined the Gera workers. They threw German police from the windows of their barracks. Russian reinforcements were called, this time they came with tanks.

The workers concentrated their anger against the German Communist officials who acted as agents of the government. At Rathenow they killed a factory guard when he tried to stop the strikers from entering the plant. At Erfurt they hanged two Red policemen from lamp posts.

By Saturday, June 20th, the Russians had sent twenty-five thousand troops to Berlin from their three-hundred-thousand-man occupation force at nearby Potsdam. In every major city, Russian power supplanted East German puppet police power. The Minister of Justice was purged. One half of the German police were demobilized as unreliable and sent into the plants to work.

In small but significant numbers Russian soldiers defected to the workers of East Germany, as became apparent when the demonstrations subsided and eighteen Russian soldiers were speedily executed for mutiny.

Twenty to thirty thousand strikers were jailed; untold dozens were executed; families of convicted strikers were driven from their homes and sent to concentration camps. But on June 22, the city of Leipzig, showplace of East German Communism, was still paralyzed by a general strike.

Strikes by the workers in the rest of Eastern Europe followed. The Russian bureaucracy slept uneasily and Beria, who was directly in charge of the satellites, was to feel it most keenly for it was the beginning of *his* end.

Above all, it was the regaining of the workers' confidence in the struggle for freedom. The East Germans wrote a glorious page in this struggle for they answered, in an unmistakable affirmative, *Can* man achieve freedom out of the totalitarianism of our age?

Even the slave laborers in Vorkuta heard this answer. Whereupon they wrote the second page in the new struggle for freedom.

2) *"Russia Is More Than Ever Full of Revolutionaries"—Vorkuta, July 1953*

The impulse to organized resistance, which sparked through the slave labor camps in the Siberian wastes with Stalin's death, was re-kindled by the East German events and burst into an open strike by ten thousand miners in the slave camps at Vorkuta. That was July 1953. Two Germans, former inmates of the Vorkuta camps, Dr. Joseph Scholmer[227] and Brigitte Gerland,[228] have told the story of those heroic days. They were two of the several thousand German inmates who had suddenly been amnestied for the show at the Big Four Ministers' Conference in Berlin in January, 1954.

"You all seem to be so skeptical about the chances of a revolution in Russia. I am not sure myself. But, believe me, Russia is more than ever full of revolutionaries." Thus Brigitte Gerland addressed her co-journalists attending that conference in 1954. Her audience was very skeptical because she was not telling a tale of woe, but of revolt. She would have found sympathetic listeners had she engaged in an abstract discussion of whether a revolt *can* occur under a police State, but not when she related that one *has* happened.

Prior to June 17th, all the preparations for resistance to the totalitarian rulers were based on the eventualities of war and the slave laborers looked to the Western rulers. When Stalin died in March, 1953, hope spread through the camps. But all that came from the Eisenhowers and Churchills were condolences to the Russian leaders who continued the Stalin regime. Gloom spread throughout the slave labor camps until the June 17th revolt in East Germany showed that liberation can be achieved only by the workers themselves. The Russian political prisoners followed up with their revolt.

Here is how Dr. Scholmer, who had actually participated in the strike, described it: "A strike of more than ten thousand miners lasting for several weeks with all the usual paraphernalia —strike committees, slogans, pamphlets, and of course, blacklegs

—a strike similar in every respect to that other historic strike, in the Lena Goldfields Company's mines in Siberia in 1912, when the Tsarist police fired into the strikers just as the Communists were to do in 1953."[229]

Nothing shows the uncertainty and insecurity of these totalitarian rulers, armed to the teeth and with all the power and terror in their hands, as the caution with which the government at first dealt with the strike. They sent a commission, headed by General Derevianko, to fly to the camp. When he tried to harangue the prisoners and failed, the commission returned to Moscow with the demands of the prisoners for a review of all their cases and the removal of the barbed wires. In the end, the Kremlin did what the Tsar had done back in 1912: they opened fire on the unarmed strikers killing sixty-four and wounding some two hundred. *But they could not put back what the strikers had destroyed: the myth of invincibility.*

These prisoners without any rights had dared to strike. They held out for weeks, shaking the Kremlin to its very foundations. Despite total censorship, the workers in Leningrad knew at once of the strike. A few months after, students from the Leningrad Mining Institute, working in the pits in Vorkuta, told the prisoners how everyone had talked of the strike in Leningrad: "We soon got to know you were on strike. The drop in coal was noticeable at once. We don't have any reserves. There's just the Plan, that's all. And everyone knows how vulnerable Plans are. It destroyed the myth that the system was unassailable."

Of the Western "experts" on Russia, Dr. Scholmer had this to say: "When I first mentioned the word, 'civil war', to these people they were appalled. The possibility of a rising lay outside their realm of comprehension. They had no idea that there were resistance groups in the camps. . . .

"I talked to all sorts of people in the first few weeks after my return from the Soviet Union. It seemed to me that the man in the street had the best idea of what was going on. The 'experts' seemed to understand nothing."[230]

Asked what were the motives of the strike, Dr. Scholmer said, "Oh, they were fantastically mixed. Some wanted a little better living and working conditions. Others were hoping for a 'new era' now that Stalin was dead. Some wanted to imitate the 17th of June in Germany, which we had heard described over Radio Moscow and in *Pravda*. Others wanted to destroy the system, and there was an old man in my barracks who cried over and over again, 'Have we torn down the barbed-wire fence yet? Is it down, is it down?' "

No, the barbed wire has not been torn down, and freedom from Russian totalitarianism was not won by the East German revolt either. But two new pages in history were written: whoever before June 17th had heard of a mass revolt against a totalitarian dictatorship? Whoever had, before July, heard of slave laborers forcing concessions from a police State? *Two pages in history that have shown the way to freedom.*

That is why the former inmates speak not so much of suffering as of revolt, of freedom. Not yet? "Not yet," they too say, and go back to quote the great Russian poet, Pushkin, who back in 1827 wrote to his imprisoned friends:

> *Deep in the Siberian mine,*
> *Keep your patience proud;*
> *The bitter toil shall not be lost,*
> *The rebel thought unbowed . . .*
> *The heavy-hanging chains will fall,*
> *The walls will crumble at a word;*
> *And Freedom greet you in the light,*
> *And brothers give you back the sword.*

3) Hungary, 1956—Freedom Fighters

"Russian soldiers, go home!" became the central rallying slogan of the Hungarian Revolution which broke out on Tuesday, October 23, 1956. It followed the Polish revolt of the previous week. It was distinguished from the previous revolts by the greater depth, the uncompromising stand, and the involvement of the whole population. As in all popular revolts, the soldiers came over to the side of the people. The Freedom Fighters of Hungary embraced all layers of the population: workers, youth and women; the old and the very young. They united behind a common cause

—to rid themselves of their Soviet oppressors or to die in the attempt.

Children, from twelve to sixteen years of age, were seen with
rifles and tommy-guns slung over their shoulders and hand gren-
ades in their pockets. They destroyed Soviet tanks by diverting
the attention of the gunners to the rooftops, then dashing in under
the elevated guns to throw gasoline over the tank and set it afire.
Others led the tanks down narrow streets where they were am-
bushed and unable to turn around. One thirteen-year old veteran
of this kind of fighting was asked where they learned to do these
things. She said, "All of us kids were trained in the party."

The attempts of the workers to seize oil fields, rail centers,
steel factories and means of communication and to run these by
revolutionary committees—that is to say, workers' control of production—is the true sign of the attempts of this Revolution to affect
a total change. A general strike tied up all railroad transport as
well as most production.

Death and starvation stalked the streets of Hungary as the
rebel radio station sent out its last S.O.S.: "We are quiet. Not
afraid. Send the news to the world." The news to the world about
five days of freedom revealed more than courageous fighting. It
showed that the idea of freedom cannot be killed. That idea does
not float in heaven. People live by that idea. Overnight, the One-
Party system disintegrated and various political parties reappeared
along with small newspapers and radio stations. Hundreds of local
and district organizations, from the Hungarian Revolutionary Youth
Party to old parties, including both Smallholders and Social Democrats, appeared.

So total was the wrath of the people against Russian Communism, that the Hungarian Communist Party tried to appear in a
new guise. The temporary puppet leader, Janos Kadar, reorganized
it as the "Socialist Workers Party," but no one took that seriously.
Indeed, it was the same old Communism which, while promising
withdrawal of the Russian troops and a different way of living,
was conspiring to bring back the Russian tanks and troops in
force.

The first news to the world was about five days of freedom
from Russian tyranny, and from the Hungarian Communist, bar-

baric, ten-thousand-man secret police. And then, the news that the wrath of a people in arms was being stifled by a force of forty-five hundred Soviet tanks, crack paratroops, MVD storm guards, and a quarter of a million of Russian infantry! Yet this massacre of the daring young Freedom Fighters had not crushed the revolt. After a full week of fighting, the uranium mines were blown up. There, workers were still out on general strike and there was neither transport nor production. The Hungarian people were choosing death rather than accept Russian totalitarianism.

Even the cynics[231] who thought it wishful thinking for anyone to analyze the East German Revolt of 1953 as the beginning of the end of totalitarianism, began to look to Hungary with non-cynical hope. Many thousands fled, and every reactionary, with our own Congressman Walter of the infamous McCarran-Walter Act at the head, tried to ride on the bravery of the Hungarian revolutionaries. But the impact soon over-rode these hangers-on. The whole brunt of the fight shifted back *inside* Hungary itself. When all said that everything was over, the Hungarian Workers' Councils sprung up. Production remained the key, and the whole brunt of the struggle against Russian tyranny was born by the workers. They began to fight in the factories, which they were using as their places of refuge. The leaders of the Workers' Councils were arrested only after they left the factory and walked to the Parliament building to negotiate. The workers evolved new ways of fighting, both on the job and when they walked out on strike. For example, the miners refused to mine coal while the Russian Army remained in Hungary. Nor did they let anyone else mine the coal "for the workers." When Russian might finally asserted itself through overwhelming force the workers blew up the mines.

The revolutionary forces now unloosed cannot be overcome by sheer force. They have been forced underground, but they have not disappeared. Nor was the impact exhausted within the national boundaries of Hungary. Thousands of Communist Party members all over Western Europe began tearing up their membership cards. Ever since the end of World War II, the West European people— veering sharply against the private capitalism that they knew and hated because it had brought them two World Wars in one lifetime—had turned to Russian Communism, literally by the millions. Many now see Russian Communism as but another name for state capitalism. The tearing up of Communist Party membership cards is the first step. It is a first step that was not taken in 1953 during the East German Revolt, nor just a few months previous to the Hungarian Revolution of 1956, during the Polish Revolt, although the slogans during the latter were almost identical: "Down with this phony Communism," and "We want Bread and Freedom." It was taken only when the revolution was such a thoroughgoing one that it turned both against Russia and the satellite Communist regime in Hungary. This Western beginning may not yet reflect the deep and continuous unrest in Poland. But it is a first step in the disintegration of the mass Communist Parties in Western Europe. It is a beginning only, but it is a beginning.

SECTION TWO

THE AMERICAN SCENE

America is not exempt from the development of state capitalism, the supreme development of which we have been describing in our analysis of the Russian economy. What World War II showed as the role of the State in the economy was not a war phenomenon. The foundations for it were laid in the previous period, as can graphically be seen from a study of the Temporary National Economic Committee reports.[232] The true index of the present stage of capitalism is the role of the State in the economy. War or peace, the State does not diminish monopolies and trusts, nor does it diminish its own interference. Rather, it develops, hothouse fashion, that characteristic mode of behavior of capitalism: centralization of capital, on the one hand, and socialization of labor, on the other. The Planners form to one side, the workers to the other. The workers build their own organizations like the CIO as against the NRA; or take to wildcatting as against the labor bureaucracy.

State capitalism is not a continuous development of capitalism in the sense of a development without breaks. It is a development through transformation into opposite. Capitalism lived and progressed by free competition. Hence, it found its fullest development under a democratic bourgeois or parliamentary democracy. State capitalism means, and can only mean, bureaucracy, tyranny and barbarism as could have been seen in Nazi Germany and can be seen in totalitarian Russia. One would have to be blind not to see the elements of it everywhere, including the United States.

"Intrinsically," Marx wrote, "it is not a question of the higher or lower degree of development of the social antagonisms that result from the natural laws of capitalist production. It is a question of these laws themselves, of these tendencies working with iron necessity towards inevitable results. The country that is more developed only shows, to the less developed, the image of its own future."[233]

The same, we must add, is true in reverse. Given the context of the *world* market, and the accelerated development of a backward country once it begins "catching up" with the advanced country, the *former* shows the *latter* the image of its own future. The Hitlers, the Mussolinis, the Stalins, are not Germans, Italians and Russians only—nor are their wills theirs alone. They represent objective forces.

Stalin thought he was fashioning the State in the image of the Party. Consciously, that is what he was doing. Objectively, however, the exact opposite was true. The State transformed the Party in *its* image, which, *in turn,* was but a reflection of the production process of capitalism at its ultimate stage of development. The distinguishing feature of State monopoly, as against private monopoly, is its abolition of any difference between politics (the State) and production (the economy). The Party is the executor of the State Plan in society, as the hierarchy of plant managers, foremen, as well as "trade union representatives" execute it at the point of production. Marx knew whereof he spoke when he said that the whole of the capitalistic economy could be summed up in one phrase: "Domination of dead over living labor." By now, the "barrack-like discipline," with which this domination is exercised, has assumed, even in its living visage, a death-like mask. Terror and death are the middle names of the ruling class which calls itself the "classless intelligentsia." Once we already have at hand an actual, existing, fully-developed single state capitalist society, there is no point, however, in tracing through the economic development where state capitalism is only a tendency. Although America is headed in the same direction as Russia, Russia and America are by no means identical twins. There is something very American about the development of the "scientific individual" who labors under the illusion that he can avoid the totalitarian consequences of state capitalism. Witness the experiments and studies on the question of "human relations in industry" which mushroomed during the 1930's and again after World War II at

the very same time as we underwent the great transformation of
New Deal Planning and approached the age of Automation.

For the purposes, therefore, of tracing a difference—the "scientific individual" with, and against, the State administrator—there
is no more perfect country to watch than America which is so
barren of theoreticians that it is under the illusion that it has
escaped Marxism. The Great Divide in everyone's thinking is,
of course, the Depression. The Depression had destroyed once and
for all the workers' belief in the rationality of the economic system. Where there was employment, it soon became clear that no
more could be squeezed out of the workers on the basis of the
old economic relations. Where there was unemployment—and that
was everywhere by the millions—the chaos of capitalism was all
too obvious.

The most famous of the "human relations" studies was the
Hawthorne Project[234] undertaken by the Western Electric Company under the scientific supervision of Elton Mayo, Professor of
Industrial Research at Harvard University. What was *new* in all
these studies was that the analysts began with human relations in
industry as *the* basic problem of our day. Concerned thus, they
made a specialty of "plant interviews" and "on the spot" reporting.[235]

Elton Mayo was the first of these scientific intellectuals to discover the production code by which production workers conduct
themselves: (1) Don't be a "rate-buster" by turning out too much
work. (2) Don't be a "chiseler" by turning out too little work.
(3) Don't be a "squealer" by gossiping or complaining to a su-
pervisor about a fellow-worker. (4) Don't act like a "big-shot" or
put on airs.

By the 1940's it became quite clear that the American workers
were developing a new economic philosophy to replace the capitalistic one that Marx called "production for production's sake."
It was not too hard to sense that the ex-GI's, far from separating
themselves from the workers, were in the forefront of this destruction of the old economic philosophy. "Many others," writes Sebastian de Grazia in *The Political Community*,[236] "have documented the impersonalism of the modern scene with specialized
studies of the rooming house dweller, the hotel guest, or the mar-

ginal man. More or less, they have kept without the bounds of bias. For this reason one must turn to another source—the modern worker himself—to find protest against the competitive directive, protest unembelished with symbolism and unrestrained by fear of making moral judgments . . . :

"'Hell, supposing I do get a better job. It will be a nickel an hour more, that's all. . . . That's right. There's no sense in being pushed around by foremen if you don't have to. Mine is a Simon Legree. He jumped a guy the other day for taking too long off to go out to the can. My God! It's drive, drive, all day long. No visiting at the bench. No nothing.'

"'The son of a bitch across the street is one good reason why a lot of men are leaving that plant. Him and a lot like him. He is a foreman. He started a friend of mine running two milling machines instead of one. Jesus! Naturally Jack says no, so the foreman calls the superintendent. The superintendent says what's the matter with you GI's, are you afraid to work? Jack tells him no, I'm not afraid to work, but that's just too much; you know what you can do with your job. The bosses are just laying it on too thick. They expect too much. There are a couple of bad foremen at the plant where I work. Just a couple of days ago a GI went out to the can, and my foreman tells him he stayed too long. He said the war's over now. Can you imagine that? In another department a GI made a mistake, or didn't get his work done fast enough, or something, and the foreman says—where have you been? So the guy cracks back, 'In Italy, taking care of you.' That story did my heart good.'

"'Sure I think most of us would admit we could double our take-home if we wanted to shoot the works, but where's the percentage? A guy has to get something out of life. Now my little lady would rather have me in a good humor than have the extra money. The way it works out none of us are going to be Van-Astorbilts so why not get a little pleasure out of living together and working together?'"

This is the fact from which all contemporary sociology and social psychology begins: the rejection by the workers of all the old capitalist controls and standards.

1) *Rank and File vs. Labor Leaders*

If World War II succeeded, as it did, in helping to transform the American labor leadership, hothouse fashion, into a labor bureaucracy, and to disclose Reuther as *the* Planner who outplanned G.M.'s Wilson with blueprints to transform auto plants into bomber plants, the workers were even faster in learning to hate the labor bureaucracy on a par with management.

"Since the end of World War II, and continuing to this day," a Detroit production worker writes,[237] "the company has made changes in the shop with the help of the workers' representatives—the stewards, committeemen and union officers. After the UAW was organized, one of the worst crimes a union representative could commit was to be friendly to a foreman. I have known stewards to lose their position for being friendly with a foreman. There was a clear and decisive line drawn between the workers and the company. Any worker would have a tough time if he or she talked or kidded around with the foreman. They would be labeled a company stooge.

"In those early days, if a worker had an argument with the foreman, the foreman would try his best to settle it. The foreman never wanted the worker to call the steward. He knew the steward would defend the worker. The workers used their strength against the company even if it meant going out on strike. The union leaders were forced to go along with them. They depended on the strength of the workers. The feeling of solidarity was close and felt by the average worker. In the past five or six years there has been agitation by the union officials that the company is not too bad and that the workers who cause strikes want to starve the other workers and their families. Labor and management, say the leaders, can live peacefully side by side. The Labor leaders threaten workers who 'cause strikes.' Hundreds of workers have been fired by the company for taking strike action with the approval of the union. The other workers have been frightened by what they have seen happen. This has also tended to weaken the close relations the workers had toward each other.

"Today, the steward spends practically all of his time in the office of supervision, or walking around with his arm around company officials. They have hardly any time to talk to the workers unless it is election time. They agree with the company on most of the differences between the workers and management. When a worker has a difference with the foreman today, the foreman will say, 'Call the committeeman.' He knows how they will act. In many instances the foreman will go get the steward. He uses these against the workers. Not so long ago in my plant, the company took a worker off an operation where there were three workers doing the same type of operation. These workers put up a howl. The superintendent came up and said, 'If you don't do it, I will call the committeeman and you will have to do it anyway.' "

In this same period, this is how one committeeman described how workers keep, not only the big bureaucrats, but even the committeemen, isolated: "The burning problems in the shops today are centered not around wages so much as around the bitter hostility of the workers to their role in production. In building their unions they thought that they were creating instruments of organizing and controlling production in their own interest. The capitalists, aware of this, insisted that the unions recognize the capitalist mode of production. This is the basic conflict that the labor leadership is unable to resolve. This is the dilemma that destroys innumerable leaders who have risen out of the working class. This conflict arises constantly in many different forms. It plagues the union leaders on the local level constantly. For example, a production standard is established. The man assigned to the job refuses to perform according to standards. He is sent to Labor Relations where he is disciplined and ordered to produce as required. The committeeman who is there to represent the man can only chime in and tell the worker that on the basis of the contract, he must produce according to production standards or face discharge.

"Another example: production is set for a whole line of, say, two hundred men. The men protest the production that is set and are ready to strike. Either the company or the men call the committeeman. He tells the men that the company has the right to set the production; that it is illegal to strike; and that the men should accept the standard. The higher levels of the leadership try to solve this dilemma by fighting for concessions outside the process

of production. They give the impression of social workers in and
out of the plant. The workers are aware of this. One day, a worker
was protesting a speed-up and said to me, 'What are you going to
do about it? I know, nothing as usual. What good is the union?
Now don't tell me about the local's grocery store or about being
able to get women's clothes cheaper. Do something about the
speed-up!' "

The problem everywhere, production-wise as well as politically,
has become a battle to increase productivity. Labor leaders, engineers, businessmen, educators, and government officials collaborate in conferences on productivity that parallel the Russian
production conferences. But not much seemed to have resulted
from them until one day it became clear that while "philosophically" these conferences led nowhere, the working together of
"pure science" and practical engineering did produce a miracle.[238]
When a Ford executive coined a word for this "miracle"—AUTO-
MATION—the word took wing.

Automation has cut across the thinking of the people more
sharply than anything else since the Industrial Revolution nearly
200 years ago. At the point of production, Automation has compelled two fundamentally different class attitudes, depending on
which side of the machine you stand. If you are the one who
operates it, you feel its impact in every bone of your body: you
are more sweaty, more tired, more tense and you feel about as useful as a fifth wheel. You are never on top of the machine; the
machine is always on top of you and keeps you isolated from your
fellow-workers. In addition, you feel more isolated as more and
more of your shopmates are displaced by the monster machine.

If, on the other hand, you are the one who drives the men
and counts the production for management, you praise the machine
to the skies. This attitude of the capitalists and their agents has
acted as a brainwashing of the labor bureaucracy. Instead of listening to the specific grievances and aspirations of the workers;
instead of listening to their complaints against the conditions of
labor and new speed-ups; instead of listening when the workers
questioned the very kind of labor that would transform man into
a cog of a machine and make the machine into "the thinker," the
labor bureaucracy counselled the workers to do nothing "against"

Automation. Thus, when the miners were first confronted with
the continuous miner in 1949, John L. Lewis disregarded their
general strike and announced instead that the union was for
"progress." The working force in the mines was literally cut in
half.

When Automation reached Ford, Reuther told the auto
workers to consider "the future" which would bring them a six-
hour day, and not to fight against the present unemployment.
Meanwhile, there has been no change in the working day since
the workers, through their own struggles over decades, won the
eight-hour day.

There is not a college, from the University of Michigan to
Harvard, that does not have its Technology Project. The labor
bureaucracy appears at the conference to parrot the words of "the
educated."[239] The actual findings of "case studies" are hidden behind the windy words of labor bureaucrat and professor. Take
the case that every Detroit auto worker knows only too well—the
closing down of the Murray Body Works several years ago. Five
thousand workers found themselves with lots of time on their hands
and no money in their pockets—they were out of work. The management, however, was "forward looking." They went into another business—bowling alleys. They moved out of Detroit. The
5,000 auto workers remained in Detroit and remained unemployed.
Or take the cases of those who remain on the job in automated
plants. Contrary to the ease that push-button work was supposed to
bring about, the workers all say: the more production, the more
speed and tension.

Contrary to Reuther's abstractions[240] of every worker an engineer, there is little or no upgrading with Automation, while the
brainwashing of the labor leadership finds no need of any torture
chambers. They are all too deaf to the concrete demands of the
workers and all too willing victims of abstractions which help to
maintain capitalist exploitation. Yet precisely in the *workers'* attitudes to Automation can be discerned the pathway to totally new
relations at the point of production, and *therefore* in society.

CHAPTER SIXTEEN

AUTOMATION AND THE NEW HUMANISM

> "Technology discloses man's mode of
> dealing with Nature, the process of
> production by which he sustains his
> life, and thereby lays bare the mode of
> formation of his social relations and of
> the mental conceptions that flow from
> them. Every history of religion even
> that fails to take account of the ma-
> terial basis, is uncritical. . . . The weak
> points in the abstract materialism of na-
> tural science (are that it) excludes his-
> tory and its process."—Marx

1) Different Attitudes to Automation

1950 opened a new era in production. That was the year of
the first serious introduction of Automation,[241] in the form of
the continuous miner. The word, "Automation," had not yet
gained its present currency. The fact of Automation, however,
brought about the longest strike in the mine workers' history
since the creation of the CIO. The strike broke out in the most
modern of the mines—those where the largest coal corporation,
Consol, had introduced the continuous miner. During this nine-
months old strike, the miners turned against John L. Lewis—
another first since the creation of the CIO.

Nor did the Taft-Hartley Law, which fined their union one
million dollars, stop them. The miners were determined that no
one would do their thinking for them. They kept their thoughts

to themselves, but they showed their concern was not with the union treasury nor solely with the threat of unemployment. They were concerned with something new: something they called *"a man-killer"*—the continuous miner. The automatic miner was frightening in an entirely *new* way. The miners were concerned not just with the old grievances and hazards. This Automation was recognized as a "man-killer" in a *total* way. Soon it proved itself to be the horror the miners feared. The ceaselessness of its operation, the drive, were such that by today men with seniority are trying to use their seniority to stay off of it and are saying they'd rather be laid off than have to work on it. Back in 1949 it was not yet true. Unemployment in the coal region was at its greatest since the Depression—the continuous miner was creating ghost towns everywhere in Pennsylvania and West Virginia; the miners were literally starving because of their long strike, yet they refused to obey the order to return to work. That was the first serious break between the miners and John L. Lewis in nearly two decades.

One miner told this writer: "There is a time for praying. We do that on Sundays. There is a time for acting. We took matters in our hands during the Depression, building up our union and seeing that our families did not starve. There is a time for thinking. The time is now. What I want to know is: how and when will the working man—all working men—have such confidence in their own abilities to make a better world that they will not let others do their thinking for them."

That miner felt that the union wasn't much better than the company nowadays. The reason for this is that the rank and file had let "others"—the leadership—do their thinking and write their contracts for them. What was the point of talking about "progress" when the new machine was making a havoc of your life both on the job and *off of it?* This miner pointed out that the change the worker had brought through his activity, had somehow *turned into its opposite.* The miners would elect someone to represent them in negotiations with management. Then the first thing anyone knew was that their representative became a labor bureaucrat who turned up in the District Office, not to fight with the workers against the company but *to order* the workers to produce more. This miner wanted to know: what made the miners stick together in 1943 and tell the senators that if they were so interested in production, they could dig the coal themselves, yet no one tells the same thing to the labor leadership today. *"The working man has a mind of his own,"* concluded the miner, "so why let others do his thinking for him? If only there was *no division between thinking and doing."*

But no one heard the voice of the miner. No one listened. The daily papers were full of the fine Judge Goldsborough imposed on Lewis; and so was the United Mine Workers Union paper; as for the radical papers, they were reporting yet one more strike and, once again, expressing their sympathy.

By 1953, recession hit the United States, and in Detroit, the auto capital of the world, unemployment assumed such mass proportions that the word, "Automation," took wing. Automation is not a single machine designed for any particular industry. It is rather a method of doing things through a series of machines or mechanisms that replace men in the process of production. It results in a completely automatic, or semi-automatic, process of production, where the worker is reduced to watching the machine and to pushing buttons, while another group of men stand by to repair the machine as it breaks down.

Everyone now—from scientists who had originally predicted the most dire results from this new industrial revolution,[242] to the Ford executive who coined the word, to the businessmen's weeklies—began to blame the word, "Automation," for bringing back depression jitters. *Business Week*[243] went as far as to say that Automation was ninety per cent emotion and only ten per cent fact. The labor bureaucrats assisted by bowing before "progress" and painting the future as it *should* be instead of speaking of what is. The sharp division between the rank and file worker and the labor bureaucrat is seen nowhere so clearly as in the different attitudes each has toward Automation. Where the auto worker, for example, deals with it as it affects his daily life, Reuther speaks of the future and "the promise" Automation holds for a "vast improvement in living conditions," and "leisure."

"I do not know what he is talking about," one woman worker told this writer, "I don't have any time to breathe, much less to loll about. The work-week at Ford's now is fifty-three hours and here that man goes around talking about 'leisure.' As for working conditions, they are worse than they have ever been since the CIO first came into being. All Automation has meant to us is unemployment and overwork. *Both at the same time.*"

One miner told this writer that he lost thirty pounds in weight caused by the speed-up and tensions of automatic production. He added, that was only half of the story. The other half was safety—they just don't take out the time anymore for the right underpinnings and there has been a serious rise in accidents. "It's just not safe," he said. "I'm not working 'under protest.' I'm just not doing it. What good will working 'under protest' do me if I get killed? The company isn't going to take care of my wife and kids if something happens to me. We already had one man killed because the company tried this before. I know that I'm not going to be the next one."

In auto, too, workers now point to Automation as a safety hazard. One Detroit story read: "Worker after worker says, 'There's something about these machines that's going to mess up a lot of people.' One man said, 'We weren't on the job a day, when a man lost his finger and had the one next to it crushed. Before the week was out, another man lost a finger and a third man had three fingers chopped off by the machine.' There are signs all over the shop saying: 'Are you doing it safely?' Inside half-an-hour after the man was hurt, the workers had written under all these signs: 'This Machine Is Not Safe Enough To Do It With.'"

Far from Automation bringing new jobs, there has been a disastrous cut in employed miners from 425,000 in 1948, to 225,000 in 1955, or as much as in the whole half-century previous to that. The "new" jobs going to the young maintenance men is meant to divide up the production workers from the skilled "new scientific men," but thus far the company has not succeeded in doing that. John L. Lewis, who has always stood for "progress" in technology, got them more wages, in which the workers were not interested, instead of getting a shorter work-week and better conditions, which the miners want.

By 1955, the long Westinghouse strike finally forced everyone to admit that it was an Automation strike. They called it the first

Automation strike, and the crucial struggle was finally recognized to be that of *time study*. The electrical workers knew that the study of each motion of their hands was not to lighten their toil, but to incorporate the motion in a machine which would take away the job of a hundred and multiply by tenfold the speed of those left to operate the monster machine. The workers don't go in for abstract argumentation on leisure and plenty at some future, unspecified, time. They ask concrete questions now: (1) How much unemployment will Automation bring about? (2) Does the seniority for which he fought so hard and which protected the worker against the arbitrariness of the company's firing mean nothing under the new conditions? (3) What about the ceaseless speed-up? These machines are "'man-killers" that· are constantly breaking down, and breaking down the nervous system of the men themselves.

Whereas a Detroit radio poll showed that, next to Russia, what the workers feared most was Automation, the United States Department of Labor busily sought to reassure us about Automation—because it will not come like a tidal wave, but rather like ground swells hitting different industries at different times.[244] The old radicals pontificated that, of course, you fight alongside workers for immediate demands, but actually, capitalism can never fully institute Automation because there are too many vested interests in the capital structure as it now stands.

There is no doubt that only about one-tenth of the investment that automatic controls could "use" has been invested because of the complicating features involved, both as to pull of labor and obsolescence of material.[245] As Marx long ago put it, the final barrier to capitalism is capital itself. The tendency to stagnation and decay—as the tendency to the decline in the rate of profit—is inherent in capitalism. We see today concretely what Marx wrote of theoretically, that capitalist society must, *"under penalty of death,"* transform the worker from a fragment of a man—a living appendage to a machine—into one who is fully developed and fit for a variety of labors. Nevertheless, there is nothing "automatic" either about the collapse of capitalism or the inevitable emergence of a new society. Quite the contrary. There is no solution other than letting the "historical antagonisms" work themselves out.

The capitalist will give nothing of his free will, while the worker is being united, disciplined and organized by the very mechanism of production, to revolt against being a cog in a machine. The scientists finally admit that Automation has made everyone "jumpy." Dr. Charles R. Walker, Director of Technology and Industrial Research at Yale, reports that studies are even being conducted by medical doctors on the harmful effects of "tranquillizers," or, as the workers call them, "nerve pills," which have become so widespread. Yet all he can come up with when he views the future is: *"What can we find as substitutes for time?"* (His own emphasis.)

Contrast this intellectual attitude to that of the miner who said that *only* a new unity of theory and practice, *unified in the worker himself,* would assure the creation of a really new society. The question was: *when* would the worker gain confidence in his own abilities to stop letting "others" do his thinking for him?

The labor bureaucracy, being committed to this "progress," offers no way for the workers to express themselves except through wildcats. There were one hundred seventy such strikes in the coal fields just from January through April of 1956. Of these strikes, the one to which Lewis gave the most attention, at the forty-second annual Miners' convention, was the massive wildcat which paralyzed the entire coal industry in Northern West Virginia during the late spring of 1956. It involved the men of District 31. Lewis branded that mass eruption of miners as the work of "some individuals, ambitious in character—hoping perhaps—they would be called upon and elected to some high office." Apparently the head of the United Mine Workers' Union thinks it a shame that the miners fought to protect their lives instead of letting the company get away with having one man on a machine. Lewis wound up his blast against the miners in District 31 with this warning: "Carry the message back," he said. "Don't do it again. You will be fully conscious that I am breathing down your necks."

Everyone now knows that "full production" does not mean full employment. The Bureau of Labor Statistics shows that while national production in 1955 was up eleven per cent over 1954, employment was up only one per cent. Those who suffer most are the production workers. For example, in the chemical industry production went up fifty-three per cent in the eight years after World War II, while the number of production workers rose only 1.3 per cent—from 525,000 to 532,000. At the same time, the number of non-production workers—engineers, office workers, etc.,—rose more than seventy per cent, from 169,000 to 259,000. Despite the increase in skilled workers, this marked a gain of only fourteen per cent in total employment contrasted with a fifty-three per cent gain in product output. In the eight-year period ending in 1955, the output of goods in the electrical manufacturing industry soared eighty-seven per cent, but the number of salaried employees rose only twenty per cent. Production workers increased only sixteen per cent.

Not only in "pockets of depression," like the textile industry in New England and the South, but in auto, producing at full speed, unemployment is a steady feature. Indeed, since the end of World War II, despite the great rise in production, employment in manufacturing has slowed down to a crawl. For the time being, the armed forces and the service trades have absorbed many of the unemployed, but by no means all. Nor will they. Those who try to fool themselves—they are certainly not fooling the production workers—that expansion of service trades contains the answer should remember that anything that is not produced needs no servicing.

Finally, for the youth, factory work has no interest whatever. A young worker I met in Los Angeles said, "What skill do you need in this day of Automation? What pride can you have in your work if everything is done electronically and you are there—if you are lucky to get the job—just to blow the whistle when the machine breaks down? What about the human being?"

The todayness of Marx is truly overwhelming. His description of "the automaton," ninety years ago, fits more precisely the description of Automation than that of any present-day writers. In opposition to the liberals of his day, who saw increased production as meaning the happy life of abundance, Marx described the *concrete strife* of worker and machine when it is capitalistically controlled: *"An organized system of machines to which motion is communicated by the transmitting mechanism from a central automaton, is the most developed form of production by ma-*

chinery. . . . The lightening of the labor, even, becomes a sort of torture since the machine does not free the laborer from work, but deprives the work of all interest . . .

"By means of its conversion into an automaton, the instrument of labor confronts the laborer during the labor process, in the shape of capital, or dead labor, that dominates and pumps dry living labor power. The separation of intellectual powers of production from manual labor, and the conversion of those powers into the might of capital over labor, is . . . finally completed by modern industry erected on the foundation of machinery."

Because all science, all knowledge is today embodied in the machine, the role of the intellectual has changed from the sphere of "culture" to that of production. If, in the 1930's, our academicians discovered "the production code," and in the 1940's "the production philosophy," Automation in the 1950's has confronted them with such power that they simply, to use a Hegelian phrase, "perished." Thus, what was only an intimation, one hundred years ago, is concretely embodied today in the *class* role of the Planner. As against the authoritarian Plan that arose out of capitalistic production to discipline the worker, as against the automaton as the motive force of production, Marx pointed to the human aspect not in order to adjust it to the status quo, but to disclose a new society in which labor is not alienated, but "is itself the first necessity of living."[246]

2) Workers Think Their Own Thoughts

> "Hegel, the exponent of the dialectic, was incapable of understanding *dialectically* the transition *from* matter *to* movement, *from* matter *to* consciousness —especially the second. Marx corrected the mistake (or weakness) of the mystic."
> —Lenin[247]

What is *new* in Automation is the maturity of our age in which the totality of the crisis compels philosophy, compels a total outlook.

The struggle for the minds of men, when the tendency toward complete mechanization has reached its most acute point in Automation, cannot be won in any other way. The new impulse comes, *and can come, only from the workers*. Contrast to the chimera of the scientist who writes of "Man Viewed as Machine," the sanity of the production worker who writes that work will have to be "something totally different":

"When the women at work talked about how some day they were going to do wiring automatically, I didn't really understand the word 'Automation.' I responded to what my friend said, 'What would happen to us?' She said they would probably have to give us jobs on the machines. It was all very hazy though. Now, the word is all over the place. And it holds both fascination and fear. I saw on TV an 'automated' auto engine factory, they made one engine in fifteen minutes where it used to take nine hours. The magazine, *Saturday Review*, had a special issue on Automation. It had seven or eight different writers, some from business and one from the UAW-CIO. What gets me is how the clearest one was the industrialist. The others seemed scared to say much about what it will do to people. He doesn't care. He just says exactly what he thinks.

"There is one little paragraph of his I can't get out of my mind, '. . . another highly desirable feature of Automation in relation to labor, is the fact that machines are easier to control than people (and this is a blessing in our democratic society).' I can't tell exactly what I get from it. It's like this is it, the point of no return. He doesn't give a darn what happens to these people he talks about. And maybe I don't really understand but I think he would like to do away with one thing in this society and that is 'democracy.'

"There is something else, more time. You know, that scares me more than anything else. If I get more leisure time under this society I think I would go crazy. This is very silly because I have always wanted the shorter work day. They don't bother much about what happens to people, not just people, but the unskilled worker. They are a little scared. Not scared of what happens to the workers, but I think scared of what the workers will do to them. I can't help thinking over and over that this is it. They have

thrown so many workers into the streets with their old production methods, and now Automation. Even if the union gets the
shorter week and annual wage, what happens to all the workers
all over the country that are not working now? There are some
things about Automation that are terrific but the capitalists and
the unions can't do any good with them. We say man is able to
work, to produce, to work with, alongside, other workers. This is
life to him. Now what happens under Automation? I don't see
man working. Do the energies go toward something else? But what?
This and the leisure time is connected somewhere, though I don't
exactly know where.

"Man likes to work, to build something, but today work is so
separate from everything else in your life. Each day is divided:
you work, then you have some time in which to rest, forget about
work, escape from it. What will be with Automation? There is less
work for man (as I think of work today) but there is more time. I
am scared of more time the way things are now because more
time for the worker might be seven days a week with no pay
check at the end of the week.

"I used to be told that the fight for more leisure time was
so that the individual could have more time for art, music, literature, for study in general. That doesn't satisfy me any longer. Under
a new society work will have to be something completely new,
not just work to get money to buy food and things. It will have
to be completely tied up with life."[249]

Just as, from the first Industrial Revolution, the workers in the
factory gained the impulse for the struggles for the shortening of
the working day, and thus created a new philosophy, so from the
workers' experience with Automation comes a *new Humanism*.

The beginning of the end of state capitalism has, of necessity,
begun behind the Iron Curtain. Men everywhere breathed freer
when those under Russian totalitarian domination answered
affirmatively the question that seems to preoccupy the contemporary world: *Can* man wrest freedom from the stranglehold of the
One-Party State?

The fundamental problem of true freedom, however, remains:
What type of labor can end the division between "thinkers" and
"doers"? This is the innermost core of Marxism. The transformation

of totalitarian society, on totally new beginnings, can have no other foundation than a new material life, *a new kind of labor for the producer, the worker.*

This basic question was posed first, not behind the Iron Curtain, but on this side of it. It arose out of the new stage of production called Automation. It was posed first by the miners, who, with the introduction of the continuous miner, began to question not only the fruits of labor—wages—but the *kind* of labor. As one young worker put it when he was told that the union would now fight for a shorter work week, "The four-day week wouldn't make much difference. We are liable to wind up working the same hours as now and get overtime pay for all work over thirty-five hours. What has to be different is the way we have to work. Coming in every day and working under company discipline, afraid to stay out, is no way. Russia can't be much different. If you think about it the only reason this way of life seems to make sense is that this is the way people are used to living."

"Work that would be completely tied up with life," and "doing that would not be separated from thinking," "a new unity of theory and practice, unified in the worker himself," are in the full tradition of Marx's concept of work as human activity that develops all of man's natural and acquired talents. Thus, the workers, the American workers, made concrete *and thereby extended* Marx's most abstract theories of alienated labor and the quest for universality. Marx was right when he said the workers were the true inheritors of Hegelian philosophy. In truth, while the intellectual void today is so great that the movement from theory to practice has nearly come to a standstill, *the movement from practice to theory, and with it, a new unity of manual and mental labor in the worker, are in evidence everywhere.*

3) Toward a New Unity of Theory and Practice in the Abolitionist and Marxist Tradition

The American working class has long been a mystery to the European, worker and intellectual. Until the formation of the CIO, Europeans used to "prove" the backwardness of the American worker by virtue of the fact that he had not built industrial unions. Europeans cannot understand how it is that the American working class, the mightiest in the world, has not built a labor party of its own, as has the European working class; and how it is that no Marxist party has ever taken deep root here. Because the American worker has built no mass party, he seems apolitical. Because he is largely unacquainted with the doctrines of Karl Marx, he seems non-socialist. They admit he is very militant, but there they stop. To his own thoughts they do not listen because, being uninhibited by European tradition, he has different ways of expressing them. The truth is that the most politically advanced workers in the world, the French, thought of nothing better than what the American workers did—sitting down. Only in Spain did the outburst take the form of an outright revolution.[250] They *began* immediately with taking control of the factories. Thus, throughout the world, the workers were attempting to reorganize society by beginning with the reorganization of production relations in the factory. They did not succeed, but they tried and discovered some new truths in so doing, while the intellectuals just stuck to the old "categories," unable to move forward either in theory or in practice.

The cynic stands ready to show that despite all the hope and efforts of the 1930's, the workers did not complete a revolution, did not create a workers' state, did not build a new society. He concludes, therefore, that all the movements—including the national resistance movements during the war; the wartime wildcats and Negro demonstrations; the post-war strikes; the current colonial revolts—have been, if not for nought, certainly unsuccessful. That is true. The deeper truth, however, is that the workers *did* something, the full consequences of which we do not yet know. Certainly no fundamental problems have been solved by World War II. The crisis is now total. The H-bomb puts a question mark over the very survival of civilization as we have known it.

While the workers acted and showed they had a mind of their own, the intellectuals parroted empty phrases and ignored the workers. There has never been a greater theoretical void in the Marxist movement or out of it.

When the 1929 crash occurred, production came nearly to a standstill. Millions of workers were thrown into the streets. Now that everyone saw that production is primary, the *class* lines became, not weaker, but stronger. The New Deal is proof enough that the capitalist class too had suffered a serious split. Every serious tension *between* the working class and the capitalist class produces a rift in the camp of the ruling class itself. But that is not irreparable.

To run production in capitalist society, the capitalists sit upon the direct producers. Where there is a crisis, those bureaucrats do not get off the workers' backs. They sit the harder. The New Deal did not tamper with that relationship at the point of production. Neither did the intellectual Planners who came out of Harvard and Columbia, Yale and Princeton, Antioch and the College of the City of New York, Stanford University or the University of Chicago, etc. Just as there are only two fundamental classes in society—the working class and the capitalist class—so there are only two fundamental ways of thinking.

The 1929 crash, which shook the world to its foundations, cut sharply across the American mind, splitting it into two opposing parts: (1) The Brain Trust, or intellectual Planners, small and large. Those who invented the New Deal to save capitalism, and those who wanted "to use" the New Deal to move headlong to total planning according to the Russian model, were not so totally different from each other that they did not find intellectual cohabitation pleasant. Both had one cure for all the ills in the world. It was: Plan. (2) On the other hand, the rank and file workers tried to reorganize production on entirely new foundations by demanding that those who labor should control production. They too had but one word to describe how to do it. It was: SITDOWN. The very spontaneity of the action *created* the CIO.[251] What had been a *top committee within* the A. F. of L. overnight became a *Congress of* the greatest mass concentration of industrial workers.

While the workers were creating organizations of their own, characteristically American and specifically working class, the American intellectual was rudderless, drifting into the Communist-created Popular Front. The Russian Communists had a field day, penetrating everywhere from the Newspaper Guild to the State Department, from the labor bureaucracy in Detroit to filmdom in Hollywood. The American intellectual was not an unwilling victim. He zealously tried to influence the American worker. If he failed it was not his fault. The American intellectual has one trait in common with all intellectuals: he looks down upon the native working class as "backward." But while the Communist Party of the United States took over the American intellectual bodily, emotionally and financially, it remained without serious roots among the American working class. The intellectuals have left the Communist Party and its many fronts since then, (not always for the most principled reasons). But they expose themselves currently as still rudderless on the one question where American politics has always been expressed in its sharpest form—the Negro Question.

1956 opened a new stage in the Negro struggle for freedom. The fight down South was proceeding along two fronts: (1) school integration; and (2) the bus boycotts. Immediately, the "cultured" South asked for "understanding." LIFE magazine, so busy selling "the American way of life" abroad, responded by leading the battle of the "Northern" magazines to sell "the Southern way of life." The novelist, William Faulkner, struck the first and most telling blow by announcing that he would be willing to spill Negro blood to maintain the "Southern way of life."[252]

Oppression has ever worn a white face down South, and now, so does the degeneration of its "culture." Where, in this, are the intellectuals, North or South, who oppose this cultured blood-brother of Senator Eastland, the Nobel prize winner, William Faulkner? No doubt there are many. Where they do not keep quiet, however, they write for little journals read by radicals who need no convincing. Despite the shabby role of the American Communists on the Negro Question,[253] these intellectuals are ready to be sucked into another popular front. Yet it is not for want of American tradition. One of the most glorious pages in American history was written by the white intellectual, precisely on the Negro Question, in that very critical period preceding the Civil War.

The Abolitionists arose in America and out of America, out of its genius, with no assistance from any foreign tradition. At the same time, the masthead of William Lloyd Garrison's *Liberator* read: "The World Is My Country." The Abolitionists added a dimension to the very concept of intellectual by consciously choosing to be the means by which a social movement—the movement of the slaves for freedom—expressed itself. The intellectuals of today are busy telling us how the Communists pervert history, which is true enough. But wherein is the difference between Russians leaving out the role of Trotsky in the 1917 Revolution, and the American textbooks which do not even mention Wendell Phillips?[254] Where a Faulkner today does a lot of double-talking about being "morally" against segregation but being non-hesitant to spill the blood to preserve the alleged "underdog"—"the Southern way of life"—here is what Phillips had to say of the Southern way of life:

"And by the South I mean likewise a principle, and not a locality, an element of civil life, in fourteen rebellious States. I mean an element which, like the days of Queen Mary and the Inquisition, cannot tolerate free speech, and punishes it with the stake. I mean the aristocracy of the skin, which considers the Declaration of Independence a sham and democracy a snare—which believes that one third of the race is born booted and spurred, and the other two thirds ready saddled for that third to ride. I mean a civilization which prohibits the Bible by statute to every sixth man of its community, and puts a matron in a felon's cell for teaching a black sister to read. I mean the intellectual, social aristocratic South—the thing that manifests itself by barbarism and the bowie-knife, by bullying and lynch-law, by ignorance and idleness, by the claim of one man to own his brother, by statutes making it penal for the State of Massachusetts to bring an action in her courts, by statutes, standing on the books of Georgia today, offering five thousand dollars for the head of William Lloyd Garrison. That South is to be annihilated. (Loud applause). The totality of my common sense—or whatever you may call it —is this, all summed up in one word: This country will never know peace nor union until the South (using the word in the sense I have described) is annihilated, and the North is spread over it . . . Our struggle therefore is between barbarism and civilization."

The struggle for the minds of men today cannot be won by hollow slogans for democracy. The Europeans have seen too much of life since 1914. They aren't buying the Voice of America culture, and for good reason. They know the Negro—not only his great contributions to American culture, from jazz to historical writing. They know what he is doing presently. There is the forceful voice of the Alabama Negroes who have taken the matter of their freedom into their own hands and have never let go in all these months.

Because the spontaneity of the walkout *and* the organization of their forces to keep up the boycott was a simultaneous action, it is here that we can see what is truly historic and contains our future. Just watch how they have never let anything slip out of their hands during the boycott:

(1) They have been in *continuous* session: daily there are small meetings; three times weekly, mass meetings; at all times the new relationships.

(2) The decision is always *their own*. When the State Supreme Court handed down its decision against segregated buses and the bus company, hungry for their profits, hung up notices they would obey decisions, the Negroes said: We also asked for Negro bus drivers. To the city fathers, who proclaim segregation as the "Southern way of life," they, as Southerners, said that if they never ride the buses it will be soon enough.

(3) The organization of their own transportation, without either boss or political supervision, is a model.

Clearly, the greatest thing of all in this Montgomery, Alabama, spontaneous organization was its own working existence.

When Faulkner is the man whom Eisenhower asks to form a new organization of intellectuals to tell Europeans about American democracy and the other American intellectuals bear this silently, Europeans know that courage does not come out of thin air but out of conviction that you are part of and represent the wave of the future—as the Negro strugggle for freedom does and the "Southern way of life" does not. Under such circumstances the American intellectual struggle to win the mind of man can only be presumptuous.[255] Thus in society as a whole, as in production, the crisis is total.

Our point of departure has always been production only because to see the crisis in production means to understand it

everywhere else. Failure to see it in production means inability
to understand the crisis anywhere. This does not mean that the
crisis of our age is "limited" to production. Our age has rightly
been characterized as the crisis of the mind. It is precisely the
totality of the crisis that compels philosophy, a total outlook.
But the American intellectual has failed signally to grasp such a
total outlook. He is a man divided a dozen ways and is furthest
removed from reality.

It is not Marxists who have compelled society, at last, to face
with sober senses the conditions of labor and the relations of men
with each other. Our life and times have compelled that confrontation. In everyday life on the practical questions of the day
and in every layer of society, the great philosophic battles that
matter are precisely those over production, the role of the working
class, the One-Party State, H-bomb. Or, to put it more simply,
the critical questions are: How are workers to be made to produce
more? and: Will Civilization, as we know it, survive at all? Where
the intellectual combatants, as in America, are not professed dia-
lecticians, as many in Europe and Asia are, they are worsted in the
bargain. The seal of bankruptcy of contemporary civilization, *including the so-called Vanguard Parties,* is the bankruptcy of its
thought.

The void in the Marxist movement since Lenin's death would
have a significance only for Marxists except that Marxism is
in the daily lives and aspirations of working people. Marxism is
neither in the pathetic little theses gathering dust in small radical
organizations, nor in impressively big tomes gathering dust on the
shelves of large conservative universities.

The main difficulty in seeing the elements of the new society
in the present is that workers repeat many of the ideas of the
ruling class until the very day that an explosive break actually
occurs. Take the tremendous movement which created the CIO.
Who would have thought, in 1935, when John L. Lewis proposed to
William Green the formation of some industrial unions, that the
unskilled workers would break out in the gigantic sitdown strikes
that challenged private property? Nobody, absolutely nobody. Not
even the workers themselves knew the world-shaking passions and
forces that lay behind their restlessness and bitterness, and that

they would express themselves simply in *sitting down*. When the reporters came to ask Lewis whether he had ordered the sitdown, it was obvious that the very word, let alone the action, was as strange to him as to the reporters. It was obvious he had not thought of it, far less ordered it, although he knew enough of leadership to be "for" it.

He was taken by surprise not because he was "merely" a trade union leader whose head was full of beourgeois ideas. No, not even the founder of Marxism—who stood for a new society and predicted its inevitable coming when all others saw only the solidity of the old, the *status quo*—did not, and could not have foreseen the spontaneous action of the French working class in "storming the heavens" and creating the Paris Commune. No single human being, nor even the Bolshevik Party of Lenin, could have predicted, far less organized the Soviet. No one could have guessed it was coming until it came. But isn't it obvious now, that the Russian workers, in their own way and among themselves, were coming to the conclusion that they wanted something other than parliamentary democracy? They thought so as far back as 1905 when they created the St. Petersburg Soviet. No one told them to. No one organized it. No one made a new category out of it when it did arise. The only ones who *remembered* the 1905 Soviet, and held fast to that vision and that act, were the Russian workers. They recreated them in 1917, this time on a national scale.

The first day that happened, Lenin, as we saw, was still repeating that it was necessary to combine legal and illegal work when, in actuality, the masses had already created open, mass, tremendous organizations. The next day he finally saw. When he did, he didn't say, "I always thought so; haven't I said . . . etc., etc." No, he recognized the *new in fact and in theory* and reorganized all—all without exception—*all* of his old categories: from the democratic dictatorship of the proletariat and peasantry, to the vanguard nature of the Party and its leadership. Now, he said, the Russian reality had shown that the rank and file of the Party were ten times more revolutionary than the leadership, and the great masses outside the Party ten times more revolutionary than the party.

If, in 1917, it was clear that the Russian workers moved beyond parliamentary democracy, it should have been clear in 1936-1937 that the American workers had moved from the question of who owned the property, to the question of who controlled production. The workers didn't start any *arguments* about private property. They merely *sat down* at the machines they had always operated, and said they would not leave until the conditions of labor were changed.

Only after the first great outburst do the masses begin to bring their energies and their years of thought to bear upon the problems that face them. Then, day by day, and minute by minute, their own class ideas and class program rapidly unfold. This has once again grown as big as life and as final as death in the Hungarian Revolution which was begun by the whole population, including intellectuals. But, as it developed, the whole brunt shifted to the Workers' Councils, that is, to the workers *in the factories*. Their action once again made obvious that the workers had a mind of their own long before the outbreak, and which was sustained long after the defeat. As in 1917 the Russian workers alone remembered the Soviet of 1905, so this time not alone the Hungarian but the world working class will remember the Hungarian Workers' Councils.

The working class has not created a new society. But the workers have undermined the old. They have destroyed all the old categories; they have no belief in the rationality either of the economic or of the political order. The "vanguard," on the other hand, has done nothing. It is stuck in the mud of the old fixed categories, chief of which is "the Party to lead." In the face of the movement from practice to theory—during the 1930's, and again during the 1940's, and especially during the present period of Automation—the Trotskyists and other radical parties continue to repeat the outlived thesis of the "vanguard party" Lenin espoused back in 1902-03. This makes their intellectual abdication as complete as if they had never broken from the Communist Parties. It is equally true of those unaffiliated Marxists who, being incapable of breaking out of the old categories, let alone creating new ones, are compelled to return to Bukharin's attitude of blaming the workers for the betrayal of the Second International. When

Lenin accused Bukharin of having allowed the imperialist war to suppress his thinking, he accurately analyzed these present-day Marxist intellectuals, who would rather blame the workers, *as a class,* than face the challenge, to reorganize *their* thinking, that is being hurled at them by the new Humanist impulses from ever-deeper strata of the workers. Affiliated or unaffiliated, "the party to lead," has them all by the throat.

It goes without saying that the past masters at that are the Communists. The capitalist mentality of all these Planners is shown nowhere as clearly as on the question of Automation. No private property capitalist has ever dreamed more fantastic dreams of push-button factories without workers than the present rulers of Russia. The totalitarian bureaucracy hopes through Automation to overcome the Russian resistance to the Plans. At the same time, these bureaucrats think they have it all over "the capitalist world" because they can repeat Marxist phrases about the end of the separation between mental and manual labor. Some sound exactly like Reuther and his "every worker an engineer." On the eve of the Geneva Congress, in 1955, the official papers, *Pravda* and *Izvestia* were filled with articles on, "What Is Holding Back Automation?" Then they held an All-Union Conference of Industrial Personnel and issued "An Appeal to All Workers, Engineers, Technicians and Employees in the Soviet Union" to learn from the experience of "the production innovators." The Russian worker took it to mean more speed-up and continued his resistance. The following year, the Twentieth Congress of the Russian Communist Party, which so loudly proclaimed "De-Stalinization," continued the Stalinist line of production and more production, with the following new twist. Bulganin said, "Great harm is caused to technical progress in our country by underestimating the achievements of technology abroad. . . . The main thing is not to discover first but to introduce first. . . . Industry must be redesigned to provide proper incentive to technical innovation." The "redesigning" turned out to be the application of Automation in such a way as to teach the workers respect for the intellectuals who are the "production innovators." The Russian workers are no different than the American workers: they too want to know what happens *after?*

Where the workers *begin* with the questions—What happens *after* the conquest of power? Are we always to be confronted with a new labor bureaucracy which is to end in the One Party State?— the "vanguard" has nothing to say but, "First do this and follow me." The Capitalist ideologist is as good at giving commands: "Look at the new wonders of Automation, and follow me." Everyone is ready to lead; no one to listen.

Intellectual sloth just accumulates and accumulates to the point where the self-complacent "scientific individual" is permitted to write, with impunity and unthinkingly, of "Man Viewed as Machine." Evidently no human passion nowadays is beyond a mathematical formula that can forthwith be made practicable in "a buildable machine."

What they all forget is that a new society is THE human endeavor, or it is nothing. It cannot be brought in behind the backs of the people, neither by the "vanguard" nor by the "scientific individuals." The working people will build it, or it will not be built. There is a crying need for a new unity of theory and practice which begins with where the working people are—*their* thoughts, *their* struggles, *their* aspirations.

This is not intellectual abdication. Intellectual abdication took place during the long Depression because intellectuals had no philosophy or method of thought, and just drifted into the camp of the fellow travellers or outright followers of "the Party line." Intellectual abdication reappeared when McCarthyism so panicked them that they willingly, and without the duress of Moscow Trials, participated in public confessionals. Intellectual abdication reigns supreme when "scientific men" are allowed to take command of the field of thought as if that too were a "buildable machine."

Intellectual growth will first begin when new ground is broken. The elements of the new society present in the old are everywhere in evidence in the thoughts and lives of the working class. Where the workers think their own thoughts, there must be the intellectual to absorb the new impulses. Outside of that there can be no serious theory. Philosophy springs from the empirical sciences and actual life, but incorporation of these laws and generalizations into philosophy, Hegel showed, "implies a compulsion of thought itself to proceed to these concrete truths." Hegel knew whereof he spoke when he told the intellectuals of his day that "the sense of bondage springs from inability to surmount the antithesis, and from looking at what *is* and what happens as contradictory to what *ought* to be and happen."[256]

The modern intellectuals will lose their sense of guilt and bondage when they will react to "the compulsion of thought to proceed to these concrete truths"—the actions of the Negro school children in Little Rock, Arkansas, to break down segregation, the wildcats in Detroit for a different kind of labor than that under present-day Automation, the struggles the world over for freedom. The alignment precisely with such struggles in the days of the Abolitionists and of Marx is what gave these intellectuals that extra dimension as theoreticians and as human beings which enabled them to become part of the new society. It will do so again. Once the intellectual accepts the challenge of the times, then the ideal and the real are seen to be not far apart. The worker is right when he demands that work be "completely different, and not separated from life itself," and that "thinking and doing be united." Once the theoretician has caught this, *just this,* impulse from the worker, his work does not end. It first then begins. A new unity of theory and practice can evolve only when the movement from theory to practice meets the movement from practice to theory. The totality of the world crisis has a new form—fear at the "beep-beep" from the new man-made moon. The American rush "to catch up" with the *sputnik,* like the Russian determination to be the first to launch the satellite, is not in the interest of "pure science" but for the purpose of total war. Launching satellites into outer space cannot solve the problems of this earth. The challenge of our times is not to machines, but to men. Intercontinental missiles can destroy mankind, they cannot solve its human relations. The creation of a new society remains *the* human endeavor. The totality of the crisis demands, and will create, a total solution. It can be nothing short of a New Humanism.

CHAPTER SEVENTEEN

THE CHALLENGE OF MAO TSE-TUNG

A. Communist Counter-Revolutions

> "There are people that think that Marx-
> ism can cure any disease. We should tell
> them that dogmas are more useless than
> cow dung. Dung can be used as ferti-
> lizer."—Mao Tse-tung

1) Of Wars and Revolutions as an "Eight-Legged Essay" [257]

The Sino-Soviet rift has produced a raft of r-r-r-revolutionary
statements from the Chinese Communist Party that picture Mao as
a "Marxist-Leninist" in unsullied revolutionary armor who carries
on a single-handed global struggle against "revisionism." The West's
daily press does nothing to upset the simplicity and coherence of
this fairy tale because it is all too eager to stress the power rift
between Russia and China. The battle of quotations that first broke
out openly in 1960, with Mao leaning heavily on Lenin's *State and
Revolution,* and Khrushchev favoring Lenin's *Infantile Sickness of
Leftism in Communism,* is, to use a phrase of Mao's on another
occasion, an "eight-legged essay." In the process all words have lost
their meaning.

---

* I wish to thank a young scholar, Jonathan Spence, for some of the
research for this chapter, and I am indebted for his knowledge of the
Chinese language. The analysis of the material and the political conclusions are, naturally, mine alone.

The whole history of Mao proves him to have been a fighter, not against "revisionism," but against "dogmatism," the present revolutionary-sounding statements that thunder out from Communist China notwithstanding. Mao's accusation of Khrushchev as a coward who moved over from "fear of nuclear blackmail" to "fear of revolution," and Khrushchev's expression of "sadness" that the "Chinese comrades" could join the reactionary "atom mongers and madmen," are no more than tools forged to serve the narrow purpose of power politics. This is not to say that the ideological battle is without influence on the power struggle, and, moreover, has a logic of its own. But we must not let the fact that both contestants call themselves Communist hide their class nature: both are capitalistic to the marrow of their bones. State-capitalism changes the form, not the content, of these totalitarian regimes. It is no accident that the propulsion toward open conflict came from internal, not external causes. 1959, the first breaking point between Russia and China, was not only the year of Khrushchev's visit to the United States where he helped create the "spirit of Camp David"; nor is it only the year of China's first incursion into Indian territory. It is the year of crisis within Russia and within China, especially the latter. This was brought about by a combination of natural calamities and an inhuman drive by the totalitarian rulers to industrialize, collectivize and "communize" the vast land with one "Great Leap Forward." Instead of achieving overnight any new social order, 650 million human beings[258] were to face famine and near famine conditions. The voices of revolt came from within, not from without, mainland China. The battle of quotations, however, are directed toward the outside. Because these two state-capitalist regimes calling themselves Communist are involved in a contest for influence over the new African, Asian and Latin-American world, where the Marxian theory of liberation is a polarizing force for freedom fighters, the battle is fought out in the language of "Marxism-Leninism." Because ours is not only a nuclear age but the age of the struggle for the minds of men, any contest with "the most vicious enemy, American imperialism," requires that one have ideological as well as power "positions of strength." It is within this context that we must view the challenge of Mao Tse-tung, and, indeed, it is within this framework that Mao threw down the gauntlet to Khrushchev for leadership over the entire Communist world.

To crown his world ambitions Mao has not shirked from taking on responsibility for a possible nuclear holocaust. The Chinese rulers have shocked all mankind by their cynical statements that China would suffer "least" were such a holocaust to break out. "Even if 200 million of us were killed, we would still have 400 million left." [259] Mao has laughed at "nuclear war blackmail" branding all who fear nuclear war as cowards and "revisionists." As Hongqi (Red Flag) put it: "The modern revisionists are panic stricken by the policy of nuclear war blackmail. They develop from the fear of war to the fear of revolution." [260]

This glorification of revolution is not meant for mainland China, however. It is directed against other lands. The Chinese masses would like nothing better than a revolution against their ruling class and its head, Mao Tse-tung. For one brief period voices were heard, loud and clear, in uncompromising opposition to the single party state. They were, as they expressed it, "blooming and contending" in line with Mao's speech "let 100 flowers bloom, let 100 schools of thought contend." This opposition was soon ruthlessly crushed.

It is impossible to understand the situation the Chinese rulers face now, either internally or externally, without understanding the critical years 1956-1957. Just as the Hungarian Revolution was not only a national revolution, so the discontent in China was not confined to its borders. Both events mark an historic turning point in world development as well as in class relations within state-capitalist societies.

1956 opened a new world epoch in the fight for freedom. The year began with Khrushchev, in February, calling for de-Stalinization. He hoped this would guarantee the containment of revolutionary unrest. The year ended with the Hungarian Revolution showing, beyond any peradventure of doubt, that what the Freedom Fighters want is freedom from Communism.

In February, 1957, Mao felt certain that it was still safe for him to act the benevolent "sun" [261] that would allow "100 schools of thought to contend." The Chinese people "bloomed and contended" so vigorously that they exposed the contradiction, the lie, antagonistic contradiction between rulers and ruled, thus giving the lie to Mao's claim that he is an exponent of the Marxist theory of liberation.

The bureaucracy's incredible fanaticism and blindness to reality and to logic meant that everything had to fit into its world. If people could not be "remolded" to fit, they had to be destroyed. We face, as the starkest and most palpable reality today, what the great German philosopher Hegel—analyzing the abstract philosophic development of the "Spirit in Self-Estrangement"—had called "the absolute and universal inversion of reality and thought, their entire estrangement one from the other." [262]

The brief period of open dispute in China, from May 8 to mid-June, 1957, illuminates both the Sino-Soviet dispute, and the fundamental struggle of China and Russia against the United States. The life and death question of war and revolution is thereby brought into focus. Though the right to any freedom of expression in China was short-lived, and though the official sources[263] did not by any means reveal the full extent of the opposition, the true sweep of freedom broke through these barriers as well as through the barriers of language. Just as the Hungarian Freedom Fighters spoke in a more universal language than Magyar, and the Swahili language of the African revolutionaries is understood by all, so, for the same reasons, we feel at one with the Chinese. They all speak the human language of freedom. Let's listen to the voices of revolt.

2) *Voices of Revolt*

Lin Hsi-ling, age 21: "True socialism is highly democratic, but the socialism we have here is not democratic. I call this society a socialism sprung from a basis of feudalism." The People's Daily, June 30, then continues, "She called them (certain phenomena in the life of our society) a class system, saying that it (i.e., class system) had already entered all aspects of life . . . she said with ulterior motives that the social productive forces in both the Soviet Union and China were very low and that these two countries had not yet eliminated class differences . . . Moreover, quoting Engels' theory that one country cannot construct socialism and Lenin's dictum that socialism is the elimination of class, she arrived at the conclusion that present-day China and Russia are not socialist. She loudly demanded a search for 'true socialism' and advocating using explosive measures to reform the present social system."

Chang Po-sheng, head of the propaganda department of the Communist Youth League in the Normal College of Shenyang: "All kinds of important questions are decided upon by six persons —Chairman Mao, Liu Shao-ch'i, Premier Chou En-lai and those above the rank of the Secretary General of the Party center. The destiny of six hundred million is dictated by the pen of these six men and how can they know the actual situation? At best they can make an inspection tour of the Yellow River and swim the Yangtze." (Shenyang Daily, June 11).

"Since last year, workers in the province have involved themselves in thirteen strikes and trouble-making incidents." (Reported by New China News Agency, Canton, May 14).

Trade Unions called "Tongues of the Bureaucracy." "Trade unions were cast aside because they were concerned with production and not with the workers' welfare . . . that is why some workers in Canton, Changsha, Wuhan, Hsinhsiang and Shikiachwang dubbed their trade unions 'workers' control departments' led by the administration, 'tongues of the bureaucracy,' and 'tail of the administration,' etc. . . . Is it not a 'crisis' in the trade union work that trade unions are divorced from the masses to such a degree?" (From Li Feng's "On an 8,000-li Tour of Hurried Observations," People's Daily, May 9).

Ko P'ei-chi, Lecturer, Department of Industrial Economics, China People's University in Peking: "When the Communist Party entered the city in 1949 the common people welcomed it with food and drink and looked upon it as a benevolent force. Today the common people choose to estrange themselves from the Communist Party as if its members were gods and devils . . . The party members behave like plain-clothes police and place the masses under their surveillance. The party members are not to be blamed for this, for the party organization instructs them to gather information . . . The masses may knock you down, kill the Communists and overthrow you. The downfall of the Communist Party does not mean the downfall of China. This cannot be described as

unpatriotic for the Communists no longer serve the people . . ."
(Reported in People's Daily, May 31).

Huang Chen-lu, editor of the school paper at the Normal College of Shenyang: "The Communist Party has 12 million members,
less than two per cent of the total population. The 600 million
people are to become the obedient subjects of this two per cent of
the people. What sort of principle is this!" (Reported in Shenyang
Daily, June 11).

Su P'ei-ying. China Democratic League, and Engineer of Tientsin Civil Housing Designing Board: "When the Communists first
entered Tientsin, they said it was a revolution and our revolution
was not a change of dynasties. They way I look at it now is that
the revolution was worse than a change of dynasties and living in
such a society is heartbreaking." (Reported in New China News
Agency, June 9).

Lung Yun, Vice Chairman KMTRC[264]. "During the Second
World War, the United States granted loans and leases to her allies.
Later, some of these allies refused to pay back the loans, and the
United States excused some from repayment. It will take our
country more than ten years to repay the loans from the Soviet
Union, if we can ever repay them. Besides, we have to pay interest
to the Soviet Union. China fought for socialism, but look at the
result." (Reported by the New China News Agency, June 18, as
"Lung Yun's Absurd Views").

Tai Huang, New China News Agency journalist, who had
joined the Communist Party in 1944: "The old ruling class has
been overthrown, but a new ruling class has arisen. The evolution
of this will lead to an amalgamation with Taiwan." NCNA,
Peking, August 17, continues its report: "After the outbreak of
the Hungarian incident, Tai Huang disapproved of the dispatch
of the Soviet troops to help Hungary to suppress its counter-revolutionary rebellion . . . He slandered the people's journalistic
enterprises as a 'policy to make the people ignorant.' He mali-
ciously attacked the leaders of the New China News Agency everywhere."

NCNA, Canton, May 14: "The Communist Party Kwantung
Committee has courageously and thoroughly exposed the contradictions found in current work in Kwantung . . . the contradictions

between the leadership and the masses. These find main expression in undemocratic behaviour on the part of the cadres which leads to the practice of having work carried out by coercion and command and the violation of law and discipline; the refusal to make public the accounts which has permitted quite a number of co-operative cadres to indulge in corrupt practices; the non-participation of co-operative cadres in manual work and the payment of compensation wages to them at too high a rate. All this dissatisfies the masses . . . From last winter, a total of 117,916 households have pulled out at different times from co-operatives in the province. At present, 102,149 households have rejoined."

Suddenly, six weeks after the open forums first started, the Communist rulers called an abrupt halt to the "100 flowers" campaign. It was felt that, instead of 100 flowers, they found 1,000 weeds and, "of course," weeds must be rooted out. The road that had led to those six weeks was a tortuous one. Mao's original speech, "Let 100 flowers bloom, let 100 schools of thought contend," which had been delivered as far back as May, 1956, and was intended for intellectuals only, had never been published. Nevertheless the limited freedom expanded itself. China was confronted with student strikes and worker strikes. Meanwhile, the Hungarian "thaw" had developed into a full-scale revolution. Mao still thought he could limit the Chinese thaw by fitting the limited freedoms into the vise of single party domination. Thereupon, (February 27, 1957) he delivered a new speech, "On the Correct Handling of Contradictions Among the People." He redefined "contradiction" (Mao's favorite thesis) to where both it and freedom lost all meaning. He further redefined "the people" to where they were either "people" or "enemies." Mao put so many limitations to the permissible contradictions that "blooming and contending" was diverted. Even then, however, he felt called upon to introduce so many "additions" to the text of his speech that when it was finally published, on June 18, 1957, "the correct handling of contradictions" soon turned into a relentless hunt for "rightists." The right to free expression ended abruptly, ruthlessly.

Whether this took the form of outright execution, as in the case of the three student leaders at Hanyang, who were hanged before the horrified eyes of 10,000; or whether it took the form of sending "rightists and intellectuals" to work in the fields, or to serve prison terms, the shock was not exhausted by the typical totalitarian state's crushing of the opposition. Far from retreating in the face of widespread opposition, Mao soon came out with a real brainstorm called "The People's Communes."

3) "The People's Communes"

The first "model Commune" had been initiated in April, 1958 and was named "Sputnik." The name was not chosen accidentally. The October, 1957 Russian launching of the sputnik produced two very different reactions on the part of Khrushchev and Mao. The former knew that Russia's "superiority" over the United States was not "total." He knew, also, the cost of crushing the Hungarian Revolution and bringing the whole of Eastern Europe back under full Russian control. At the same time, the one billion dollars[265] in short-term credits to Eastern Europe prevented aid to China in as massive doses as had been previously given it. Above all, the Hungarian Revolution blew sky high, not only Hungary's State Plan, it undermined also Russia's Five Year Plan. This was scrapped and Khrushchev began to think of some substantial trade, on a long-term loan basis, with the United States. Hence, the Manifesto of the ruling Communist parties, in November, 1957, was by no means limited to exorcising "revisionism." It also reaffirmed the line of "peaceful co-existence."

Mao, who was present, thought otherwise. He believed that the sputnik had produced so radical a shift in the world balance of power that the Communist orbit could now undertake little wars, "just wars" and all sorts of adventures with which to taunt U.S. imperialism. While he signed the "unanimous statement," he decided upon a very dramatic departure not only vis-a-vis the United States, but a dramatic short-cut to try to outstrip Russian Communism. This illusion of Mao's was fostered by one bountiful harvest, and his vainglorious confidence that he could, by militarizing labor, outstrip science.

What Mao's "People's Communes" far outstripped was Stalin's dictum "to liquidate the kulak as a class." In these "Communes" all the peasants—of China's population of 650 million, no less than

500 million are peasants—were to be herded into barracks-like quarters where they were to function "along military lines," working from sun-up to sundown. After dinner they were either to attend meetings, or work in fields, or on construction, or in steel "mills"—or wherever they might be ordered to work. Then Mao planned to organize "Communes" in the cities. This total regimentation and militarization of labor was called "mass mobilization," or "mass line." This, said Mao, was going to unleash such vast productive forces that they could accomplish in one decade what it took four decades to accomplish in Russia. Moreover, the fantasy went on, they could go, "without interruption," to Communism.

The totalitarian state was in so great a hurry that in eight months it herded 120 million peasant households—formerly in 740 thousand agricultural producers' cooperatives of 160 families each—into 24,000 "People's Communes" each averaging no less than 5,000 families. This, it was claimed, "liberated" tens of millions of women from household chores. They therefore had to work alongside their men in the field full time; their children were taken away from them, and sent to nurseries; old parents were sent to "old peoples' happy homes." All eating was done in public mess halls, hence the women who were "freed" from household chores had to cook, instead of for one family, for approximately 8,000.

"The People's Commune," read the Chinese Communist Party's Central Committee Resolution, "is the combination of industry, agriculture, commerce, education and military affairs within the scope of their activity." [266]

Pretentious claims were made that steel was being produced on the farms. Actually only a low-grade of pig iron—full of slag, and quite useless to the steel mills—was produced at the cost of transporting the bulky ore to the farm kilns. In the end, Peking itself had to admit that in 1958 no less than 3.08 million tons of "locally made pig iron" had to be scrapped because it was no good for industrial purposes. Instead of unleashing vast productive forces, all that the "mass line" unleashed were aching backs, and miserable barracks conditions of work and of living. The chaos, disorganization, intolerable living conditions, inhuman relationships, and just plain exhaustion compelled even the totalitarian bureaucracy to call a halt and proclaim benevolently that "ten to twelve hours was sufficent" to work; that calisthenics and meetings should not take all the rest of the time since "people should sleep eight hours." The determination persisted for the recognition of personal freedom. Hence, a new dictum: "Members of the Commune are directed to lead a collectivized life. Each person must work ten hours and engage in ideological studies for two hours a day. They are entitled to one day of rest every ten days . . . The CCP committee rules that all members are free to use their time as they wish outside of the ten hours of labor and two hours of ideological study each day; that husband and wife may have a room of their own; that members are permitted to make tea and other refreshments in their own quarters for themselves; and that women members may use their spare time to make shoes and mend clothes . . . The Commune members have enthusiastically welcomed the small personal freedoms granted them by the CCP committee." (From a New China News Agency report of November 20, 1958) .

While the Communes never did develop as the over-all form of production in industry, industry was alleged to have met its production targets "so far ahead of time" that a halt could be called. Once again it was to be recognized that while industry is "the leader" agriculture remains "the basis." There is no doubt that some progress was made, if the measure of progress is not the way in which people live, but the way industry is developed. Irrigation projects were constructed with forced labor, and the rate of industrial growth far outdistanced that in another Asiatic country—India.

Whatever attraction the fantastic goals set for 1958 had for the underdeveloped countries, if the gullible thought that ordering the masses about like soldiers and making them work endless hours would produce industrialization overnight, if the cynical failed to recoil from the "Communal living" which was short on sex life and love, and long on public mess-halls and work, the present famine conditions compel second thoughts. Here are the figures:[267]

	First Claims on 1958 Output	Revised Claims on 1958 Output
Steel (million metric tons)	11.08	8.00
Grain (million metric tons)	375.00	250.00
Cotton (million metric.tons)	3.32	2.1

No current statistics are released for agriculture.[268] It is known, however, that while the word "Commune" is retained, it is actually the production brigade rather than the whole Commune that has become the operational unit. The large production brigade embraces from 200 to 300 families, equivalent to what it was in agricultural producers' co-ops, or a single large village; and the small production brigade consists of only forty families. Again, while the large production brigade has the right of ownership, the small production brigade has the right of use of labor, land, draft animals, and farming tools and equipment.

The "new" method of work follows along the road of the First Five Year Plan modeled on the Russian line, rather than the lines of departure mapped out with "The Great Leap Forward." The blame is placed on those who didn't understand, and thus are in need of yet a new rectification campaign since there are those "who have taken advantage of the difficulties created by natural calamities and shortcomings in basic-level work to carry out destructive activities."

The dictum is: "Reform some comrades who are crudely unconcerned with details, unwilling to understand and often have no idea whatsoever of complete conditions, but yet who direct production." The "new" principle has all the sound of sweated piece-work pay, thus: "The principle of exchange for fair prices, distribution according to work, and work-more-earn-more." [269]

We must not think, however, that the recognition of a need for technological build-up, or the need to concentrate on agricultural production, or the need for "specialists" and "lowering of production costs" means the abandonment of the Chinese Communist "three-sided banner" that is, socialist construction, the "Great Leap Forward," and the "Commune."

Directed to the Afro-Asian world was the claim that it is possible for the underdeveloped areas to go uninterruptedly from industrialization into "Communism," and that "the mass line" can achieve greater miracles than advanced science.

Khrushchev didn't have to wait two years for the revised figures on the achievements of the "Great Leap Forward" to be published for him to know the preposterousness of the so-called simultaneous development of agriculture and industry in a country that had no advanced technological base for either. Nor did he appreciate Mao's attempt to transform the fantasy into a "theory" to prove the superiority of the China Road over Russia's more arduous long road to "Communism." The breaking point, however, came, not on the question of the "Commune," but at a time when Mao tried to tell him how to conduct the struggle against the United States. He disregarded Mao's opposition to his meeting with Eisenhower, and arrived in the United States on September 15, 1959. The "spirit of Camp David" for a summit was adhered to until the U-2 spy plane incident in May, 1960. It is true that these considerations of power-politics, and not any theoretical differences, are the basic reasons for the different interpretations from Moscow and Peking on war and revolution. The objective forces that compel the different interpretations are, however, by no means exhausted by pointing to the obvious power-politics involved. Mao's and Khrushchev's "theories" are as objectively founded as are their power politics. It is, therefore, necessary to trace them through to their sources.

B. The Dialectic of Mao's Thought From the Defeat of the 1925-27 Revolution to the Conquest of Power

> ". . . in place of revolt appears arrogance."—Hegel

Different conditions produce different modes of thought. The twenty-two year long struggle for power—from the defeat of the Chinese Revolution of 1925-27 to Mao's assumption of full power in mainland China in 1949—determined the dialectic of "Mao's Thought" as a corollary to Stalin's long series of basic revisions of Marxism which ended in its total transformation into opposite— the monolithic single party state power of totalitarian Communism. To this, and not to Marxism, Mao made two original contributions: (1) the role of the Army, in and out of state power; and (2) "Thought Reform," that is to say, brainwashing which, as the natural adjunct to his "four-class politics," is applied equally to all classes. These are the underlying premises of all of Mao's actions and writings, including the two essays officially cited to prove the "originality of Mao's Thought as creative Marxism": *On Practice,* and *On Contradiction.* We must never forget that the transformation into opposite is not just an academic question. It is objectively grounded. To grasp the ideology at its source, however, we cannot begin with Mao's conquest of power in 1949, much less with the Sino-Soviet Rift beginning in 1958. Its true beginning is the defeat of the 1925-27 Revolution. Indeed, Mao dates the Chinese Revolution from its defeat because it is then, as he puts it, that the "Revolutionary War" began. In this case we are willing to follow Mao's method of back-dating because it is there that his undermining of Marxism began.

1) Defeat of Revolution

The defeat of the 1925-1927 Chinese Revolution meant the defeat of the peasantry as well as the proletariat. However, where the proletariat could not in any way escape the counter-revolutionary vengeance of Chiang in the cities where his power—state and military, prison and police—was centered, it was possible, in the vast land of China, to find some escape in the mountainous countryside.

Very early during his running from Chiang's endless "extermination campaigns," Mao must have decided that warlordism is no accidental feature of Chinese life, and that "mass power" too should be coordinated with the military. Guerrilla war, and not peasant revolution, was soon made into a theory. The "Red" Army, and not the poor peasants, became the new all-encompassing reality— political as well as military, philosophic as well as economic. The Party armed with military might won support from the peasantry when it took over in a definite piece of territory and fostered agricultural reform. But whether or not it had such wide support, its military control of an area gave the Party state power over the peasantry. This is the quintessential element. Theory can wait.

This is why Mao did not make his only original and moving piece of writing of spontaneous peasant revolt and organization— "Report on an Investigatoin of the Peasant Movement in Hunan," February, 1927—into a theory of the role of the peasantry in revolution.[270] Mao had no disagreement with Stalin's policy of "The

Bloc of Four Classes," which contributed no small share to the defeat of the Revolution. Despite its revolutionary fervor when it reports the actual revolutionary actions of the peasantry, Mao's Report describes divisions of society as those between "good gentry" and "bad gentry," "corrupt officials" and "honest ones," and speaks of "a new democratic order," not of a social revolution and a new classless society.

The peasant revolts which have characterized the whole of Chinese history since before Christ, deeply characterized, of course, the 1925-27 Revolution. But Mao's "Red Army," which arose after the defeat of the Revolution including the peasantry in Hunan, did not spring from any large scale spontaneous peasant movement. Quite the contrary. "The Red Army had no support from the masses. And in many places it was even attacked like a bandit gang." [271] When asked whether his Army hadn't included some lumpen-proletariat and even some bandit chiefs, Mao's answer was characteristic, that is to say, practical: They were excellent fighters. The Army was kept disciplined and in action. By the time of Chiang's fourth extermination campaign, it was capable of the historic military feat, the phenomenal long march, which began in October, 1934, into the vastness of China, and stretched over no less than 6,000 miles.

What, however, is forgotten in the oft-telling of this military exploit—I leave aside the decisive role of Chu Teh because it does not change the character of Maoism—is that the long march meant also stops; conquests of villages; acquisition of food supplies by whatever means; and the final method of establishing power when it did set itself up as the supposed "Soviet Republic." The so-called Soviet areas always coincided with the Red Army's sphere of action including the setting up of the "Soviet" from above by the Chinese Communist Party. One thing is clear and indisputable and absolutely new: Never before had a Marxist leader built an Army where there was no mass movement and called the territory of its operation a "Soviet Republic."

The running for safety, the need to survive, the compulsion to protect oneself, was to be elevated into "a theory of revolution." Not only that, every aspect of this survival was so transformed. For example, early in his career, Mao was ruthless against opponents, more ruthless against revolutionary opponents than he was against Chiang Kai-shek. Thus Li Li-san, who tried to base himself on the urban proletariat and some revolutionary Marxist principles, had to be destroyed. Thus, Mao liquidated the Kiangsi Soviet which, in 1930, tried to base itself on the city. As he himself put it to Edgar Snow, the rebels were "disarmed and liquidated." [272] Thereby, Mao completed what the counter-revolutionary Chiang Kai-shek achieved with the defeat of the 1927 Revolution—physical divorce of the Party from the working class.

He repeated this in 1936 as he moved again "to liquidate" Chang Kuo-t'ao[273] who opposed his "peasant Soviets." Mao followed the same policy after his new united front with Chiang in the war against Japan, when he moved against Trotskyists who stood for a "third front" or "Lenin front." Indeed, he branded these as the "principal enemies," which means that fighting against them took priority over fighting either Chiang or Japan.

The struggle against "dogmatists" characterized Mao, in action and in theory, before and after power. We will not get the slightest whiff of fighting "revisionists" until Mao has to fight Khrushchev for power within the Communist world and suddenly finds it necessary to appear "orthodox." The pretense of orthodoxy is strictly limited to the world outside of China. Since the concrete there gives the lie to this claim of orthodoxy, the emphasis is on Mao's "original contributions." Original they truly are. Indeed they have nothing whatever to do with Marxism as was seen over and over again on his road to power. His outflanking of the cities was of one piece with his appeal to the workers, not to revolt, but to continue production, and remain at work while he "took the cities."

Mao's "orthodoxy" has more than a tinge of "originality" since he feels compelled to transform his road to power into a universal theory applicable to all, and especially so to the under-developed countries. Thus, a recent article in Hongqi (Red Flag) Number 20-21, 1960, called "A Basic Summing Up of Experience Gained in the Victory of the Chinese People's Revolution," expansively states, over and over again, that the road to power was the establishment of "small revolutionary bases in the rural areas," the moving from "a few" of these to "many," and thus encircling "the cities by the rural areas (led) to the ultimate taking over of the cities."

And again: "Com. Mao Tse-tung maintained that, above all, the bases in the country which at the beginning were small in area and still few in number should be firmly held and continuously expanded and developed. In this way, it would be possible 'to come ever nearer the goal of attaining nation-wide political power.' "

Mao is not stressing the role of the peasantry as against that of the city workers in order to give the peasantry a special role in the revolution. On the contrary, he denigrates the early peasant Soviets in China, of which he was a leader, but not yet the undisputed leader. Here is how he analyzed that period: "We must by no means allow a recurrence of such ultra-left, erroneous policies as were adopted toward the petty and middle bourgeoisie by our party in the period from 1931 to 1934 (the advocating of uneconomically high standards in working conditions; excessively high income-tax rates; . . . the shortsighted, one-sided view of the so-called 'welfare of the toilers' instead of making our objective the development of production, the prosperity of our economy, the taking into account of both public and private interests and benefits of both labor and capital.)" [274]

Mao launched his new policy by securing Chiang Kai-shek's release after his own Kuomintang subordinates had kidnapped him at Sian in December, 1936. Mao then had Chiang re-instated as head of the united national forces. This is what it meant:

"Our policy is to rely on the poor peasants and maintain a stable alliance with the middle peasants in order to destroy the system of feudal and semi-feudal exploitation by the landlord class and the old type of rich peasants. The land, the properties which the landlords and rich peasants receive, must not exceed those which the mass of peasants get. But neither should there be a repetition of the ultra-left, erroneous policy carried out between 1931 and 1934, the so-called policy of 'distribute no land to the landlords and poor land to the rich peasants.' It is necessary to heed the opinion of the middle peasants . . . if they do not agree, concessions should be made to them." [275]

And again: "We have already adopted a decision not to confiscate the land of the rich peasant . . . we are not confiscating the

property and the factories of the big and small merchants and
capitalists. We protect their enterprise . . . The common interests
of both capitalists and workers are grounded in the struggle against
imperialist aggression . . . What we consider the most important
is that all parties and groups should treat us without animosity
and bear in mind the objective of the struggle against Japan for
salvation of the country. We shall hereafter consider of no importance any difference of opinion on other questions." [276]

In a word, Mao "supports" the poor peasant, the revolutionary
peasant, like a rope supports a hanging man. Only after the abrogation of the Land Law of the first "Soviet Republic" which had
stipulated the confiscation of the land, without compensation, of
all landowners above middle peasant—and only after the total disintegration of the proletarian leadership—did Mao finally (1937)
become the undisputed leader of the Chinese Communist Party.

He is "for" the peasant when he wants to fight the city worker.
He is "for" the poor peasant as he moves against the landlord who
opposes him. When he needs the landlords as "part of the nation"
that opposes Japan, he promises them their rights, and he even
collects their rent for them in this period! The only peasant he is
truly for is the peasant *Army*. Of all the Communists in power,
only the Chinese list the Army along with the Party as the two
instruments of power. Since the attempt to establish Mao as
nothing short of "the greatest and most outstanding revolutionary
leader, statesman and theorist of Marxism—Leninism in the modern
era" begins with establishing him as "the philosopher" who wrote
"On Practice," [277] and "On Contradiction," [278] it is to these we turn.

2) The "Philosophy" of the Yenan Period: Mao Perverts Lenin

> "We are opposed to the die-hards in the
> revolutionary ranks . . . We are opposed
> to the idle talk of the 'left.' "—Mao Tse-
> tung.

The drastic change from the first "Soviet" period (1928-34) to
the second (Yenan period, 1935-1945) was naturally questioned by

many Communists. When some in his "Red Army" called the merger with the Chiang regular Army "counter-revolutionary," Mao replied that they were "dogmatists." This political struggle underlies the period of Mao's alleged original contribution to the philosophy of Marxism.

Objective research has since cast considerable doubt as to the date (1937) when the essays "On Practice" and "On Contradiction" were written; they weren't published until 1950-52.[279] We, however, are willing to accept the official date for their writing at face value because they are objectively, subjectively, for yesteryear and for today, so very Maoist that it does not matter that Mao may have back-dated them to make them appear prescient or re-written them to suit his present style. The point is, in order to sell the policy of class collaboration, Mao evidently thought a frontal attack on "dogmatists" would be insufficient. Hence he chose the form of "Philosophic Essays." These are so filled with empty abstractions that it is difficult to discover either his subject or his aim.

In "On Practice," Mao writes, "The epistemology of dialectical materialism . . . regards human knowledge as being at no point separable from practice." If knowledge is at no point separable from practice, he would have done well to tell us what practice he is talking about. But, no, Mao is anxious to make this reduction of theory to "practicality" appear to be based on nothing less authoritative than Lenin's *Philosophic Notebooks.* Mao quotes Lenin's sentence, "Practice is more than cognition (theoretical knowledge)." He fails to tell us, however, that Lenin was only restating Hegel's analysis of the relationship of the Practical Idea to the Theoretical Idea before the two are united, as Lenin puts it, "precisely in the theory of knowledge."

Far from theory being reduced to "practicality," Lenin asserts, in the very section from which Mao quoted one sentence, the following: "Alias: Man's consciousness not only reflects the objective world, but creates it." Since this preceded the quotation Mao used, it would have seemed impossible for even a Confucian like Mao so totally to have misunderstood its meaning—unless, of course, he had set out deliberately to pervert Lenin. In any case, the world the sophist Mao created was for such a low purpose—to compel obedience to a new united front with Chiang—that one hesitates to dignify the writing as "philosophy."

Only because this state-capitalist tyrant rules over no less than 650 million souls is one compelled to attempt an analysis of his "original contribution to Marxism."

Evidently, Mao failed to convince his hearers or his readers (we are not told which) because he soon followed with still another "philosophical essay," once again directed against the dogmatists," and this time called "On Contradiction." We are told that it was delivered as a lecture at the anti-Japanese Military and Political College in Yenan, August, 1937.

In "On Contradiction" Mao used some "practical" examples. This has at least one virtue: it shows exactly how he has to rewrite his own previous period of rule in order "to balance" the mistakes of "dogmatists" against those of the Kuomintang. It turns out that only *"after* 1927 (my emphasis—R.D.), the Kuomintang turned in the opposite direction" from the "revolutionary and vigorous" period of united front in 1925. The defeat of the Chinese Revolution is now laid at the door of "Ch'en Tuh-siuism," that is to say, the revolutionary Trotskyist leader, Ch'en Tuh-siu! Even the loss of "Soviet China" (now called merely "revolutionary bases") is blamed, not on Chiang's extermination campaigns, but on the "mistakes of adventurism."

"Since 1935," Mao pompously continues amidst a great deal of pretentious phrasemongering on the philosophic meaning of "Contradictions," "it (the Communist Party) has rectified these mistakes and led the new anti-Japanese united front." It follows that after "the Sian Incident in December, 1936, it (the Kuomintang) made another turn," obviously in the "right revolutionary direction" since they are once again in a united front. In "On Contradiction," this demagogic class collaborationist says benignly, "We Chinese often say: 'Things opposed to each other complement each other.'"

So permeated to the marrow of his bones is Mao with Confucianism that it is doubtful he is even conscious that he is thereby perverting in toto the Hegelian-Marxian theory of development through contradiction. Seen in all its profundity for the first time by Lenin, in 1915, as he re-read and commented upon Hegel's *Science of Logic,* this development through contradiction, transformation into opposite, helped Lenin get to the root of the collapse of established Marxism, the Second International. Blind to the developing oppositions, contradictions, antagonisms, Mao on the other hand invented a "truly original" division in the concept of contradiction, which he called "Principal Aspect of the Contradiction." This division between "the principal contradiction" and "the principal aspect of contradiction" permits Mao to make as complete a hash of philosophy as he has previously made of history. Thus it turns out that under certain conditions, "even principal contradictions are relegated temporarily to a secondary, or subordinate, position" and because of "uneven developments" and "mutual transformations," the economic basis becomes "subordinated" while "political and cultural reforms become the principal and decisive factors." Trying to make up for this insipid subjectivism, Mao proceeds to tell his readers that Communists "of course" remain materialists since "as a whole," they see that "material things determine spiritual things . . ." All one can say of such a hodge-podge is what Kant said of "the cosmological proof," that it was "a perfect nest of thoughtless contradictions."

A recent traveler to China cited what a local party secretary from Shensi said: "Through the study of theory, I clearly understood the principles of uninterrupted revolution and of revolution by stages and put them into concrete application in pig breeding." [280] Senseless as the local party secretary's statement is, it is only the logical conclusion of "The Leader's" reduction of theory to "practice" compelling the Chinese to follow his dictum that "dogmas are more useless than cow dung."

Before, however, we flee in disgust from the vulgarities that pass for "philosophy," and become too anxious to dismiss what totalitarian China lovingly calls "Mao's thought," let us bear in mind his present power. Let us remember, also, that when Mao made the Chinese Communist Party accept the new united front with Chiang and initiated his "three-thirds" principle—that one-third Communist Party members, one-third Kuomintang, and one-third non-party people constitute the administration in Communist areas—the fight against Japan stiffened. This was the period when visiting foreign journalists, whose cultural standards were greater than those of Mao's cohorts, were impressed with his "exciting

speeches on culture." Wearied of the Kuomintang corruption and
its ineffectualness in fighting Japan, they were impressed by the
Communists, not only in the fight against Japan, but in the dedi-
cation "to go to the people," i.e., to establish schools among the
peasants in remote areas, and proceed with agricultural reforms.
Still others, including many of the bourgeoisie and landlords, were
attracted by the moderate agricultural program, and hence, many
anti-Communists began accepting the Chinese Communists as mere
"agrarian reformers." Mao contributed nothing to Marxian philosophy, and denuded its politics of its class content. But he certainly carved out an original road to power. It is this which we
must look at again from still another aspect which he calls "three
magic weapons."

3) "Three Magic Weapons"

Stalin's rationalization for transforming the workers' state into
a state-capitalist society was called "building socialism in one country." It was based on the supposition that this could be done if
only Russia were not attacked from the outside. To assure this
Stalin transformed the world Communist movements into outposts
for Russia's defense. He allotted them no independent class role
to play. In the case of China it resulted in the elaboration of "the
bloc of four classes" which effectively subordinated the Chinese
Communist Party to the Kuomintang which helped defeat the 1925-
1927 Revolution. The "bloc of four classes," renamed the policy
of the "united front," became the warp and woof of Mao's thoughts
and actions both as he strove for power and after he achieved it.

What Stalin had used for the outside, Mao applied inside
China. Mao is a positivist. He is positively "magical" in seeing
"positive" elements in all classes. It stood him in good stead on
the road to power; and when he achieved it, he proceeded to
liquidate "the bureaucrat capitalists" not the capitalists as a class;
the "bad gentry" and not the landlord as a class. He feels positive
he can "remold" the capitalists and landlords mentally. This is
where his "rectification campaigns" differ from Stalin's purges:
he is so blind to the actualities of the class divisions tugging at his
rule that he believes in "a world of Great Harmony," where all
contradictions, of course, "complement each other."

A recent article from Hongqi[281]—"The United Front—A Magic Weapon of the Chinese People for Winning Victory"—sheds more light on the united front as the actual "philosophy" of the de-classed concept of "contradiction." Truly it is "the magic weapon" by which Mao swears throughout his development, in and out of power. As Mao made it the very warp and woof of existence and thought in 1937, the recent article from the fortnightly of the Central Committee of the Chinese Communist Party extends its existence to the present day. It was "the magic weapon" after he consolidated power in mainland China and, in 1952, when Mao began his three "antis" campaign—anti-corruption, anti-waste, and anti-bureaucratism. It continued into the later campaign of the five "antis"—anti-bribery, anti-tax evasion, anti-theft of state property, anti-cheating on government contracts, and anti-stealing of economic information for private speculation. So much for the period in which he tried to break the back of the private capitalists and landlords whom he brought with him from the anti-Japanese war, and as he laid the basis for state-capitalism in the economic foundation as well as in the political structure.

He then had to increase his campaign against the proletariat and peasantry and intellectuals who still thought this meant a move to socialism. The "rectification campaign of 1957-1958" is not accidentally launched under the same "philosophic" banner of 1937, only this time "On Contradiction" gets extended to "On the Correct Handling of Contradictions Among the People." Simultaneously, the vise of the single party state rule is clamped on the "100 schools of thought contending."

A perennial mathematician of sorts, Mao had, "as early as 1939, on the basis of the rich historical experience of the Party over a period of 18 years," expanded the single magic weapon into "three magic weapons":[282] "the united front, armed struggle, and Party building are the three fundamental problems of the Chinese Communist Party's three magic weapons, its three principal magic weapons, for defeating the enemy in the Chinese Revolution."

Since he is supposed to be a Marxist revolutionary, this leader "of the bloc of four classes," having state power in addition to these "three magic weapons" of "the united front, armed struggle and Party-building," remembers that he is supposed to stand for proletarian revolution and the rule of the proletariat. To a man in command of "magic weapons" this obligation presents no problems. "The people's democratic dictatorship" in China, says Mao, functions indeed "under the leadership of the working class." How? To the Chairman of the Communist Party, the one and only ruling party in China, it is all as simple as jumping through a hoop: the proletariat lives "through the Communist Party." Mao makes it easy indeed as he moves to sum up and reduce the "three magic weapons" into the single omnipresent one: "To sum up our experiences and concentrate it into one point, it is: the people's dictatorship under the leadership of the workingclass (through the Communist Party) and based upon the alliance of workers and peasants." [283]

For one ready, with one great leap, to go directly to "communism," he cannot, needless to say, stop long at this "alliance of workers and peasants" before he jumps into the "world of Great Harmony": "Bourgeois democracy has given way to people's democracy under the leadership of the working class, and the bourgeois republic to the people's republic. This has made it possible to achieve socialism and communism through the people's republic, to abolish classes and enter a world of Great Harmony." [284]

C. Oriental Despotism, Brainwashing—Or the Economic Compulsion Of State-Capitalism

In contrast to the panegyrics from Chinese Communist sources, scholars are once again reviving the appelation of *Oriental Despotism*.[285] A good dose of this thesis has even affected one Marxist who made an original study of *Mao's China*, correctly designating it as a state-capitalist society.[286] There is so much war-lordism in Mao; so solid a substratum of Chinese nationalism underlies his revision of Marxism; so thoroughly saturated with Confucianism is "Mao's Thought"—and the state-capitalist society he established is so great a tyranny—that it is all too easy to arrive at such a seemingly logical conclusion as "Oriental Despotism." That nothing quite misses the mark by so great a margin is obvious from the total overhaul of Chinese society, its family life as well as its industry, its ruling ideology as well as its agriculture.

Neither Chinese economic development nor the Sino-Soviet dispute is greatly illuminated by harking back to the past of any alleged continuous development called "Oriental Despotism." At the same time the fact that Mao's China is vying also with India for influence in the Afro-Asian and Latin American worlds compels a second look both at the ideology and economics of present-day China.

1) In Agriculture

The victory of Mao is not rooted in some sort of unchanging Oriental despotism resting on a static agricultural mode of production. The very opposite is true. There have been so many changes in the agricultural pattern of China in the single decade of Mao's rule that it looks as if there were no points of "equilibrium" at all. The fact, however, is that it is the state-capitalist structure which keeps it from collapsing now in its period of crisis, and underlies all agricultural changes from the first land reform, upon gaining power, until the "People's Commune."

Thus, the land redistribution of the period from 1950 to 1953 left a mere three million peasants unaffected. To say that this gave the land to the peasants would be the greatest hoax ever perpetrated on the perpetually betrayed poor peasants. The redistribution made the average land-holding per capita something under 2 mou (1/6th of an acre equals 1 mou). The redistribution did eliminate 20 million landowners; it is estimated that no less than five million were killed. Obviously there weren't as many as five million top capitalists and landlords in the exploitative class. The pattern of Mao's ridding China of revolutionary opposition, as well as "counter-revolutionaries," has been to brand all opposition as "bureaucrat capitalist" or "rich landlord" or "rightist." This stood him in good stead for it allowed hundreds of thousands to be sentenced to forced labor and sent to build roads and irrigation projects.[287] At the same time, enough "bad gentry" and capitalists were liquidated to assure full state power to the Communist Party, which had come to power with their help. And enable it to turn against the peasants who had been granted 2 *mou* but could not possibly eke out a living from it.

The first period of cooperatives proceeded, however, at a slow pace, with peasants being encouraged to form mutual aid teams and small cooperatives. By 1955, the tempo had quickened to such an extent that no less than 96 per cent of the peasant households were reported as organized in cooperatives. The peasants were permitted to have "ownership" of their lands, private property was allowed, and they could work 10 per cent of their land for themselves. This was the period when high increases in production were attained, and when the bountiful harvest created the foundation for Mao's brainstorm about the formation of "People's Communes."

Instead of "the Great Leap Forward," we know the results of this 1958 phantasmagoria, dealt with above. Nevertheless, it would be wrong to dismiss the impact on the non-industrialized world of what the Chinese totalitarian rulers called the "uninterrupted revolution"—"a revolution without pause" that, moreover, can be accomplished, without high technology, by the mere application of a "mass line."

As *Hongqi* recently put it:[288] "Before it was possible to equip agriculture with machinery it was possible to develop agricultural and productive forces and thereby promote the development of industry." Not in any way deterred by thus standing matters upside down, our Chinese theoretician proceeds to develop the concept of "simultaneity" as the new basis of "the worker-peasant alliance": "That basis is, as Comrade Mao Tse-tung points out, 'simultaneously, gradually, to bring about on the one hand, socialist industrialization and socialist transformation of handicraft industry and capitalist industry, and commerce, and, on the other, the socialist transformation of agriculture as a whole through cooperation. In that way we shall . . . let all people in the rural areas enjoy a common prosperity.' "[289]

It is obvious that "prosperity" has become famine, but what has this to do with Oriental despotism? Far from an Oriental despotic ring, it has a most modern ring which lends it appeal to overpopulated Asia and underpopulated Africa.

2) Military and Industrial

Nor is Mao's victory accountable solely to the fact that Chiang Kai-shek's regime was so corrupt and discredited that it literally fell apart by itself. Although that certainly helped Mao's Army achieve power, we fly in the face of the facts of Mao's military exploit in the "Long March," as well as the organization needed for bare existence for two decades in isolation from all urban centers, if we limit Mao's victory to Chiang's ineffectuality. Mao's rule, no doubt, has its roots in old China, both its magnificence and its corruption, its war lords and Mandarins. What needs analysis, however, are the distinguishing marks which set off one epoch from another, not the similarities which blur what is new, what is of our age.

Our age is the age of state-capitalism, national revolutions and workers' revolts. Unless one is ready to base himself on the masses who alone can initiate a truly new social order, one has no place to go but to state-capitalism. This is so not only irrespective of personal traits but even of the basic factor that China is over-whelmingly agricultural. Insofar as China is concerned, indus-trialization has come so late on the stage that, either a new human basis will be laid for it, or the exploitative industrial form will need to go via state-capitalism. The very occupation and indus-trialization of Manchuria by Japan, for example, meant that a great deal of industry became "ownerless" once China regained its independence. Even Chiang Kai-shek recognized what would next have to be done: "We must adopt a planned economy," he wrote in 1943 in his *China's Destiny*. "It is imperative that we eventually accomplish the objective of 'transforming' capital into state capi-tal." The minute Mao consolidated his power in mainland China, this is precisely what he embarked on—statification of industry. And, it needs to be added, with the same method of exploitation of the masses as Chiang or any other capitalist would have followed.

The First Five Year Plan (1953-1957) began with substantial aid from the Soviet Union, mainly in the form of 156 complete projects and key industries—iron and steel plants, oil refineries, chemical works, power plants. For the first time state ownership was fully established, and the workers were forever admonished

about "production and more production." This part didn't change
from the May Day slogans of 1950 when he allowed private capitalists to function: "Members of the Chinese working class! Consolidate your ranks and unite with the national bourgeoisie." Just as,
in 1947, he stressed that he was "for both labor and capital,"
"reasonable profits" were greatly encouraged, first for private capital, and now for the State. The five "antis" campaign was launched
as the capitalists amassed too much profit—and the "rectification
campaigns" proceeded apace when the workers struck against inhuman working conditions, whether that was 12 hours of labor, or
lack of any freedom in their personal lives. The State moved from
joint private and state enterprises which it had called state-capitalist
to "socialism," that is to say, real state-capitalism. The appeal to
the capitalists to remain managers of business did not stop. Thus:
"If you do a really good job in developing your business, and train
your children to be first-class technical experts, you will be the
obvious people to put in charge of the nationalized enterprise and
you may find that you earn more as managers of a socialist enterprise than as mere owners." No doubt many of them have become
managers of industry.

The workers were forbidden to strike. The trade unions were
made into pure organs of disciplining the workers and seeing that
production plans were carried out. Forced labor was a regular
feature of Chinese state-capitalism calling itself Communism. It is
not in this that it differs from its Russian model. It does differ in
its concept of "thought reform."

3) Brainwashing

Brainwashing, as a word coined in the Korean War to denote
either forced or genuine changing of sides on the part of American
soldiers joining the Chinese, gives the appearance of yet one more
form of the confessionals made so famous during the infamous
Moscow Frame-Up Trials. No doubt there is much of that in them.
What is new in Mao's perennial "rectification campaigns" is that
they are neither limited to the "foreigner" or "enemy," nor meant
as a purge limited to members of the Party. No. Mao has raised
the concept of "thought reform" both to a philosophic category
and a veritable way of life.

While he has not succeeded in brainwashing the Chinese, he has succeeded in brainwashing certain liberals outside of China who take this belief in thought reform to mean that there is no violence against the people. Contrary to Stalin, these believers in Mao's order maintain that Mao has not killed "the general staff of the revolution." As "proof" they point to the fact that those in command are the very ones who led the "Revolution." This crude misconception conveniently forgets that, with the defeat of the 1925-1927 Revolution, Chiang Kai-shek did for Mao what Stalin had to do for himself—kill or imprison the revolutionaries, including Ch'en Tu-hsui. This is first of all, but not all. For even in those years when Mao did not have full power, he was ruthless against revolutionary opponents. We saw this in 1930 when the workers under Li Li-san attacked Changsha and held the city for a few days, whereupon Mao "disarmed and liquidated the rebels." This was repeated in 1936 with Chang Kuo-t'ao. And again during the war with Japan when he "liquidated" the Third Front. There were no Trials comparable to the Moscow Trials after Mao Tse-tung gained power in mainland China only because the "general staff of revolutionary war" were those who followed his class collaborationist path to power, and state-capitalist rule in power.

The one grain of truth in the apologia is that Mao believes in "thought reform." However, this is not for the reasons the apologists give. No, it is for the needs of a state-capitalism that must be developed in an overwhelmingly agricultural land, and therefore wishes to convince part of the capitalist and landlord class to remain as managers of the state economy in the hope of obviating the inevitability of proletarian revolution.

The most amazing feat of brainwashing is neither that made famous in Korea among American soldiers, nor that within China once power was achieved. The phenomenal aspect is that achieved among intellectuals who do not have state power and are supposedly giving their lives to achieving workers' power; in a word, the petty-bourgeois Marxist intellectual. The inescapable fact is that in this epoch of state-capitalism the middle class intellectual, as a world phenomenon, has translated "individualism" into "collectivism," by which he means nationalized property, state administration, State Plan. The post-war years gave this phenomenon the appearance of a new emanation from the under-developed countries. In actuality, the only thing that distinguishes the brain-washers from the capitalistic Brain Trust of the New Deal days is that their master, Mao Tse-tung, was once a Marxist revolutionary himself and is adept in the use of Marxist terminology. This now has expanded itself into a challenge to Khrushchev, or more precisely, Russia's leadership of world Communism. The fact that Mao has also captured the non-existent imagination of the Trotskyists who, despite Trotsky's historic and theoretic fight against Mao, have all become "Maoists" to an embarrassing degree is only further proof of the administrative mentality of the intellectuals in a state-capitalist age who have made such a fetish of the State Plan that they, literally, are begging to be intellectually raped.[290] They do not even flinch in the face of a possibility of thermonuclear war so long as they will die for the right "principles." We must, therefore, analyze further the Sino-Soviet conflict. In doing this let us not forget that which the "left" Communist splits, East and West, disregard with such bohemian abandon: the power politics behind the conflict.

D. CAN There Be War Between Russia and China?: The Non-Viability of State-Capitalism

1) 1960-62: Preliminary Sparring

In 1960 China took advantage of the 90th anniversary of the birth of Lenin (April 22) to transform the power conflict into a "theory of revolution." It was called "Long Live Leninism," and appeared as an "Editorial" in Red Flag, No. 8, 1960 (translated in the Peking Review, No. 17, 1960).

This "Editorial" is a full-sized pamphlet of some 40 pages. It is heavily sprinkled with quotations from Lenin, which stress proletarian revolution. While the editorial itself plays down "modern science" (that is, ICBM's, H-bombs, and sputniks) as mere "specific details of technical progress in the present-day world," it unleashes an attack on "modern revisionism" in a way that makes it very easy to read "Khrushchev" where the editorial says "Tito." Since all the proofs of the war-like nature of the United States are drawn from the period after Khrushchev's visit with Eisenhower, it is easy to see that "the inevitability of war" is, in truth, not a question of Lenin's theory, but is specifically directed against Khrushchev's policy of peaceful co-existence.

Khrushchev correctly judged that lengthy editorial on Lenin as a new stage, not merely in "Mao's Thought," but in Mao's ambitions for leadership in the Communist orbit, in influence over the underdeveloped areas, and in planning the strategy of any war with the United States. It is rumored that a discussion between Russia and China regarding a joint Pacific Fleet was cancelled by Khrushchev for fear that Mao would push him into a war over the Formosa Straits.[291] The "Editorial," however, was a still-birth. The May 1, U.S. U-2 spy plane over Russia made it so. It also gave Khrushchev the opportunity he needed not only to break up the summit conference he had heretofore planned, but also to convoke an international conference of the Communist world to discipline Mao. Khrushchev's appearance at the UN was part of the preparation for this conference. In the well known shoe-pounding incident at the UN Khrushchev got his opportunity to announce to the whole world that he is not only master of the Communist world, but the only hope of the new world opened up by the African Revolutions.

On Dec. 7, 1960, Khrushchev convened the 81 Communist Parties for a conference in Moscow.[292] There he transformed his UN speech into the new Communist Manifesto which declared Russia to be "the first country in history to be blazing a trail to communism for all mankind." The overwhelming majority of the Communist Parties present in Moscow demanded Mao sign the Declaration so that a "unanimous" Communist front be shown American imperialism. Mao could not refuse to do so without exposing the fact that China considered Russia to be the enemy. Mao signed, but continued his independent road not only in China but throughout the third Afro-Asian-Latin American world.

China's signature to the 1960 Moscow Manifesto did not stop its deviationary road along its own national interests any more than France's signature to NATO stopped De Gaulle from seeking his own glory road. The post-war world of the 1960's, is, after all, a very different world from what it was in the late 1940's when both Europe and China lay in ruins, and each had to accept aid and, with it, the "philosophy" underlying the Marshall Plan and the Warsaw Pact respectively. Mao is trying to do with a barrage of revolutionary phrases what De Gaulle is trying to achieve with spoutings about "French grandeur." In both cases, however, the split within their respective orbits is due to national ambitions for world expansion.

The initiative, however, had returned into Khrushchev's hands after the U-2 spy plane discovery. He used it to isolate China further. In 1961 the Draft Program for the 22nd Russian Communist Party Congress relegates the Chinese Revolution to the total of 11 words. This was done, not because it is the program of a national party, the Russian, but because Russia as a world phenomenon began the 20th century with the 1917 Revolution as a new epoch and continued it with the 1957 Sputnik which outdistanced even the United States. Moreover, Khrushchev insisted, this Russian age is not only different as against the United States, but as distinct from China, because the Russians are "building Communism." [293] No wonder Khrushchev at the Congress itself chose to attack Albania (meaning China) and Chou En-lai chose to walk out after defending Albania (meaning China), and challenging Russia's right to bring such disputes into the open without "prior consultation" with the Communist world. These attacks and defenses are as counterfeit as the "theories" in which Mao and Khrushchev wrap themselves as they carry on their bitter competition.

The October 22, 1962 confrontation of J. F. Kennedy and Nikita Khrushchev over missiles in Cuba, the historic moment when the whole world held its breath for fear of nuclear holocaust, gave Mao Tse-tung the opportunity to regain the initiative in the Sino-Soviet conflict. The moment Khrushchev backed down when Kennedy made it clear he was ready to plunge the world into nuclear war unless Khrushchev removed those missiles from Cuba, Mao launched the new stage of conflict by accusing Khrushchev of "cowardice in the face of imperialism." Then he moved to take over "leadership" of the "socialist world" by demanding that it come to his support in the Sino-Indian war.

*2) New Dateline: Peking, June 14, 1963: "A Proposal Concerning
the General Line of the International Communist Movement"* [294]

The new, the qualitative difference in the Sino-Soviet conflict
crystallized into an open challenge theoretically as well. It took the
form of a "letter" of the Central Committee of the Chinese Communist Party (CC of the CPC) to its Russian counterpart, dated
June 14, 1963, and entitled "A Proposal Concerning the General
Line of the International Communist Movement." Soon thereafter it was published as a pamphlet in a dozen different languages
of East and West.

China's industrial development may lack everything from steel
to dams and atomic energy. Its Army, however, has everything
from overwhelming numbers to military equipment. In the first
instance, it is the largest land army in the whole world, and in the
second instance it has the most modern equipment on the Asian
continent. Russian humor may have pinpointed Mao's historic
image when it says history will record him "as an athletic failure
in the broad jump." But he was no failure in the Sino-Indian War.
As "Mao's Thought" thrives on military engagements, it has given
birth to yet a new crop of "theories." These are developed with
much subterfuge and great wordiness in the 61-page June 14th
"letter." They add up to a single and total ambition for world
mastery.

In five different ways the June 14th "letter" states that "the
touchstone of internationalism" (p. 10) should no longer be the
defense of Russia. The first reason given for the new thesis is that
the defense of the Soviet Union was originally the touchstone of
internationalism because it was the only "socialist country" but
"Now that there is a socialist camp of thirteen countries" the whole
"socialist world" has become that "touchstone of internationalism."
"Therefore," reads the second point of indictment against Russia,
referred to as "anybody": "If anybody . . . helps capitalist countries attack fraternal socialist countries, then he is betraying the
interests of the entire international proletariat and the people of
the world." (p. 10) The accusation of betrayal is obviously aimed
at Russia for its failure to support China's invasion of India. The
third variation of "Russia no longer" is an appeal for adherents

within the country under attack since the "step back in the course of historic development" is declared to be tantamount to "doing a service to the restoration of capitalism." Yugoslavia is named as the culprit but, clearly, Russia is meant.

The Manifesto of the Central Committee of the Chinese Communist Party is now prepared for the big jump, the shift from proletarian revolutions to national struggles "since" the countries of Asia, Africa and Latin America are "the storm centres of world revolution dealing direct blows at imperialism." (p. 12) "In a sense, therefore, the whole cause of the international proletarian revolution hinges on the outcome of the revolutionary struggle of the people in these areas . . . " (p. 13)

This shift of pivot—the fourth variation on the theme, "Russia no longer"—is supposed to be based on Lenin's thesis (at the Second Congress of the Communist International, 1920) about the imperative duty of the proletariat of the technologically advanced countries to unite with the peasant masses in the colonial countries struggling to free themselves from imperialism. Lenin's new point of departure in the theory of non-inevitability of capitalist development for backward economies is based on a big "if": *if* "aid of the proletariat of the most advanced countries" is extended unstintingly. Lenin stresses that the only proof of proletarian internationalism, therefore, is for the Russian proletariat to extend this aid along with the theory and practice of revolution. All of this is reduced by Mao to a matter of his competition with Khrushchev as to who will "lead" this new, third world. In the process, Mao moves away from his concept of the division of the world into two camps, "the socialist countries" against "the capitalist countries." Although he had taken great pains to bring this concept in as a substitute for the class struggle in each country, he now disregards it. In order to reintroduce his old, ruinous "four class policy" he broadens the concept of "the people" to include "also the patriotic national bourgeoisie, and even certain kings, princes, and aristocrats who are patriotic." (p. 15)

By the time Chinese Communism reaches the fifth and final theme of its international manifesto of "never, no, never again Russia"—this time directed against Russia being "a state of the whole people building communism"—we are suddenly confronted with the most sinister of all theories of retrogression. Over and over again "A Proposal Concerning the General Line of the International Communist World" proclaims that "for a very long historic period after the proletariat takes power" (p. 36); "for decades or even longer after socialist industrialization and agricultural collectivization" (p. 37) have been achieved, "the class struggle continues as an objective law independent of man's will." (p. 36) This holds true in all "socialist countries." Now whatever the subjective impulse for concocting this—all too transparently it is meant to lay the foundation for opposition to the 22nd Russian Communist Party Congress which enunciated that Russia was "building Communism"—it is the most serious of all theories of retrogression. We now have not only the retrogression of capitalism to fascism, but the retrogression of socialism, that is to say, a supposedly classless society, to one in which "there are classes and class struggles in all socialist countries without exception." (p. 40) Surely no more deadly deviation has ever been proclaimed "a principle of Marxism-Leninism."

Where the tiny state power of Yugoslavia, in 1948, when it fought the giant, Russia, for national independence, could not allow itself any new glory roads a la De Gaulle in the Western camp, Mao's delusions are as vast as the Chinese continent—and not only as it is now constituted, but as it was at the height of its imperial glory under the Yuan and Ming Dynasties when China conquered Burma, Thailand, Indochina Peninsula, debarked troops to Indonesia, imprisoned the king of Ceylon and once even imposed annual tribute from the Moslem world or at least from the Holy City of Mecca. Before 1962 only Nehru had questioned the map included in "A Manual of History" which was published in Peking in 1954.[295] This shows a great part of the Soviet Far East as well as the Republic of Outer Mongolia, North and South Korea, Cambodia, Thailand, Malaya, Burma, Assam (about 50,000 miles of Indian territory, in fact), Butan, Sikkim, Nepal, the island of Sakhalin as well as some islands in the Philippines, as having been part of China.

When, in 1962, Khrushchev dared to quip at Mao's phrase about "cowardice in the face of the imperialists" by saying it ill-behooves Mao to speak so when he is doing nothing presently to

322   MARXISM AND FREEDOM

drive the imperialists from "his own territory—Taiwan, Hong Kong, Macao," the *People's Daily* and *Red Flag* hit back with: "Certain persons would like us to raise the questions of unequal treaties here and now . . . Have they realized what the consequences of this might be?" Whereupon the Chinese began explaining "the imperialist encroachments on Chinese territory (1840-1919). Period of the Early Democratic Revolution." And, in expanding themselves on what Tsarist Russia took from "old China," the present Chinese rulers included territories taken from Emirs and Khans who most assuredly did not consider themselves vassals of the Emperor of China. (Nor, for that matter, did Mao's dream of China's past glories stop itself from designating as an "imperialist encroachment" Thailand's becoming independent; that too "belonged" to China of the Emperor and he means "to redress" some day the borders of what the CC-CPC designates only as "old China.")

Mao opts for nothing short of mastery of the world, of the Communist world to begin with. Though, for tactical reasons, and because of the withdrawal of Russian technical aid, China had to fall back on a variation of "the theory of socialism in one country" ("Every socialist country must rely mainly on itself for its construction." p. 45), the CC-CPC challenges not only Russia but the majority of the presently constituted Communist world. It warns that "one should not emphasize 'who is in the majority' or 'who is in the minority' and bank on a so-called majority . . ." (p. 47). In the place of following majority rule, he proposes the rule of "unanimity," that is to say, China's right of veto over policies formulated by Russia and the majority of other Communist Parties. Thus, the present Sino-Soviet conflict differs fundamentally not only from Yugoslavia's 1948 conflict with Stalin for national independence, but also from Mao's own differences both in 1957 and in 1960 when the conflict could be hushed up because it was fought within the Communist world.

The one and only thing that both Khrushchev and Mao prove, the one and only thing that is beyond the peradventure of any doubt is the non-viability of their "new" social order. *The non-viability of state-capitalism as a "new" social order is proven by the same laws of development as that of private capitalism, that is to say, the compulsion to exploit the masses at home and to carry on wars abroad.* A shocking question faces us now: *Can* there be a war between two regimes calling themselves Communist?

3) Back to "Wars and Revolutions": Russia and China At War?

The challenge to totalitarian power that was issued by the Hungarian Revolution of 1956 brought Russia and China closer together than they had ever been, either in Stalin's era or in Malenkov-Khrushchev's times. The class content of the counter-revolutionary crushing of the proletarian revolution is crucial to all else that has happened since. Directly after the show of solidarity with Russian imperialism against the Hungarian revolutionaries, China, as we saw, moved toward expanding its own state power.

Despite De Gaulle's derisive question, "The ideological split? Over what ideology?" his display of arrogance at his news conference on July 29, 1963, could not clothe his nuclear ambition as Mao does his. Its death features stood out in all their goriness: "France will not be diverted by Moscow agreements from equipping herself with the means of immeasurable destruction possessed by other powers." By contrast, Mao was enabled to exorcise Khrushchev for "servilely meeting the needs of United States imperialism" by his agreement to a treaty which "undertakes . . . to refrain from causing, encouraging, or in any way participating in, the carrying out of any nuclear weapon test explosion, or any other nuclear explosion, anywhere . . . " This, said Mao, means "out and out betrayal" of "the socialist countries and all oppressed countries" since it would keep them "from acquiring nuclear weapons" while consolidating the United States' "position of nuclear monopoly." The superiority of arguments, carefully clothed in Marxist garb, however, cannot be maintained when both contestants are so clothed.

For the time being no war is in the offing between Russia and China. From Russia's side, this would make no sense not only because it is the "have" nation, but also because it certainly would break up the international Communist movement that still considers the State Plan as a fundamental division between itself and "the bourgeoisie." From China's side, such a war would be suicidal not only because Mao isn't strong enough to challenge the Russian goliath, but also because he is a firm believer in the infamous Dulles policy of negotiating from "positions of strength." Those he will not have unless he first wins to his side both the West European and the Asian Communist Parties which are in power (North Korea, North Viet Nam), and also the African non-Communist world—or that of Latin America.

Moreover this struggle between state-capitalist powers is taking place in a nuclear age. Because the opposition of all the peoples of the world to nuclear war is total Khrushchev would like nothing better than to reduce all his differences with Mao to a disagreement on "peaceful co-existence." As *Izvestia* put it, Russia was not surprised that militarist, reactionary forces in the West were "atom mongers and madmen," but it was most "sadly" surprised to find that the "Chinese comrades should join their voices to the screams of those madmen." Indeed, so total is the opposition to nuclear war that the only two countries which dared openly oppose the Nuclear Test Ban Treaty—Mao's China and De Gaulle's France— had to claim that they did so "in the name of peace." Mao went so far as to offer counter-proposals for nothing short of "complete, thorough, total and resolute prohibition and destruction of nuclear weapons." That did not prevent him from attacking the actual treaty not only as "a big fraud" and "betrayal of the Soviet people," but also as an exposure of "the servile features of those who warmly embrace imperialism. The exposure," he said, "of these freaks and monsters in their true colors is an excellent thing for the revolutionary struggle of the peoples and the cause of world peace." (*People's Daily*, Aug. 2) Mao, indeed, is no less scared of a nuclear holocaust than the rest of the world. But he does not allow the question mark this puts over the very survival of civilization to divert him from his feeling that this time the "have" nations—the United States and Russia—will first of all eliminate each other!

There is no doubt that China expounds a global strategy basically different from that of Russia. It alone has the audacity to speak of a time to follow a nuclear war when "socialism will be built on its ruins." Nevertheless, this is not the point in the Sino-Soviet conflict. Nor is that divisive and decisive point to be found in China's recent attempts to exclude Russia from Asian and African meetings on racial grounds. Both points are only the culmination of something that began as Mao strove for power. It had been obvious in all Mao's fights with Stalin and as soon as the Chinese Communist Party took power it demanded that "Mao's Thought" become the underlying theory for all conquests of power in "colonial countries."

This theme was muted during the Korean War of 1950-53 and again in the "joint" Khrushchev-Mao 1957 Manifesto against the proliferation of polycentrism. Naturally, every ruling class has found it easy to support revolutions—abroad. But, whereas new ruling classes, when they first come on the historic scene, proved themselves full of vitality because they did have a wider support among the masses than the old ruling classes they overthrew, the State Planners of today feel compelled to embark on wars before ever they have proved their right to historic existence on native soil.

Wars and revolutions are not synonymous. They are opposites. Here, then, are the actual consequences of Mao's revolutionary thunder since he won power against Stalin's advice to maintain his coalition with Chiang Kai-shek: 1) China embarks on wars only when it is sure to win, as against Tibet first, and limited to incursions into borders of India now; 2) When it suits its purpose, China peacefully, or, more correctly, shrewdly "co-exists" with European imperialist outposts on its own territory, like Hong Kong and Macao; 3) If Mao, whose "Thought" could exude nothing more original than "a four-class policy," is nevertheless more adept than Khrushchev in the use of Marxist terminology to hide his territorial ambitions, he is no "braver" in facing a challenge from the greatest military power in the world—the United States. Mao has backed down more times, not only on Taiwan, but on Quemoy and Matsu, than did Khrushchev when he saw that Kennedy was actually ready to go to nuclear war over missiles in Cuba; 4) Despite his revolutionary thunder, in the abstract, Mao is, in the concrete, an expert in imperialist maneuvering and in dubbing even "fascist regimes" as "peace-loving." Thus, before the Sino-Indian war, Mao called the military regime in Pakistan "fascist," but the moment China was engaged in war with India, Mao lost no time in making a deal

with Pakistan which had suddenly become a "peace-loving nation";
5) Nor does his "revolutionary defense" of the Afro-Asian world
he hopes one day to dominate keep him from excluding other
Communist lands whom he calls "revisionist" while including, as
we saw, "the national bourgeoisie, and even certain kings, princes,
and aristocrats who are patriotic."

The odd mixture of Mao's opportunism and adventurism, the
ordinary imperialist power struggle (both within the Communist
world and outside, as in the conquest of Tibet, incursions into
Indian territory, and covetous glances cast from Burma to Viet
Nam, and from Nepal to Laos) cannot be separated from the
struggle for the minds of men. It is here that the irresponsible
abuse of Marxist language—on the question of "revolutions without pause" proceeding in a straight line from State Plans to "Communism"—makes it imperative to show, not only the blind alley
into which the dialectic of Mao's thought has led and from which
it may catapult the world into a nuclear holocaust, but also to show
that which is opposite from both the state-capitalist powers and
the general global struggle with the United States for world domination. That is to say, it is imperative to illumine the path of
freedom.

In Place Of A Conclusion: Two Kinds of Subjectivity

> " . . . the transcendence of the opposition
> between the Notion and Reality . . . rest
> upon this subjectivity alone." — Hegel's
> *Science of Logic*

> " . . . in this *(Science of Logic)* most ideal-
> istic of Hegel's works, there is the least
> idealism and the most materialism. 'Con-
> tradictory' but a fact!" — Lenin's *Philo-
> sophic Notebooks*

Two kinds of subjectivity characterize our age of state-capitalism and workers' revolts. One is the subjectivism that we have been

considering—Mao's—which has no regard for objective conditions, behaves as if state power is for herding 650 million human beings into so-called "People's Communes," as if a party of the elite that is armed can both harness the energies of men and "remold" their minds. We have seen the results of this type of subjectivism permeated with, to use a Hegelian phrase, "a certainty of its own actuality and the non-actuality of the world," ready to ride the whirlwind of a nuclear holocaust.

The second type of subjectivity, the one which rests on "the transcendence of the opposition between the Notion and Reality," is the subjectivity which has "absorbed" objectivity, that is to say, through its struggle for freedom it gets to know and cope with the objectively real. Its maturity unfolds, as Marx put it in *Critique of the Hegelian Dialectique* "when actual corporeal Man, standing on firm and well rounded earth, inhaling and exhaling all natural forces . . . does not depart from its 'pure activity' in order to create the object . . . We see here how thorough-going Naturalism, or Humanism, distinguishes itself both from Idealism and Materialism, and, at the same time, is the truth uniting both."

Our epoch is the epoch of the struggle for the minds of men. To engage in this struggle, and clear one's head, it appears to me necessary to focus on these two types of subjectivity of which I can give here* only a few indications.

In 1956 these two types of subjectivity came into head-on collision in Hungary.[296] The Hungarian Revolution put an end to the illusion that workers or peasants or intellectuals can be brainwashed. It put an end to the pretense that Communism and Marxism are one. It raised the banner of Marxist Humanism as freedom *from* Communism. In the great tradition of Marx who had written that Communism is "not the goal of human development, the form of human society," the Hungarian Freedom Fighters moved away from totalitarian state centralization to decentralized Workers' Councils, Youth Councils, Councils of Intellectuals—that is to say a form of rule where the individual and society are not opposed to each other because the freedom of the individual is the proof, the only proof, of the freedom of all.

---

* This is the burden of my new work in progress.

This outburst of elemental activity and organization of thought was bloodily suppressed by the counter-revolutionary might of Russia which, with the help of its Chinese cohorts, branded this Humanism as "revisionism." Mao had good reason to help his Russian partner because, as he himself put it, "Certain people in our country were delighted when the Hungarian events took place. They hoped that something similar would happen in China . . ." [297] To the extent that Mao was able to suppress his opposition without an open civil war, to the extent that he usurped the Marxist banner—both in general and in the specific use of one word, "Commune," that has always stood among Marxists for self-liberation (the Paris Commune of 1871)—to that extent some newly independent African nations were attracted to it.

However, just as it is impossible to hide the hunger rampant in the so-called "Peoples Communes," [298] so it is impossible to cover up the fact that within China, as within each modern country, there is a fundamental division into classes. Mao has no magic by which to turn these antagonistic contradictions into a mere difference between what he calls the "old" and the "new." Far from being a mere opposition between the existent and the not-yet existent, it is an open struggle between two antagonistic forms of reality that co-exist. *The co-existence of oppressor and oppressed is the determining factor also in proving the non-viability of Chinese state-capitalism that calls itself Communist.*

Mao admits that, just as under ordinary private capitalism, the basic contradictions in Chinese society "are still those between the relations of production and the productive forces, and between the superstructure and the economic base." This is precisely the fatal flaw which, in 1943, compelled the Russian theoreticians to revise Marx's economic theory of value.

No matter by what name they are called, capitalistic relationships, at the point of production, reveal their exploitative nature. Why Russia "chose" to revise Marx's economic theories, and why China "chose" to revise Marx's philosophy, is due both to the totality of the world crisis and to the important industrial differences between the two countries.

Russia has become an important industrial land, a country that possesses values. China is a vast underdeveloped land, whose main possession is not the machine, but 650 million human beings.

It is precisely this backwardness which has pushed China forward to pose—only to pose but not to solve—its crisis in human terms. It cannot hide, however, the duality, the irreconcilable duality between China's new ruling class and the millions it exploits. Nor can it cover up the fact that the division of the world into two nuclear giants fighting for world domination—the United States and Russia—extends to the little Caesars in each camp—not only de Gaulle in "the West" but Mao in "the East."

Mao's failure to grasp dialectic logic has nothing whatever to do with "understanding philosophy." Dialectic logic is the logic of freedom and can be grasped only by those engaged in the actual struggle for freedom. Therein lies the key to the fulfillment of human potentialities and therein lies that new relationship between theory and practice which could lessen the birthpangs of industrialization. Anything else is the type of subjectivism which hides Mao's compelling need to transform the struggle for the minds of men into a drive to brainwash them.

The remorseless logic of this engulfed Mao himself and led him to elaborate a theory, not of revolution, but of retrogression. The objective compulsion for such "theories" flows, of course, from the brutal form of state-capitalism characteristic of China. Just as the bankruptcy of capitalism in general was accompanied by the bankruptcy of its thought, so the extension of state-capitalism into the misnamed "communes" was accompanied by Mao's threadbare thought, the true end of the absence of any philosophic method. Where Stalin, when admitting that the operation of the law of value in his "socialist country," felt compelled to force a separation between the law of value and the law of surplus value in order to try to deny the existence of classes under socialism, Mao proclaims this loudly as "socialism." Despite this thoroughly capitalistic concept of socialism; despite the concrete and total exploitation of the Chinese masses; despite the concrete invasions by China of other lands; and despite the voices of revolt within China itself against its Communist masters, Mao's abstract revolutionary thunder abroad gets the supports of militants, especially intellectuals, in and outside of the Communist Parties. It is a sad commentary on our times and exposes how totally lacking in any confidence in the self-activity of the masses are today's claimants to the title, "Marxist-Leninist." Their militancy gains momentum only where there is a state power to back it up. It is the mark of our state-capitalist era that our "revolutionary" petty-bourgeoisie fears the self-mobilizing of the proletarian masses even more than do the powers that be, and seem incapable of acting without the support of a state power.

The subjectivity of the millions struggling for freedom, on the other hand, poses the need for a new relationship between theory and practice. The freedom struggles are not limited to Hungary or Africa, Russia or China; they include the United States[299] and Western Europe as well. The challenge is for a new unity of Notion and Reality which will release the vast untapped energies of mankind to put an end, once and for all, to what Marx called the *pre*-history of humanity so that its true history can finally unfold.

CHAPTER EIGHTEEN

CULTURAL REVOLUTION OR
MAOIST REACTION

NOW THAT THE CULTURAL REVOLUTION has slowed its pace, there is time to take a closer look at this startling phenomenon.

The Red Guards may appear to have emerged out of nowhere but on August 18, 1966 they arrived one million strong in paramilitary formation to hear Defense Minister Lin Piao, Mao's "closest comrade in arms," explain the big-character poster *"Bombard The Headquarters."* They learned that the headquarters were those of the Communist Party where they would find "persons in authority taking the road back to capitalism." When these teenagers streamed out of the square they seemed armed with something hardier than "Mao's Thought."

For the next month the bourgeois press had a field day describing the rampage against "all the old" in China, from Confucian texts and priceless art treasures, to many Communist leaders. It was even more bizarre to follow the young Maoists' attacks on Western imperialism, not so much the living, barbarous U.S. imperialism that was raining bombs on a Communist ally, North Vietnam, but against "Hong Kong haircuts" and the "bourgeois-feudal reactionary music of Bach, Beethoven and Shostakovitch."

Within a couple of months these teen-age hooligans were doing more than roaming the streets, putting dunce caps on "anti-revolutionaries." By the end of 1966, a proliferation of Red Guard and "Red Rebel" groups had abandoned their forays against foreign embassies to go into formerly forbidden ground, the factories and fields. "Seize control committees" tried to oust established factory managers while imitating them in lording it over the workers and forbidding strikes. Soon not only the Western press but the official Chinese press was talking of "civil war."

But where was this civil war? In Sinkiang, where army units disobeyed the seize control committees? In a "handful" of anti-Maoists within the Communist Party? And if it existed only in Mao's over-active imagination, what was its purpose? What objective conditions impelled the transformation of the Cultural Revolution into what Hegel might have called "a giddy whirl of self-perpetuating disorder?" To what extent was its disorder its order, that is, planned from above? To what extent had its internal dialectic propelled it beyond the boundaries set for it?

The anti-Maoist bourgeois press, the Maoists and their apologists all describe the Cultural Revolution as nothing short of a "second revolution."[1] The bourgeois analysts depict Mao as a man looking back nostalgically to the days of the Long March and slipping into occasional fits of paranoia. The Maoists and their apologists paint a portrait of Mao (there are 840 million actual portraits[2]) which shows him forever young, forever moving forward, forever combatting those Party, State and army bureaucrats who would lead the new generation from the path of "uninterrupted revolution" to the path of revisionism.

Factual information about events in China is hard to find. But the value of this description of a "second revolution" can be assessed. What is necessary is, first, to see China in its world context, especially in the period immediately preceding the Cultural Revolution and, second, to keep one's presuppositions aside so that the dialectic of the Cultural Revolution can be followed in and for itself. This is particularly important because the origins of the Cultural Revolution are tangled inextricably with the course of the war in Vietnam.

The Crucial Year: 1965

WHEN MAO CAME TO POWER in China he saw no need for mass partici-

1. "Mao's Second Revolution," K. S. Karol, *New Statesman*, Sept. 1966. Mr. Karol has since outdone himself by explaining that the deification of Mao's Thought is needed to preserve "the legitimacy of the Chinese Revolution and the socialist perspective that it has opened before the country." See the Introduction to his book on China, reprinted as "Why the Cultural Revolution?" *Monthly Review*, September 1967.
2. *Peking Review* #31, July 28, 1967: "More than 840 million copies of portraits of Chairman Mao, or over five times the number produced in the preceding 16 years, were printed in the eleven months from July 1966 to the end of May 1967 . . . There are 33 different portraits of the great leader of the world's people."

pation in any "uninterrupted revolution." Indeed, it was not until seven years later, in 1956, that he saw a need to convene a Congress of the Chinese Communist Party, which had last met eleven years before, in 1945. The 1956 Congress declared China to be "state capitalist,"[3] a formulation with which this author agrees. Within a month the Hungarian revolution erupted. It was soon followed by voices of revolt in China,[4] whereupon Mao thought up the Great Leap Forward, which would bring China "directly to Communism," bypassing both capitalism and "socialism." Instead, it brought the country to the edge of famine. Shortly thereafter, Mao stepped down as head of state, while retaining his post as Chairman of the CCP.

The American decision to bomb North Vietnam in February 1965 put the Communist world to the test. China, which had pictured itself as the besieged fortress, had to face the fact that U.S. imperialism had turned North Vietnam into a genuinely besieged fortress. Kosygin's visit to Peking immediately after seemed to bode a closing of Communist ranks, or at least a united front to help Hanoi. But nothing of the sort happened. Mao had quite a different perspective. For him, 1965 was to see the turning point in the struggle for world dominance. Against the U.S.-NATO axis and the Moscow-Warsaw axis he projected a Peking-Djakarta axis. Nothing, least of all a united front with Russia to help the Vietnamese fight U.S. imperialism, could be allowed to interfere with that perspective and the strategy that flowed from it. Where the others were ready to hold world perspectives in abeyance once the strategy of a Peking-Djakarta axis disintegrated, Mao became all the more adamant in his single-minded view of China as the center and sole leader of "world revolution," to which Vietnam must be subordinated.

In September 1965, an attempted coup against military leaders in Indonesia failed. On October 1, the military started a bloodbath against Communists and other oppositionists which resulted in the slaughter of hundreds of thousands. Any perspective of a Peking-

3. *Documents of the First Session of the First National People's Congress of the People's Republic of China.* Foreign Language Press, Peking, 1955. Repeated in *Eighth National Congress of the CCP*, Vol. 1 (Documents), Peking, 1956.
4. The best work is *The Hundred Flowers Campaign and the Chinese Intellectuals*, by Roderick Macfarquhar (New York: Praeger, 1960). See also *Communist China: the Politics of the Student Opposition* by Dennis Doolin (Stanford Univ. Press, 1964).

Djakarta axis was quashed for the forseeable future. Despite more recent[5] attempts to rewrite the history of the Indonesian Communist Party (KPI), in October 1965 not even Mao could think of a way to lay the blame for the greatest disaster in Communist history at the door of "Russian revisionism." Aidit, the KPI leader, had aligned his party with China as soon as Mao came to power. Peng Chen acknowledged that Aidit's ascendency dated from his acceptance of Maoism.[6] If the KPI's line was characterized by class collaboration rather than struggle,[7] if "peaceful coexistence" underlay all the KPI's actions, it was at the direction of the Chinese Communist Party. In short, the collapse of the Peking-Djakarta axis was the result not only of counter-revolutionary terror in Indonesia but of the class collaborationist line of the KPI which prepared the way for it. And that line was laid down in Peking.

For Mao, the Indonesian crisis was a test of the ability of his Central Committee to draw "the correct conclusions." Apparently many of the members failed this test. Not only was pressure for a united front with Russia exerted by outside Communist parties, including the North Korean, but reports leaked from the Japanese CP indicate that Liu Shao-sh'i was not the only Chinese leader who pressed for such a united front. For Mao this was the last straw. His own cadres had not properly understood the tale of "sitting on the mount and watching the fight of the tigers." The Russians did understand the tale: "From all this it becomes clear that the Chinese leaders need a lengthy Vietnam war to maintain international tensions. . . . There is every reason to assert that it is one of the goals of the policy of the Chinese leadership in the Vietnam question to originate a military confrontation between the USSR and the United States."[8] The Chinese Central Committee, however, still had to learn who the main enemy was.[9]

5. *Peking Review* #30, July 21, 1967.
6. *Peking Review*, June 4, 1965. Also reprint Aidit's and Sukarno's speeches.
7. For further discussion of the KPI, see my three articles, "Indonesian Communism: A Case of World Communism's Decomposition" in *News & Letters* (Detroit), October and November 1965.
8. From a "secret" letter of the CPSU to other CPs, published by *Die Welt* (Hamburg) and reprinted in the New York *Times*, March 24, 1966.
9. Edgar Snow wrote as far back as 1962 that "China's preoccupation with the United States as the main enemy might veer elsewhere." (*The Other Side of the River*, p. 671.)

No wonder the Cultural Revolution had been limping along, restricted to the arts. The leadership would have to be shaken up, hardened or discarded. Mao decided to "disappear."

The Chinese press and the wall posters now reveal that during the critical period from November 1965 to May 1966, when Mao dropped out of sight and the speculations in the Western press ranged from "ill health" to "perhaps even death," he had left the "oppressive atmosphere" of Peking to prepare the Proletarian Cultural Revolution. When he returned he was ready to take on not only the foreign parties but his own Central Committee as well as readying the so-called Red Guards. He summoned a Party Plenum, the first in four years, to meet on August 1. The resolution of this body gave a categorical answer to those who had called for a united front with Russia on the Vietnam war: "The Plenary sessions maintain that to oppose imperialism it is imperative to oppose modern revisionism. There is no middle road whatsoever.... It is imperative resolutely to expose their [Russian Communists'] true features as scabs. It is impossible to have 'united action' with them."[10]

"Russian revisionism" was not alone in being rejected. The other Communist parties around the world were rebuffed; any that did not acknowledge the CCP as the sole leader of world Communism were denigrated.* Internally, the title of "Chairman Mao's closest comrade-in-arms," passed from Liu to Lin Piao. All motions were carried unanimously.

Now Mao was ready to transform the Cultural Revolution. He announced the means of this transformation, not at the Plenum, but at a mass rally in Peking. It was a "new force," divorced not only from the legal structures of Mao's Single Party-State-Army but from production itself. All schools were to be closed for an entire year. Rootless teenagers, who owed loyalty to none but Mao, who knew no world outside of Mao's China, for whom both history and revolution existed only as they "made" them, would carry through

10. From excerpts in the New York *Times*, August 14, 1966. The document in full can be found in *Peking Review*.

* China was not about to forget that Cuba had dared to make a public statement about Chinese methods and procedures being

> exactly the same as the ones used by the United States Embassy in our country ... our country had liberated itself from the imperialism 90 miles from our shores and it was not willing to permit another powerful state to come 20,000 kilometres to impose similar practices on us.

the Great Proletarian Cultural Revolution

The Red Guards

"Shoot Brezhnev!" "Burn Kosygin!" These were some of the posters carried by the Red Guards who surrounded the Russian Embassy in Peking, marching, singing, shouting and harassing anyone who ventured out for food. But this was not exclusively an anti-Russian act; it was part of the process of "hardening" the Chinese and some self-created havoc in China was not viewed as too high a price to pay for achieving this objective.

When the Sino-Soviet conflict first burst into the open in 1960, the Chinese masses were confused and dismayed. As one refugee told me:

> We had no specific love for the Russians; there had actually been very little contact between Russians and Chinese. But the regime itself had always played up the Russians as the greatest friends we had, and Stalin's *History of the Communist Party* had been studied as much as any work by Mao. And now all we heard about them was that they were "revisionists." Somehow, instead of hatred against the Russians, a feeling of utter isolation descended upon all of us.

No feeling of isolation ever bothered Mao. He is forever ready to make a "Great Leap Forward" over objective conditions, confident that will and hard work, especially hard work by 700 million souls, can achieve miracles, "Make one day equal twenty years." Standards for the miraculous work were spelled out by the CCP as follows: "Each person must work ten hours and engage in ideological studies for two hours a day. They are entitled to one day of rest every ten days . . ."

The voices of revolt heard during the brief period of the "One Hundred Flowers" campaign and again after the disastrous "Great Leap Forward," which brought the country to near famine, were silent during the development of the Sino-Soviet conflict. Despite the absence of similar manifestations of opposition, Mao nevertheless insisted on the creation of Red Guards for his new Great Leap Forward.

While in 1960 the Chinese masses were dismayed at their isolation, in 1966 it was the Russians who were dismayed. For the Red Guards, the enemy was not only "Russian revisionism" but Russia itself. Mao's favorite statement remained: "You learn to make revolutions by making them just as you learn to swim by swimming."

The Red Guards were told daily that they were, indeed, "making revolution." So satisfied was Mao with the work of the Red Guards in the months of August and September that he was thinking of institutionalizing them.

This new leap, like its capitalized predecessor, tripped over the objective conditions it scorned. In the course of the Maoist terror mass opposition surfaced. Somehow the "handful" of anti-Maoists had managed to "dupe" so many that the ruling clique admitted that "perhaps we are temporarily in a minority." Even more important, the opposition had roots directly in production, in the factories and the fields. They were, in fact, the proletarian and peasant masses. They wore no red armbands, waved no books of quotations from Mao but they went out on unprecedented strikes and fought pitched battles with the Red Guard "seize control committees" that invaded their factories.

Mao, like other rulers, capitalist and Communist, is so convinced of the backwardness of the masses that he was taken by surprise. At first he said that the masses had been "duped by the economists, the revisionists." Since the Red Guards were his creation and he had been so satisfied with their vicious vandalism against the "old culture" and "persons in authority taking the road back to capitalism" during the months of August and September, he had now to decide whether to permit them to shift from these attacks into an assault on "management" of production. He permitted wall poster criticism of Chou En-lai who had asked the Red Guards to keep out of production and away from the agricultural communes. The *Red Flag* then began to write against "phoney" Red Guards who "wave the red flag to attack the red flag." Finally, however both the *People's Daily* and the *Red Flag* printed editorial warnings to "industry" that it was not sacrosanct.

OF ALL THE MYTHS CREATED by the "Cultural Revolution," none is a greater hoax than the myth of Mao's dependence on, and confidence in, the youth. His readiness to turn away from his old "comrades-in-arms" was not designed to leave the fate of "the world revolution," Sino-centered, in the hand of the youth. As Mao himself had told Edgar Snow in 1965, "the youth could negate the revolution."[11] The

11. The interview granted Edgar Snow in January, 1965, was published in *The New Republic*, February 27, 1965.

Army alone had always enjoyed his confidence. On the other hand, at no time did he trust the youth, in or out of power. His suspicion of the young rose to fever pitch in 1958 when it became clear that they were in the forefront of the opposition both to his Thought in the 100 Flowers Campaign and to his Great Leap Forward. He sent them to build the dams, not to become the "ruling cadres." There is no country on earth where the leadership is kept in such old hands. The average age of Politburo members is close to 70; even the alternate members average 63. For a brief moment in 1964, it looked as though Mao might entrust some serious responsibilities to the Communist youth organization when he spoke to it about "successor generations." However, even that brief moment in the sun was eclipsed by the slogan "Learn from the Army." And, indeed, in the whole of 1965, it was the Army that was to be emulated, especially since it "studies Mao's Thought." Not only was the plan jettisoned but so was the whole youth organization when suddenly (or so it seemed), the Red Guards were created.

Far from proving Mao's unshakeable confidence in the youth, the formation of the Red Guards was a manifestation of his belief that the country, including the youth, had to be "shaken up," had to be made literally to live by and sleep with "the little red book" at their sides.

In this shake-up no one knows how many have been arrested, taken to prison, tortured or actually beaten to death; estimates run as high as 60,000 prisoners and thousands beaten to death,[12] but the talk now of the "indiscipline"[13] of Red Guards does not augur well for them either. In any case, the masses, workers and peasants, did rise up against the new terror. The bitter and bloody struggles had begun. Nothing helped much. The point of no return had been reached. The deluge came. Soon the press in the West and in China

12. Stuart Schram, who has been an analyst quite sympathetic to China, and stressed the great achievements of Mao, has made this estimate in the revised 1967 edition of his *Mao Tse-tung*. The official broadcasts and statements speak only of "masses," never reporting actual figures of the total number arrested, beaten and humiliated, much less those actually killed.

13. When Mrs. Mao Tse-tung made her first attack on the Red Guards in September 26, 1967, she told them: "It's a mistake to go running around the streets. Last year was the time to kindle the flames of revolution. To go into the streets now is precisely the wrong thing to do." By December 1967, Lin Piao reminded the Red Guards that they must remember that the Red Army "cherishes" them and they must therefore obey and reveal their own "selfish" shortcomings.

itself was talking of "civil war."

In reality, what followed can best be called a "preventive civil war," deliberately provoked by Mao. But in provoking it he sealed the fate of his regime. The immediate outcome of the current struggle cannot affect that fate. In unleashing this struggle he has laid bare not only the divisions in the ruling stratum but the *class* divisions between rulers and ruled. Mao is caught by the objective conditions of a world divided between two and only two giant industrial powers. He does not have the advantage Stalin had, the use of world CPs as outposts of his foreign policy. He has no confidence in the world proletariat, and the Chinese proletariat has no confidence in him. They are finished with "Great Leaps Forward" that throw them backward. In this situation, to take the rootless elements and transform them into the tools of the ruling clique is the only answer, and it is no answer. Mao, his heirs and his "cultural revolutionaries" cannot escape the non-viability of the state capitalist system they have created, the end product of which is "Mao's Thought."

Revolution or Retrogression?

SOME SELF-STYLED REVOLUTIONARIES are ready to forgive Mao every crime in the book and leave a few blank pages for those he might invent later, on the ground that he is the foe of U.S. imperialism which is the chief enemy of world revolution. They are ignorant of fundamental class divisions within each country, China included, and illogically link those opposites, war and revolution.

Fighting wars is Mao's specialty. He knows the problems far more intimately than he knows Marxism, and on guerrilla warfare he is a genius. But the problems he now faces at home, on his Russian borders,[14] and in the struggle against "Russian revisionism" cannot be solved by guerrilla warfare. Neither at home nor abroad is he leading a fight against hated enemies—the ruling class he, him-

14. "Tensions on the China-Soviet Border" by A. Doak Barnett, *Look*, October 3, 1967. Includes a map detailing disputed borders which China now says were gotten through "unequal treaties."

self, represents or an imperialist occupying power. Rather, Mao's fight is directed against the Chinese masses at home and Russia abroad. The world hadn't learned of the Sino-Soviet conflict until 1960, but in fact, Mao's price for helping Russia crush the Hungarian Revolution and resisting Poland's challenge to Russia's leadership of the Communist world was the 1957 nuclear pact. It was only when "in the spirit of Camp David" Khrushchev reneged on sharing Russia's nuclear know-how with China that Mao turned against the policy of "peaceful co-existence" he had devised at Bandung. Mao's substitute for the policy of "peaceful co-existence" was the declaration that the underdeveloped countries were "the storm centers of world revolution." Throughout the period of 1960-64, while these ideological battles were splitting the Communist parties, what China was, in fact, concentrating on was the creation of its own *force de frappe*. China's first atomic explosion in 1964 came

---

"Cultural Revolution" in Life, Work, Love in China

"Then there are other workers concerned only with love and romance, pandering to low tastes, claiming that 'love' and 'death' are eternal themes. All such bourgeois revisionist trash must be resolutely opposed."

> **Hold High the Great Red Banner of Mao Tse-tung's Thinking; Actively Participate in the Great Socialist Cultural Revolution, Peking Review, April 29, 1966**

"In recent days, in certain enterprises and units, incited and organized by certain leadership persons, a handful of freaks and monsters have cheated the misled members of the worker ·Red Guard units and some worker masses to put forward many wage, welfare and other economic demands to the leadership and administrative departments of the units. They are reckoning up old and distant accounts, and are even waging a so-called 'resolute struggle' all night long . . .
"In recent days, one group after another of misled workers and some rascals have gone to Peking to 'report conditions' . . . large numbers of people have left their production posts, and some enterprises are threatened with a stoppage of production."

> —Foochow notice reproduced in **The China Quarterly,** April-June, 1967.

With Mao Tse-tung's thinking for our weapon, and with Chairman Mao's support for us revolutionary rebels, we dare to embrace the universe and seize the moon and the giant sea-turtle; we dare to touch the tiger's buttocks and put our hands in the hornets' nest; we dare to pull the local emperor off his horse.

> Radio Foochow, January 7, 1967.*

on the eve of Khrushchev's fall. The following year his answer to those who wanted to enter into common action with Russia when the United States began to rain bombs on North Vietnam was to devise "a spontaneous, new type of organization" (the Red Guards) that would teach his leadership how Sino-centered "world revolution" is.

For some Western students of China, Mao's aim in the formation of the Red Guards was to create "an organization of a new type with built-in safeguards against bureaucracy,"[15] as if a new type of organization can be created by ukase. Those who mix erudition with apologetics tell us—in the words of one apologist—that Mao has always been fearful of "concentrated bureaucratic power." It is a

15. *Mao Tse-tung* by Stuart Schram (Penguin, 1967). The most perceptive and scholarly analysis of the national streak in Chinese Communism is a study of a founder of Chinese Marxism, *Li Tt-Chao and the Origins of Chinese Marxism* by Maurice Meisner (Harvard, 1967).

With victory, certain moods may grow within the Party—arrogance, the airs of a self-styled hero, inertia and unwillingness to make progress, love of pleasure and distaste for continued hard living.

> **Quotations from Chairman Mao Tse-tung** (Peking: Foreign Languages Press, 1966).*

For a year the whole country has been alight. . . . Now in the second year it is the year for grasping victory. . . . The third year is for winding up. Then after an interval of a few years we will start again.

> Chou En-lai's speech, May 26, 1967, to a mass rally at the Chinese Academic Sciences. **K'o-chi Chan Pao** (Scientific Fighters' News), June 2, 1967.*

"I also saw the reason for the different names given him [Mao]—'great teacher, leader, commander-in-chief, helmsman'—and the reason why everyone studies his works. I do not claim to know in what form Mao will lead; I recalled that in 1958 he gave up his government tasks because he had more important things to do. He may give up some of his present jobs and titles to 'successors.' But Mao himself seems likely to plan and lead the anti-imperialist struggle for decades. I think he may really outlast it. Even through a nuclear war."

> Anna Louise Strong, **Letter from China**, October 20, 1966, describing **Mao Tse-Tung on Tien An Men**, at the October celebration where he made no speech.

> * Reproduced in **Asian Survey**, Winter, 1968.

little difficult to believe that a man who heads a vast totalitarian state and who whipped out a para-military organization overnight is so revolted by bureaucratic power. It is no less difficult to believe the writer who sees "something profoundly anti-organizational" in the formation of Mao's Guards. But, then, Prof. Schurmann thought that the purpose of the bloody Russian purges in the 1930s was to advance "the sons of workers into cadre positions at all levels of the organizational system." And now he sees that the "sons and daughters of the poor are coming into leadership positions in China."[16] Contrast this to the testimony of a young refugee from Mao's China who told me that living conditions had become so bad that the African students who had come to China looked rich by comparison: "We were very interested in these new arrivals, their countries, their revolutions, but we were not permitted to fraternize with them. They were ghettoized both as to living quarters and any socializing. We also wanted to ask them for things we were short of. And we were stopped from doing that. We all felt very frustrated. I felt more strongly than ever that things were reeling backwards."

In this state capitalist age, revolution and counter-revolution are so interlocked that even those who understand the relationship of thought to objective conditions speak of Mao's "revolutionary fervor" and "revolutionary voluntarism." Hegel, instead of praising Stoicism, saw it as "a general form of the world's spirit only in a

16. Franz Schurmann's major work, *Ideology and Organization in Communist China*, is introduced modestly with the words: "The writing of this book has been like the Chinese Revolution, a long process climaxed by an act." But despite seven years work in Chinese, Japanese, and Malayan documents, this "act" failed to analyze the army. The work was going to press when Lin Piao made his famous speech on "People's War," likening the industrial nations to the City and the underdeveloped countries to the Country which surrounds the City and wins, just as Mao did in China. Professor Schurmann at once rushed into print, as though the army never existed until Lin's speech: "After I had completed this book, I realized that I had omitted an important area of organization: the army." By that time another "area of organization," the Red Guards, had arisen, and this time he was ready with an analysis. It seems that "thousands of young students swarmed into the streets and formed the red defense guards." (*New York Review*, October 20, 1966.) Since testifying to the spontaneity of this mass movement, he has written·nearly everywhere (*Diplomat*, Sept., 1966, and his reply to Professor Levenson's criticism in *New York Review* especially) on the thesis that "Mao Tse-tung has always been fearful of concentrated bureaucratic power and the present purge may be said to conform to his general approach to politics." He fails to enlighten us as to why all the "built-in deterrents against bureaucracy" required either the purge or the "spontaneous Red Guards."

time of universal fear and bondage."[17] Marx saw the need to listen to impulses from a new, objective revolutionary force, the proletariat, and to transcend the ideas of others, whether bourgeois idealists, radical putschists or anarchist voluntarists, before a truly revolutionary philosophy of liberation could be elaborated. Lenin saw the need to show that, although "the petty bourgeois in a frenzy may also wish to smash up the state," what distinguished Bolshevik violence was that "we recognize only one road, changes from below—we wanted workers themselves to draw up, from below, the new principles of economic conditions."[18] As against these discoverers of the dialectic of thought and the dialectics of liberation, men who could not conceive of the shaping of history without a "Subject," today's self-styled revolutionaries think it enough for "the supreme commander and great helmsman" to order social change for it to be realized. But is that revolution? or liberation?

They see the enemy as "Russian revisionism." Russian Communism has, of course, not only revised Marxism but transformed it into its opposite. But that opposite is the very foundation of "Mao's Thought." In his recent, most basic,[19] and most revolutionary-sounding challenge to "Russian revisionism," A *Proposal Concerning the General Line of the International Communist Movement*, Mao says:

> For a very long historical period after the proletariat takes power, class struggle continues as an objective law independent of man's will. . . . For decades or even longer . . . for an entire historical period . . . there are classes and class struggles in all socialist countries without exception.

He repeats this theme over and over, concluding that it may remain true "perhaps for even a century."

But if classes and class struggles continue under "socialism," what is the point of overthrowing capitalism? Surely no more deadly deviation has ever been proclaimed as "a principle of Marxism-Leninism." This is not a theory of revolution. It is a theory of retrogression, all the more serious since it is proclaimed not in the name

17. *Phenomenology of Mind*, p. 245. This work is finally available in paperback.
18. *Selected Works*, Vol. VII, p. 377.
19. The Plenum resolution in August 1966 reiterates this to be "The programmatic document" that must continue to be studied since it gives a "scientific Marxist-Leninist analysis of a series of important questions concerning the world revolution of our time . . ."

of fascism but of Marxism-Leninism.

Mao has always propounded "protracted struggle," raising it to
the level of theory. But to the masses this is not theory, it is the
weight of exploitation they have had to endure in all class societies,
except that it was not called "socialism." One Communist refugee,
after telling about work during the "Great Leap Forward" ("the
most primitive labor imaginable, as if we were to build a whole dam
by hand. We lacked even such simple devices as a block and tackle
to lift heavy rocks. These had to be pushed into place by sheer brute
force.") insisted that the worst was not the work but the discussion
meetings that followed:

> We didn't know which was the hardest to bear—the labor, the food, or
> the meetings. We had to describe what we did that day, and we had to
> speak about our attitude to what we did. Although I had volunteered for
> the job—the Great Leap Forward sounded great to me at Peita (Peking
> University)—I now began to feel as if all our labor was forced labor. I
> kept my tongue, but you couldn't always keep quiet, since if you kept
> silent your team leader would see you afterwards and ask what was the
> matter. I felt like I was nothing more than an ant, not only because of
> the unthinking labor but because you so often said yes when you meant
> no. . . . Moreover, my own experience kept intruding into the study of
> Mao's Thought; they didn't jibe either theoretically or practically. But I
> didn't dare say so, out loud or even to myself.

A spectre is haunting Mao, the spectre of the Hungarian Revolution. To this day he boasts that he urged Khrushchev to send the
tanks into Budapest. To this day Mao's China has consistently
fought the humanism of Marx:

> The modern revisionists and some bourgeois scholars describe Marxism as
> humanism and call Marx a humanist. . . . In particular they make use of
> certain views on 'alienation' expressed by Marx in his early *Economic-
> Philosophic Manuscripts*, 1844. . . . In the early stage of development of
> their thought Marx and Engels were indeed somewhat influenced by
> humanist ideas. . . . But when they formulated the materialist conception
> of history and discovered the class struggle as the motive force of social
> development, they immediately got rid of this influence.[20]

A basic document of the Cultural Revolution, "Raise High the
Great Banner of Mao Tse-tung's Thought and Carry the Great
Proletarian Cultural Revolution Through to the End," openly
admits: "If serious steps were not taken to remold them [the intel-

20. The Fourth Enlarged Session of the Committee of the Department of
Philosophy and Social Science of the Chinese Academy of Sciences, held on

lectuals] they were bound at some future date to become groups like the Hungarian Petofi Club."[21]

The Red Guards were intended to be the agents of that "re-molding." They were built outside the structure of the CCP, not so much to fight "the bureaucracy" as to force those on top and those on the bottom to face the realities of China's position in a world divided between two industrially advanced lands. In such a world, a technologically backward country like China that has no perspective of world revolution "in our time" feels compelled to drive the masses all the harder. Under private capitalism this was known as primitive accumulation; under state capitalism, calling itself Communism, it is called, internally, "fighting self-interest,"[22] and, externally, "Mao Tse-tung's Thought Lights Up the Whole World."[23] The country it now lights has already sunk to the barbarity and depravity of televised public executions. The "self-interest" it now fights is not so much that of "the main person in authority taking the road back to capitalism" as the interests of the Chinese masses, including those they now call "phoney" Red Guards: "large scale struggles of masses with masses, work stoppages . . . armed struggle against real Red Guards." As we enter 1968, the issue has not been decided; despite the command of the Army, that permanent restorer of class order, not all of the rival Red Guard groups in factories and communes have joined "a single organ based on systems." While Mao, on his 74th birthday, holds to his "theory of revolution," that the success of socialism "requires from one to several centuries," the masses see only retrogression down that road. As one refugee from Mao's China expressed it:

October 26, 1963, was especially devoted to the problem. See *The Fighting Tasks Confront Workers in Philosophy and the Social Sciences* (Peking, 1963).
21. *Peking Review*, quoted by Ellis Joffe in his important article, "Cultural Revolution or Struggle for Power," *China Quarterly*, July-September 1966, which has a special section on "China Mid-1966." Especially important on the cultural aspects in the article, "The Fall of Chou Yang" by Merle Goldman who has just published an excellent work not limited to the present Cultural Revolution.
22. *Peking Review*, Nov. 24, and Dec. 1, 1967. See also the article from Hong Kong by Charles Mohr in The New York *Times*, Dec. 31, 1967.
23. On December 26th, Mao's birthday, the official Chinese news agency announced that no less than a half billion copies of Mao's writings have been published this year in 23 languages, proudly pointing out that, whereas before the Cultural Revolution, only 13 plants were publishing his works, now there are 180 plants, and they publish in foreign languages as well.

Retrogression, that's it. That really is it. Mao is a retrogressionist. That's the word that escaped me when I said everything seemed to be reeling backwards. That word hadn't come into my consciousness because I was afraid to face its consequence. But retrogression does really sum up Mao's Thought. . . . Humanist tendencies are very strong among the Chinese. It can raise their spirits once more. I believe the youth stands ready to make a new revolution.

Whether or not the Peking University student is right or wrong in her analysis of the present situation, it is clear that the forces unleashed by the "Cultural Revolution" have by no means been stilled. And Mao's latest campaign against the "ultra-leftist" concept of "doubting all and overthrowing all" is proof of the fact that the "Cultural Revolution" has escaped the confines set for it.

NOTES

1. Daniel Guérin, *La Lutte de Classes Sous La Première République*, two volumes, Paris 1946.

2. The reader should also consult *The French Revolution* and *After Robespierre: Thermidorian Reaction* by Albert Mathiez.

3. Cf. Marx: "The revolutionary movement which began in 1789 in *Cercle social*, which in the middle of its course had as its chief representatives *Leclerc* and *Roux* and which was temporarily defeated with *Baboeuf's* conspiracy, brought forth the *communist* idea which Baboeuf's friend *Buonarroti* reintroduced into France after the Revolution of 1830." (*The Holy Family*, pp. 160-1.)

4. The quotations of Varlet, Roux, and Leclerc are from Daniel Guérin, *op. cit.*

5. Frederick Engels, in his *Peasant Wars in Germany*, has pointed out that the sixteenth century German Reformation betrayed the peasant revolts by not giving them the land and, as a result, the country itself "disappeared for three centuries from the ranks of countries playing an independent part in history." The question of land and the peasant as the prerequisite for a successful revolution was brought home to us in the Civil War. We suffer still from this incomplete revolution in the South where the Negro did not get his "40 acres and a mule." To deal with it here, however, is out of the scope of the present work.

6. Quoted by Herbert Marcuse, *Reason and Revolution*, p. 79.

7. In his penetrating introduction to Hegel's *Early Theological Writings*, Richard Kroner, who, it need hardly be stressed, is no Marxist, has this to say: "Perhaps young Marx, reading this, found the germ of his future program. In any case, foreshadowed in the words ('mind of his own') is the pattern of the labor movement which was to make the proletarian conscious of his existence and to grant him the knowledge of having a mind of his own."

8. See Appendix A, "Critique of the Hegelian Dialectic."

9. *Phenomenology of Mind*, p. 80.

10. *Philosophy of Mind*, paragraph 482, pages 401-02.

11. Anyone who gets a headache grappling with the metaphysical struggles of consciousness and self-consciousness leading to the "Absolute," has the difficulty primarily because of one failing—the failure to hold firmly to the actual historic periods Hegel had in mind when he described the development of "pure thought" from the rise of the ancient Greek city-state through the French Revolution. Once he does hold firmly to the historical development, he can see in the *Phenomenology of Mind* not only the past but the present as well, the daily life experiences common to all of us. Who hasn't seen the "Alienated Soul" or "Unhappy Consciousness" among his restless friends— the tired radicals who cannot find a place for themselves in or out of the bourgeois fold, fall into "a giddy whirl of self-perpetuating disorder," and

land on the green couch? Who hasn't seen "the true and virtuous" among
the labor bureaucrats turning away from reality "in a frenzy of self-conceit"
because they have given their "all" for the workers only to be repaid in
wildcats? Indeed the *Phenomenology* contains both the tragedy of our times
and its comedy.

¹². *Philosophy of Mind*, par. 482, p. 101.

¹³. *Science of Logic*, Vol. II, page 476.

¹⁴. *Reason and Revolution*, page 252.

¹⁵. *Philosophy of Mind*, paragraph 481, p. 100.

¹⁶. This speech is reproduced in *Essays on Literature, Philosophy, and
Music*, by Andrei A. Zhdanov, pages 67-68.

¹⁷. *Ibid.*, page 71. The lowest of all today's sophists is the head of the
Chinese Communist Party and State, Mao Tse-Tung, who recently (June 18,
1957) caused a world sensation with his speech, "On Contradiction," in which
he proclaimed, "Let a hundred flowers bloom. Let a hundred schools of thought
contend." Mao has ridden this single track, which he calls "Contradiction,"
ever since 1937. At that time, he directed his attack against "dogmatists" who
refused to reduce all contradictions in the anti-Japanese struggle and submit
to "the leadership of Chiang Kai-Shek." In 1952, Mao introduced a new set of
definitions into "Contradictions," this time applying it to those who opposed
the Chinese Communist Party taking sole power in China. By June 18, 1957,
after editing with a heavy hand the speech he delivered on February 27th to
the Supreme State Conference, he reduced the struggle of class against class
to a contradiction *among* "the people" while he became the champion, *at one
and the same time,* of the philosophy of a hundred flowers blooming *and one,
and only one Party, the Chinese Communist Party ruling.* Outside of the exploitative class relations themselves, nothing so clearly exposes the new Chinese
ruling class as their threadbare philosophy. (See *Selected Works of Mao Tse-
Tung.*)

¹⁸. See: *Question of Philosophy*, (the official Russian quarterly philos-
ophic journal) No. 3, 1955; available in Russian only. See also in Chapter
III of this book the section "Communism's Perversions of Marx's Economic-
Philosophic Manuscripts."

¹⁹. *Philosophy of Mind*, paragraph 576, p. 197.

²⁰. See Appendix A, *Critique of the Hegelian Dialectic*.

²¹. *Logic*, paragraph 122, p. 229.

²². This author found the most valuable books in this vast field to be
The Industrial Revolution in the Eighteenth Century, by Paul Montoux,
and, of course, the pioneering work by the late Arnold Toynbee, *Industrial Revolution of the Eighteenth Century in England.*

²³. Ure, *The Philosophy of Manufacture.*

²⁴. The only two works by Proudhon that are easily available in America
are: *General Idea of Revolution in the 19th Century*, and *Proudhon's Solution of the Social Problem.*

²⁵. Letter of December 28, 1846, from Marx to P. V. Annenkov. All
letters of Marx and Engels cited hereafter, unless otherwise specified, are
from the *Selected Correspondence*. The dates, rather than the page numbers
are given so that they can just as easily be located in any edition in any language.

26. Unfortunately there is no American translation available, but Marx's devastating answer quotes substantial sections of Proudhon's argument.

27. *Deutsch-Französiche Jahrbucher.* Only one issue appeared, February 1844.

28. Preface to *A Contribution to the Critique of Political Economy.*

29. Quoted by Franz Mehring in his biography of Karl Marx.

30. In this respect Herbert Marcuse's *Reason and Revolution* is a truly pioneering and profound work, and I would here like to acknowledge my debt to it.

31. *The Holy Family,* p. 254.

32. Except where otherwise specified all quotations in the remainder of this chapter are from Marx's Essays in Appendix A.

33. Marx did not know the Existentialists of our day. Yet all one needs to do to see *their* "yearning for a content" is to substitute the word, "Existence," for the word, "Intuition": "This whole Idea behaving in such a baroque way . . . is nothing more than mere abstraction, the abstract thinker, who, made clever by experience and enlightened beyond truth, has decided, under many false and still abstract conditions, to abandon himself. . . . The mystical feeling which drives the philosophers from abstract thinking into intuition is boredom, the yearning for a content." Marx annihilates the empty fantasies of our modern intellectuals. Where they keep separating the question of personality from the mode of production as if seeing, touching, hearing, talking, feeling exist outside of productive man, Marx analyzes the development of all of man's senses as the development of the history of the world. Where they keep identifying their feeling of nausea with that of the objective world, Marx shows that the subject and object are one *when* "new passions and new forces" (the proletariat) put an end to class society as the *pre*-history of humanity and thus create the conditions for a truly human life. (Contrast the Early Works of Marx, in Appendix A, with Jean-Paul Sartre's *Being and Nothingness*.)

34. CAPITAL, Vol. I, p. 835.

35. Letter from Marx to Schweitzer, January 24, 1865.

36. See *The German Ideology.*

37. In their *Private Property and the Modern Corporation.*

38. *Questions of Philosophy,* No. 3, 1955; available in Russian only.

39. My emphasis—

40. See "The Russian Scene," in Part V.

41. Francois Fejto, ed., *Opening of an Era: 1848.*

42. *The Class Struggles in France,* 1848-1850 (included in Karl Marx, *Selected Works,* Vol. II). Since Marx's shorter works appear in many different editions no page numbers to these are cited here.

43. "Address to the Communist League, 1850," (included in *Selected Works,* Vol. II).

44. *The Eighteenth Brumaire of Louis Bonaparte* (included in Karl Marx, *Selected Works,* Vol. II).

45. Quoted by David Footman in his biography of Lassalle, *Ferdinand Lassalle, Romantic Revolutionary,* p. 158.

46. Marx: "He got angry with me and my wife for laughing at his plans and calling him a BONAPARTIST. . . . Finally he convinced himself I was too 'abstract' to understand politics. . . . We agree in nothing except a few ultimate aims."

47. Letter of April 9, 1863.

48. Despite the mountain of books on the Civil War, its full history is yet to be written. In the opinion of this author there exists only one serious work, for example, on the much maligned period of the Reconstruction— W. E. B. Du Bois' *Black Reconstruction.* Of necessity I limit myself here to the impact of the War on the workingmen's movement in Europe and on Marx's works.

49. Of this great movement too, there is no definitive work. Some of the best works of the Abolitionists remain in obscure pamphlets, the most remarkable of which was the one written in 1829 by David Walker. So extraordinary a sensation was caused by the appearance of his pamphlet entitled, "Appeal to the Colored Citizens of the United States," that legislatures in the South were called into special session to enact laws against free Negroes as against slaves for reading it. They put a price of $10,000 on the head of the author. 50,000 copies of this 76-page pamphlet were sold and circulated from hand to hand. Those who could not read had others read to them. The academic historians have yet to bring Walker out of obscurity. The *antebellum* South trembled at the simple words of this obscure Negro who told them prophetically that race prejudice would yet "root some of you out of the very face of the earth."

50. Consult the autobiography of Frederick Douglass. The Communists hope to ride to glory on the fact that they are publicizing the writings and works of the great Negro Abolitionists like Frederick Douglass, Sojourner Truth, Harriet Tubman, and others. The Communists will not succeed. The proof lies in the spontaneity of today's Negro struggles which completely ignore them.

51. The text of Phillips' speech, entitled, "The Cabinet," can be found in Wendell Phillips, *Speeches, Lectures and Letters,* first published in Boston, 1864, and difficult to obtain. Fortunately, many of these will soon appear in a book by Oscar Sherwin, *Prophet of Liberty: The Life and Times of Wendell Phillips.*

52. *The Civil War in the United States,* by Karl Marx, pp. 279-80.

53. Interestingly enough a non-Marxist Hegelian group came to the support of the North. It was the famous "St. Louis group" of intellectuals who, having become critical of the philosophies of Emerson and Thoreau, organized themselves for the study of Hegel's works. Led by the New Englander, W. T. Harris and the German emigrant, Brokmeyer, they made the first English translation of Hegel's *Science of Logic;* by 1867 they founded the first definitely philosophical periodical in this country, "The Journal of Speculative Philosophy." (See *A History of American Philosophy* by Herbert W. Schneider, Columbia University Press, 1946). Brockmeyer, incidentally, later became Lieutenant-Governor of Missouri.

54. CAPITAL, Vol. I, p. 329. All references to this work are to the standard Charles H. Kerr edition.

55. Marx and Engels: *The Civil War in the United States,* p. 252.

56. More popularly known as the *Critique of Political Economy.*

57. Karl Marx, *A Contribution to the Critique of Political Economy,* pp. 33-34.

58. *Grundrisse der Kritik der Politischen Oekonomie, 1857-1858.* Available only in German. Marx-Engels-Lenin Institute, Moscow, 1939. It is a sad

commentary on the state of contemporary Marxist scholarship that these have yet to be analyzed.

59. Letter from Marx to Engels, January 8, 1868.

60. CAPITAL, Vol. I, p. 297.

61. "What a distance we have traveled." CAPITAL, Vol. I, p. 330.

62. See Engels' Preface to CAPITAL, Volume II.

63. CAPITAL, Vol. I, p. 239.

64. This material has never been published in the exact form in which Marx left it. In 1905, Karl Kautsky, to whom Engels entrusted the manuscript, took some liberties with the structure and published it under the title *The Theories of Surplus Value*. To this day, except for one volume published in the United States under the title, *A History of Economic Doctrine*, the work is unavailable in English. For the past decade, the Russian Communists, who now own the manuscript, have been promising to publish it in its original form, but they have not done so. (Eng. tr. by T. McCarthy.)

65. See Appendix B.

66. *The Civil War in France*, (included in *Selected Works*, Vol. II).

67. *The Civil War in France*.

68. This does not appear in the English editions. The International Publishers edition, edited by Dona Torr, does include some material from the French edition that is not in the standard Charles H. Kerr edition.

69. CAPITAL, Vol. I, p. 82.

70. *Speech at the Anniversary of the PEOPLE'S PAPER*, April 1856. (included in *Selected Works*, Vol. II).

71. CAPITAL, Vol. I, p. 93, footnote.

72. CAPITAL, Vol. I, p. 689.

73. *Civil War in France*, (included in *Selected Works*, Vol. II).

74. CAPITAL, Vol. I, p. 48.

75. *Correspondence of Marx and Engels*, letter of August 24, 1867.

76. *Critique*, p. 299.

77. CAPITAL, Vol. I, p. 195-196.

78. CAPITAL, Vol. I, p. 258.

79. CAPITAL, Vol. I, pp. 357-8.

80. CAPITAL, Vol. I, p. 361.

81. *Poverty of Philosophy*, p. 157.

82. CAPITAL, Vol. I, p. 364.

83. "A work of art that wants the right form is for that very reason no right or true work of art. . . . Real works of art are those where content and form exhibit a thorough identity. . . . The content of Romeo and Juliet may similarly be said to be the ruin of two lovers through the discord between their families: but something more is needed to make Shakespeare's immortal tragedy."—Hegel's *Logic*, p. 243.

84. See Hegel on "The Third Attitude to Objectivity": "What I discover in my consciousness is thus exaggerated into a fact of the consciousness of all and even passed off for the very *nature* of the mind." (Hegel's *Logic*, first Wallace translation; in the second, more accessible edition, the wording is slightly different, see page 134.)

85. CAPITAL, Vol. I, p. 654, footnote.

86. *Archives of Marx and Engels,* Russian edition. Vol. II, (VII), p. 69. This is the famous "Chapter VI," or original ending of CAPITAL, when it was in manuscript form. It is unavailable in English.

87. *Ibid.,* p. 35.

88. CAPITAL, Vol. I, p. 217.

89. CAPITAL, Vol. I, p. 327

90. CAPITAL, Vol. I, p. 463.

91. CAPITAL, Vol. I, p. 53.

92. *Philosophy of Manufacture.*

93. CAPITAL, Vol. I, p. 476.

94. CAPITAL, Vol. I, p. 787.

95. CAPITAL, Vol. I, p. 823.

96. CAPITAL, Vol. I, p. 533.

97. CAPITAL, Vol. I, p. 534.

98. CAPITAL, Vol. I, p. 671.

99. CAPITAL, Vol. I, p. 636.

100. CAPITAL, Vol. I, p. 640.

101. CAPITAL, Vol. I, pp. 836-837.

102. CAPITAL, Vol. I, pp. 836-7.

103. CAPITAL, Vol. I, p. 690.

104. CAPITAL. Vol. I, p. 693. Different as the situation appeared in Hitler's Germany and in Stalin's Russia, the capitalist law of population held true, although unemployment assumed a very different shape. See Part V.

105. In the final edition, the part became separate chapters of Part VII.

106. CAPITAL, Vol. I, p. 837.

107. CAPITAL, Vol. I, p. 708.

108. CAPITAL, Vol. I, p. 709.

109. CAPITAL, Vol. I, p. 837.

110. CAPITAL, Vol. I, p. 835.

111. CAPITAL, Vol. I, p. 649.

112. This analysis includes also *Theories of Surplus Value,* which Marx had intended as Book IV of Vol. III (of CAPITAL), but which have not been translated into English to this day, except for the first part. (See footnote 64).

113. It wasn't only the Marxists who saw that this division had more theoretic sense than all that political economy has produced on the question of the "market." After the 1929 crash, some academic economists realized that if they were going to get any distance in understanding the crisis, they would have to understand production better. By 1942, Joan Robinson asserted that with this division of total output into two, and only two major groups, Marx had devised "a simple and penetrating argument." (Cf. Joan Robinson, *An Essay on Marxian Economics,* p. 51.)

114. *Theories of Surplus Value,* Vol. I, Part II, p. 170, Russian ed.

115. CAPITAL, Vol. III, p. 396.

116. CAPITAL, Vol. I, p. 647.

117. CAPITAL, Vol. II, pp. 475-6.

118. Chapter I of V.I. Lenin, *The Development of Capitalism in Russia,* Russian edition. This chapter has been omitted from the English edition.

119. What complicated the argument was that most of her critics were reformists. She, however, attacked both reformists and revolutionaries indiscriminately, and labeled all her critics "epigones."

120. Page 401, Russian edition.

121. *Theories of Surplus Value*, Vol. II, Part II, page 161, Russian edition.

122. CAPITAL, Volume I, page 810.

123. Engels, *Herr Eugen Dühring's Revolution in Science*. A shortened and popular version of it, "Socialism, Utopian and Scientific," is included in *Selected Works*, Vol. II.

124. CAPITAL, Vol. I, p. 842, the Dona Torr, International Publishers edition.

125. Nothing is simple these days. In 1931 Russia found out that, although she had complete monopoly of everything including sales, her tractors just couldn't "compete," that is to say, stand up in production. To buy tractors from Ford meant, however, to pay in gold-standard money at a time when the agricultural crisis in her country made it impossible to have agricultural products to sell to get the money. At another time when she wanted to dump wheat on the international market she found doors closed there. See Part V.

126. Hegel, "Logic," Paragraph 81, p. 148.

127. Letter of July 11, 1868.

128. CAPITAL, Volume I, page 59.

129. CAPITAL, Volume I, p. 659.

130. CAPITAL, Volume II, pp. 132-133.

131. CAPITAL, Volume III, p. 58.

132. CAPITAL, Volume III, page 966.

133. CAPITAL, Vol. I, p. 647.

134. CAPITAL, Vol. I, p. 239.

135. CAPITAL, Vol. III, p. 568.

136. CAPITAL, Vol. III, p. 293.

137. CAPITAL, Vol. III, pp. 954-955.

138. CAPITAL, Vol. II, p. 503.

139. CAPITAL, Vol. III, p. 955.

140. *Grundrisse*, p. 596, German only, (see footnote 58).

141. Originally, Marx had intended to end Volume I with a Chapter VI, entitled, "The Direct Results of the Process of Production," which would have summed up the volume simply and made the transition to Volume II without anticipating its problems and results. Then, both because of health and because of his deepened comprehension of the subject, he rewrote the last part as the "Accumulation of Capital." It was this section, again, which had undergone the greatest revision for the second edition of CAPITAL. The original ending can be found in the *Archives of Marx-Engels, Vol. II (VII)*, both in the original German and in Russian translation. The best way to follow the changes in "Accumulation of Capital," is to get the Dona Torr edition which singles out the changed passages and publishes them separately at the end of the volume. The Kerr edition, which is the standard edition and which has been used here, publishes the French edition as corrected by Marx, but the changes are not singled out.

Marx's "Accumulation of Capital," in Volume I, anticipates Volumes II and III, in the same manner in which the "Absolute Idea," in Hegel's *Science of Logic*, anticipates the *Philosophy of Nature*, and *Philosophy of Mind*, which ultimately completed his philosophic system. Marx's letter to S. Meyer, April

30, 1867, on his health, says: "I laugh at the so-called 'practical' men and their wisdom. If one chose to be an ox one could of course turn one's back on the agonies of mankind and look after one's own skin. But I should really have regarded myself as *unpractical* if I had pegged out *without completely finishing* my book, at least in the manuscript."

142. Joseph A. Schumpeter, *A History of Economic Analysis.*

143. Letter of April 10, 1879; *Letters on Capital*, Russian edition.

144. In this Hegel was not as far distant as would appear at first sight. Cf. his: "The Idea is not so impotent as merely to have a right or an obligation to exist without actually existing." Hegel's *Logic*, p. 12.

145. Hegel's *Science of Logic*, Vol. I, p. 73, footnote.

146. See G. D. H. Cole: ". . . the earlier International Congresses which helped to prepare the way for the Second International have been largely forgotten, and with them the close connection of the entire movement in its early stages with the struggle for the eight hours' day and with the American initiative in this respect. . . . The actual resolution adopted . . . was as follows: . . . 'In view of the fact that a similar manifestation has already been decided on for May 1st, 1890, by the American Federation of Labor at its Congress held at St. Louis in December 1888, this date is adopted for the international manifestation.'" (*The Second International*, p. 9).

147. See especially the pamphlet, "Imperialism: a Popular Outline," and the article, "The Split in the International," included in Lenin's *Selected Works*, Vols. V and XI, respectively.

148. I am, of course, not referring to Communists who have perverted Marxism into its opposite, but to Trotskyists and similar radical groupings.

149. Not only was Engels' critique, written in 1891, not published until 1901 (*Neue Zeit, Jahrg., 2, Vol. I, 1901*), but it made no impression on the living revolutionaries even then. It took the actual collapse of the Second International before Lenin "discovered" this criticism.

150. Marx was most critical of the program which served as the basis for the unity. In fact, he was going to disassociate himself publicly from the new organization. Meanwhile, he satisfied himself with a fundamental theoretical attack known as the *Critique of the Gotha Programme*. This was not made public until 1891, as the German Social Democracy prepared for the Erfurt Congress, when Engels insisted on its publication. (Included in Marx-Engels *Selected Works*, Vol. II.)

151. See Ruth Fischer, *Stalin and German Communism.*

152. The last principle was greatly tampered with. As soon as Karl Liebknecht, the leader of the youth, wrote his pamphlet *Militarism and Anti-Militarism*, which earned him an eighteen month jail sentence, the pamphlet was promptly repudiated by the Party, Liebknecht was replaced by another leader, and the youth was placed under the strict discipline of the Party. That was 1907. As we shall show when we take up the 1905 Revolution, the degeneration had already set in.

153. Trotsky was in jail, but his theory of permanent revolution, and his writings on the history of the Soviet had been published.

154. Both in St. Petersburg and in Moscow the Soviet worked in closest collaboration with the socialist parties, although these socialists had for so long wrangled about what attitude to take toward the Soviet. Four volumes of original documents of the 1905 Revolution have now been published in

Russian. The American reader can get it only from secondary sources; both Cole's previously cited work on the *Second International* and Deutscher's *Prophet Armed: Leon Trotsky* carry summaries of the events.

155. Lenin, *Selected Works*, Vol. VII, p. 251.

156. Lenin, *Selected Works*, Vol. VII, p. 261.

157. That the Party was corruptible to begin with could be seen even from the corridor gossip which had it that one of the leaders of "the revolutionary wing" said to Bernstein, "But such things you speak about should be done, not said." Those who insist on seeking the "roots" of Stalinism in Leninism would, if they were truly objective, find a whole forest of "roots" for the One-Party State concept in the Second International's *ukase* that only one Social Democracy exist in each country.

158. It should be born in mind that Lenin did not know most of Marx's *Early Philosophic Essays*. These were not published until after the Russian Revolution, when the Marx-Engels Institute bought the Archives from the Second International. Lenin's return to the philosophic foundations was through his own reading of Hegel.

159. All quotations from Lenin's *Notebooks* can be found in Appendix B, *Lenin on Hegel's Science of Logic*.

160. It is no accident that the favorite book in Russia has become this very same *Materialism and Empirio-Criticism*, which has undergone innumerable editions. These editions make a hash of Lenin's relation to the dialectic by including two pages from his *Philosophic Notebooks* as if they and the book on *Materialism* were one continuous development. At the same time, not a single scholar in the Marx-Engels-Lenin Institute has been able to make a single contribution to thought in their editions of the *Notebooks*. The Russian conception of the backwardness of the Anglo-Saxons is such that they have never even bothered to make a translation of the *Notebooks* for the American and English public. The first English translation of the *Notebooks* is included as Appendix B of this book.

161. Quoted by O. H. Gankin and H. H. Fisher, *The Bolsheviks and the World War*, p. 219.

162. *Ibid.*, p. 222.

163. *Ibid.*, p. 223.

164. *Ibid.*, p. 225.

165. *Ibid.*, p. 226. This is even more true in our epoch of state capitalism. It is this which compelled Mao Tse-Tung to try to hide his totalitarianism under the slogan, "Let a hundred flowers bloom, let a hundred schools of thought contend." In admitting the existence of contradictions in the "Peoples' Republic," he said that to do otherwise would be "to fly in the face of objective reality." That, most certainly, is true. But this precisely is the supreme manifestation of the class character of the Chinese regime. The one thing this "haughty vassal . . . in the interests of state-power" (to use a Hegelian phrase) forgot is that 600,000,000 human beings will not long be bottled up in contradictions. They are sure to find their way *out of* "contradiction" to the true revolutionary solution. (For an objective analysis of Chinese economy, see: *An Economic Survey of Communist China*, by Yuan-Lu Wu, Bookman Assoc., N. Y., 1956.

166. "Discussion on Self-Determination Summed Up," is part of Lenin's *Collected Works*, Vol. XIX, which contains the best material on the National Question available in English.

167. Lenin, *Selected Works*, Vol. V, p. 303.

168. From the Trotsky Archives at Harvard College Library, as quoted in Richard Pipes, *The Formation of the Soviet Union, Communism and Nationalism, 1917-1923*.

169. Quoted by Lenin in what, unfortunately, is his most popular pamphlet in the "vanguard parties" to this day: *What Is To Be Done?* It has undergone innumerable editions as a separate pamphlet and is included both in his *Collected* and *Selected Works*.

170. *Selected Works*, Vol. II, Part II, "The Second Congress and the Split in the R. S. D. L. P."; Vol. III, Part V, "The Party in the Period of the Revolution of 1905-07"; Vol. IV, Part II, "The Years of Revival (1912-1914)." It is clear from Lenin's voluminous writings on the "organization question" that *one organization of thought* determined his concept of organizational life, and *another* determined that of the established Social Democracy. It was certainly no accident that the latter was so thoroughly Lassallean in practice.

171. *Works*, Volume VIII, page 37 (Russian edition).

172. As early as 1903 Lenin had repudiated some of the connotations of "vanguard." At the August 4th session, of the 1903 Congress, Lenin stated: "I will now go over to the disputed place in my brochure, which called forth here so many interpretations. . . . It is clear that here the principled formulation of a serious theoretical question (the working out of an ideology) has been mixed up with the single episode in the struggle against Economism, and in addition this episode has been presented entirely incorrectly. . . . We all know now that the Economists bent the stick in one direction. To straighten the stick it was necessary to bend it in a different direction, and this I did. I am certain that the Russian Social Democracy will always with energy straighten out the stick, twisted by every opportunism, and that our stick will therefore always be the straightest and most appropriate to action."— *Works*, Volume VI, pages 21-3, Russian.

173. The tendency that wanted to function "legally," that is to say, only to the extent permitted by the Tsarist Autocracy, and proposed that the underground organization be "liquidated."

174. *Selected Works*, Volume III, page 500.

175. *Works*, Volume VIII, page 140 (Russian edition).

176. A slight variation from this first translation appears in Wallace's second edition of *Science of Logic*, p. 258.

177. *London Conference of 1871*, pages 49-59 (Russian edition, 1936).

178. *Selected Works*, Volume XI, *The Split in the International*.

179. *Collected Works*, Vol. XX, Book I, p. 55.

180. *Selected Works*, Vol. VI, p. 232.

181. *Civil War in France*, (included in Marx's *Selected Works*, Vol. II, p. 495).

182. Lenin, *Selected Works*, Vol. VII, p. 277.

183. Lenin, *Selected Works*, Vol. IX, pp. 419-22.

184. The most lively account of all positions are to be found in the Stenographic Report of the 9th Congress of the R. C. P., but that is unavailable in English. The English reader will therefore have to follow all the trade union platforms from Lenin's criticism of them. Volume IX, of his *Selected*

Works, is indispensable for that.

185. *Selected Works,* Vol. IX, p. 9.

186. *Stenographic Report of 9th Congress,* March 1920, Russian.

187. *Ibid.,* p. 124.

188. No one is as inventive in creating new words as those who try to hide an ugly truth. Thus, the Social Revolutionary, I. N. Steinberg, has invented for the word, counter-revolution, the expression, *"revolution within the revolution,"* as the explanation of Kronstadt. See his *In the Workshop of the Revolution,* p. 296.

189. Lenin, *Selected Works,* Vol. IX, p. 19.

190. From the *New Program* of the R. C. P., requoted by Lenin during this debate. See, Vol. IX.

191. See Trotsky's *Works,* Vol. XV, p. 245, Russian edition.

192. See Lenin's *Selected Works,* Vol. IX, p. 24. It happened, as it so often happens in history, that in the 1920-21 debate, Stalin, a man who appreciated what a majority means, supported Lenin who then had the majority behind him. But in his concept of Plan he not only had the administrative *attitude* of Trotsky; he possessed the *brutality* to carry through the Plan to the bitter end of establishing state capitalist barbarism. (See Part V of this volume.)

193. Lenin, *Selected Works,* Vol. IX, p. 429.

194. Lenin, *Selected Works,* Vol. IX, p. 440.

195. *Selected Works,* Vol. IX, pp. 253-54. See also, Lenin's *Collected Works,* Rus. Ed., Vol. XXVI: "To put life into the Soviets, to attract the non-party people, to have the work of the party people checked by non-party people. . . . We are badly executing the slogan: arouse the non-party people, check the work of the party by the non-party masses." (p. 474, 475.)

196. Because Lenin, at that Congress, spoke of a state capitalism that is "not written about in books," that "exists under Communism," some Marxists have denied that Russia is an "ordinary" state capitalist society. The Russian Communists are banking on just such a misreading of Lenin's warning about "a return backwards to capitalism."

197. *Selected Works,* Vol. IX, p. 346.

198. *Selected Works,* Vol. IX, p. 347.

199. *Selected Works,* Vol. IX, p. 348.

200. First published in 1932 by Leon Trotsky. See *The Suppressed Testament of Lenin.*

201. *Leninski Sbornik,* No. 11. Russian ed. Unavailable in English.

202. Unavailable in English. There are some Marxists who first now wish to take that work as a new point of departure. Evidently anything is good enough to avoid working out for oneself an analysis of one's own epoch!

203. *Leninski Sbornik* (Lenin's Miscellany), No. 11, p. 360. Russian only.

204. *Ibid.,* p. 362.

205. See *The Stenographic Report of the Tenth Congress of the R. C. P.,* Russian. The essence is repeated in almost all of Trotsky's criticisms of the "tempo" of the Five Year Plans. See also his "Letter to the Bureau of Party History," in *The Stalin School of Falsification,* especially pp. 28-30 and 64-65.

206. His reaction to V. P. Milyutin's writing on a single economic Plan

is typical: "Milyutin writes rubbish about the Plan. The greatest danger of all is to bureaucratise this matter of a plan of State economy.

"That is a great danger. Milyutin does not see it.

' "I am very much afraid that, even though you approach the matter from another angle, you too do not see it. We are poor, starving, ruined beggars.

"A complete, a complete and real plan for us now would be a bureaucratic Utopia.

"Do not run after it!"

(Letter to Krzhizhanovsky in *The Letters of Lenin*, p. 464.)

207. CAPITAL, Vol. I, p. 652.

208. CAPITAL, Vol. I, p. 827.

209. *Bulletin of the Opposition.* Russian only.

210. See: J. H. Meizel and E. S. Kozera, *Materials for the Study of the Soviet System*, p. 202. A valuable job has been done here for the American reader to acquaint him with the actual laws through translations.

211. Abigniew K. Brzezinski, in his book, *The Permanent Purge*, has compressed valuable facts on purges, although the book suffers from its thesis that everything, from a debate to the holocaust of 1937, is a "purge," and yet, to him, the Moscow trials were only "show."

212. Leon Trotsky, *The Revolution Betrayed.*

213. CAPITAL, Vol. III, p. 1027.

214. This table shows the class division in Russia in 1939, when the population was 169,519,127. The headings are mine but the categories in the tabular breakdown are from the official statistics of the *Central Administration of National Economy*, 1939.

215. See, *The Permanent Purge*, by Zbigniew K. Brzezinski.

216. Anyone interested in this aspect can consult Hodgman, *Soviet Industrial Production, 1928-1951*. By now the books on Russian economy are endless. This was not true when the author first analyzed the Five Year Plans from original Russian sources.

217. A new study of "Real Wages in the Soviet Union, 1928-1952" has been made by Janet G. Chapman, which claims real wages have been cut to 37% of the 1928 figure. (See: *Review of Economics and Statistics*, January, 1954.)

218. The 1913 figures are from Prokopovicz's *Bulletin*, No. 1-2; 1928 prices are abstracted from *Statistical Handbook* (in Russian); 1940 figures for beginning of year from "Monthly Labor Review." The 1926 study, including quantities, was reproduced in *International Labor Review.*

219. Naturally the Russian sources play up the "free social benefits" and no doubt in hospitalization, rentals, etc., the Russian worker today has "privileges." That in no way changes the fact that food is *the* main item in his budget.

220. Professor Colin Clark, who was one of the first to present *A Critique of Russian Statistics*, estimated that the most rapid advance in economic progress from the turn of the century to 1940 was made by Japan. (See his *Conditions of Economic Progress*. Also see the following studies of Japan: *Industrialization of Japan and Manchukuo, 1930-1940*, by Schumpeter, Allen, Gordon and Penrose; *The Economic Strength of Japan* by Isoshi Asha, and *Industrialization of the Western Pacific*, by Kate Mitchell, 1942.)

221. I once discussed purges with an auto worker. He said, "Purges are not just a Russian thing. They take place all the time in America too, without

benefit of spectacular trials. That is the character of American mass production. The biggest purge that took place in American industry was when Henry Ford II took over. He wiped out from the top down.

"Two examples: 1) They introduced a new model on a truck job. They had a hard time getting production organized. Trucks weren't coming off the line either in quantity or quality. So they began to purge the lower levels of foremen. No improvement. So they clipped the top guy. Two more followed him. Finally they got the line rolling. 2) On a tractor job, they introduced a new model and couldn't get quantity or quality. They began to eliminate foremen on the lower level. No results. They wiped out the top guy, replaced him with another guy and wiped this one out too. Finally they got one.

"But everybody knows, from top to bottom, that these purges don't do it. After many months of hit and miss it gets going, but the purges take place anyway."

222. This was first revealed in the article in *Pod Znamenem Marxizma*, (*Under the Banner of Marxism*) No. 7-8/1943. However, the magazine did not reach this country until 1944, at which time I translated it into English and it was published in the *American Economic Review*, No. 3, 1944, under the title, "Teaching of Economics in the Soviet Union." See also Will Lissner in the *New York Times*, October 1, 1944. The controversy in this country, on the startling reversal in Marxian teachings, continued in the pages of the *American Economic Review* for an entire year and I replied with my rebuttal, "Revision or Reaffirmation of Marxism," *American Economic Review*, No. 3, September 1945.

223. Engels long ago noted that statification in and by itself "does not deprive the productive forces of their character of capital": "The more productive forces it (the modern state) takes over, the more it becomes the real collective body of all the capitalists, the more citizens it exploits. The workers remain wage-earners, proletarians. The capitalist relationship is not abolished; it is rather pushed to an extreme. But at the extreme it changes into its opposite. State ownership of productive forces is not the solution of the conflict. . . ." (*Herr Eugen Dühring's Revolution in Science*, p. 290; known popularly as "Anti-Dühring." It is the book on which Marx collaborated. It was written after the French edition of CAPITAL.)

224. Trotsky often spoke of this, I know, but neither in 1923 nor when he formed the Left Opposition and was expelled had he revealed the full text. This is from the Trotsky archives at Harvard College Library and is quoted in *The Formation of the Soviet Union, Communism and Nationalism, 1917-1923*, by Richard Pipes.

225. See Varga's *Changes in the Capitalist Economy as a Result of World War II*, 1946; in Russian only.

226. Tito's defection did not signify any fundamental change in production relations *in* Yugoslavia. True to his Russian model, the trade unions had been liquidated into the State, the guiding principle of factory directors was to sweat the workers "*by thoroughly utilizing working hours.*" This Article (14) of the Five Year Plan, introduced in 1947, was not changed after the break with Russia and the introduction of a "New Law on Peoples Committees." Tito's nationalism is Stalinism in Yugoslav dress. The fact that Tito's country is very small and very backward, and independent of Russia, does not make his "so-

cialism" any different so far as the Yugoslav workers are concerned. They
continue to labor under the same state capitalist exploitative conditions. The
break from Russia, however, was a blow to that pole of world capital. That
America recognized this at once is seen in the aid granted Yugoslavia.

227. *Vorkuta*, by Dr. Joseph Scholmer.

228. See also: *Russia's Slaves Rebel*, by Brigitte Gerland, which appeared
serially in *The London Observer*, during January and February, 1954.

229. *Vorkuta*, p. 234.

230. *Ibid.*, p. 301.

231. Although the resistance to Hitler in Germany and Austria is outside the scope of this book, the author would like to call attention to
The Twilight of Socialism, by Joseph Buttinger, which details the history
of the Revolutionary Socialists of Austria, who were the only Socialists to
fight the Hitler thrust directly. It is true that some of those heroic fighters
are no longer sure that they are Marxists. Contrary to the cynics of today,
however, these actual fighters against fascism search for "a point from
which they can go forward . . . to one truth they cling: that man must
not remain forever under the blind sway of social conditions,' that he can
rise up successfully against an order that denies his humanity. , . . In this
deepest sense, the Austrian Revolutionary Socialists have not failed. Their
socialism lives on, like seed beneath the snow. In every country they have
brothers, including some of other name, brought up in other schools. Everywhere, individually or in small groups, they search for a new way. Gradually
they will be joined by other men, thrust into thought and action by the curse
of social disaster. They will not be units of a mighty host in the near future.
But even if their spirit cannot prevail in politics for many years, the needs
of the time will call them, sooner or later. Going his own way, even the
loneliest will some day encounter brothers, at home or abroad. And wherever
in the world they meet, however different their tongues, they will know and
embrace one another, and wonder what had made them think they were
alone." (Pp. 549-550.)

232. These studies, made under Congressional authorization, investigated
the concentration of economic power and were prepared immediately prior to
American entry into World War II. There are too many monographs to
list here. Among the most instructive is monograph number 22, "Technology
in Our Economy," U. S. Government Printing Office, Washington, 1941. The
post-war period is reported in *Economic Concentration and World War II*,
U. S. Government Printing Office, Washington, 1946.

233. CAPITAL, Vol. I, p. 13.

234. See both *The Human Problems of an Industrial Civilization*, The Macmillan Co., New York, 1933; and, *The Social Problems of an Industrial Civilization*. Harvard University Press, Boston, 1945.

235. Alvin Gouldner, *Wildcat Strikes*; 1954.

236. Sebastian de Grazia, *The Political Community*; pp. 103-104.

237. "Changing Relations in the Shop," by Charles Denby, *News & Letters*,
September 21, 1955.

238. See: *Automatic Control*, by the editors of Scientific American, 1955.
A Review of Automatic Technology, U. S. Department of Labor, 1955. *A Special*
Report on Automation, Business Week, October 1, 1955. *Man and Automation*,
Report of the Proceedings of a Conference sponsored by the Society for

Applied Anthropology at Yale University, December 27, 28, 1955. *Automation*: *Materialen zur Beurteilung der ökonomischen und sozialen Folgen*, by Friedrich Pollock (Frankfurter Beitrage zur Soziologie, 1956).

239. See: *Man and Automation*, Technology Project, Yale University.

240. Put into resolution form by the April, 1957, UAW Convention as "opportunities they offer us to usher in a golden age of plenty for all mankind." (*Automation and the Second Industrial Revolution*, Resolution No. 14.)

241. I am excluding the oil and chemical industries which preceded the epoch of Automation. While it is true these industries were the first to be automated—indeed Automation is the basis of their becoming big industries—they seemed to be, and were, the exception rather than the rule.

242. See: Norbert Wiener, *The Human Use of Human Beings*.

243. "*Automation*, the Facts Behind the Word. Special Report"; October 1, 1955.

244. *A Review of Automatic Technology*, U. S. Dept. of Labor, 1955.

245. See: Leontief's article, "The Economic Impact," in Section II, "The Second Industrial Revolution," of *Automatic Control*.

246. *Critique of the Gotha Program*, (included in *Selected Works*, Volume II).

247. See Appendix B.

249. "Working for Independence," by Angela Terrano, *News & Letters*, January 6, 1956.

250. Since the Spanish Revolution of 1937, the theoretical void has engulfed also the Anarchists and Anarcho-Syndicalists who had ended up as part of Government, which they had always theoretically disclaimed. What is far worse than becoming bound to Russia by gold payments was to become prisoners of administrative thinking.

251. Nothing discloses the intellectual void among the present labor leadership as the fact that it has not produced a single serious piece of analysis, much less a definitive history, of the CIO. It is of course no accident that the labor bureaucracy is incapable of being the historian of labor. Not only does it bear no resemblance to the men and women who created that organization; it tries hard to forget its own origin.

252. Mr. Faulkner's later denial that he had said "if I had to choose between the United States and Mississippi, I would choose Mississippi even to going out and shooting Negroes in the street" is even more barbaric than his original statement. "Of course I didn't say that," reads the U. P. dispatch of March 16, 1956 from Oxford, Miss., "because I don't believe it's come to that." But just in order to make sure where he will be when it does "come to that," he used all his fictional skill to rewrite history and make "that white embattled minority who are our blood and kin" appear as the "underdog." It appears that after centuries of being the oppressors as well as the provocateurs of a Civil War these "underdogs" must be allowed to work their way out "morally." (See the original interview Faulkner gave Russell Warren Howe, New York correspondent for the *London Sunday Times*, February 21, 1956, published in *The Reporter*, March 22, 1956; then his statement of being "grossly misquoted" to the U. P., March 16, 1956; both reprinted in *The Montgomery Advertiser*, Montgomery, Alabama, March 17, 1956. Also "A Letter to the North" by William Faulkner in LIFE, March 5, 1956.)

253. Nothing is more ludicrous in this shabby role than their veering between the two extremes, depending on which wind blows from the Kremlin:

(1) of reducing the Negro question to the absurdity of demanding *"for"* the Negroes "Self-Determination in the Black Belt;" and (2) asking the Negroes to forget their fight for democratic rights the minute Russia became an ally of America during World War II.

254. 1958 finally saw the publication of a biography of Phillips. *Prophet of Liberty: the Life and Times of Wendell Phillips,* by Oscar Sherwin, Bookman Associates, New York.

255. The only thing that tops Henry Luce's attempt to sell "the American way of life" abroad is the bombastic presumptuousness of his high-powered publicity attempt to sell the American public Djilas's *The New Class* as something "that will rock Marxism."

256. Hegel's *Logic,* paragraph 147, p. 269.

257. Mao Tse-tung, *On Contradiction,* International Publishers, New York, 1953.

258. 650 million was the figure used in 1959. In 1958 it was 600 million. Since 1960 the population references have jumped all the way to 700 and even 750 million. There is no accurate count.

259. Statement of the Chinese War Minister to Sam Watson of the British Labour Party, quoted in *Time,* Dec. 1, 1958.

260. Quoted by Thomas Perry Thornton in his "Peking, Moscow and the Underdeveloped Areas" in *World Politics,* July, 1961.

261. Chinese children must learn the rhymes:

"Mao Tse-tung is like the sun:
"He is brighter than the sun . . . "

And one Chinese governor came up with this one:

"The sun shines only in the day, the moon shines only at night.
"Only Chairman Mao is the sun that never sets."

(Quoted in *Mao's China* by Ygael Gluckstein)

262. *Phenomenology of Mind,* p. 541, The Macmillan Co., New York.

263. The indispensable book for the English reader is *The Hundred Flowers Campaign and the Chinese Intellectuals* by Roderick MacFarquhar (Stevens and Sons Limited, London: Frederick A. Praeger, New York). It has a minimum of comment and a maximum of translations from official Chinese sources. The quotations used here are all from that book.

264. Revolutionary Committee of Kuomintang. As all parties permitted to exist in China, it had to accept "the leadership of the Communist Party." In the case of Lung Yun, who was born in 1888 and had been a member of the Kuomintang Central Committee, 1931-49, but expelled from it for defecting to the Communists, he had been given high governmental posts in Communist China.

265. See *The Sino-Soviet Dispute,* documented and analyzed by G. F. Hudson, Richard Lowenthal and Roderick MacFarquhar; Frederick A. Praeger, New York, 1961. Also see *The Sino-Soviet Conflict, 1956-61* by

Donald S. Zagoria, Princeton University Press, 1962; and *The New Cold War: Moscow v. Pekin* by Edward Crankshaw, Penguin Books, Middlesex, England, 1963.

266. *Communist China Digest*, May 2, 1960.

267. Consult Chapter 3, "Economic Development," *Communist China and Asia* by A. Doak Barnett, Harper Brothers, New York, 1960; *Mao's China* by Ygael Gluckstein, Allen and Unwin, London, 1957. See also Chao Kuo-chun, *Economic Planning and Organization in Mainland China, 1949-57.*

268. One of the best books on agriculture is *Agrarian Policy of the Chinese Communist Party, 1921-1959* by Chao Kuo-chun, Asia Publishing House, New Delhi, 1960.

269. Quoted by H. F. Schurmann in his "Peking Recognition of Crisis," *Problems of Communism*, September-October 1961.

270. The report is included in *A Documentary History of Chinese Communism* by Brandt, Schwartz and Fairchild. Harvard University Press, Cambridge, Mass., 1952. Also see *Soviet Russia and The East, 1920-27*, a documentary survey by X. J. Eudin and Robert C. North, Stanford University Press, 1957.

271. From "The Military Bulletin of the Central Committee," Shanghai, quoted by Harold Isaacs in *The Tragedy of the Chinese Revolution*, 1938 edition.

272. Edgar Snow, *Red Star Over China*. Consult also *Stalin's Failure in China, 1924-27*, by Conrad Brandt. Harvard University Press, Cambridge, Mass., 1958.

273. *Chinese Communism and The Rise of Mao* by Benjamin Schwartz. See also Robert North, *The Kuomintang and The Chinese Communist Elites*.

274 Quoted by John Kautsky in *Moscow and the Communist Party of India*, Technology Press of MIT and John Wiley and Son, New York, 1956.

275. *On the Present Situation and Our Tasks*, December 25, 1947. Foreign Language Press, Peking, 1961.

276. Address to the members of the All-China Salvation League, quoted by Isaacs, ibid.

277. International Publishers, n.d. Judging by the reference notes which go through the year 1949, this pamphlet was probably published in 1950.

278. International Publishers, New York, 1953; Foreign Language Press, Peking, 1961.

279. "How Original Is 'Maoism'?" by Arthur A. Cohen in *Problems of Communism*, November, December, 1961.

280. Audrey Donnithorne, "Economic Development in China," in *The World Today*, April, 1961.

281. Translated and published in *Peking Review*, June 16, 1961.

282. Ibid.

283. *Selected Works of Mao Tse-tung*, Vol. IV, Foreign Language Press, Peking, 1961.

284. Ibid. Also see, George Paloczi-Horvath, *Mao Tse-tung, Emperor of the Blue Ants*, Doubleday & Co., Inc., New York, 1963.

285. *Oriental Despotism* by Karl A. Wittfogel, Yale Univ. Press, 1957.

286. Ygael Gluckstein thus spoils an otherwise fine study, *Mao's China*, which we recommend.

287. Ibid. Also the *China Quarterly* carries competent current articles, and the *Peking Review* gives the official Chinese Communist view.

288. Translated and published in the *Peking Review*, May 26, 1961.

289. Mao Tse-tung, "The Question of Agricultural Cooperation," quoted above, ibid.

290. I do not mean to say that had the Trotskyists followed Trotsky's "line" they would have had "the correct solution." Far from it. The fact that Trotsky had never accepted the theory of state-capitalism and to his dying day maintained, in his theory of permanent revolution, his underestimation of the revolutionary role of the peasantry, precluded that. (See my pamphlet, *Nationalism, Communism, Marxist-Humanism and the Afro-Asian Revolutions*, pp. 21-22. News & Letters, Detroit, Mich., 1959: Cambridge, England, 1961.) What I do mean is that Trotsky wrote voluminously against the class-collaborationist policy of Stalin for China, against Mao Tse-tung's military conception of encircling the towns instead of appealing to the proletariat within them to rise and lead the struggle of the peasantry, and against the concept of a "Soviet China" — in caves! (See Leon Trotsky: *Problems of the Chinese Revolution*, with Appendices by Zinoviev, Vuyovitch, Nassunov and others, Pioneer Publishers, 1932; *The Permanent Revolution*, Pioneer Publishers, 1931; Introduction to Harold R. Isaacs' *The Tragedy of the Chinese Revolution;* Appendices II & III to *The History of the Russian Revolution*, Simon & Shuster, 1937; "Summary and Perspectives of the Chinese Revolution" in *The Third International After Lenin*, Pioneer Publishers, 1936; and *Stalin*, Harper & Bros., 1941.) Leon Trotsky's widow, Natalia Sedova, was so shocked when the French press (*France-Soir*, Nov. 7, 1961) attributed to her the statement that Leon Trotsky was "the spiritual father of Mao Tse-tung" that she wrote them (Nov. 9) indignantly:

"1—A great revolutionary like Leon Trotsky could not in any way be the father of Mao Tse-tung who won his position in direct struggle with the Left-Opposition (Trotskyist) and consolidated it by the murder and persecution of revolutionaries just as Chiang Kai-shek did. The spiritual fathers of Mao Tse-tung and of his party are obviously Stalin (whom he always credits as such) and his collaborators, Mr. Khrushchev included.

2—I consider the present Chinese regime, the same as the Russian regime or all others based on the latter model, as far from Marxism and the proletarian revolution as that of Franco in Spain."

291. See Edward Crankshaw in *The London Observer*, February 12 and 19, 1961.

[292]. The English translation, released by *Tass* was published in *The New York Times*, Dec. 7, 1960. In view of the fanciful interpretation by Russian "experts," especially Isaac Deutscher (*Reporter*, Jan. 5, 1961) about how the "compromise" between Khrushchev and Mao was achieved at this meeting of the 81 Communist Parties which was supposed to have been "very nearly a revival of the old Communist International," it is important to get "first reactions" and compare them with the present stage of the Sino-Soviet rupture. See my analysis of this "New Russian Communist Manifesto" in *News & Letters*, January, 1961.

[293]. See the Draft Program of the 22nd Russian Communist Party Congress released by *Tass* July 30, and published in *The New York Times*, Aug. 1, 1961. Consult also "The 22nd Party Congress" by Merle Fainsod, issued as a special supplement of *Problems of Communism*, Nov.-Dec. 1961.

[294]. Issued in English by *Foreign Language Press*, Peking, 1963. The page numbers cited here are to this edition. The reply of the Central Committee of the Russian Communist Party on July 15 was published in *The New York Times*, July 15, 1963.

[295]. This map is reproduced in the *New Republic* of 4/20/63 in an article, "China's Borders," the third of a series of articles by J. Jacques-Francillon. The other articles appear in the issues of 3/16/63 and 3/23/63. (See also B. Shiva Rae's article in the *National Observer* of 7/23/63.)

[296]. By now the books on the Hungarian Revolution are legion, and yet few go fully into the Workers' Councils, and fewer still bring out the Humanism of Marxism as it developed in the disputes among Communists. Nevertheless, the following are the best in presenting the record of the revolutionaries and the type of eye-witness accounts that concentrated on them: *The Hungarian Revolution*, a White Book edited by Melvin J. Lasky, Praeger, 1957; *Behind the Rape of Hungary* by F. Fejto, N. Y., McKay, 1957; *Imre Nagy on Communism: In Defense of the New Course*, Praeger 1957. Consult especially *The Review*, published by the Irme Nagy Institute, No. 4, 1960; Vol. III No. 2, 1962. "My Experiences in the Central Workers Council of Greater Budapest" by Miklos Sebestyen. The magazine *East Europe* also carried (April 1959) "Eyewitness Report of How the Workers Councils Fought Kadar." Also consult "Spontaneity of Action and Organization of Thought: In memoriam of the Hungarian Revolution," published by the Marxist-Humanist Group of Glasgow, Scotland, November, 1961.

[297]. Mao Tse-tung, *On the Correct Handling of Contradictions Among the People*.

[298]. See "Hunger in China, Letters from the Communes — II," Introduction and Notes by Richard L. Walker, special supplement to *New Leader*, May 1961.

[299]. See *American Civilization on Trial*, second edition, *News & Letters*, Detroit, Mich., August, 1963.

SELECTED BIBLIOGRAPHY

To this day there is no complete collection of Marx's writings. The closest to being complete are the Marx-Engels *Collected Works*, published in Russian by the Marx-Engels-Lenin Institute in Moscow (K. Marx and F. Engels, *Collected Works*, Volumes 1-15, 17-19, 21-29, published between 1928 and 1948). Also available in Russian are K. Marx and F. Engels, *Archives*, Volumes 1-5, edited by Ryazanov, and, after 1924, Volumes 6-8 and 10-13, edited by Adoratsky. Nor are Lenin's complete works available in English. I have used the third edition of Lenin's *Collected Works*, published in the original Russian in 1937, as well as the *Leninski Sbornik* (Miscellany), Volumes 1-35, published in Moscow between 1924 and 1945.

Again, the only complete material available of the early congresses of the Russian Communist Party are in the Stenographic Reports in Russian. The one most often referred to in this book is the Stenographic Report of the Ninth Party Congress during which the famous trade union debate of 1920-1921 was concluded. The English reader is referred to Volume IX of the *Selected Works* of Lenin. Finally, the most complete materials on the Five Year Plans are, of course, in the original Russian. There is obviously an abundance of material on the Russian economy available in English, but I refer to very few of these since they are preponderantly interpretations of the original Russian material which I have cited in the text. One of the few exceptions is the *Quarterly Bulletin of Soviet Russian Economics*, edited by Prokopovicz and published in Prague until the beginning of World War II. Some of the numbers of this *Bulletin* were translated into English in the late 1930's, but these are available in very few American libraries.

Every one of Stalin's speeches and writings since Lenin's death are, on the other hand, available easily and in too many editions to cite. They can be obtained from International Publishers, New

York. The English editions published by the Moscow Foreign Language Publishing House are also available in America. I have therefore cited only the date on which the speeches were delivered. These will be found in the text itself rather than in this bibliography.

This bibliography is intended as a guide for the average American reader who wishes to proceed to a further study of Marxism. I have therefore not listed any of the foreign language references here. Where it was impossible to avoid reference to these works, they will be found in the footnotes. What is true of the Russian is true also of the reference works in French and German. The only exception is the significant study of the class struggles in the French Revolution by Daniel Guérin because it is the only recent work on the topic: *La Lutte de Classes Sous la Première République*. In a word, this bibliography limits itself to references which are readily accessible to the English reader. Of necessity, therefore, it is not an exhaustive but a selective bibliography and not even all the works cited in the footnotes are listed here.

A final word on the American scene: Though there seem to be few references listed here for Automation, those listed do reflect the different attitudes ranging from the abstract scientific to the reactions of production workers. These are the times through we are living and innumerable articles and monographs are appearing in the current press.—R. D.

A.   *1776 to 1883*
Dealt with in parts I, II, and III of the text

Hegel, Georg Wilhelm Friedrich, *Logic;* translated from *The Encyclopaedia of the Philosophical Sciences,* by William Wallace; Oxford University Press, New York. 1892 and 1931.

————, *Phenomenology of Mind, The;* translated by J. B. Baillie; The Macmillan Co., New York, 1931.

————, *Philosophy of Fine Art, The;* 3 Vols.; G. Bell & Sons, London, 1920.

————, *Philosophy of History, The;* tr. by J. Sibree; Willey Book Co., New York, 1944.

————, *Philosophy of Mind;* translated from The *Encyclopaedia of the Philosophical Sciences,* by William Wallace; Oxford University Press, Oxford, 1894.

————, *Philosophy of Right;* translated with notes by T. M. Knox; Oxford University Press, Oxford, 1945.

————, *Science of Logic;* 2 Vols.; translated by W. H. Johnston and L. G. Struthers; The Macmillan Co., New York, 1951.

————, *Selections;* edited by J. Lowenberg; Charles Scribner's Sons, New York, 1929.

Marx, Karl and Frederick Engels, *Capital;* 3 Vols.; Charles H. Kerr & Co., Chicago, 1915.

————, *Civil War in the United States, The;* International Publishers, New York, 1940.

————, *Contribution to the Critique of Political Economy, A;* Charles H. Kerr & Co., Chicago, 1904.

————, *Dialectics of Nature;* International Publishers, New York, 1940.

————, *German Ideology, The;* International Publishers, New York, 1939.

————, *Herr Eugen Dühring's Revolution in Science;* Charles H. Kerr & Co., Chicago, 1935.

————, *History of Economic Theories from the Physiocrats to Adam Smith;* The Langland Press, New York, 1952.

————, *Holy Family, The;* Foreign Languages Publishing House, Moscow, 1956.

————, *Letters to Dr. Kugelmann;* International Publishers, New York, 1934.

————, *Poverty of Philosophy, The;* Charles H. Kerr & Co., Chicago, no date.

————, *Selected Correspondence;* International Publishers, New York, no date.

————, *Selected Works;* 2 Vols.; International Publishers, New York, no date. These volumes contain, among others, the following fundamental shorter works: *Manifesto of the Communist Party; Wage-Labour and Capital; Value, Price and Profit; Germany: Revolution and Counter-Revolution; Address of the Central Council to the Communist League; Class Struggles in France, 1848-50; Eighteenth Brumaire of Louis Bona-*

parte; Civil War in France; Address to the General Council of the International Working Men's Association; Critique of the Gotha Programme; Socialism: Utopian and Scientific.

Ricardo, David, *Political Economy and Taxation;* London.

Smith, Adam, *Wealth of Nations, The;* Modern Library, New York, 1937.

Supplementary Material

Beard, Charles A. & Mary R., *Rise of American Civilization, The;* The Macmillan Co., New York, 1945.

Commons, John R., *History of Labour in the United States;* 2 Vols; The Macmillan Co., New York, 1921.

Douglass, Frederick, *Life and Times;* De Wolfe, Fiske & Co., Boston, 1893.

Du Bois, W. E. B., *Black Reconstruction;* Harcourt, Brace & Co., New York, 1935.

Fejto, Francois, *Opening of an Era: 1848;* A. Wingate, London, 1948.

Footman, David, *Ferdinand Lassalle: Romantic Revolutionary;* Yale University Press, New Haven, 1947.

Garrison's Children, *William Lloyd Garrison,* told by his children; 4 Vols.; The Century Co., New York, 1885.

Guérin, Daniel, *La Lutte de Classes Sous La Première République;* 2 Vols; Paris, 1946.

Hobson, John A., *Evolution of Modern Capitalism, The;* The Macmillan Co., New York, 1949.

Jellinek, Frank, *Paris Commune of 1871, The;* Victor Gollancz, London 1937.

Lefebvre, Georges, *Coming of the French Revolution, The;* Vintage Books, New York, 1957.

Lissagaray, Prosper O., *History of the Commune of 1871;* Reeves & Turner, London, 1886.

Mantoux, Paul, *Industrial Revolution in the Eighteenth Century, The;* Harcourt, Brace & Co., New York, 1928.

Marcuse, Herbert, *Reason and Revolution: Hegel and the Rise of Social Theory;* 2nd edition; Humanities Press, New York, 1954.

Mathiez, Albert, *After Robespierre: Thermidorian Reaction;* A. A. Knopf, New York, 1931.

————, *French Revolution, The;* A. A. Knopf, New York, 1928.

Mehring, Franz, *Karl Marx, the Story of His Life;* Covici, Friede, New York, 1935.

Parrington, Vernon L., *Main Currents in American Thought;* 3 Vols.; Harcourt, Brace & Co., New York, 1930.

Phillips, Wendell, *Speeches, Lectures, and Letters;* 2 Vols; Lee & Shepard, Boston, 1891.

Proudhon, Pierre J., *General Idea of Nineteenth Century Revolution;* London, 1923.

Sherwin, Oscar, *Prophet of Liberty: Life and Times of Wendell Phillips;* Bookman Associates, New York, 1957.

Toynbee, Arnold, *Industrial Revolution of the Eighteenth Century in England;* Longmans, Green & Co., New York, 1920.

B. *1889 to 1924*
            Dealt with in Part IV of the text

Lenin, V. I., *Collected Works;* International Publishers, New York 1927-1942. This series consists only of a few odd volumes which cover Lenin's writings for the periods indicated in parentheses: Vol. IV (1900-02); Vol. XIII (*Materialism and Empirio-Criticism*); Vol. XVIII (1914-15); Vol. XIX (1916-17); Vols. XX and XXI (1917).

————, *Letters of Lenin;* Harcourt, Brace & Co., New York, 1937.

————, *Selected Works;* 12 Vols.; International Publishers, New York, 1943. This is a comprehensive selection of most of Lenin's fundamental writings. Vol. IX of this series is essential for an understanding of the problems after the Revolution; it includes the Trade Union Debate, the New Economic Policy, and Lenin's last address to the R.C.P.

Trotsky, Leon, *First Five Years of the Communist International, The;* 2 Vols.; Pioneer Publishers, New York, 1945 and 1956.

————, *History of the Russian Revolution, The;* 3 Vols.; Simon and Schuster, New York, 1937.

————, *Our Revolution;* Henry Holt & Co., New York, 1918.

————, *Suppressed Testament of Lenin;* Pioneer Publishers, New York, no date.

Supplementary Materials

Bunyan, James and Fisher, H. H., *Bolshevik Revolution, 1917-1918, The;* Stanford University Press, Stanford, Calif., 1934.

Carr, Edward H., *Bolshevik Revolution, 1917-1923, The;* 3 Vols.; The Macmillan Co., New York, 1952.

Cole, G. D. H., *Second International: 1889-1914, The;* 2 Vols.; St. Martin's Press, New York, 1956.

Deutscher, Isaac, *Prophet Armed, Trotsky: 1879-1921, The;* Oxford University Press, New York, 1954.

Fischer, Ruth, *Stalin and German Communism: A Study in the Origins of the State Party;* Harvard University Press, Cambridge, 1948.

Gankin, Olga H. and H. H. Fisher, *Bolsheviks and the World War, The;* Stanford University Press, Stanford, Calif., 1940.

Hobson, J. A., *Imperialism;* George Allen & Unwin, London, 1938.

Krupskaya, Nadezhda K., *Memories of Lenin;* 2 Vols; International Publishers; New York, no date.

Luxemburg, Rosa, *Accumulation of Capital;* Yale University Press, New Haven, Conn., 1951.

Pipes, Richard, *Formation of the Soviet Union, Communism and Nationalism, 1917-1923, The;* Harvard University Press, Cambridge, 1954.

Steinberg, I. N., *In the Workshop of the Revolution;* Rinehart & Co., New York, 1953.

Wolfe, Bertram D., *Three Who Made a Revolution;* The Dial Press, New York, 1948.

C. From 1924 Until Today
Dealt with in Part V of the text

Alinsky, Saul, *John L. Lewis;* G. P. Putnam's Sóns, New York, 1949.

American Economic Review, September, 1944, "Teaching of Economics in the Soviet Union," translated from *Pod Znamenem Marxizma* ("Under the Banner of Marxism"), No. 7-8, 1943.

Business Week, "Special Report on Automation," October 1, 1955.

Buttinger, Joseph, *In the Twilight of Socialism;* Frederick A. Praeger, New York, 1953.

Clark, Colin, *Conditions of Economic Progress,* Macmillan, 1951.

Dallin, David J. and Boris I. Nicolaevsky, *Forced Labor in Soviet Russia;* Yale University Press, New Haven, 1947.

Dunayevskaya, Raya, "New Revision of Marxian Economics," *American Economic Review,* September, 1944.

———, "Revision or Reaffirmation of Marxism? A Rejoinder," *American Economic Review,* September, 1945.

Fainsod, Merle, *How Russia Is Ruled;* Harvard University Press, Cambridge, 1953.

Gordon, Manya, *Workers Before and After Lenin;* E. P. Dutton & Co., New York, 1941.

Gouldner, Alvin, *Wildcat Strikes;* Antioch Press, Yellow Springs, Ohio, 1954.

Harris, Herbert, *American Labor;* Yale University Press, New Haven, 1939.

Jasny, Naum, *Socialized Agriculture of the USSR, The;* Stanford University Press, Stanford, Calif., 1949.

Lens, Sidney, *Left, Right & Center;* Henry Regnery Co., Hinsdale, Ill., 1949.

Meisel, James H. and Edward S. Kozera, *Materials for the Study of the Soviet System;* 2nd edition; The George Wahr Publishing Co., Ann Arbor, Michigan, 1953.

Mills, C. Wright, *New Men of Power;* Harcourt, Brace & Co., Inc., New York.

National Resources Committee, *Structure of the American Economy: Part I, Basic Characteristics;* U. S. Government Printing Office, Washington, D.C., June, 1939.

News & Letters, Bi-Weekly published at Detroit, Mich. Specific numbers quoted are mentioned in the text.

Reuther, Walter, *Impact of Automation,* December 1955. UAW, Detroit, Mich.

Robinson, Joan, *Essay on Marxian Economics, An;* Macmillan & Co., London, 1942.

Scholmer, Joseph, *Vorkuta;* Henry Holt & Co., New York, 1955.

Schumpeter, Joseph A., *History of Economic Analysis;* Oxford University Press, New York, 1954.

Scientific American, Editors of, *Automatic Control;* Simon and Schuster, New York, 1955.

Souvarine, Boris, *Stalin;* Longmans, Green & Co., New York, 1939.

Trotsky, Leon, *Revolution Betrayed;* Doubleday, Doran & Co., New York, 1937.

————, *Stalin School of Falsification, The;* Pioneer Publishers, New York, 1937.

U. S. Dept. of Labor, *Review of Automatic Technology, A;* U. S. Government Printing Office,. Washington, D.C., 1955.

Walker, Charles R., *American City;* Farrar & Rinehart, New York, 1937.

Wiener, Norbert, *Human Use of Human Beings, The;* Doubleday Anchor Books,

Wu, Y. L., *An Economic Survey of Communist China;* Bookman Associates, New York, N. Y., 1956.

Yugow, A., *Russia's Economic Front for War and Peace;* Harper & Brothers, New York, 1942.

INDEX